Introductory Psychology

Introductory Psychology

A text book for health students

edited by
John C. Coleman
*The London Hospital Medical College
University of London*

Routledge & Kegan Paul
London, Boston and Henley

First published in 1977
by Routledge & Kegan Paul Ltd
39 Store Street,
London WC1E 7DD,
Broadway House, Newtown Road,
Henley-on-Thames,
Oxon RG9 1EN and
9 Park Street,
Boston, Mass. 02108, USA
Reprinted 1980
Set in Monotype Imprint
and printed in Great Britain by
Redwood Burn Ltd
Trowbridge and Esher
© Routledge & Kegan Paul Ltd 1977
No part of this book may be reproduced in
any form without permission from the
publisher, except for the quotation of brief
passages in criticism

ISBN 0 7100 8442 0 (c)
ISBN 0 7100 8443 9 (p)

Contents

	INTRODUCTION Dr John C. Coleman	vii
	CONTRIBUTORS	ix

Part One Fundamental Processes of Psychological Functioning

Chapter 1	RELATIONS BETWEEN PSYCHOLOGY AND PHYSIOLOGY Dr Irene Martin	3
Chapter 2	PERCEPTION Dr R. P. Power	32
Chapter 3	MEMORY Dr Harry Kay	74
Chapter 4	LEARNING Mr Dougal Mackay	95
Chapter 5	EMOTION Dr Irene Martin	125

Part Two Human Growth and Development

Chapter 6	INTELLIGENCE Professor H. J. Butcher and Mr F. S. Stevens	155
Chapter 7	PERSONALITY Dr Gordon Claridge	175
Chapter 8	CHILD DEVELOPMENT AND ADOLESCENCE Professor B. M. Foss	220
Chapter 9	ADULTHOOD AND AGEING Professor D. B. Bromley	245

Part Three Social Psychology as Related to Medicine

Chapter 10	**MAN AS HIS OWN OBSERVER** Mr J. J. M. Harbison and Joan I. Harbison	283
Chapter 11	**ATTITUDES** Dr Alan Richardson	298
Chapter 12	**COMMUNICATING WITH THE PATIENT** Dr P. Ley	321
	INDEX	344

Introduction

John C. Coleman

This book is intended for students at the introductory or pre-clinical level. The book reflects the belief of each of the contributors that psychology can be, not only of interest, but of direct relevance to those studying medicine and related subjects at this level. The material has been chosen with this specific goal in mind. The book is divided into three sections, each of them pertinent to medicine and health care in different ways.

Part One concerns Fundamental Processes of Psychological Functioning. This section should be of help to the student in understanding both his own functioning, with respect to perceiving, remembering, learning and so on, as well as that of the patients with whom he will come into contact. Part Two is entitled Human Growth and Development. This is often the area of greatest interest to students, and has obvious relevance not only to the individual's own growth process, but to numerous medical specialities such as obstetrics and gynaecology, paediatrics, geriatrics and general practice. Lastly Part Three concerns Social Psychology as Related to Medicine. Here topics of particular importance in health care have been discussed, and the student should find these chapters especially useful when he or she first starts to think about some of the strengths and weaknesses inherent in medical practice.

For the teacher of psychology in the medical context the book will, it is hoped, provide material upon which to base either a short or a fairly extensive introductory course. It must be pointed out, however, that each chapter reflects the individual bias of the author concerned, and the book should not be seen as a definitive text. It is rather a set of writings by a number of well-known psychologists which may form the basis for discussions in lectures or seminar groups. It should also constitute the background reading for each topic, encouraging students to think carefully about the issues involved. If it manages to do this the book will have been a success.

Introduction

Finally I should like to express my gratitude to John Graham-White. The original idea for this book was his, and he was responsible for a large proportion of the early work. I am sorry that he was not able to complete it, but I hope that he will feel pleased with the end result.

Contributors

D. B. Bromley, BA, PhD, FBPsS, Professor of Psychology, University of Liverpool.

H. J. Butcher, BA, PhD, Professor of Developmental Psychology, University of Sussex.

Gordon Claridge, BA, PhD, DSc, Lecturer in Abnormal Psychology, Fellow of Magdalen College, Oxford.

J. C. Coleman, BA, PhD, Senior Lecturer in Clinical Psychology, The London Hospital Medical College.

B. M. Foss, Professor of Psychology, Bedford College, University of London.

J. J. M. Harbison, BA, MSc, Principal, Social Research, Statistics and Economic Unit, Dept of Finance, N. Ireland.

Joan I. Harbison, BA, MSc, Lecturer, Stranmillis College of Education, Belfast.

Harry Kay, MA (Oxon. and Cantab.), PhD, Vice-Chancellor, University of Exeter.

P. Ley, BA, DipPsychol, PhD, FBPsS, Senior Lecturer in Clinical Psychology, University of Liverpool.

Dougal Mackay, BA, MSc, Principal Psychologist, St Mary's Hospital, London.

Contributors

Irene Martin, PhD, Reader in Physiological Psychology, University of London.

Roderick Pakenham Power, MA, PhD (Sydney), FBPsS, Senior Lecturer, School of Behavioural Sciences, Macquarie University, Australia.

Alan Richardson, PhD, Reader in Psychology, The University of Western Australia.

F. S. Stevens, BSc, DipEd, ABPsS, Principal Lecturer in Psychology and Senior Educational Lecturer, Manchester Polytechnic.

Part One

Fundamental Processes of Psychological Functioning

Chapter one

Relations between Psychology and Physiology

Irene Martin

Many people are unsure what psychology is and should be about. They hesitate over its methods of investigation and measurement, and remain uncertain about the background of thought that guides its operations. Yet it holds an unquestionably significant role in the biological sciences, linking with the physiological sciences on the one side and social and anthropological studies on the other. It is with the former link that we are primarily concerned in this chapter, although, as we shall see later, the intricate set of interrelations is expanding to include clinical areas such as psychiatry, psychosomatic medicine and even general medicine.

Psychology has inherited a great diversity of viewpoints, and the apparently divisive features of its interests and problems can more readily be understood in historical perspective. In the first place, however, we must admit to a certain arbitrariness in any subject-matter; what we define as psychology today depends on what topics are regarded as important and what questions can be meaningfully asked. A hundred years ago psychology would have been very differently defined.

The earliest and most influential traditions were those of religion and philosophy; hence arose problems centred on the soul, spirit, will, consciousness and, of course, the mind. Many of the speculations verged on mysticism and were essentially outside any scientific framework as we would conceive it today. Many of the questions asked (and answers sought) were of a metaphysical nature. It was difficult to know how to view man; he appeared to be both an immaterial soul and a material body.

Questions about mind–body relationships figure very largely in the history of psychology. In pre-Darwinian days it was believed that man was differentiated from lower animals in that he alone possessed a rational soul; and it was frequently hypothesized that this soul (or mind) operated from very different laws from those that governed the more machine-like operations of the body. Of all philosophers, Descartes is most famous for his dualistic view of mind and body. According to this view, the body which was physical could be explained on mechanistic lines. Like the rest of the physical world it could be treated by the quantitative techniques of the physical scientist. The workings of the mind, on the other hand, could not be treated by quantitative techniques; they could only be understood by introspection, by the analysis of our own consciousness. This dualistic outlook resulted in a dualistic psychology: on the one hand mechanistic and objective so far as physiological mechanisms were concerned; on the other hand introspective and subjective so far as mental life was concerned.

The influence of Darwinian biology began to be felt in psychology at the end of the nineteenth and the beginning of the twentieth century, when Darwinian biologists started to study man in the same sort of way as they studied animals, and to use the same sort of explanatory account of human behaviour. Psychologists appreciated the opportunities afforded by the biological outlook. They began to see different problems they could study. Armchair philosophizing, preoccupation with unanswerable questions on the nature of the mind and the soul, the use of introspection and self-analysis as techniques for obtaining data, all these were dropped. Psychology became the study of behaviour, objective, scientific and devoted to the observational and experimental method. This dedication to a biological approach shifted the emphasis in psychology from mind to behaviour, from mental events to the kind of behavioural adaptation processes which had been evolved in the struggle for survival. Psychologists began to assert that psychology need never use the terms consciousness, mental states, mind, content, introspection. It was no longer a study of consciousness but a study of behaviour, of the organism's adaptation to its environment, of stimulus–response interaction.

This 'behaviourist' group of psychologists were very keen to model themselves on the physical scientist; and to begin the task of studying behaviour within the laboratory they were necessarily forced to use relatively simple forms of experimental subjects. In this way the white rat became greatly favoured. Problems of motivation, of learning, of intelligence and anxiety were studied in this context. The theories which were developed were simply extended to man. In this era, which lasted until about the half-way mark of this century, interest in human experience declined within academic, experimental psychology. It could not fail to remain of significance in applied areas and in allied clinical disciplines such as psychiatry. Hence the controversy and bewilderment about psychology: is it about man and his experiences (as the layman would suppose) or about seemingly insignificant bits of behaviour in special strains of rats? To the clinician, the contents of the 'mind' – how a person verbalized his thoughts and feelings – would always seem of importance. To the experimental psychologist such private verbalizations were of little use in building up a quantitative set of data from which general laws – of learning, memory, intelligence, etc. – could be built.

A further and more recent influence on psychological research has been that of technological development. It is about a hundred years since the first recordings were made of electrical activity from the surface of the brain. It is now possible to implant electrodes to provide information about the brain's activity, to inject pharmacologic agents to alter it, and to make precise lesions within the central nervous system. In a way, although the brain was a 'thing' which could be viewed, its workings had been just as mysterious as those of the mind. With the new techniques which became available, the activity of the brain could be studied in the normal, awake individual during states of psychological interest such as emotion, sleep, excitement and learning. Subject-matter divisions have been revised and a large number of hybrids developed: psychopharmacology, psychoneurology, psychosomatic medicine, psychophysiology and psychobiology, all concerned with the interaction between mind and brain in scientifically discoverable ways.

This chapter will be concerned with empirical studies from such disciplines. It will attempt to illustrate in outline the kind of experiments which have been carried out linking mental events such as thoughts, ideas, memories, perceptions, with physiological activity such as autonomic arousal and cortical alerting, and with their effects on observable behaviour. Such investigations are carried out from differing angles. For example, there are experiments which use drugs known to produce an altered bodily state (like adrenaline) and which examine how the individual's perceptions, attitudes and subjective awareness of events might change. This approach is to manipulate the bodily state and to assess what psychological changes follow as a consequence. The converse approach would be to manipulate psychological factors (for example, by discussing the individual's attitude to his work and family), on the hypothesis that a reappraisal of himself in relation to others might be followed by an alleviation of somatic symptoms. The assumption underlying this work, although not often made explicit, is that of a symmetrical interaction between mind and body.

The philosophical aspects of the mind–body relationship are discussed as much today as they have been for decades. Attempts to resolve the relation between mental events and physical processes have ranged from 'dualism', where mind and body though interacting are interpreted as essentially different from one another, to the 'identity theses' or 'double-language' hypothesis, in which it is argued that the two languages (mental and neural) do share a common referent, namely brain processes. It can be argued that 'mind' and 'body' are only two ways of describing observed events, i.e., two different kinds of language.

One way in which the languages may differ is in their level of explanation. This then raises the controversy of reductionism versus holism, i.e., the allegedly fundamental distinction between atomistic, micromechanistic terms of explanation on the one hand, and the concept of wholeness on the other. The former finds its most outspoken contemporary advocates in the field of molecular biology. The latter view is often expressed in the concept of the system as a whole. General systems theory is a discipline concerned with properties and principles of 'wholes' or systems in general, irrespective of their particular nature and the nature of their components. The best-known of the various systems approaches is cybernetics, the theory of communication and control, with its basic concepts of information transfer and feedback (see Koestler and Smythies, 1969, for a forceful and lively defence of holism and rejection of reductionism).

The idea of treating the brain formally as a communication system is helpful in bringing psychological and physiological data to bear jointly on the same problems, despite the different terms in which they are expressed. Recent theory construction in cybernetics, information theory and general systems theory make use of constructs which are neither physical nor psychological, but are applicable to both fields. In this way the problem becomes the formulation of a generalized theory within which both psychological and neurophysiological constructs appear as specifications.

Implications of mind–body issues may be detected in views on illness and disease expressed by clinicians. Typically, for example, the doctor and his patient oscillate between two mind–body theories: interactionism and independence. An interactionist statement would be of the order: 'The body influences the mind and the mind influences the body.' Belief in independence is illustrated in such remarks as: 'There's nothing physically wrong with you; it's all mental.' It is felt that practical consequences of these ways of thinking arise in the handling of specific patients. One is that if a disease is called 'psychological' there is the hazard of not looking for 'physical' causes. Conversely, if a disease is called 'physical' there is likely to be no serious search for 'psychological' factors in its aetiology.

Recent thinking, however, tends to refute the conflict between mind and body. 'Mind' and 'matter' are abstractions that are becoming increasingly inadequate in modern science; are we justified in claiming the 'reality' of minds, brains and bodies? The concept of 'matter' in the classical sense is abandoned in modern physics. Similarly, the concept of 'mind' may be an inadequate label for a complicated dynamic process. Possibly, expressions such as 'mental' and 'physical' are nothing more than ways of analysing our experience. They may no more correspond to something in reality than do such concepts as 'the Equator' or an 'engram'. These arguments are based on the nature of our immediate experience and the way we interpret and label this experience.

This kind of controversy well illustrates the metaphysical speculations from which psychologists wanted to be free. It was no doubt with relief that they turned to more tangible problems of observable behaviour and measurement. In many ways the present period is preoccupied with the refinement of both physiological and psychological measurements. We can measure physiological changes both from the body surface and from deeply lying structures of the brain with considerable degrees of accuracy and safety. We can measure overt behaviour with an array of methods. This mass of information can be sorted and analysed by computers. Introspective experience, too, is being subjected to analysis and measurement by a variety of techniques. We can begin to measure moods, feelings, judgments, opinions, attitudes and other aspects of experience through careful construction of questionnaires, tests and scales. The results of all these efforts are that a many-sided view can be obtained on such traditional categories of human experience as, say, anxiety. As discussed in the chapter on emotions, we can attempt to measure anxiety by taking careful notes of the patient's own self-reports, by measuring his behaviour (that is, what he actually does) in situations which he judges to be anxiety-provoking, and by recording physiological changes indicative of emotion, such as cardiovascular activity, sweating, tremor and so on. All these many measures comprise the state we label 'anxiety'. It is inappropriate to ask which of them all is the 'best' measure of anxiety. Our answer would be that experience, physiological change and external behaviour are all part of what we call anxiety, and that the many components interact with one another. Classical physiology tolerated only one unknown quantity in its equations, and held there could be only one thing at a time under investigation. Contemporary views of science accept that we have to deal with the interaction of many variables and unknowns. It becomes necessary to study the complex pattern of responding, and to try to determine how the overall pattern is organized in the efficiently functioning individual, as well as in cases of pathological anxiety.

Of the many interdisciplinary studies which have emerged in the past few decades, we shall examine a few in which psychology and physiology profitably interact. These are physiological psychology, psychophysiology, and psychosomatic medicine.

Physiological psychology

This is the oldest of the three disciplines and has produced a considerable amount of information on such topics as sleep and waking, on the brain centres which regulate drives and emotions, and on the neural concomitants of learning. As its name implies, its emphasis is on manipulation of the physiology of the organism, with a view to studying the effects of such manipulation on behaviour. The nature of the work typically involves infra-human animals, since its procedures are often inappropriate to human experimentation. These frequently include recordings from implanted electrodes, stimulation of brain centres, and experimental lesions.

The primary focus is on those physiological processes and their anatomical substrates which intervene between the arrival of sensory signals in the central nervous system and the elaboration of appropriate responses to them. The area includes investigations of the brain mechanisms that underlie emotion, memory, thinking, learning, drives (hunger, thirst, sex), and various other aspects of motivation and behaviour.

The contribution of technical developments to this area of study is very considerable. Although microelectrodes have been used for many years to record the electrical activity of the brain, these experiments required the use of anaesthesia and immobilizing drugs which altered the state of the nervous system. The recent development of techniques for chronically implanting electrodes in the brain and stimulating by radio has enabled physiological psychologists to study the effects of electrical stimulation of the brain on behaviour without the complicating effects of having to restrain and to anaesthetize the animal. Such methods enable records to be taken of the electrical activity of the brain during many different kinds of behaviour.

The results of this kind of work demand a revision in our previous concept of how the brain works. They make it clear that the various ganglia lying at the base of the brain, and various subcortical structures such as the hypothalamus, play an intrinsic part in higher mental functions of all kinds. Until such discoveries were made, the study of how the brain handles complex behaviour was almost exclusively focused on its uppermost covering layer, the neocortex. It was thought that the more important kinds of mental function such as thinking, remembering and learning were in some way localized in the network of nerve cells that make up the neocortex, and attention had been primarily focused on the primary sensory and motor areas, and on the so-called associative areas.

One of the interesting discoveries of the past few decades concerns the role of the reticular formation in sleep and wakefulness. Striking effects on activation levels are exerted by the meso-diencephalic system, composed of the reticular formation and the diffuse thalamic projection system. Studies have shown that the classical sensory pathways, as they pass through the lower brain stem, give off collaterals which set up recurrent discharges in the reticular formation. The effect of this lateral stimulation is transmitted upwards in the brain, where it produces widespread cortical arousal (i.e., fast, low amplitude, desynchronized activity) associated with behavioural activation (tension of skeletal muscles, increased autonomic activity, respiration, etc.). Conversely, the production of large experimental lesions in its cephalic portion results in chronic loss of wakefulness, the animal appearing as though asleep.

Current evidence points to reticular deactivation as the physiological basis for sleep, and two possible sets of mechanisms have been proposed: one a passive and one an active process. The central reticular structures are normally 'energized' as a result of combined peripheral sensory stimulation via sensory collaterals and physical, biochemical and hormonal changes in the *milieu intérieur*. When these are blocked or missing, reticular deactivation occurs. Such deactivation may result from either a reduction in outside stimulation or diurnal biochemical and hormonal variations, or from both. Normal sleep-preparatory behaviour would lead to a reduction in both types of stimulation. These processes are those of passive reticular deactivation. However, two types of active influence on the reticular system have been described: those ascending from bulbar structures and those descending from the cortex. Figure 1.1 is a diagrammatic representation of some of these processes.

There has been much speculation concerning the significance of the reticular activating system in the perception of external stimuli. It has been debated whether cortical registration of afferent stimulation can occur by way of the afferent pathways in the absence of reticular formation activation of the cortex. Under deep anaesthesia, when the electrocortical activating role of the reticular system is reduced or abolished, evoked potentials at the cortex may be elicited as well as before. This suggests that the elimination of reticular system activity has not prevented the transmission of sensory messages over the classical sensory pathways and via the specific relay nuclei of the thalamus to the primary receiving areas. However, behaviourally, the animal does not respond to these messages in a discriminative way. Thus the inference can be drawn that, for perception to occur, elaboration and integration of messages received at the cortex is dependent upon the reticular activating system and probably also the diffuse projection nuclei of the thalamus.

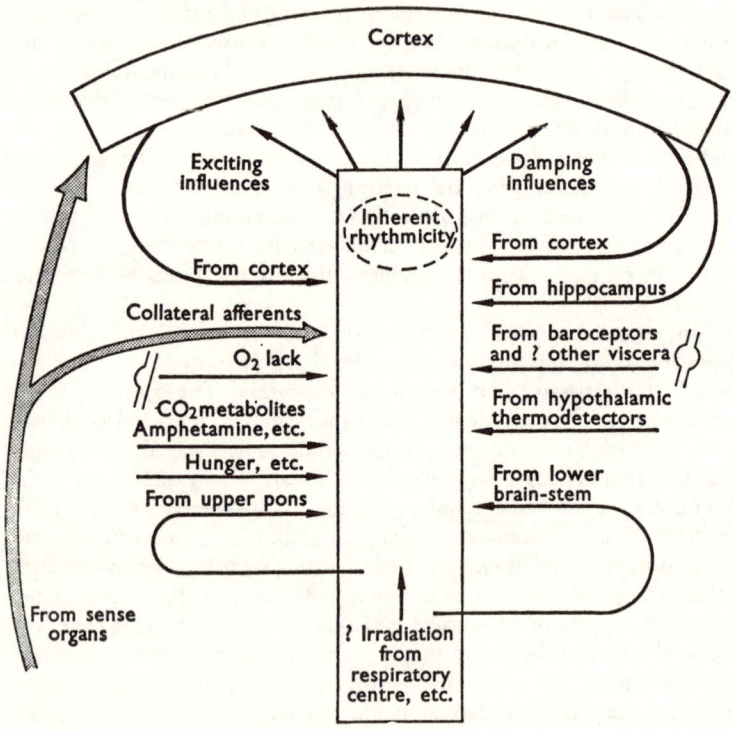

Figure 1.1 The factors that maintain the dynamic equilibrium of the upper reticular formation and the consequent level of sleep-wakefulness (reproduced from Oswald, 1962)

The role of the reticular formation has been implicated in the orienting reaction, a response to novel or significant stimuli which involves alerting, turning towards the source of the stimulus, and a large number of concomitant physiological changes. The purpose of these changes is to make the animal sensitive to incoming stimuli so that it is better equipped to discern what is happening and to mobilize the body for whatever action may be necessary. Typically, the response pattern will weaken to repetitions of the stimulus. This has led theorists to propose that there is an analysing mechanism, possibly located within the cortex, which assesses the significance and novelty of incoming stimuli. According to this conception, incoming stimuli leave traces of their characteristics within the nervous system. These traces are 'neuronal models' which preserve information about the intensity, quality, duration, etc. of past stimuli and with which new stimuli are compared. Various theories have been proposed concerning the type and site of these models and their relationship to factors of perception which underlie attention and reaction to events in the external environment.

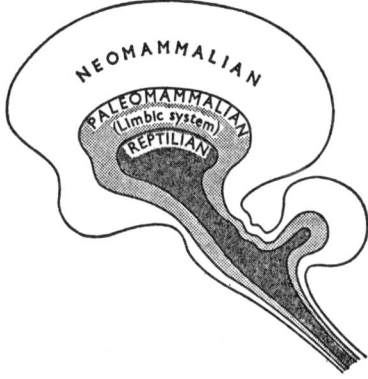

Figure 1.2 In evolution, the human brain expands in hierarchic fashion along the lines of three basic patterns referred to in the diagram as reptilian, paleomammalian and neomammalian. As indicated in parentheses, the limbic system conforms to the paleomammalian (from Maclean, 1975)

Contemporary research is also adding to our knowledge of the physiological basis of emotion. In 1937 the neurologist Papez proposed a theory of emotion that involved many structures of the brain either considered to be primarily olfactory in function or not known definitely to have any function at all. These included the hippocampus, fornix, mammillary bodies of the hypothalamus, and cingular gyrus; they were shown to belong together in one system, the limbic system. It has since been proposed that in its evolution the primate forebrain expands along the lines of three basic patterns that may be characterized as reptilian, paleomammalian and neomammalian (see Figure 1.2). There results a linkage of three cerebrotypes which are different in chemistry and structure and which in an evolutionary sense are aeons apart (Maclean, 1975). The three brain types are extensively interconnected and functionally dependent, yet each cerebrotype seems to have its own special kind of intelligence, its own special memory, its own sense of time and space, and its own motor and other functions. Whereas intellectual expression may be carried out by the use of verbal symbols which require a well-developed cortex, emotional expression can be achieved by the more primitive neural mechanisms of the limbic system, using a sort of 'organ language' instead of words. To this system is ascribed the mediation of emotional experience and expression and it has been emphasized that it occupies a strategic location for the correlation of feelings, particularly those arising from the internal organs of the body.

In early experiments attempting to locate the site of emotional expression, relatively complete ablations of the cerebral cortex (total decortication) were carried out in a variety of experimental animals, typically cats and dogs. A state of sham rage was described in these animals, characterized by easily aroused displays of anger to trivial stimuli and a relative inability to co-ordinate a directed attack. Displays of rage have also been elicited in cats by stimulating the hypothalamus: again the label 'sham' was applied inasmuch as the aggressive activity seemed not to be directed toward specific objects in the environment, the reactions ceased abruptly at the end of the stimulus, and the animals might continue to lap milk, purr, or respond to petting during hypothalamic stimulation, despite a concurrent display of rage.

Compared with the animal data, relatively little is known about the effects of lesions on human emotions. Much of the information which is available relates to accidental lesions. One such study on the emotional life of paraplegics and quadriplegics noted that subjects with cervical lesions described themselves as acting emotional but not feeling emotional. A typical report was: 'Seems like I get thinking mad, not shaking mad, and that's a lot different.' Clinical studies have frequently reported emotional changes following psychosurgical operations such as prefrontal leucotomy, and after neurosurgery for illnesses such as Parkinson's disease, but the evidence is inconsistent and difficult to interpret.

Particular attention has been given in experimental studies to the hypothalamus, which is believed to be the focal, organizing structure of emotional behaviour. The classic experiments that point to the importance of the hypothalamus were made with dogs and cats, in whom the complete rage response could be elicited only so long as the hypothalamus was intact. With sections below the hypothalamus, emotional responses became fragmentary. The conclusion was, therefore, that there is some mechanism in the hypothalamus for organizing the somatic patterns of emotional response.

It is known that the main centres for integrating patterns of autonomic effects is in the hypothalamus. The experiments of Hess (1954) had shown that the posterior portion of the hypothalamus, in the area of the mammillary bodies, is organized as a sympathetic integrating system. He called this portion of the hypothalamus the 'ergotrophic' zone. Stimulation of this zone in cats allowed to move freely produces general features of alertness and arousal, even aggressiveness if stimulation is continued. Hess suggested that this posterior part of the hypothalamus is concerned with the autonomic support of such defensive reactions as flight and attack.

In contrast, stimulation in the front of the hypothalamus leads to different types of both autonomic and behavioural responses. Electrical stimulation of this area, called the 'trophotrophic' zone, gave rise to responses of a parasympathetic type, with slowing of heart rate and dilatation of the blood vessels in the stomach and intestine. The animals became calm and drowsy. These results suggest that the trophotrophic zone is organized to deal with vegetative events like digestion and metabolic processes of repair.

In his explicit descriptions of affective responses following stimulation of the entire diencephalic system, Hess has provided much evidence for the integration and co-ordination of sympathetic and parasympathetic responses at the level of the hypothalamus. More recent research has advanced our understanding of the interaction between hypothalamic and pituitary functioning.

This interaction is believed to play an important role in the physiological basis of motivation. Most basic motivational forces arise from some physiological need state, for example the organism's energy and fluid balances, which are usually maintained within rather narrow limits. Some compelling drives, however (such as sexual motivation), cannot be traced to specific needs or deficiencies and may not be expressed in overt behaviour. Sexual motivation is of particular interest to physiological psychology because it demonstrates very clearly the close interaction between environmental and organismic variables. On the one hand sexual motivation is very closely related to various secretions of the endocrine system, but although hormonal mechanisms are indispensable to sexual drive and behaviour they are not by themselves sufficient to elicit sexual motivation; rather, they prime the organism to respond appropriately. Given a physiologically ready organism, sexual motivation seems to be aroused very directly by the stimulus of the sexual partner.

Hypothalamic mechanisms also attract a major share of experimental and theoretical attention in physiological studies of hunger and thirst, which have been carried out for many years. Theories come and go, and still no entirely satisfactory account of eating and drinking behaviour is forthcoming. Electrical stimulation or extirpation of relatively small and well-defined regions of the ventral aspect of the diencephalon produce drastic and sometimes irreversible changes in food intake and food motivation. Hyperphagia and obesity following injury or tumour growth in the general region of the hypothalamus have been reported in the clinical literature for over a hundred years. The hypothalamus is directly connected to all regions of the central nervous system that influence feeding behaviour; and it is often thought that the hypothalamus may contain the master control which integrates the information from both peripheral and central sources. Future research in this field will have to concentrate on the physiological mechanisms that excite or inhibit the hypothalamic centres and on the integrative processes that translate the resultant hypothalamic activity into overt behaviour.

Other areas of investigation carried out along similar lines are concerned with reproductive behaviour and its wide range of activities: maternal, nesting, sucking and contact behaviour, hoarding, homing and migration. This kind of behaviour is of great interest to ethologists, who have studied it typically in natural surroundings and have put forward several theories of instinctive activity. In addition to ethological investigation a considerable amount of laboratory work has been accomplished. This work is as sophisticated on the behavioural side as on the physiological. Analysis of the maternal behaviour in some mammals and birds, for example, suggests several distinct and essential activities: nest-building, behaviour during birth, retrieving the young, and suckling the young. In most of these instances, an essential factor in the instigation of the behaviour is said to be an internal state, a specific hormonal condition, or a deficit of specific substances in bodily tissues. The precise ways in which these various elements of behaviour are affected by hormones and by brain lesions leads to the conclusion that they are complexly and variously controlled within the nervous system and in conjunction with appropriate environmental conditions. A thorough summary of the factors involved in reproductive behaviour, emotion and in drives such as hunger and thirst, can be found in Cofer and Appley (1964), Grossman (1967), and Morgan (1965).

Another topic which must be mentioned in this section is that of learning and its physiological mechanisms. Several kinds of learning have been examined in these experiments, usually classical conditioning, instrumental learning and discriminative learning (see Chapter 4). The main method for studying neural aspects of learning was the brain lesion, mostly in the cerebral cortex. With the advent of stereotaxic methods of making lesions deep within the brain, more information has been obtained from subcortical regions. One approach is to correlate recorded electrical events with the behavioural phenomena of conditioning. Such events may be electroencephalographic, i.e., changes in the rhythmic patterns of the brain, and evoked potentials, recorded either by gross electrodes or from microelectrodes in single units. A novel stimulus typically desynchronizes cortical alpha rhythms, and also produces fairly widespread evoked potentials in the brain. They may be recorded in the primary sensory pathways and the indirect reticular pathways, as expected, but they may also appear in many other places and in cortical areas not directly related to the sensory system being stimulated. On repeated presentation of the stimulus the alpha and evoked responses typically habituate. With the development of the conditioned response, however, the evoked potentials become more widespread and larger in amplitude.

These studies of changes in electrographic response during learning represent a more technically sophisticated variant of ablation studies, in the sense that information is obtained about the detailed changes of activity in specific anatomical regions. However, the functional role of such involvement remains obscure. As conditioned responses are established, the pattern of electrical reaction to the conditioned stimuli shifts, which suggests that the participation of particular regions varies at different stages of the formation of the response.

Any physiological theory of learning must account for the way that a memory trace is laid down in the nervous system. Earlier experiments in which learning (usually conditioning) was followed by ablation of various cortical regions had yielded little positive clues about where the memory trace is localized. Rather, they gave rise to the feeling that memories are not localized but are multiply represented throughout different regions of the cortex. Subsequent electrophysiological research has confirmed and extended this view. It seems reasonable to conclude that learned behaviours are mediated by systems which are anatomically extensive and involve many brain regions.

A major contradiction to this conclusion may lie in the permanence of certain apparent memory defects in man, such as agnosias and apraxias, which are extremely discrete. These defects presumably arise from localized tissue destruction. Neural mechanisms which mediate the storage and access to elements of symbolic language in man may possess somewhat greater anatomical specificity than the mechanisms involved in the storage of the very much less precise and probably multidimensional elements which represent learned relationships in lower animals (John, 1967). Yet marked improvement in many kinds of activity seems possible after most brain lesions in man, particularly if no projection area is involved. Learning in human adults is extremely dependent upon pre-existing verbal associations, and man is particularly vulnerable to brain damage that abolishes verbal associations.

Most psychological theories have postulated two distinct memory mechanisms: one based on functional changes in the CNS to account for short-term memory; the other based on more permanent anatomical modifications to account for long-term storage. Several hypotheses have been proposed concerning the mechanism of memory. One particular hypothesis postulates structural changes, specifically that changes take place in presynaptic knobs. These are the knobs containing the synaptic vesicles from which the neuro-transmitter is secreted when an impulse terminates in their vicinity. Since acetylcholine is the principal transmitter substance in the central nervous system the theory implies that acetylcholine may somehow be involved in learning (for further discussion see Chapter 3).

With advancing knowledge in protein chemistry, attempts have been made in recent years to develop a protein theory of events taking place in learning, and quite recently the theory has been put forward that learning causes certain changes in ribonucleic acid (RNA). While there is some evidence both that the metabolism of acetylcholine and changes in RNA are involved with the memory trace, considerably more research is necessary to clarify the nature of the relationship.

Many of the experiments described in this section have referred to electrical stimulation of the brain with a view to observing the effects on eating, drinking, sleeping, sexual or emotional behaviour. It was accidentally discovered, however, that when electrodes were implanted in certain regions of the brain and the animal was able to press a lever to stimulate its own brain, it seemed to seek and to 'enjoy' this form of stimulation (see Figure 1.3). Localization experiments showed that when electrodes were implanted in the classical sensory and motor systems response rates stayed at the chance level of 10 to 25 lever presses an hour. In most parts of the limbic system, the response rates rose to levels of from 200 to 5,000 lever presses an hour, indicative of a strongly 'rewarding' effect of the electrical stimulus. In fact, electrical stimulation of some of these regions actually appeared to be more rewarding than food.

At about the same time it was also observed that stimulation of certain hypothalamic parts appeared to be 'aversive' and to motivate the animal to learn to terminate (i.e., escape) such stimulation when it is presented. These effects are observed from only a very small number of electrodes sited in the posterior and lateral diencephalon and lateral segmental regions.

It is uncertain as yet why electrical stimulation is so rewarding. One tentative conclusion is that emotional and motivational mechanisms are localized in the brain, and that brain stimulation in these regions may excite some of the nerve cells that would be excited by satisfaction of basic drives, such as hunger, sex or thirst.

Popular accounts of this research refer to the 'pleasure areas' of the brain. These are normally electrically activated by various kinds of

Figure 1.3 The brain self-stimulation circuit. When the rat presses on the lever, it triggers an electrical stimulus to its brain and simultaneously records its action via wire on the left

stimuli acting on the peripheral receptors; one semi-serious suggestion is that people seek those types of stimuli which provide maximal amounts of electrical activation in their pleasure centres!

Psychophysiology

This is one of the studies which examines relationships between bodily and mental events, usually with human subjects. In a typical experiment, physiological responses are recorded to stimuli which are designed to influence mental, emotional or motor behaviour. The general goal of psychophysiology is to correlate physiological processes with psychological constructs such as emotion, attitude, attention, motivation, learning, and personality. It differs from physiological psychology in its concentration on human subjects, its use of body surface recordings rather than implanted electrodes, and in its reliance on external stimulation (by sensory stimuli, films, conversation, and by a variety of laboratory situations which simulate real-life events) rather than on direct intervention of brain processes. As its name might imply, it concentrates rather more on the psychological than physiological side of the system; its interest in physiology is restricted to the relationship with the psychological.

It is surprising how extensive are the recordings which can be obtained from the intact skin surface. Measures of autonomic activity are quite numerous: sweating (usually of the palms), blood flow, blood volume, blood pressure, heart rate, temperature, pupillary changes, salivation, chemical variations in the composition of blood, saliva and urine. In addition, respiratory changes can be recorded, measure of skeletal muscle activity, and the electrical activity of the cortex (EEG). A number of less common measures include gastro-intestinal motility, metabolic rate, tremor, eye movements and blinks.

When a specific stimulus is applied (sudden flash of light or an unexpected sound) a number of responses can be detected. Reflex eyelid closure can occur within the first 100 msec., as well as muscular components of the startle reflex. Various components of the cortical evoked response occur within the 50 to 300 msec. range. The pupil will begin to dilate with onset latencies between 300 and 400 msec. Many of these responses will be completed or in the process of recovery by the time that EEG changes are observed; autonomic effects like change in heart rate, sweating and blood pressure are even slower.

Latencies of peripheral responses can be partially understood in terms of transmission rates along effector fibres and innervation of peripheral end organs. The amplitude of a response, its duration and recovery are far less clearly understood. They will relate to properties of end organs and undoubtedly to homeostatic factors that act to reduce the disturbance. They also seem to relate to a variety of psychological factors.

In a typical psychophysiological experiment a stimulus or situation is presented which is expected to produce a certain psychological reaction, possibly of anxiety or frustration, interest or attention. Concomitant physiological recordings show how the subject becomes activated at the initial presentation of the stimulus, and how response characteristics reflect the nature of the stimulus material, highly emotional stimuli, for example, being typically followed by large, long-lasting, slow recovering autonomic responses. Whatever the nature of the material, however, there is usually a decline in responsivity with successive repetition, until after many repetitions of a stimulus the person may cease to respond altogether.

Considerable individual variability in responsivity has been demonstrated, and an attempt has been made to understand this in terms of the individual's basic personality traits, and also in terms of his current status, i.e., whether relaxed, anxious or aroused. One individual will orient strongly to a mild stimulus and fail to habituate to it even when it is shown to be unimportant. Some people are afraid of apparently trivial situations and overreact to them, while others are unreactive emotionally even though some degree of reaction would seem to be appropriate. Obviously the study of individual differences is important, and one area of psychophysiology attempts to relate physiological patterns of reaction to types of personality and psychiatric categories.

In the psychophysiological literature it has been useful to differentiate ongoing levels of physiological activity (those that occur, for example, during periods of rest, states of attention, thinking, sleeping) from specific responses with characteristic waveforms superimposed on these levels, generally occurring as a result of an external stimulus. It is believed that levels of peripheral physiological activity reflect underlying changes in some central sleep-waking continuum, shifting up or down as the individual becomes more alerted or more relaxed. The concept of 'arousal', 'activation', or 'energy mobilization' has been developed to refer to a behavioural continuum ranging from deep to lighter stages of sleep, to drowsiness and through to normal levels of alertness and wakefulness. A heightened level of arousal seems to be a concomitant of intense emotions, although the state of arousal *per se* is not enough to define a specific emotional state.

Individuals at different levels of arousal seem to function behaviourally at different levels of efficiency. This is another important issue in psychophysiology. Whereas the one mentioned above refers to the effects of psychological stimulation on physiological measures, the second refers to the effects of a given psychophysiological state on performance. In this context we can ask such questions as: given an excited organismic state, does the individual learn more or less quickly, and function more or less effectively? To have a highly aroused bodily state when the approaching 'danger' is no more than an important interview, a public lecture, or an oral examination may be positively disadvantageous, in that smooth action and cool thinking are disrupted. Conversely, if the individual is at a relaxed or sleepy physiological level, can he maintain adequate vigilance and remain sufficiently attentive to his surroundings, as in efficiently driving a car, for example?

Different kinds of hypotheses have been developed in connection with the short-term physiological responses which occur to specific stimuli and which have a characteristically sharp onset and more rapid recovery. These hypotheses relate to the information conveyed by the stimulus and implicate processing mechanisms of registration and storage, e.g., of information concerning the quality, intensity, duration, etc. of the stimulus. With successive repetitions of the stimulus a more detailed processing of input occurs, and it seems likely that a memory trace or 'model' of the stimulus is stored within the nervous system.

Many studies on habituation have illustrated the effects of stimulus repetition on physiological responsivity. The situation or stimulus which on first meeting fills us with apprehension will, on subsequent occasions, produce a weaker and weaker reaction, or none at all. A great deal of experimental evidence testifies to this fact, and typical habituation curves have been drawn which illustrate an initially rapid and subsequently more gradual decline in responsivity. The shape of the curve is dependent upon a number of factors, which includes stimulus quality, intensity, interval between successive presentations, and ongoing level of organismic arousal. Curves of habituation have been obtained for all kinds of behavioural, physiological (e.g., autonomic) as well as neuronal responses to stimulation.

There are exceptions to this widely observed phenomenon of habituation, and there is evidence that when strong emotions like fear are involved an opposite process (sensitization) can take place. In a primitive and changing world, there is obviously some need to be on guard against possible dangers. If we are alone in a house at night, we might be selectively tuned to certain sounds: footsteps, for example. If an unexpected sound occurs, we orient to that sound; that is to say, we will probably turn to its source in such a way that our receptors (ears in this instance) are better placed to hear further sounds. Bodily changes occur as indicated above. These may have many functions. Increase in EEG activity may be a concomitant of an alerted mental state; increases in autonomic activity may prepare us for some form of action.

Attention is narrowed to the source of the stimulus. It can be seen that there are many interrelated psychological and physiological changes. These generally seem to fall within the category of alerting and attending, and remain relatively contained unless we cognitively assess the situation to contain 'real' danger. If this does occur, and we decide that the sound is that of an intruder, obviously a strong physiological fear/alarm reaction will occur and some form of planned action will take place. The whole bodily system is then thrown into preparation for emergency action; adrenaline is released, the sympathetic nervous system becomes increasingly active and redistributes blood to the muscles as required for immediate and sustained muscular effort. This preparation for emergency action is of primitive origin and obviously had more adaptive significance in the past than it has today. Nevertheless, the mechanism still seems present within us and, coupled with processes of learning, may account for the way in which we acquire many seemingly irrational fears.

Bodily activation probably occurs most strongly and diffusely in states of intense emotion, but psychophysiological studies aimed to distinguish patterns of reaction peculiar to specific emotions have met with no great success. Apart from some evidence for differences in fear and anger, there is little to show that emotions can be distinguished by the pattern of reaction. Indeed, sympathetic activity seems to be a concomitant of almost every emotion; heart rate is elevated in love as in fear. It is, of course, possible that more refined techniques of measurement will reveal more subtle patterns and changes than have so far been detected. It is also possible that when we can obtain telemetric recordings in 'real-life' situations rather than in artificial laboratory situations we shall get clearer and better differentiated patterns of reactivity. It also seems to be the case that physiological arousal accompanies states which we would not normally identify as emotional. These include interest, attention and expectancy. Indeed, it is possible that bodily changes are at best rather limited in their variety as indicants of emotion – more strictly, it may be our awareness of such changes which is limited – and what makes us differentiate a rich inner emotional life is not so much altered physiology as attitudes, perceptions and cognitive states. Many workers would assign the differentiation of emotions as much to cognitive assessment of the environment as to an altered physiological state. Evidence to support this view comes from those studies in which adrenaline has been administered. Although exogenous administration of adrenaline produces all the sympathetic-like changes associated with fear, it has never been clearly established whether the subject really experiences fear. It has been suggested that peripherally released catecholamines acting directly on the brain or via visceral proprioceptors represent limited and rudimentary components of an emotional state and that some component is missing: this is the subject's cognitive evaluation of the situation as fear-producing or not. To understand human emotion fully, the expectancies, perceptions and judgments of the individual must be examined, as well as recordings of physiological change.

There can be little doubt that learning plays a large part in emotionality. The list of stimuli and situations which men and women find fearful is extremely lengthy. They include fears of small animals such as spiders, birds and cats; of thunder, of being confined in small spaces, of being exposed in wide-open space. They fear each other; they fear meetings, public talks, and so on. Hence the interest in the mechanisms of learning; what are the conditions which make for learning to fear so much? Why are fears retained through adult life even though the suffering individual knows they are inappropriate?

The rationale which lies behind techniques of behaviour modification as applied to the treatment of certain psychiatric conditions is that if a condition is learned then possibly it can be unlearned. Although some individuals may have learned to attach fears and anxieties to all sorts of stimuli and situations, there may be ways to modify if not eliminate such fears. Because the pattern of anxiety is so complex and involves not only the physiological state of the individual but also his perceptions and attitudes it may be necessary to try to unlearn both inappropriate physiological reactions and inappropriate psychological reactions and to re-learn new, more adaptive ways of responding.

Many studies have concentrated on the modification of physiological responses using operant conditioning techniques, more popularly called bio-feedback techniques. Impressive evidence has been accumulated that, with appropriate training, heart rates can be accelerated or decelerated, intestinal activity, blood pressure and EEGs increased or decreased, gastric blood flow raised or lowered. Studies with human subjects have been equivocal. It is not always clear whether they gain control over muscular relaxation, heart rate or blood flow directly as a result of the reinforcing reward schedule which is applied, as in the animal studies, or whether via effects of respiratory changes, alterations in muscle tension, or visual imagery of particular scenes. Certainly many individuals are capable, through imagination of emotional or relaxing events, of markedly increasing or decreasing physiological activity. It would be expected that an alteration in physiological levels would influence the subject's attitudes to and perceptions of his fear. Conversely, there are attempts to reduce physiological levels via cognitive-verbal control, as when the subject instructs himself: 'I feel relaxed, calm, and in control.' Such suggestions, if applied in appropriate ways, also help the individual to exert control over his own internal state.

Some psychophysiological research has been carried out in certain types of psychiatric patients. It has long been felt that anxiety states are characterized by a highly active sympathetic nervous system, such that they are in a constant state of autonomic arousal which is difficult to damp down, and which leads them to learn new emotional responses too rapidly. Other studies have examined the autonomic and motor reactions of depressives before and after treatment, in an attempt to understand the slow thinking and retarded action which are frequently reported. Hypotheses have been made concerning a possible reduction in normal levels of arousal and attempts made to differentiate types of depressive illness according to the pattern of psychophysiological responsivity which they show.

Along similar lines, psychophysiological reactions of schizophrenics have been studied. These patients show psychological withdrawal from their environment but, far from being unreactive, some seem to be physiologically over-aroused and highly reactive to certain kinds of stimuli. Research into EEG, heart rate and skin resistance activity has led to the suggestion that there is a tendency for acute and/or paranoid patients to be responsive to their environment and to show less habituation than normals, whereas the chronic or regressed patient tends to be slow in response and to show fewer and smaller responses. Work showing that schizophrenics experience more difficulty than normals in switching attention between modalities, and that distractability is heightened, adds to the view that attention is an important aspect of psychological deficit in these patients. This kind of clinical research, however, is attended by many problems: those of diagnosis both within and between cultures, of acute v. chronic, of differing therapies (especially drugs) and effects of institutionalization, to name but a few.

Psychosomatic medicine

As its name implies, psychosomatic medicine concerns itself not only with a physiological but also a psychological approach to general medicine. As with physiological psychology and psychophysiology, it studies the interaction between mental and physical processes. Although both are probably involved to some extent in all diseases the problem of showing a cause and effect relationship between, say, an emotion and the pathological state is a difficult one. Over the years it has seemed that in certain illnesses emotional antecedents were more frequent or striking than in other diseases, and these have come to comprise a list which is identified as psychosomatic. It traditionally includes ulcerative colitis, peptic and duodenal ulcers, rheumatoid arthritis, essential hypertension, asthma and allergic illnesses such as hay fever and dermatitis, and coronary thrombosis. There is no general agreement on which illnesses are psychosomatic, the only common characteristic being the assumption that sustained or strong emotional disturbance plays a part in causing, aggravating, or maintaining the localized morbid process that is the disease in question.

A variety of explanatory hypotheses concerning the psychosomatic illnesses have been put forward over the years. In general, it is true to say that a psychoanalytic outlook has gradually been replaced by a more experimental approach. During the early phase of psychosomatic studies, when the psychoanalytic outlook dominated, the most frequently employed methods were biographical study (to determine personality-type and the timing of emotional crises) and the psychoanalytic study of psychic structure and conflict. This necessarily involved a retrospective examination of the patient's personal and social relationships, early mother–child interactions being considered particularly significant.

An illustration of this approach can be found in Alexander's conclusion that the gastric symptoms of duodenal ulcer are connected with 'intense oral-receptive tendencies' and a more or less repressed wish to be loved: the oral tendencies were opposed to the desire for activity and independence so that a conflict was generated. The symbolic value of an ulcer is brought out in the assumption that oral-receptive traits betoken a regressive tendency which leads the patient back to his infantile wish to be fed and so puts his stomach constantly into a state of readiness for food. There are many weaknesses in this type of psychoanalytic investigation: often a reliance upon a single patient or a very few patients, failure to demonstrate that a particular conflict-situation is specifically related to the disease, and a failure to recognize that other causal factors may be involved. Moreover, there is insufficient evidence for the belief that these patients can be cured by intensive psychotherapy.

Another quite popular hypothesis concerns what has been called 'organ vulnerability'. This suggests that a particular organ or function in a particular individual is especially liable to respond to psychological stress by exhibiting pathological changes. This hypothesis can be considered alongside the general evidence concerning visceral and other physiological reactions in response to stressful stimuli.

The sympathetic nervous system in general serves to provide emergency responses originally conceived to be flight or fight reactions. Under sympathetic arousal the heart beats faster and increases the amount of blood pumped out with each beat. Superficial blood vessels and those going to the gastro-intestinal tract constrict and blood pressure increases. Arteries serving the large muscles dilate and so their blood supply is increased. Pupils of the eyes dilate, increasing the amount of light impinging on the retina and thus improving visual acuity. The adrenal medulla secretes adrenaline which, besides reinforcing other sympathetic effects as it circulates in the blood, also causes the liberation of blood sugar from the liver, thus making available a larger energy source for the muscles. Breathing becomes faster and deeper so that more oxygen is available for metabolism.

During sleep, cardiovascular functions are reduced. The heart beats more slowly and the volume of blood pumped with each stroke is less. The blood flow to the periphery of the body is minimal, but that supplying the gastro-intestinal tract and the other abdominal organs is greater. Blood sugar is stored in the liver as glycogen. Digestive processes are increased, both in movement of the gastro-intestinal tract and the flow of digestive juices. Altogether the picture is one of rebuilding or restoring and is quite the opposite of the massive expenditure of energy seen in the catabolic (sympathetically dominated) states.

It has been suggested that some people show a dominance of parasympathetic or sympathetic features, that there is an imbalance towards one or the other system. Some individuals have been shown to give an unusually strong sympathetic response to injection of adrenaline, but only a slight parasympathetic response to atropine. On the other hand some show slight responses to sympathomimetic (adrenaline) and sympatholytic (ergotamine) drugs, but excessive reactions to parasympathomimetic (pilocarpine) and parasympatholytic (atropine) drugs.

This idea of a general sympathetic or general parasympathetic dominance has not, however, been too strongly supported by research evidence; what has emerged in such investigations is that there seems to be a tendency for individuals to respond with a particular physiological pattern to stressful stimuli. In normal, non-hospitalized subjects it has been shown, for example, that one individual may show a particularly large blood pressure change, and relatively little change in other systems. Another may show profuse sweating, another marked tremor. In other words it has been suggested that under stress the widespread sympathetic reactivity which occurs is patterned in a particular way for different individuals, with some responses being far more dominant than others. This has been termed 'individual response stereotypy' and is related to another principle, that of 'symptom specificity'. This states that, for patients with a somatic symptom, the physiological mechanisms underlying the symptom is specifically responsive to activation by stressful stimuli. Thus a patient suffering from severe headaches may show marked increases in muscle tension of the neck and head in stressful situations; another with high blood pressure may show marked changes in this system when stressed.

This particular area of research – of measuring different kinds of physiological reactions to different stresses – has produced many interesting findings in the past few decades. Experimenters have attempted to observe physiological changes to a wide variety of stressors. Those working with laboratory animals have demonstrated that situations involving a response in the animals which could best be described in the language we use for human emotions (fear, rage, pain) were accompanied or followed by visceral responses which if long sustained could conceivably be expected to lead to a morbid tissue change. These latter have been found to occur, but after such extensive and prolonged stress (e.g., severe pain and cold) that the applicability of the findings to human subjects remains uncertain.

The current popularity of the stress concept in psychobiology stems largely from the work of Selye (1956) who sees stress as the state of the organism following failure of the normal homeostatic regulatory mechanisms of adaptation. A main key to the understanding of Selye's concept of (systemic) stress is the distinction he makes between the specific effects induced by a stressor agent and the effects induced by such stimulation which are not specific to it. Thus, he observes that whereas one stimulus (e.g., cold) may produce a vasoconstriction and a second stimulus (e.g., heat) a vasodilation, both (or either) if applied intensely or long enough produce effects in common that are not specific to either stimulus. These common changes, taken together, constitute the stereotypical response pattern of systemic stress. Selye defines stress as 'a state manifested by a syndrome which consists of all the nonspecifically induced changes in a biologic system'. Thus it has its own characteristic form of expression, but no particular, specific cause.

The syndrome by which the stress state is made manifest is called the General Adaptation Syndrome (GAS). Its characteristic pattern includes three stages:

(1) Any systemic stress (i.e. one which affects large parts of the body) elicits an essentially similar syndrome, namely: the discharge of adrenocorticotrophic hormones (ACTH) into the blood stream, which stimulate the adrenal cortex to secrete various hormones. Major changes include adrenocortical enlargement, thymico-lymphatic involution and intestinal ulcers. This syndrome is the alarm reaction, and it includes both the initial shock phase of lowered resistance and a counter shock phase in which defensive mechanisms begin to operate.

(2) The second stage is the stage of resistance. It is one of acquired adaptation, because it helps the acquisition and maintenance of bodily resources to fight the stress.

(3) Finally, when exposure to stress is continued too long or the

stress is too severe, there comes the third stage, one of exhaustion. This is the result of prolonged over-exposure to stress. Adaptation wears out and many symptoms of the alarm reaction reappear, for instance gastro-intestinal ulcers and destruction of lymph cells.

This theory is very well presented in Selye's (1956) book, *The Stress of Life*. As can be seen from Figure 1.4, it implicates the pituitary-adrenal system, thus supplementing the earlier work which involved autonomic/adrenal medulla stress responses.

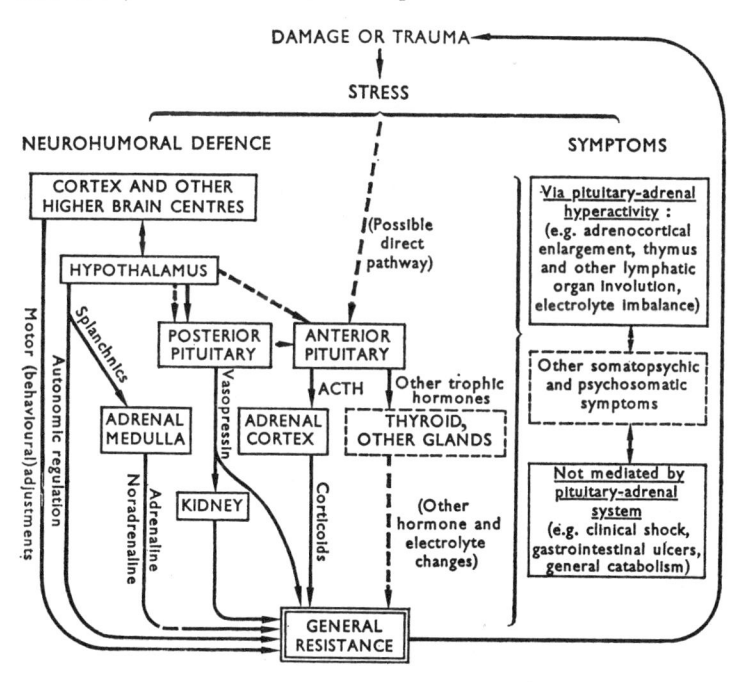

Figure 1.4 Partial schema of stress syndrome. (Solid lines represent known relations, broken lines uncertain relations) (reproduced from Cofer and Appley, 1964)

Experimenters using human subjects have attempted to observe physiological effects in a variety of experimental and real-life stresses; for example, in parachutists preparing for jumps, in students about to sit examinations, and in viewers of different types of film. In all these situations where emotional involvement is high there is a large increase in such physiological reactions as heart rate, muscle tonus, respiration, sweating and blood pressure. This type of work allows one to observe the relationship between physiological changes and different types of emotional stress, although most of the work so far has involved fear and anxiety.

In a more clinical setting, some ingenious work has been carried out with fistulous patients in whom gastric functions can easily be observed. It was found that fright, shame and gloom were accompanied by pallor of the gastric mucosa and decreased activity; anger, anxiety and hostility, on the other hand, were associated with humid, reddened mucosa, active secretion and increased motility. Experiments carried out on patients with duodenal ulcer indicate that unpleasant effect was mostly associated with a rise in acidity and in motility which was greater and lasted longer than in normal subjects.

All the recent experimental research shows just how much more complex the visceral discharge is than it was once assumed to be. Indeed, there are few physiological reactions of the organism which involve as many organs and systems and such profound changes as are seen in emotion. It is hardly surprising that repeated exposures to these effects may well alter the reactivity of the person and even induce permanent anatomical damage in various organs. Unfortunately, the long-term studies necessary to determine whether the particular pattern of autonomic reactivity observed in normal persons subjected to different stresses would result in frank psychosomatic illness have not been carried out. It would indeed be of interest to see whether the constitutional pattern of response suggests a proneness to disease in any particular system.

We can therefore sum up (after Lewis, 1967) the aim of research in this area as trying to demonstrate the following:

(*a*) that a characteristic type of personality and physique is associated with a particular pathological condition of the body;

(*b*) that a conflict, emotional upheaval or environmental 'stress' has closely preceded the onset of a pathological condition;

(*c*) that conflict or emotional stress under experimental conditions produced physiological changes which could, if severe or repeated, contribute to the development of a pathological condition;

(*d*) that a particular organ or function in a particular individual is especially liable to respond to psychological stress by exhibiting pathological changes; and

(*e*) that morbid tissue change can be induced regularly by emotional stress.

None of these hypotheses can be described as firmly supported by experimental evidence, but all have something to commend them. It is to be hoped that future research in these areas will prove to be more definitive, and it should perhaps be mentioned that it is only during the past few decades that a shift has occurred from clinical observation to laboratory research. The sweeping generalizations regarding the nature and influence of psychological variables in the causation of bodily disease which characterized the earlier phase of psychosomatic medicine have largely been replaced by careful research design. This frequently involves extensive control data, and the taking into account of many relevant factors such as age, sex, socio-economic status, personality, as well as the range of physiological factors involved.

The nature of the stressor agents which produce severe emotional disturbances has not in the past been very precisely defined. Although difficult to study, it has become widely accepted that one of the major stresses in life centres on interpersonal interrelationships. Since man is a tribal creature with a long period of development, he depends for his very existence on the aid, support and encouragement of those about him. He lives his life so much in contact with men and is so deeply concerned about their expectations of him that perhaps his greatest threat is their disapproval and rejection. The rapid increase in coronary heart disease, for example, speaks for human physiologic changes which have occurred far faster than could be accounted for on a genetic basis alone. Therefore recent attention has been focused upon man's environment and psychosocial *milieu* in search of broader aetiologic explanations of this disorder. (It is not denied, however, that proper attention must be paid to differing physiological and genetic predispositions to the disease.)

Investigators both in the USA and Europe have found certain psychosocial characteristics to occur commonly among subjects with coronary heart disease. Some have commented on the myocardial infarction patient's propensity to devote a tremendous share of his energies to his work. Others have noted the patient's high level of aggressiveness, competitiveness and strivings against time deadlines. In sum, psychosocial factors which have come to be suspected as predisposing to the development of coronary heart disease have been those which deal primarily with work behaviour, use of leisure time, home problems, and life problems and satisfactions.

However, it is obviously the case that the existence of an apparently stressful environment does not in itself trigger severe emotional reactions. It seems to be something, rather, in the individual's attitude to that environment which predisposes a maladaptive response. Recent work on what has been termed the 'specificity of attitude' hypothesis in psychosomatic disorders states that there is a specific relation between the attitude which a person develops towards a stressful situation and the physiological changes which occur in response to that situation.

The concern of this chapter has been with interrelationships between physiology and psychology, and experimental work has been described which illustrates some of the ways this interrelationship has been studied in the laboratory. With the rapid advances of technique in this area it has become possible to replace the immobilized, anaesthetized animal preparation with a freely moving, relatively normally functioning animal. Such an animal is able to interact much more naturally with its environment, albeit a restricted laboratory environment. When we come to study man, we have to add to the physiological data his subjective feelings and reports in order to understand more fully states like anxiety and pain. The next chapter will examine such states as emotion in more detail. This cross-sectional description must then be seen in perspective so that we can examine its causes (i.e. antecedents) and its consequences (i.e. behavioural interaction with the environment).

The conventional model of brain function as adopted from traditional physics conceives of the organism as an essentially inert system which is activated only by external factors. Modern biology, on the other hand, teaches us that the organism is not an ordinary physical system, that is, one corresponding to conventional (or rather, obsolete) physical theory: it is an open system, and among the characteristics of open systems is that they not only respond to stimuli but also show inner, self-regulatory activity.

We know little, as yet, about the effects of environmental stresses, including the effects of our normal social environment, on physiological and psychological reactions. The earlier analogues borrowed from physical systems spoke of 'principles of stability' according to which the tendency of the organism was to release tensions and come to rest in a state of equilibrium. This passive, automaton-like process is far from adequate in describing the active participation, the use of feedback, and the whole variety of coping processes which seem to characterize man's attempt to deal effectively with his environment.

References

Cofer, C. N. and Appley, M. H. (1964). *Motivation: Theory and Research*. London: Wiley.

Grossman, S. P. (1967). *A Textbook of Physiological Psychology*. New York: Wiley.

Hess, W. R. (1954). *Diencephalon: Autonomic and Extra-pyramidal Functions*. New York: Grune & Stratton.

John, E. Roy (1967). *Mechanisms of Memory*. New York: Academic Press.

Koestler, A. and Smythies, J. R. (eds) (1969). *Beyond Reductionism: New Perspectives in the Life Sciences*. London: Hutchinson.

Lewis, A. (1967). *Inquiries in Psychiatry: Clinical and Social Investigations*. London: Routledge & Kegan Paul.

Maclean, Paul D. (1975). 'Sensory and Perceptive Factors in Emotional

Functions of the Triune Brain', in *Emotions – Their Parameters and Measurement* (ed. L. Levi). New York: Raven Press.
Morgan, C. T. (1965). *Physiological Psychology* (3rd ed.). New York: McGraw-Hill.
Oswald, I. (1962). *Sleeping and Waking*. Amsterdam: Elsevier.
Selye, H. (1956). *The Stress of Life*. New York: McGraw-Hill.

Suggestions for further reading

Chalmers, N. *et al.* (eds). *The Biological Bases of Behaviour*. Open University Set Book. London: Harper & Row 1971.
Pribram, K. (ed.). *Brain and Behaviour* (4 vols). Harmondsworth: Penguin 1969.

Chapter two

Perception

R. P. Power

Introduction

Perception is the process by which an organism obtains information about the states of its own internal organs and the states of the world about it. We come in contact with the environment through the various senses, which are listed in Table 2.1. In a chapter as short as this it is not possible to consider the different sensory systems at great length, and the main emphasis will be on vision and audition. The physiology of the receptor organs and the study of sensory processes, the way in which incoming information is encoded and transmitted to the cortex, will be largely ignored in this chapter. Readers will have access to standard works on physiology, and for a discussion of sensory processes can refer to a paperback book by Mueller (1965) or to a more recent publication by the Open University (1972), *Biological Bases of Behaviour*, Units 5–7. Recently developed psychological techniques which enable inferences to be made about the visual cortex are described by Blakemore (1973). He also gives a readable account of the physiology of the system.

The first broad topic considered here is the way in which people keep in touch with their environment, and the sensitivity of some of the perceptual systems. The organization of sensory input to give a meaningful picture of the world is described, and then the factors which govern attention. These two topics cover experience which is fairly common to most people, and the next deals with individual differences in the way things are perceived. The development of perception in infancy is then discussed, and the chapter concludes with consideration of what happens when sensory input is transformed to give new relationships between objects, and a description of some illusions.

It might be thought that anatomists and physiologists should be able to answer the questions posed above. They have discovered a great deal about the structure and function of the systems, but they are a long way

Table 2.1 Sensory modalities

Modality	Proximal stimulus	Receptor	Cortical projection area	Dimensions of the experience
Vision	Electromagnetic waves (390–700μ)	Rods and cones in the retina	Occipital lobe	Hue, intensity and saturation
Hearing	Pressure waves usually in air	Hair cells in the inner ear	Temporal lobe	Pitch, loudness and timbre
Smell	Molecules in the air	Hair cells in the upper part of the nose	Olfactory fibres do not reach the cortex	Camphoraceous, musky, floral, pepperminty, ethereal and pungent
Taste	Molecules in solution	Hair cells mainly on the tongue	Parietal lobe	Sweet, salty, sour and bitter
Pressure	Deformation of the skin	Nerve endings in the skin	Parietal lobe	Extent, duration and intensity
Temperature	Temperature changes from adaptation level	Nerve endings in the skin	Parietal lobe	Cold to hot
Pain	Intense stimuli or injury to tissue	Nerve endings in the skin	Parietal lobe	Sharp, dull and throbbing
Kinesthesia	Movement of joints and muscles	Nerve endings in muscles, tendons and joints	Parietal lobe	Position and load
Equilibrium	Body movement and acceleration	Hair cells in the semi-circular canals and vestibular sacs of the inner ear	Cerebellum	Movement in three planes and body position

from complete answers, and may never be able to provide them. One reason is the incredible complexity of the systems at the peripheral, intermediate and central levels: it was as recently as 1962 that Hubel and Wiesel (Hubel, 1963) were able to record in the visual cortex responses to lines of different slant. Another is that past experience affects considerably the way in which things are perceived.

Even so, the problem may seem slight. Objects in the environment, or events inside the organism, emit energy of various types which impinges on the receptors, which excite the relevant projection areas. These are summarized in Table 2.1. (The energy from the object is often called the distal stimulus and the energy impinging on the receptor the proximal stimulus.) But the example in Figure 2.1 shows that other factors are involved. Although an infinite number of distal

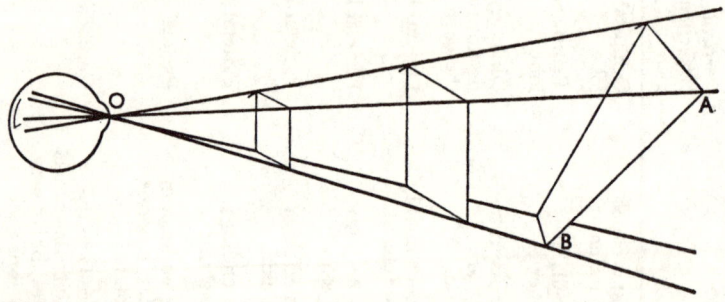

Figure 2.1

stimuli (of different sizes, shapes, etc.) can produce a proximal stimulus of identical shape and size, organisms will normally discriminate between them. From this example it can be seen that an object of a certain size subtends a certain visual angle (AOB in Figure 2.1), but at twice the distance the object would need to be twice the height and four times the area to subtend the same visual angle. But although an object of constant size projects an expanding and contracting image as it approaches and recedes it is judged to be of relatively constant size. This is just one of the many cases where the percept is similar to the distal object rather than the proximal stimulus, raising a question to be considered later; namely, how it is that such objects are perceived as constant.

Spatial localization

One of the principal activities of the visual and auditory systems is the localization of objects and events in space. The haptic (kinesthetic and touch senses) system is rarely used by people with normal vision to locate objects. The other systems, like taste and smell, are not particularly useful for this purpose.

Table 2.2 Cues to depth

1. *Muscular*	3. *Pictorial*
Accommodation of the lens	Relative size
Convergence of the eyes	Interposition
2. *Parallax*	Linear perspective
Binocular parallax	Texture gradients
Retinal disparity	Cast shadows
Seeing behind objects	Attached shadows
Double images	Familiar size
Monocular parallax	Aerial perspective
Head movement parallax	Field position
Motion parallax	

Many cues (sources of information) to localization are known, and the most frequently discussed are listed in Table 2.2. (1) The muscular cues involve signals about the state of the eyes; (2) binocular parallax is concerned with the slightly different images of the two eyes and monocular parallax with head or object movement; and all the cues in (3) can be reproduced in two dimensions and are those used by artists to represent distance.

(1) *Accommodation* involves focusing the image on the retina, and is the change in curvature of the lens in response to a near or far object, the lens becoming more spherical for near and flattening for far objects. *Convergence* is direction of the eyes inward so that the two images of the object fall on corresponding parts of each retina (the receptor surface). These two processes are essential for clear vision, but although for a long time it was thought that the feedback from the muscles involved functioned to signal depth, it seems that this is of limited use. Accommodation is ineffective at distances greater than one metre; and convergence, if used at all, does not function at more than fifteen metres.

(2) The parallax cues, on the other hand, are of considerable use. *Retinal disparity* is largely responsible for the three-dimensional 'look' of the world. It occurs because the eyes, being about seventy millimetres apart, as shown in Figure 2.2a, have slightly different images, which are fused to give perception of distance. This was demonstrated in 1838 by Wheatstone, who presented slightly different drawings of an object (as would be projected to each eye) to each eye, and found that a strong impression of depth was given. Although disparity and the other binocular cues are useful, it is still possible to make very accurate

judgments of distance with one eye. Another binocular parallax cue is *seeing behind objects*: this is shown in Figure 2.2a and can be demonstrated simply by holding an object at arm's length, and closing first one eye and then the other. Crossed and uncrossed *double images* are illustrated in Figure 2.2b. If a near object (N) is fixated, a far object (F) will be

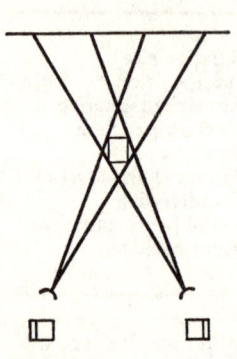

Figure 2.2a 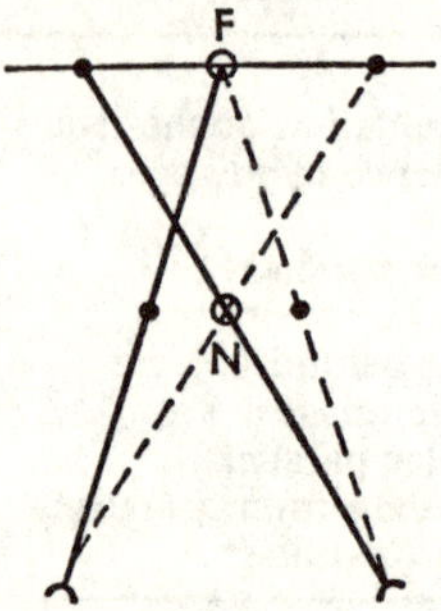 *Figure 2.2b*

seen as two objects (this can easily be demonstrated by holding one finger in front of the other, and fixating the near finger), F being seen on the right by the right eye, and on the left by the left eye (close one eye, then the other, to observe this). But when F is fixated, N is seen on the left by the right eye, and on the right by the left eye.

The other forms of parallax can operate with only one eye. *Monocular parallax* can be induced by *head movements*; if the head is moved from side to side images of near objects move more rapidly across the retina than far objects. Similarly, with *motion parallax*, if two objects are moving at the same speed, the nearer will project an image which moves faster than the further object.

(3) The remaining cues can be used by an artist on a two-dimensional surface. With *relative size* the larger of two or more similar objects (Figure 2.2c) will be judged as closer, other things being equal. *Interposition* (Figure 2.2d) is a very powerful cue to relative distance: one object partially overlapping another must be closer. *Linear perspective* (Figure 2.2e) is a powerful and well-known cue: an impression of depth

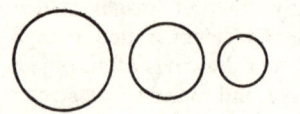

Figure 2.2c 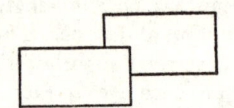 *Figure 2.2d* 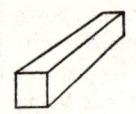 *Figure 2.2e*

arises from parallel lines converging in the distance. *Gradients of texture*, less obvious, follow the same rules as linear perspective: the elements and interstices making up a receding surface (Figure 2.2f) project smaller and closer images, but a vertical surface is suggested when the elements remain the same size and distance apart (Figure 2.2g). A variation in the rate of change indicates a contour (Figure 2.2h). Shadows, whether attached (Figure 2.2i) or cast (Figure 2.2j)

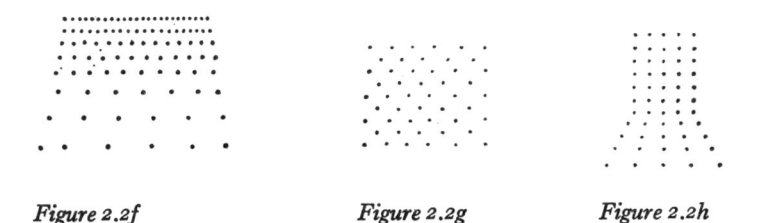

Figure 2.2f   *Figure 2.2g*   *Figure 2.2h*

act as cues. *Attached shadows* give information about shape, whereas *cast shadows* give information about position as well. It has always seemed likely that knowledge of the size of an object, its *familiar size*, would help judgments of distance, but the difficulty of eliminating all other cues has made this difficult to demonstrate. It has recently been shown, however, that knowledge of the size of an object can act as a cue to distance (Figure 2.2k). In conditions where all other cues to

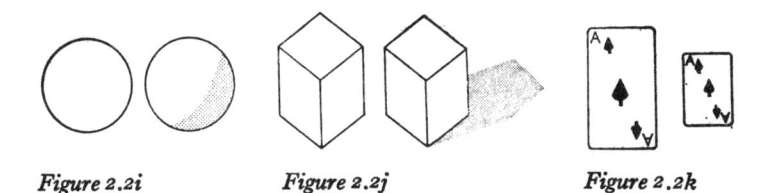

Figure 2.2i   *Figure 2.2j*   *Figure 2.2k*

depth are eliminated, the distance of a normal-sized playing card is somewhat underestimated, a double-sized playing card is judged to be nearer still, and a half-sized playing card as further. *Aerial perspective*, the tendency for distant objects to appear less clear, desaturated (colours washed out) and taking on the ambient hue is difficult to demonstrate experimentally, but observation shows that where a strong wind has removed smog distant objects look sharper and closer. *Field position* depends on the fact that objects on the ground are higher in the visual field the further away they are, and that objects on the ceiling plane, or in the sky, are lower the further they are. Its effectiveness as a cue to distance is uncertain, since in most situations field position is inextricably bound up with other cues.

This list is not fully exhaustive, but the main cues have been mentioned.

The relative efficacy of these cues has often been considered. Clearly interposition is very powerful, as are parallax and linear perspective. Texture gradients are rather less powerful, although effective, but it is not yet possible to rank the others. It should also be noted that it is usual for several of these cues to be available, and it is said that our judgments are 'over-determined'. If, therefore, one or another of the cues fails we can still make accurate judgments.

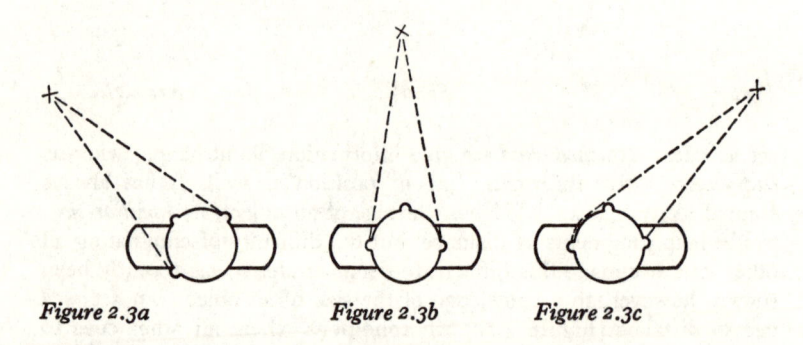

Figure 2.3a *Figure 2.3b* *Figure 2.3c*

It has generally been held that auditory localization involves fewer cues than visual localization. If a sound source is to one side then the sound waves will take a little longer to reach one of the ears (Figure 2.3c). This difference provides three cues; time differences, phase differences and intensity differences (Rosenzweig, 1961). With *time difference* the time taken to reach the ear nearer the sound will be less than the time taken to reach the other ear. Since the time taken to reach the second ear is greater there will be a *phase* difference in the waves at any given moment: one ear may be stimulated by the peak of a wave as the other is stimulated by the mid-point of the wave. With *intensity differences* the ear away from the sound source is 'shadowed' by the head and the waves are therefore attenuated.

Phase differences are more important for the localization of low frequency sounds and intensity differences more important for high frequency sounds. The auditory system is very effective in detecting these differences: for instance differences of thirty microseconds lead to a judgment that a sound is to one side. Since these cues depend on a differential stimulation of the two ears it follows that a sound is judged to be in the median plane (a plane drawn through the middle of the nose and the centre of the head) when there are no differences. But the observer cannot, without moving his head, tell whether the sound is dead ahead, above or behind, since none of these positions lead to differential stimulation.

These statements apply to pure tones, the stimuli most frequently used until recently in auditory experiments, but with more complex sounds localization is rather better than the analysis suggests. It seems that the pinna, the external ear, produces complex transformations in sound waves which assist localization.

These binaural cues have been extensively investigated, but relatively little attention has been paid to monaural cues. Intensity will decrease as distance increases, but although monaural people move their heads about when attempting to locate a sound source, it is not known just what information they are using, although it is clear that the pinna is involved.

One factor often overlooked in consideration of spatial localization is that the observer needs to know the position of his head. For instance, stimulation of the two ears will be identical for a sound 45° to the left of the median plane, whether the head is in the normal position or turned to one side (Figure 2.3). Thus when making judgments we must constantly monitor information from the kinesthetic and equilibrium systems involved in head movements.

Speech perception has recently attracted much attention, although the research is still in relatively early stages. The principal tool for analysing speech is the sound spectrograph, which shows graphically the frequencies produced and how they change during articulation of a syllable. Sound spectrograms show that most speech sounds involve several different frequencies at the one time. For instance the sound 'u' in the word 'sun' involves bands of frequencies between 200 and 800 hz, 1,000 and 1,500hz, and 2,800 and 3,400hz. These bands are known as formants. In order to establish the features necessary for perception of a given speech sound a computer-controlled speech synthesizer can be used to produce and manipulate patterns of formants and listeners can then be asked to report what they hear.

Speech sounds can be continuous or discontinuous. Examples of continuous sounds are vowels and fricatives (e.g., the 's' in 'Sue'), vowels being produced with a relatively open vocal tract and fricatives with it relatively closed. Fricatives may be voiced (air forced over vibrating vocal cords: 'z' as in 'zoo') or voiceless (vocal cords relaxed and not vibrating: 's' as in 'Sue'). Discontinuous sounds (e.g., plosive consonants: 'b', 'd') occur when pressure is suddenly released after the vocal tract has been completely closed.

Plosive consonants may be voiced ('ba', 'da', 'ga') or voiceless ('pa', 'ta', 'ka'). The difference which leads to a syllable being perceived as 'ba' and another as 'pa' is the time which elapses between opening the lips and the voicing of the vowel. For 'ba' it is less than about 40 milliseconds and for 'pa' it is longer. Although it is not obvious to a listener or a speaker, frequency analysis of the letters 'b' and 'p' show them to be very similar, and it is the elapsed time before voicing occurs which determines the percept.

The distinction between voiced and voiceless sounds refers to the 'manner' of production. A third manner is that of nasal sounds (e.g., the consonants in the syllables 'am', 'an', 'ag') produced when the velum, the soft palate, is lowered and air travels through the nose.

A final distinction is between places of production. Bilabial sounds are produced when the lips are closed, alveolar when the tongue is pressed against the alveolar ridge, the ridge behind the front teeth, and velar when the back of the tongue is pressed against the velum.

Table 2.3 Manner and place of production of sounds. In each case it is the pronunciation of the last letter of the syllable which is being considered

		Place of production		
		Bilabial	Alveolar	Velar
Manner	Voiced	ab	ad	ag
of	Voiceless	ap	at	ack
production	Nasal	am	an	ang

The sorts of sound produced by various combinations of manner and place of production are shown in Table 2.3. Attempts are being made to produce machines which will talk, and these are described by Flanagan (1972), and a more detailed analysis of phonetics and speech perception is given by Miller (1951).

Constancy in perception

Perceptual constancy refers to the tendency of judgments of objects to remain the same despite variations in the proximal stimulus. An example of this was given earlier: an object is judged to remain the same size even though the retinal image expands and contracts as the object approaches and recedes. Studies in which constancy is reduced or eliminated show the way in which it operates. Holway and Boring (1941) systematically studied the effects on size judgments of reducing information about the distance of the stimulus. The task of the subjects was to judge the size of illuminated discs placed at various distances down a long corridor. These objects increased in size so that they all subtended the same visual angle. If size constancy was perfect then the objects should have been judged to increase linearly with distance. On the other hand, if no constancy occurred, then the objects should be judged as the same size, since all projected identical images. Results very close to constancy were obtained with (1) binocular and (2) monocular vision, but when the subjects observed (3) monocularly with head movements eliminated, constancy was considerably reduced, and it was reduced even further when (4) black curtains were hung along the corridor to reduce the effect of shadows on the floor. They concluded that reduced information about distance reduced judged constancy of size.

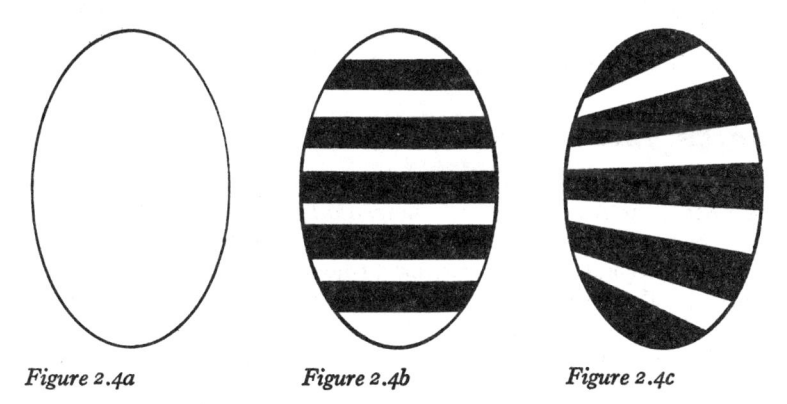

Figure 2.4a   *Figure 2.4b*   *Figure 2.4c*

Similar rules apply to judgments of other types. Our judgments of shape show constancy: we normally judge a dinner plate as circular, even though we usually see it from a position at which it projects an elliptical image. But if an ellipse is observed with information about its slant eliminated, subjects cannot judge either its shape or slant with any accuracy. For instance if an elliptical shape (Figure 2.4a) is presented in the fronto-parallel plane, a plane at right angles to the line of sight, it will be judged to be at any of a wide variety of angles when other cues to depth and distance are eliminated. On the other hand if a regular pattern is placed on the surface then its slant will be judged fairly accurately. It is also possible to give misleading information: if a perspective transformation (Figure 2.4c) of pattern 2.4b is placed on the surface, then the right-hand side will be consistently judged as closer. Thus, although judgments of objects normally show constancy it is possible to eliminate constancy or alter it in a systematic fashion by manipulating the cues described in the previous section.

Brightness and colour constancy also occur: snow looks white even when in deep shadow and coal looks black in bright sunlight, even though the coal may be reflecting more light. But if the snow and coal are inspected through a tube which permits nothing but the coal or snow to be seen then the snow may be judged to be the darker. It is not the fact that we know coal is black and snow white, since the same effect occurs with unknown black and white objects.

From these examples it can be seen that constancy operates when objects carry their own information (cue of familiar size), when parallax can operate, or when they are seen in relation to their surroundings. With shape we can judge the slant of the plate, and this allows us to judge correctly its shape; and with brightness the relationship between amount of light reflected by the object and its surroundings allows us to judge the brightness of the object. This principle is known as relational determination (Wallach, 1963).

Sensitivity of the perceptual systems

Although organisms can locate and effectively deal with objects in space they can respond only to a limited range of stimuli. For instance, humans can respond to tones with a frequency of between 20 and 20,000 cycles per second (cps), whereas bats, who use echoes to locate objects, can respond to sounds with a frequency of over 100,000 cps. The study of the limits of physical stimuli to which responses can be made, and the relationship between amount of physical energy and strength of sensation is known as psychophysics. When preparing a psychophysical scale the first point to establish is the absolute threshold, the minimum amount of energy required to produce a response, and the second point is the terminal threshold, the maximum amount of energy to which a response can be made. The terminal threshold can be difficult to establish since it is sometimes hard to know when, for instance, loudness or heat turn to pain. Once these thresholds have been established the physical continuum between them can be divided into just noticeable differences (JNDs), a JND being the physical increase necessary to produce a judgment of different.

One interesting feature of psychophysical scales is that for most of their length the increase in physical energy required for a JND is a constant fraction of the stimulus being judged. This is known as Weber's law, after its discoverer, and can be stated as $\Delta I/I = k$, where I is intensity of the stimulus, ΔI the increment necessary to produce a judgment of different, and k the Weber fraction. For instance the Weber fraction for weight is about 1/40; this means that a weight of one pound requires an increase of about 1/40 of a pound for a difference to be detected, and that a weight of 40 pounds requires an increase of one pound for a difference to be detected. When psychophysical scales are constructed it is possible to compare the relative sensitivity of the sensory systems: the smaller the fraction the more sensitive the system. For instance humans are very sensitive to small changes in pitch, the fraction being 1/333 at 2,000 cps, and relatively insensitive to changes in loudness, the fraction being 1/11. Observers can be compared as well as systems; the more sensitive the observer the smaller the fraction. These examples will give some idea of the sensitivity of the systems: against a bright sky a wire 1/16 inch thick can be detected at half a mile by an experienced observer, or measured in another way, only about 7 light quanta are necessary to stimulate the eye. The ear is so sensitive that the minimum energy required to produce a response cannot be directly established but it has been calculated that the threshold amplitude of a sound wave is about 10^{-9}cm, which is smaller than a light wave.

Sometimes it is possible to be affected by sources of information which we cannot consciously identify. An experienced clinician may have a 'feeling in his stomach' about a diagnosis, but he will find it difficult to explain rationally by just what symptoms he is affected. Knowledge of results can help to improve decisions: if, during a psychophysical study, the person being studied is given knowledge of results, then he will have a lower absolute threshold, and his Weber fraction will be smaller.

So far the sensitivity of the systems has been considered without much reference to situations in which the data are collected, but when stimuli are near threshold level thresholds are affected by the expectancies and motives of the observer. In an experiment designed to establish a threshold the experimenter will normally include some catch trials: that is, trials on which no stimulus is present at all. This is done to keep the subjects alert, but even the most alert subject will occasionally respond on a catch trial. This has been investigated, and it has been shown that if there are a lot of catch trials, there will be a tendency for an observer to ignore some signals, and if there are not many catch trials he will tend to respond when there is no signal present. Thus changes in the frequency of catch trials will lead to changes in the threshold value obtained, since the subject's expectancies will be affected.

The motivation of the subject is also important, and will affect the sorts of error made. For instance a radiologist examining X rays of the chest during a mass screening knows that it is unlikely pathology will be present in any given case. Given that at early stages the symptoms will be minimal (near threshold), from the principles mentioned so far it might be assumed likely that they will be missed. But the cost of missing a signal is high. This situation can be illustrated by a 'payoff matrix', with the radiologist's responses on the top, the state of the world on the side and the payoff in the cells, as below:

		Pathology detected	
		YES	NO
Pathological symptom	PRESENT	Chance of saving life	Chance of person dying
	ABSENT	Unnecessary alarm	Bored radiologist

Since the consequences of missing a signal are so drastic it is likely that the operator will detect even a rare signal. This sort of task has been studied by manipulating monetary rewards. For example, see below:

		Response	
		YES	NO
Signal	PRESENT	£1	−£2
	ABSENT	−50p	£1

Here a false alarm (saying 'Yes' when there is no signal) is penalized less than a hit (a correct detection) is rewarded, but the opposite could be arranged, and the subject's behaviour would vary accordingly, since his behaviour must change to maximize his payoff. Note that the bad error of missing a signal is penalized quite heavily. By means of these techniques the effect of motivation on thresholds can be studied.

An experiment which demonstrates the effect of motivation on accuracy of diagnosis was carried out by De Dombal *et al.* (1974). They compared senior surgeons with a computer-aided system of diagnosis for acute abdominal pain, and found that the clinician's diagnostic performance improved markedly during the period he was being compared with the computer and then reverted to the original level.

One way of improving performance of operators in situations where the frequency of signals is low is to introduce artificial signals from time to time in order to keep the expectancy of the operator high.

Psychophysical procedures suggested by Stevens (1968) are more direct than the JND type of scale. Stevens suggested that we should measure sensations directly by assigning magnitudes to our experiences. The experimenter might say that light A has a brightness of 10 arbitrary units, and then ask the observer the value of light B; or he might ask the observer to adjust a tone so that it was half as loud as another tone, or twice as loud. Or instead of using numbers the experimenter might ask the observer to match one sensation with another, a loud noise requiring a stronger handgrip than a softer one. These procedures are very adaptable, and can be used in contexts other than of direct perception. For instance, a group of Swedish university students were asked to assign numbers to certain occupations as an indication of preference. They gave values of about two for a factory worker, four for a hairdresser, nineteen for an architect and twenty-seven for a physician. Such scales can have most of the properties of more usual measures, such as length. Sellin and Wolfgang (Stevens, 1968) asked various groups to give numbers to the seriousness of criminal acts. Stealing $5 was given a value of one, as was breaking and entering a building. A separate estimation of breaking in and stealing $5 was given the value two, showing that judged seriousness was additive. Similarly, although stealing $20 was worse than stealing $5, it was not very much more so, and for the offence to be judged as twice as serious the amount needed to be about sixty times greater.

The procedures described are discussed by Woodworth and Schlosberg (1954), Galanter (1962), Stevens (1968) and, more technically, by McNicol (1972).

Perceptual organization

The proximal stimulus normally consists of a variety of colour patches of different shapes and sizes, changing constantly with movements of both the body and objects. Perception, however, as has been shown, is of stable objects and events. This means that the stimulus input must be organized by the observer, and some of the laws which govern this organization have been established. It should be noted that the laws rarely operate in isolation, and one may well overrule another, so each should really read, 'all other things being equal . . .'.

Figure and ground. Probably the simplest form of organization is figure and ground: the figure is that part of the visual field which stands out from the background and is normally the object being observed. This ability to distinguish figure from ground seems to be present from birth. Although it is possible to concentrate exclusively on the ground, perceptually the figure usually appears to be the centre of attention: it stands out from the ground, is better defined, localized and more solid. The contour separating figure and ground seems to belong to the figure. The ground, in contrast, seems less well structured and to extend continuously behind the figure. Physically the figure is usually smaller, in the centre of the field of vision, bounded by a continuous line, and is a meaningful whole. Figure-ground relationships also occur with hearing: the meaningful message is heard against a background of relatively uniform sound. In music the melodies stand out from the accompaniments, the solo instrument from the orchestral ground, or the heartbeat from other noises heard through a stethoscope. Under some conditions there will be a reversal of figure and ground (Figures 2.5a, b and c), and when this happens the contour bounding what was previously the figure seems to change to what was previously the ground. Some of the other principles can be seen in Figure 2.5a. For instance, the smaller area tends to be seen as figure; it tends to stand

Figure 2.5a *Figure 2.5b* *Figure 2.5c*

out, is more solid and is the centre of attention. Figure 2.5b shows that when the light and dark areas are similar reversals occur with greater frequency, and Figure 2.5c shows that the change in rate of reversal is not due to the black-white relationship in Figure 2.5a. This type of reversal may occur spontaneously, or may be under voluntary control, as occurs when listeners choose to concentrate on soloist or orchestra.

Closure. Very often observers organize a group of elements into a figure, or perceive a pattern as more complete than it is, and this is known as closure. It is demonstrated in Figure 2.5d, and usually occurs

Figure 2.5d

Perception

when the organized elements convey more meaning, or present a simpler percept, than do the single units. Closure can be so powerful that observers are not normally aware of it. For instance, there is the blind spot in the visual field caused by the optic tract leaving the eye. Since there are no receptors there can be no sensory input, yet a gap is not perceived. The existence of the blind spot can be easily demonstrated. Close the left eye and fixate the right on the cross of Figure 2.5e. If

✗   ●

Figure 2.5e

the book is now held about twelve inches from the eye the circle will disappear since it is falling on the blind spot. It may be necessary to move the book a little nearer or further since the blind spot is not in quite the same position for everyone. Closure may occur in cases of scotoma (an area in the retina which is blind due to trauma to the visual system). After some time the patient will cease to notice the gap, or at least its full extent.

Proximity. Objects which are close to one another tend to be grouped together. For instance the first block of dots in Figure 2.5f tends to be perceived as four vertical columns, but when the relationship between them is changed as in the second block they become four rows. When they are uniformly spaced as in the third block there is a tendency to switch from one form of organization to another. Proximity effects also occur with auditory perception: two taps alternating with a slightly longer period of silence are organized into a pattern. Once a perceptual pattern is established small departures from it, such as an irregularity in heartbeat, can easily be detected.

Figure 2.5f   *Figure 2.5g*

Similarity. Other factors can overcome proximity, as with Figure 2.5g. In this case similarity of some elements leads them to be organized as units, and the similarity of the others leads them to be grouped into other units or ignored.

Fundamental Processes of Psychological Functioning

Good continuation. Good continuation leads to the simplest possible percept, and can overcome the other principles. Figure 2.5h is perceived

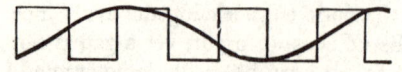

Figure 2.5h

as a sine wave superimposed on a square wave, even though the enclosed elements make up a figure somewhat like Figure 2.5i.

Figure 2.5i

These principles can work together or in opposition. For instance, the first six elements in Figure 2.5j are grouped on the basis of proximity, but the next six show that this can be disturbed by closure, or closedness with the next three whole units.

Figure 2.5j

A well-organized pattern can be transposed without destroying its character. A melody can be played in another key, higher or lower on the scale, on different instruments or louder or more softly and still be readily recognizable, just as a photograph can be in black and white, or colour, or larger or smaller, without presenting any difficulty in recognition. In these cases what is preserved is the relationship between the elements. Despite such preservation, the negative photograph of a face is very difficult to identify.

Perception

Once what appears at first sight to be a random pattern of lines is given meaning it suddenly achieves organization and is much easier to retain. The pattern in Figure 2.5k has no particular meaning (see what it is like before reading on) and it would be very difficult to retain unless you are told it is a washerwoman and her bucket. It could now be reproduced easily many years later.

Figure 2.5k

In general we seem to arrange sensory input to produce the simplest pattern (Figure 2.5h makes this very clear). As Hochberg (1964) points out, the two drawings in Figure 2.5l are geometrically equally satisfactory representations of a wire cube, yet one is clearly perceived as three-dimensional and the other as two-dimensional. This occurs, he says, because in one case the three-dimensional percept is simpler, and in the other the two-dimensional percept is simpler. This is referred to

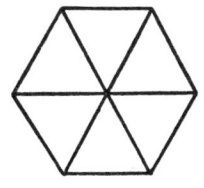

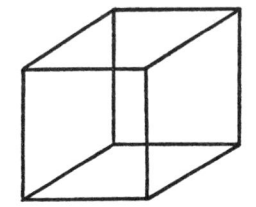

Figure 2.5l

as the minimum principle. The laws given above are all examples of the principle, but attempts to set up objective rules for simplicity are only recent. With a series of figures of the type shown in Figure 2.5l ranging from those which invariably give a two-dimensional percept to those which invariably give a three-dimensional percept, it has been found that as the number of angles, the number of continuous lines, and the average number of different angles increases, the tendency to see the two-dimensional arrangement decreases and the tendency towards a three-dimensional percept increases.

Attention and habituation

The environment is normally full of objects and events to which we can pay attention, but in general we ignore most of them, and concentrate on items of interest. On occasion, of course, some items demand, and get, attention. This gives a useful distinction between internal and external determinants of attention, or, in other words, voluntary and involuntary attention.

Voluntary attention is obviously a function of a person's interests, needs, motives and emotional state. *Interests* may be long- or short-term; long-term interests determine the things people pay attention to: a dentist will tend to notice poor teeth or dental work, whereas a medical practitioner will tend to notice other sorts of physical abnormality, and a psychiatrist will notice oddities in behaviour. Short-term interests govern selective listening. At a party when many people are talking, it is fairly easy to select first one voice to listen to and then another. A tape recording of the same party will present a confused jumble which it is very difficult or impossible to sort out. This occurs for two reasons: the binaural cues mentioned earlier are missing and the recorder will eliminate some of the frequencies. It is for these reasons that some people forced to rely on hearing aids have difficulty in a crowd. *Needs*, taken as body deficits, will lead organisms to notice sources of food when hungry, liquid when thirsty, and so on. *Motives* also govern attention: for example, people are interested in themselves; and it has been shown that although a person concentrating on a message delivered to one ear will not normally hear words delivered to the other ear, he will often notice his own name even when it is no louder than other words which are ignored. *Emotional state* may lead a jealous man to pay attention to a compliment to his wife or girlfriend, whereas a person who is not jealous might not notice it.

Involuntary attention is influenced by features of objects and events such as intensity, novelty, contrast, repetition and movement. *Intensity* of the stimulus is clearly important: a loud sound, a bright light and an intense pain all demand attention. In this case it is often the sudden onset which is important. A quite intense stimulus can often be ignored when it persists over time. For instance, the quite loud sounds from a railway carriage can be ignored in favour of the less intense sounds from someone speaking. Similarly cessation of an intense stimulus attracts attention. Thus it is really changes in intensity which are important, rather than the absolute level of intensity. *Novelty* is also important: if something is to be noticed it is given a new shape and colour, a fact utilized by advertisers and package designers. *Incongruity* is probably a special case of novelty: a woman with a long beard would be noticed. *Repetition* helps to attract attention, partly because a repeated stimulus is often a more intense stimulus, and partly because the first occurrence serves to signal that there is something happening, and the second identifies it. Most of us give a double knock on a door, and this may be because we recognize the value of repetition. *Contrast* is also effective: a white figure on a black ground will stand out well, whereas a light grey on a dark grey will not be nearly as successful. *Movement* is used by advertisers, who construct flashing and moving signs in order to attract attention.

These factors all have one thing in common; change; even repetition means constant change. The biological utility of noticing change is, of course, very great. In general it is more important to know when something has changed, than to know that it has remained the same. The fact that continual stimulation of the one set of receptors leads to a breakdown in perception will be discussed later.

Probably each of these determinants rarely operates alone. A moving advertising sign has changes in intensity, it repeats, has contrast with its background, appears to move and very likely has some degree of novelty, so the division given above is somewhat arbitrary. Another problem is that consideration of these factors may be misleading: several soap-powder manufacturers may study the rules and produce packages, each of which in isolation might be very attention-getting, but which when placed near one another in a supermarket are very similar. In this case an old-style packet, or a plain white one, might be the most successful.

The other side of attention is habituation or adaptation. This can also be voluntary or involuntary. Very often observers are quite unaware of involuntary adaptation. For instance if you stare at a coloured square for half a minute it will look much the same during that period. But if, on the other hand, you cover half of it, and stare at one point on the border for half a minute, then move the cover and look at the centre of the patch, the side at which you were looking will appear very desaturated. This is an example of the general rule that continued stimulation leads to a decrease in response, even though we are not aware of it. The physiological correlate of this process is a decrease in rate of response on the part of the sensory nerves involved. Dark and light adaptation is also involuntary: after a few minutes in a dark room the eyes adapt, and previously invisible objects can be seen. The reverse process also occurs, but with greater rapidity: it takes about twenty minutes for full dark adaptation, but adaptation to light takes only two or three minutes. Such effects can be very subtle: many cases have been reported where a person adapts to very gradual increments in stimulation, such as a gas leak, or smell of burning, and thus does not notice the danger.

Adaptation of this type leaves after-effects: for instance, if a colour patch is fixated for half a minute, and the gaze is then transferred to a neutral surface (grey or white) a negative after-image will be seen. This is the complementary colour of the original patch: with red it is green, with yellow it is blue, and vice versa. This occurs because there are three types of receptors for coloured light; cones which respond maximally to red, green and blue light. If, say, the red receptors have been stimulated for some time, they will respond less when white light, a mixture of all colours, is observed, but the other receptors will respond at a high rate, and the colour to which they normally respond will be perceived (Brindley, 1963). The after-effects of light and dark adaptation are well known: inability to see in dim light, and dazzle in bright light.

Adaptation also occurs with the other systems. A constant odour rapidly ceases to be noticed. This is involuntary, since it cannot be reinstated by attending to it: a hard sniff which reinstates it is changing the amount of the stimulus which is passing the receptor surface. Up to this moment you were probably quite unaware of the feel of your clothes and pressure from your seat. This is a mixture of voluntary and involuntary adaptation, since attention can reinstate the feelings, but not to the extent felt on first contact. It is said that we adapt least to pain.

One final question related to attention is whether observers can pay attention to more than one thing at once. In general the answer is no, but there are exceptions. One was mentioned earlier, a person noticing his own name even when concentrating on something else. Sometimes two signals can be perceived at once if they are short and the number of possible messages is low. For instance, at a busy airport there is a constant stream of incoming messages, and the traffic controller will often hear two call signs occurring simultaneously, and be able to detect them correctly, but he will hear only one of the subsequent messages. It seems that this occurs because there is a short-term store for incoming messages, and the call signs of nearby aircraft are known, so after a short time in the store the expected signal is processed. But the messages following the call sign exceed the capacity of the store, and could be one of many possible messages, so the system cannot cope with them. Thus except for special cases it seems that it is impossible to pay attention to more than one thing at a time (Broadbent, 1962).

Although this rule is often claimed to be a general law, it applies only to messages which have similar modes of presentation: for instance, in the example quoted the messages were both auditory. But if the modalities are different then we can attend quite well to two inputs. It has been shown (Allport, Antonis and Reynolds, 1972) that people can attend to, and repeat back, continuous speech at the same time as noticing features of complex scenes, or even while sight-reading piano music. In both experiments the performance was good, and in the case of sight reading it was as good as with undivided attention.

It was mentioned that continual stimulation of the one set of receptors leads to a breakdown in perception. This has been studied by placing subjects in a situation in which sensory input is reduced to minimal levels, and also by fixing an image on the retina.

The first type of study was initiated by the Canadian government in order to study 'brainwashing' (Heron, 1961). The subjects were placed in a sound-proofed cubicle, with the temperature kept steady, they wore translucent goggles which prevented patterned vision, and cotton gloves and cardboard tubes on their arms to reduce haptic input. They lay on a soft bed and were given no idea of time. After two or three days performance on various intelligence test items decreased, and the subjects were more susceptible to propaganda. They reported confused thoughts, and were unable to concentrate on problems. Hallucinations were experienced by most subjects, some being so vivid that they thought the experimenters were projecting images on the goggles. After subjects left the cubicle, perception was disturbed for some time. Thus isolation and reduction of input is very disturbing, although subjects in experiments soon recover. Deprivation of this type might seem far removed from situations in which people normally find themselves, but there is evidence (Bennett, 1961) that airforce pilots flying jet aircraft solo or cut off from other members of the crew have similar experiences. In these cases the pilots have been flying straight and level above 20,000 feet and thus have had little to do. The pilot is strapped in his seat, often cannot see the wings or nose of the plane, and is subject to monotonous noise. Some pilots have become so disturbed that they could not return to flying such aeroplanes, although they are still capable of flying piston-engine planes at lower heights.

In the other type of study an image is projected to the retina in such a fashion that the same set of receptors is constantly stimulated. Normally any given receptor is constantly being stimulated by fresh input, partly because of voluntary eye movements, and partly because the eye is in a state of constant tremor (Fender, 1964). To overcome ocular tremor a small viewing device is attached to a contact lens which moves with the eye. This is illustrated in Figure 2.6. Under these conditions the image fades and disappears. It can be reinstated by switching off the light illuminating the pattern and switching it on again.

Thus monotonous and reduced input leads to gross disturbances in perception, and steady stimulation of the one set of receptors leads to loss of perception.

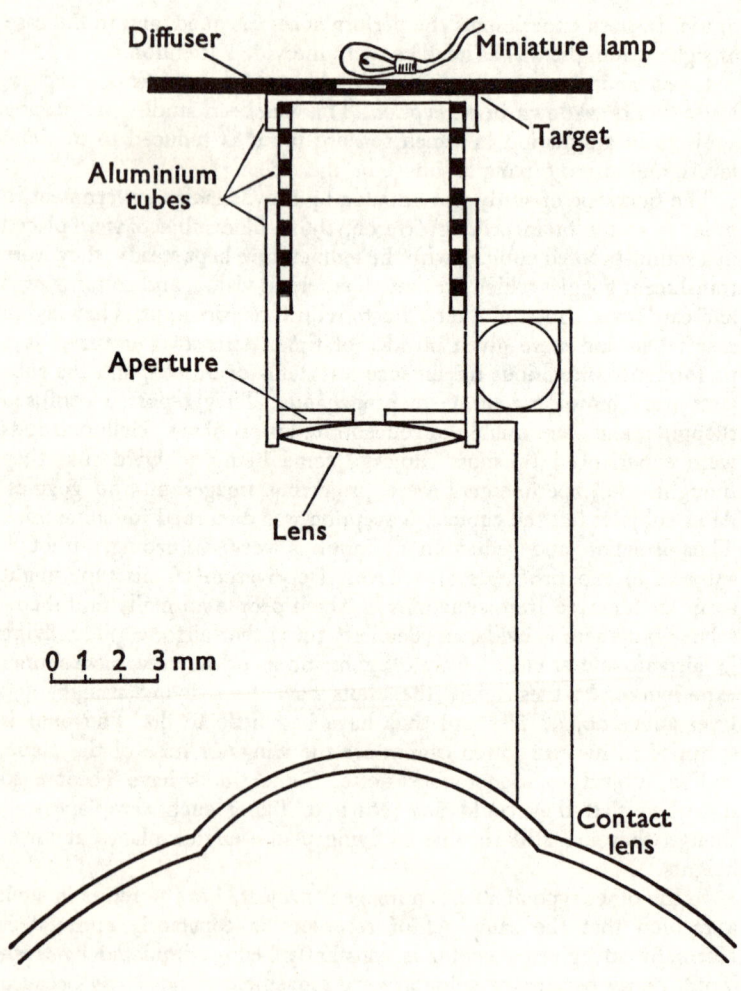

Figure 2.6

Other central effects on perception

In the section on attention it was shown that needs, interests and motives lead us to attend to some things and ignore others. Since these variables exert their influence through the central nervous system they are referred to as central effects. Factors which actually distort the way in which things are perceived will be considered in this section: 'distort' in this context means that one person will perceive things differently from another, or that things will be perceived, or even not perceived, because of their emotional connotations. Although of interest, these effects are small. Because we need to have a fairly undistorted knowledge of the world there would have been fairly strong natural selection for perceiving things as they really are.

In studies of the effect of central process on perception it is often difficult to know whether the effects occur on the input side, actually affecting perception, or on the output side, affecting responses rather than actual experience. This complex problem, not considered here, is discussed by Garner, Hake and Eriksen (1956). This section will simply be concerned with experiments seeming to demonstrate that sets, expectancies and motives do affect perception.

A set is a readiness to respond in some fashion, and may be the result of some known or unknown past experience. Unknown past experience may function in reactions of people with left- and right-wing political views to a picture of strikers picketing a factory. The left-wing group might describe the faces as showing 'grim determination to defend their rights', and the right-wing as showing 'savage aggression at society'.

Control of sets or expectancies is demonstrated in an experiment by Kelly (1950). The experimenter told a class that as their usual lecturer was away and the class was to include discussion, he would give a brief description of the personality of the replacement. Half of the students were given a sheet describing 'a rather cold person, industrious, critical, practical, and determined' (Kelly, 1950, p. 433), and the other half were given the same description, except that the words 'rather cold' were changed to 'very warm'. The lecturer arrived and took charge of the discussion. Afterwards the students were asked to give their impressions of him. The analysis of these impressions showed that the students who were told he was warm described him as 'more considerate of others, more informal, more sociable, more popular, and more humane' (p. 435) than did the others. In addition to analysing what the students said about the lecturer the experimenter had noted the number of times each student had taken part in the discussion, and he found that the behaviour of the two groups was different: those told he was warm participating more.

Clearly expectancies were affecting both reported experience and behaviour, but it should be made clear that sets can have only a limited effect. When the experiment was repeated with a lecturer who was actually colder this difference was apparent in the absolute ratings of the subjects, who were nevertheless affected by the set. Thus the set had an effect, as did the real personality of the lecturer.

Another feature of Kelly's experiment worth noting is that 'warm' or 'cold' was placed at the beginning of the description of the personality. There is considerable evidence that an adjective introduced at the beginning of a description has a primacy effect: that is, it has a much greater effect than when introduced later in the description.

Other 'preinformation' factors which affect judgments are known as halo effects and stereotypes. A halo effect occurs when a favourable or unfavourable judgment of one aspect of a person leads to favourable or unfavourable judgments of other aspects. This effect is typically seen in interview situations, and is very difficult to avoid: it is usual for an interviewer to use a separate scale to rate the various aspects of the person, and he is trained to disassociate his ratings one from another. It might be thought that a halo effect was operating in Kelly's experiment, but it must have been something more than that, because the students told that the lecturer was 'warm' did not rate him as significantly higher on intelligence than students told he was 'cold'. Stereotypes are judgments about a class of people based on limited information: examples are that Germans are militaristic, French great lovers, Americans extroverts, and British cold. Most people feel that they are not influenced by stereotypes, but it is fairly clear that they are. For instance Warr (1969) has obtained data which show that university students, when told only that a person is 'intelligent' think him likely to be confident, tolerant, reliable and conscientious and unlikely to be domineering, dull, selfish and irresponsible. Similarly, when told that a person is a musician they think him likely to be imaginative, sensitive and passionate and unlikely to be lazy. A mixture of these influences can have quite considerable effects, such that beliefs about the nature of an illness may affect observations and their interpretation. For instance Rosenhan (1973) arranged for several volunteers to present themselves at different mental hospitals where they claimed to 'hear voices', one of the classical symptoms of schizophrenia. After admission the 'patients' did not mention this or any other symptom, and engaged in generally normal behaviour. They found that normal behaviour was often interpreted as symptomatic of schizophrenia, and that all signs of normality were ignored by the psychiatrists, psychologists and nurses. It was the 'real' patients who realized that the volunteers were normal.

The value of an object can also affect the way in which it is judged. Lambert, Solomon and Watson (1949) divided fifty-four nursery-school children into experimental and control groups. The experimental group had to turn a handle eighteen times to receive a poker chip, which when placed in a slot led to the delivery of a sweet. After ten days they no longer received a sweet when they turned the handle, but the next day they did. The control group simply received a sweet when they turned the handle: thus a poker chip had no chance to become valuable. Both groups were asked to judge the size of the poker chip before the experiment began, and on the tenth, eleventh and twelfth days. On the first day, and after no reward, the judgments of both groups were about the same, but after ten days' reward the experimental group judged the poker chip to be larger, as they did when it again achieved value.

One area of perception which interests many people is 'subliminal perception', or perception 'without awareness'. The most controversial aspect of this topic concerns perceptual defence: the tendency not to report the presence of unpleasant or threatening stimuli under conditions when similar but neutral or non-threatening stimuli are reported. Interest in this effect originally came from clinical observations which seemed to demonstrate that people may utilize a 'defence mechanism' which enables them to misperceive or not notice a stressful object or situation. Beginning in 1947 a series of experiments has been carried out in an attempt to show that the effect occurs. For instance McGinnies (1949) exposed neutral words (e.g., apple, dance) and 'emotional words' (e.g., raped, bitch) in a tachistoscope (a device for presenting stimuli for brief, controlled periods of time), gradually increasing the exposure time from 0·01 seconds until the subject could correctly report the word. In addition he measured the galvanic skin resistance of the subjects (the resistance of the skin is thought to decrease as emotion increases). McGinnies found that the emotional words required a greater exposure period and that the galvanic skin resistance was lower for these words just before they were recognized, and thus concluded that there was an emotional response to the stimuli before the subjects could report them, and that this response delayed recognition.

Other investigators, however, pointed out that these results could be due to factors other than perceptual defence. For instance, it was suggested that subjects could be reluctant to pronounce the emotional words, and would thus wait until they were quite sure that they were seeing them correctly. Another criticism was that the emotional words are not seen written as commonly as the neutral words, and thus the effect could be due to lack of familiarity with the words. (It is known that the more frequently a word has been seen the easier it is to recognize.) More recent experiments in which these factors have been controlled do, however, seem to demonstrate that the effect does occur (Worthington, 1969).

Given that the effect does occur, the next problem is how to explain it, since at first glance it seems to suggest that there is a censor who looks at incoming stimuli and decides what shall be seen. In order to account for the effect Dember (1960) has suggested that we make affective (emotional) and identifying responses to stimuli, that the affective responses occur more rapidly than identifying responses, and that if these arouse an unpleasant response this will inhibit the identifying response.

Subliminal perception has been a cause for concern since newspaper reports that the words 'eat popcorn' when flashed on a cinema screen below threshold for conscious perception led to greater consumption of popcorn. It was felt that unscrupulous advertisers and politicians might take advantage of the method to promote their own interests. However, there is no convincing evidence that subliminal perception can be effective in such situations. The main reason for its ineffectiveness is that a stimulus which is below threshold for a particular individual but high enough to affect behaviour will be above threshold for other individuals. Thus the phenomenon is a very small effect which can be demonstrated in a laboratory, but not in uncontrolled situations. It is, of course, of considerable theoretical interest.

Many other experiments have demonstrated cognitive effects on perception and it can be concluded that central processes affect the way in which the world is perceived, but also that the real nature of the objects in the environment exerts considerable control over perception.

Development of perception

The principal methods used in studying the development of perception are observation and experiments with babies and children, and these have been supplemented with cross-cultural studies. In some cases experiments with animals have been used since it has not been possible to subject children to necessary experimental controls, such as rearing in the dark. There has been considerable dispute about the extent to which perception is innate, that is simply a function of the structure of our perceptual systems, and to what extent it is a function of learning. This dispute has by no means been fully resolved, but as techniques have improved in the last few years it has become clear that a good deal of perception is rather more innate than had been thought.

Cross-cultural studies have shown that many pictorial cues have to be learned. For instance Hudson (1960) presented outline drawings (see Figure 2.7) to black and white Africans of various ages and degrees of education. The drawings included a man, an elephant, a tree and an antelope, and the relationship between these elements was shown by various combinations of the cues' relative size differences (small elephant, large man), interposition (one feature partially covering another) and linear perspective (a path with converging edges). The subjects were able to identify the objects in the pictures, but ability to interpret the depth relations between the objects was a function of education; illiterate people and those living outside school-dominated areas being less able

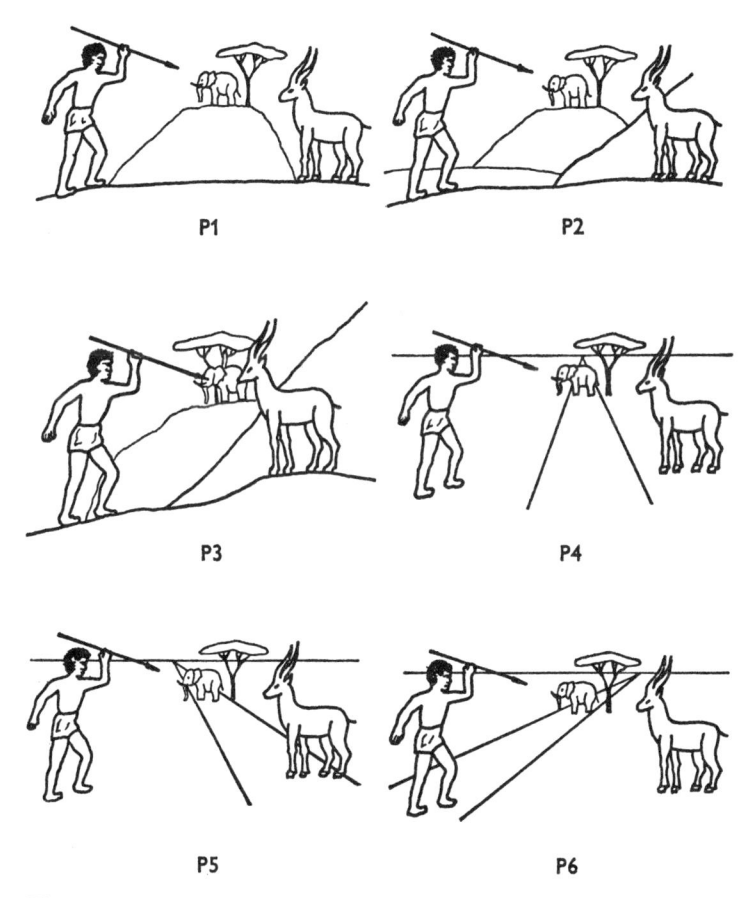

Figure 2.7

to use the cues. It was found that the cue of interposition was the most effective and linear perspective the least. So judging depth in pictures seems to depend on learning to ignore cues which indicate that the picture is flat, and to interpret those used to represent depth in drawings. Since the subjects who could not adequately interpret the pictures were able to deal effectively with a real three-dimensional environment it is important that studies on development utilize real objects rather than representations. Other cross-cultural studies of perception are described by Deregowski (1972), Lloyd (1972), and Segall, Campbell and Herskovits (1966).

A large number of studies have been carried out on the development of perception in children, and they have been well summarized and evaluated by Gibson (1969). It seems that at first the attention of infants is 'captured' by objects: that is, they seem to make no decision about the objects to which they will pay attention. For instance, at first infants will observe one object for a very long time: up to thirty-five minutes by the ninth or tenth day. Since they are fixating objects it is clear that they are discriminating figure from ground. Visual following of a moving object also occurs at this early stage. By one month there seems to be more voluntary control, and movement of an object at the periphery of the visual field leads to eye movements which bring it to the centre of the field of vision.

The type of stimulus which has been most commonly used with young children is the human face: it is, obviously, a frequent and important part of the child's environment, and two- to six-day-old children respond to a face or a representation of a face. The face is a complex object, capable of complex transformations, and research has been directed towards establishing what features of it attract attention. The results of this research are not always clearly interpretable, but it is known that young children will smile in response to an oval frontal rather than profile view, that a nodding motion is superior to a still face in eliciting this response, and that the presence of eyes also helps. By three months the eyes attract considerable attention (possibly because they move independently in the face), but if the face is cut off below the eyes this produces a turning away response. By five months the mouth becomes more important, but still individual faces are not discriminated: discrimination occurs at about six to seven months. By eight months smiles and frowns are responded to appropriately. This skill in recognizing faces keeps developing until the age of fourteen years.

A question of considerable interest has been whether perceptual constancy is a function of learning, and recent evidence shows that it is present in very young babies: too young for them to have had much chance to learn it. The technique for studying constancy with babies between forty and sixty days old has been developed by Bower (1966). In his experiments the babies were placed so that a left turn of the head closed a microswitch, which in turn activated a counter so that the number of turns could be counted. The child was rewarded for turning his head to the left when the training stimulus was present by having the mother or experimenter pop up from behind a screen and say 'peek-a-boo'. With partial reward ('peek-a-boo' about every fifth turn) a child can emit about 400 such responses in a twenty-minute session.

In one experiment babies were reinforced in the presence of a twelve-inch cube at three feet. After training of this type the original stimulus and others differing from it in various ways (same or double size at double the distance) are presented and the number of responses to each counted. It is argued that the baby will respond more to stimuli it considers most like the original stimulus. As a result of experiments with a variety of stimuli and observation conditions (monocular, binocular, with and without head movement parallax) Bower concluded that children of two months, who have had no chance to learn through interaction with objects, have size and shape constancy, and that the cue used is head movement parallax.

Human infants can crawl after about six or seven months: other animals can move about much earlier, some just about as soon as they are born. The visual cliff (Gibson, 1969) consists of a sheet of heavy glass, with a board (of suitable width and height for the species concerned) down the centre. On one side of the board is a 'shallow' and on the other a 'deep' section, made by placing patterned sheets of hardboard under the glass at appropriate depths. The glass serves two functions: it acts as a safety net, and equalizes auditory and tactile cues. In one experiment children between 6·5 and 14 months were placed on the board, and the mothers called to the children from the deep and shallow sides alternately. Nine of the children did not leave the board, possibly because they could not crawl adequately, but twenty-four of the twenty-seven who did would crawl on to the shallow side, but not the deep. The remaining three crawled on to both sides. So it seems that most children, by the time they can crawl, can perceive and avoid a dangerous drop. By implication, then, it would seem that many cases of babies falling off high objects are failures of motor co-ordination rather than of perception. By varying the patterns on the floors (e.g., by having a large pattern on the deep side and a fine one on the shallow side so that both subtend the same visual angle) Walk (Gibson, 1969) has fairly convincingly shown that the cue the children use is motion parallax. It is impressive that two different series of experiments, using quite different techniques, confirm the use of motion parallax by infants. Although children of this age have not had much chance to learn about cliffs, it could be argued that somehow learning had taken place, so a variety of animals which can see and locomote when very young were tested. (If necessary they were reared in the dark until they could both walk and see.) Even at one day chickens, kids and lambs did not go off the deep end so it does seem that this ability is independent of specific learning. This tendency is clearly very strongly inbuilt; even after neodecortication a cat avoids the deep side.

What, then, can be said about the role of learning in the development of perception? Clearly some abilities are innate (use of motion parallax), and some have to be learned (perspective in pictures). Further studies are required before it can be determined just which abilities are innate and which are learned (binocular parallax is present by age two, but it is not known whether this is a result of learning or maturation, or some interaction between the two), and how learning and maturation interact. It can be said that with human children there is an innate capacity for selective visual exploration: certain features of objects attract and hold attention, but do not elicit any very specific responses. In this they are unlike some other species, which may make very specific responses to very specific stimuli: baby herring gulls will gape for food in response to a mark of particular shape and colour on the parent's beak, but will not do so if this mark is changed (Tinbergen, 1951). Experience and learning can change this behaviour with children in two ways. Experience modifies selective attention (to eyes and mouth), and learning results in identifying responses to specific classes of events and objects (smiles and frowns).

Response to transformed input

In this section the effects of systematic distortion of visual input (e.g., inverting the retinal image) will be considered. These studies are useful for several reasons. One is that it is known that 'normal' eyes have aberrations, but these are not noticed since the perceptual system copes with them; and systematic studies of distorted input will help in understanding this process. It is also important for ophthalmologists to know what sorts of distortion produced by prescribed lenses will disappear over time, and what can be done to speed up the process. Divers experience distortions due to refraction caused by the air-water interface of their masks, and they have to adapt to objects which appear larger, closer and further from the median plane than they really are. It is useful to know how well they can cope under various conditions, and how adaptation might be speeded up. Related problems exist when surgeons examine the interior of the body using optic devices.

In some early studies the subject wore a lens which inverted the retinal image. This was done because the retinal image is normally inverted (Figure 2.1) and it was of interest to know whether a subject would come to perceive the new image as upright. It was hoped that such a study would give information about the way in which perception develops in infants, but adults already have a long history of learning, and thus for them it is a case of learning to cope with a rearranged visual input, whereas the child is coping with a whole new set of experiences. In experiments with lenses objects are usually still recognizable; that is, meaning is preserved but the relationship between the elements is distorted, and the relationship between these elements and the subject is changed. If prisms are worn in front of the eyes so that the visual field is rotated, say 10°· to the left, all straight vertical lines become curved, coloured fringes appear along vertical edges, and right angles appear acute or obtuse. When the head moves from side to side objects shrink and grow in a rubbery fashion. The sort of question now being investigated is what changes when such lenses are worn: is it the perception of the world, or are a new set of motor responses learned? What are the conditions under which such learning takes place and what happens when vision and touch conflict?

In an early experiment Stratton (1897) wore a lens system which inverted the visual field of the right eye, the left being covered. At first he found his actions disturbed, since he would reach in the wrong direction when he wanted to pick up an object, but by the end of the eighth day visual-motor co-ordination had become quite good. When the lens was removed he experienced an after-effect for a short time, this newly learned sensori-motor co-ordination taking a while to disappear. Although it is clear that he learned to cope with a visually upside-down world it is not clear to what extent he came to perceive the world as normal. This difficulty in knowing whether the world looks normal after such an experience is brought out by a quotation from a subject in a later experiment who had worn inverting lenses for thirty days. When asked, 'Well, how do things look to you now? Are they upside down?', he replied, 'I wish you hadn't asked me. Things were all right until you popped the question at me. Now, when I recall how they *did* look *before* I put on these lenses, I must answer that they do look upside-down *now*. But until the moment that you asked me, I was absolutely unaware of it and hadn't given a thought to the question whether things were right-side-up or upside-down' (Snyder and Pronko, 1952, p. 113).

More recent studies have concentrated on rather less drastic transformations produced by prisms which rotate the visual field about 10° to the right or left. Some of these are described by Köhler (1962).

Held (1965) has maintained that for adjustment to transformed input to occur it is necessary to experience self-produced movement: that is, to have active physical interaction with the environment. It is certainly the case that self-produced movement helps adjustment to distortion, but adjustment can take place without it. For instance Weinstein, Sersen, Fisher and Weisinger (1964) have found that subjects wearing prisms, and seated in a wheelchair, when required to direct their own movement by telling a blindfolded experimenter how to move them, adapt to the prisms. Here there is no self-produced movement of the type required by Held's theory: all the subject has is a discrepancy between vision and body movement when the prisms are put on, and this is sufficient for adjustment.

The question of just what changes (the visual perception of the world, or motor learning to cope with the transformed input) in these experiments is still under investigation, but, at least in the early stages of adjustment, it seems likely that the major change occurs in motor responses. Before discussing this claim it should be noted that two processes are occurring when visual input is transformed, (1) sensory adaptation and (2) behavioural compensation (Day, 1969). The adaptation process is of the type described earlier: for instance, Rock and Harris (1967) have reported that subjects observing through a convex lens, which reduces the images of objects, adapt, since subsequently judged objects are reported as larger. The compensation process shows a change in the direction in which a person moves his arm when he is required to reach out and pick up an object: when a prism is placed in front of his eye he will at first reach to one side of the object, but after a few trials will reach accurately. When the prism is removed he will again make errors, but will soon adjust.

The adaptation change is presumably perceptual, but the major change, behavioural compensation, seems to be a change in the way the subject responds to the transformed input. That is, it is a case of motor learning: new or modified responses are learned to cope with the transformed input. It is, therefore, just like learning to draw while observing one's hand in a mirror.

It is interesting to note that when, in such situations, there is conflict between visual and haptic information subjects rely on vision (Rock and Harris, 1967). For instance if a subject is required to set a bar to the horizontal, and is allowed to run his hand along it and at the same time observe this through a lens which makes the bar appear tilted, he will ignore the haptic information and set it so that it looks horizontal, even though if he is not allowed to see the bar he will set it quite horizontal just with the haptic information. Thus much more reliance is placed on the sense of vision than on the other senses (Day, 1969). This effect is quite strong, since sculptors and potters, who are well trained in making haptic judgments, are as susceptible as an unselected group of university students (Power and Graham, 1976).

Illusions

One area of perception which has been extensively investigated for the last hundred years or so is that of illusions. They occur when some aspect of an object is perceived as distorted in a systematic fashion. Examples of some geometrical illusions are shown in Figures 2.8a–f.

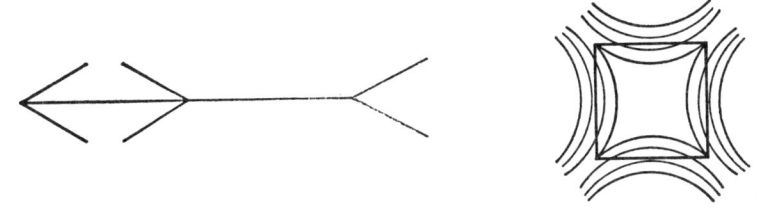

Figure 2.8a

Figure 2.8b

Although all visual, they also occur with haptic stimulation (e.g., by tracing along the components of the Muller-Lyer illusion (Figure 2.8a) with the eyes closed). Illusions can be distinguished from delusions (pathological idiosyncratic distortions) and hallucinations (experiences of objects not present) in various ways, but the most obvious is that all people, or at least all people with a European cultural

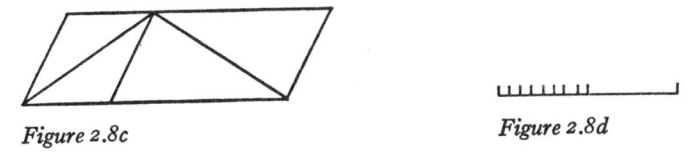

Figure 2.8c

Figure 2.8d

background, perceive the same effects to about the same extent. (It was mentioned earlier that people with different backgrounds have difficulty in perceiving depth in pictures.) Interest in illusions has two main bases. They are intrinsically interesting, and it has been suggested that by studying malfunction it might be easier to understand normal function, just as in medicine study of pathology may lead to understand-

Figure 2.8e

ing of normal function. Many attempts have been made to explain illusions, but at the moment it is necessary to agree with a recent reviewer that as far as the one theory to explain all geometrical illusions

Fundamental Processes of Psychological Functioning

goes, 'the explanation . . . now seems no closer than it was seventy years ago' (Over, 1968, p. 559). The major difficulty is that none of the current explanations can account for all the illusions, and this would suggest that it is a mistake to try and explain them all by a single principle. In fact there are quite reasonable explanations for those which involve perspective: for instance, the tunnel illusion (Figure 2.8f). In

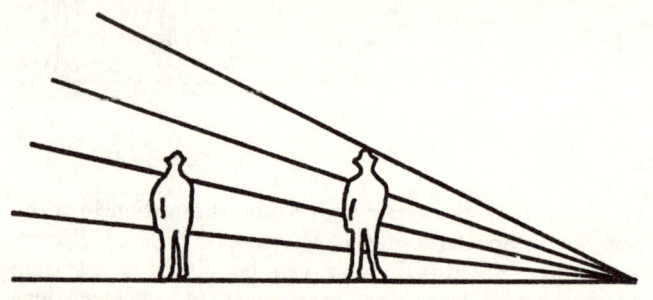

Figure 2.8f

this case there is a perspective representation of a receding surface, and the figure on the right covers more of the background. It is not surprising, then, that the men are perceived to be of different sizes. They would be of different sizes if they did, in reality, cover more of the background.

With this example the background had led to a non-veridical judgment, but normally when an object is perceived in relationship to its background constancy operates, and the object is perceived much as it really is (see the section on constancy of perception above). This suggests that the two effects, constancy and illusion, may have something in common (Day, 1972). Before pursuing this argument, examine the two outline figures 2.9a–b: with prolonged viewing they

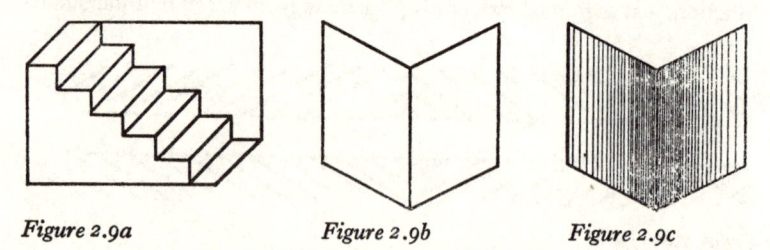

Figure 2.9a *Figure 2.9b* *Figure 2.9c*

appear to reverse in depth, first one part being seen as closer, then the other. These are ambiguous shapes, just as those in Figure 2.5 which led to figure-ground reversals are ambiguous. They are ambiguous since they have no features to determine which is the 'correct' aspect, and judgments of them fluctuate. In this they are different from illusion and constancy: in both cases the percept is determinate, either veridical or non-veridical. It has been argued (Day, 1969; Power and Day, 1973) that constancy, fluctuating judgments and illusion lie on a continuum: constancy occurring when an object is seen in a normal relationship with its background, fluctuating judgments occurring when cues to depth or distance are eliminated, and illusion occurring when the object is seen against a misleading background, as with the tunnel illusion. As can be seen from Figure 2.9c the fluctuations can be reduced or eliminated by information about the shape of the object. These three types of judgment will be considered again when illusions connected with movement are discussed.

One feature of the geometrical illusions is that they can often be obtained by successive presentation of the inducing and test portions of the figures. If the cross on the pattern of concentric lines in Figure 2.10b is fixated for 30 seconds, and the gaze is then transferred to the cross in the adjacent square, the square will probably appear distorted in the same way as the square in the simultaneous presentation (Figure 2.10a).

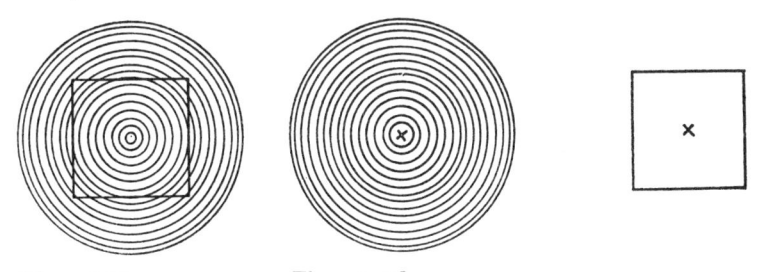

Figure 2.10a   *Figure 2.10b*

These geometrical illusions are artificial: that is, they occur because man has arranged lines in a special relationship. But the illusion that the moon at the horizon is larger than the moon at the zenith occurs naturally. A series of experiments (Kaufman and Rock, 1962) has confirmed that the illusion occurs because the moon at the horizon is seen over terrain, which makes the sky at the horizon appear further away than the sky at the zenith (Figure 2.11). It is seen as further because the terrain acts as filled space; and as was shown in Figure 2.8d filled space appears to extend further than unfilled. Since at both positions the moon subtends the same visual angle it must be seen as larger when it is seen as further. The filled-unfilled space part of the argument can be verified by cutting a hole in a card and observing the moon through it so that the terrain is invisible. The moon will appear the same size in both positions. The fact that an object subtending the same visual angle will appear larger if it is judged as further can be verified by obtaining a strong after-image (see the section on attention and habituation above) and projecting it on a near surface, when it will appear small; and then projecting it on a far surface, when it will appear large.

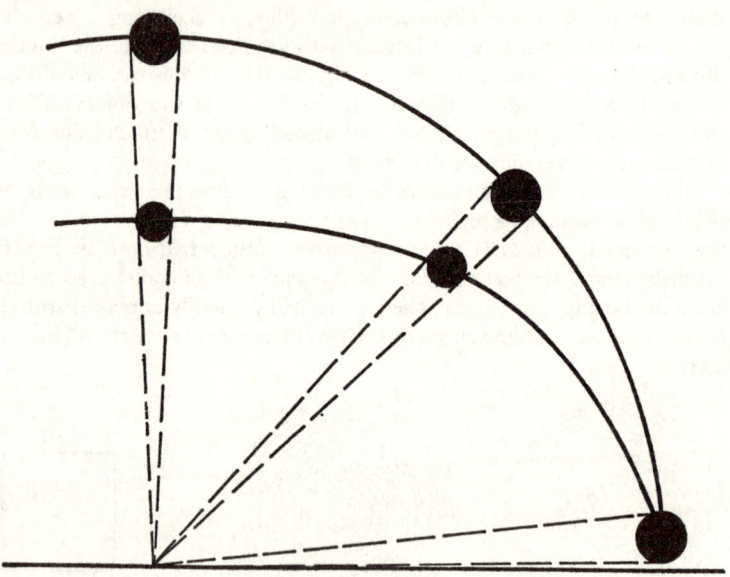

Figure 2.11

A variety of illusions connected with movement also occurs. If two lights about four or five inches apart are switched on and off in succession with an interval of a second or so, they are perceived in just that fashion. If the time interval is gradually reduced a critical point will be reached when a new percept is experienced. The percept will be of one light moving back and forth. If the time interval is reduced still further then the percept will be of two lights flashing on and off simultaneously. The laws governing this phenomenon are fairly well known. Increasing the intensity, reducing the time interval or reducing the distance will make up for the opposite change in either of the other variables, but there is as yet no really satisfactory understanding of the physiological mechanisms involved.

The autokinetic phenomenon is another example of apparent movement. If a fixed point source of light in an otherwise dark room is observed it will appear to move quite markedly. It may even appear to move in a meaningful fashion, especially if someone suggests that it is tracing a certain pattern. Social pressure of this sort will lead to quite considerable changes in reports of the effect. The conditions under which the phenomenon occurs are known: it is the absence of a frame of reference, but the mechanism is not fully understood.

As well as apparent movement of stationary objects, incorrect judgments of movement can be obtained. For instance if a luminous dot in an otherwise dark room is surrounded by a luminous square, movement of the dot to the left will lead to that percept, but so will movement of the square to the right. Also any combination of movements of the dot and square will lead to the dot's being judged as moving. This effect occurs because of an assumption that the ground against which a figure is observed is fixed, rather than the figure. This accounts for the fact

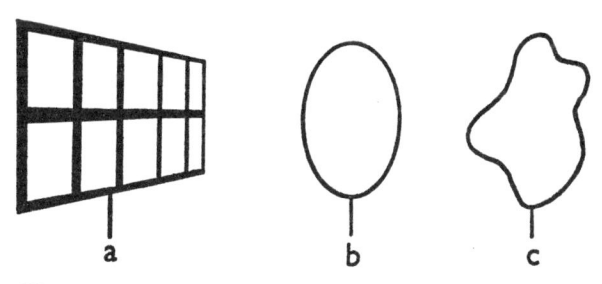

Figure 2.12

that the moon is often judged to be moving, rather than the clouds which are moving past it. This illusion, and a variety of others, are described by Kohlers (1964). One more movement illusion of a different type will be considered. If a plane shape (other than a rectangle) is rotated about an axis it will often appear to reverse its direction of rotation. One well-known shape which produces this apparent reversal of rotary motion in depth is shown in Figure 2.12a. Although it cannot be seen in this illustration, the original shape was cut and painted to resemble a perspective transformation of a window. If it is observed monocularly at short distances, or binocularly at greater distances, it will appear to reverse on most of the occasions on which it rotates into the fronto-parallel plane. The elliptical and irregular shapes shown in Figure 2.12b and c also produce the illusion, but with lower frequency. The illusion occurs because there are few cues to true rotation direction provided by the shapes, so it would be expected that shapes 2 and 3 would be perceived as rotating in one direction and then the other. Shape 1 is judged as reversing more often since it has strong but

Fundamental Processes of Psychological Functioning

misleading cues to depth, the long side being judged as closer most of the time (Day and Power, 1965). A rectangular shape does not produce the illusion since it has strong cues to direction of rotation (Power, 1967).

As with some of the geometrical illusions, the conditions under which constancy, fluctuating and illusory judgments are obtained apply here. The three objects shown in Figure 2.4 have ambiguous, valid and invalid information to depth painted on them. If the pattern is repeated on the other side, and they are rotated, shape B will be judged to rotate, shape A will be judged to be fluctuating (sometimes rotating, sometimes oscillating) and shape C will be judged to oscillate almost all the time (Power and Day, 1973).

One final odd form of perception is that of 'impossible' figures (Figure 2.13). With figures of this type attention is paid to one part at a time, and this part makes sense, but when another part is examined it becomes clear that the shape cannot be constructed.

Figure 2.13

Conclusion

In the section on illusions a continuum from constancy, through fluctuating judgments to illusion was described. This continuum can be considered in a wider context.

Some of our percepts are produced in a fairly mechanical fashion by the action of our receptor organs. We have little or no control over these processes and they act in a similar fashion for all people. Also, despite small differences between individuals, we all judge the properties of most objects in our environment fairly accurately and in a similar fashion. This must be so since we normally deal with our environment and with one another in a satisfactory manner.

Other judgments are more variable, a person judging an object or event sometimes in one way and sometimes in another, but more important, there are judgments which differ between people. These fluctuations occur because of variations in internal states or differing past experiences. Examples here would be the direction of attention, which is subject to a fairly high degree of conscious control; perceptual defence, which affects individuals differently according to what they find threatening, and is not under conscious control; and, more intermediate, there are stereotypes and halo effects which are normally unconscious but which we can, if we choose, discover something about. In these cases the stimulus situation is such that it does not force all of us to perceive in just the same fashion.

Finally, we have illusion: there are the illusions discussed in the last section, where it was shown that most people, at least in our culture, perceive things similarly but incorrectly. Where illusions are common to all there is no difficulty for the individual, although on occasion there is possible danger if a judgment is seriously in error. But if an individual persists in an illusory judgment which is not common to most people he is considered to be experiencing a delusion or hallucination. In addition to the illusions mentioned in the last section we could consider effects due to sets as cases of illusion: we have arranged the stimulus situation in such a fashion that a person or group of people will systematically misperceive a situation. Similarly, experiments with distorting lenses are experiments on illusion, since they are concerned with the systematic modification of a percept. They also show us how to overcome illusion: it is by obtaining as much information from the environment as we can, and using it to modify our percepts.

References

Allport, D. A., Antonis, B. and Reynolds, P. (1972). 'On the Division of Attention: a Disproof of the Single-Channel Hypothesis', *Q. J. Exp. Psychol.* 24, pp. 225–35.
Bennett, A. M. H. (1961). 'Sensory Deprivation in Aviation', in *Sensory Deprivation* (ed. P. Solomon). Cambridge, Mass.: Harvard University Press.
Blakemore, C. (1973). 'The Baffled Brain', in *Illusion in Nature and Art* (eds R. L. Gregory and E. H. Gombrich). London: Duckworth.
Bower, T. G. R. (1966). 'The Visual World of Infants', *Scient. Am.* 215 (6), pp. 80–92.
Brindley, G. S. (1963). 'After-images', *Scient. Am.* 209 (4), pp. 84–93.
Broadbent, D. E. (1962). 'Attention and the Perception of Speech', *Scient. Am.* 206 (4), pp. 143–51.
Day, R. H. (1969). *Human Perception.* Sydney: Wiley.
Day, R. H. (1972). 'Visual Spatial Illusions: a General Explanation', *Science.* 175, pp. 1335–40.
Day, R. H. and Power, R. P. (1965). 'Apparent Reversal (Oscillation) of Rotary Motion in Depth: an Investigation and a General Theory', *Psychol. Rev.* 72, pp. 117–27.
De Dombal, F. T., Leaper, D. J., Horrocks, J. C., Stanland, H. R. and McCann, A. P. (1974). 'Human and Computer-aided Diagnosis of

Abdominal Pain: Further Report with Emphasis on Performance of Clinicians', *Br. Med. J.* 1, pp. 376–80.
Dember, W. N. (1960). *The Psychology of Perception.* New York: Holt.
Deregowski, J. (1972). 'Pictorial Perception and Culture', *Scient. Am.* 227 (5), pp. 82–8.
Fender, D. H. (1964). 'Control Mechanisms of the Eye', *Scient. Am.* 211 (1), pp. 24–33.
Flanagan, J. L. (1972). 'The Synthesis of Speech', *Scient. Am.* 226 (2), pp. 48–58.
Galanter, E. (1962). 'Contemporary Psychophysics', in *New Directions in Psychology* (ed. T. M. Newcomb). New York: Holt, Rinehart & Winston.
Garner, W. R., Hake, H. W. and Eriksen, C. W. (1956). 'Operationism and the Concept of Perception', *Psychol. Rev.* 63, pp. 149–59.
Gibson, E. J. (1969). *Principles of Perceptual Development.* New York: Appleton-Century-Crofts.
Held, R. (1965). 'Plasticity in Sensory-motor Systems', *Scient. Am.* 213 (5), pp. 84–94.
Heron, W. (1961). 'Cognitive and Physiological Effects of Perceptual Isolation', in *Sensory Deprivation* (ed. P. Solomon). Cambridge, Mass.: Harvard University Press.
Hochberg, J. E. (1964). *Perception.* Englewood Cliffs, N.J.: Prentice-Hall.
Holway, A. H. and Boring, E. G. (1941). 'Determinants of Apparent Visual Size with Distance Variant', *Am. J. Psychol.* 54, pp. 21–37.
Hubel, D. H. (1963). 'The Visual Cortex of the Brain', *Scient. Am.* 209 (5), pp. 54–62.
Hudson, W. (1960). 'Pictorial Depth Perception in Sub-cultural Groups in Africa', *J. Soc. Psychol.* 52, pp. 183–208.
Kaufman, L. and Rock, I. (1962). 'The Moon Illusion', *Scient. Am.* 207 (1), pp. 120–30.
Kelly, H. H. (1950). 'The Warm-cold Variable in First Impressions o Persons', *J. Person.* 18, pp. 431–9.
Köhler, I. (1962). 'Experiments with Goggles', *Scient. Am.* 206 (5), pp. 62–72.
Kohlers, P. A. (1964). 'The Illusion of Movement', *Scient. Am.* 211 (4), pp. 98–106.
Lambert, W. W., Solomon, R. L. and Watson, R. P. (1949). 'Reinforcement and Extinction as Factors in Size Estimation', *J. Exp. Psychol.* 39, pp. 637–41.
Lloyd, B. B. (1972). *Perception and Cognition.* Harmondsworth: Penguin.
McGinnies, E. (1949). 'Emotionality and Perceptual Defence', *Psychol. Rev.* 56, pp. 244–51.
McNicol, D. (1972). *A Primer of Signal Detection Theory.* London: Allen & Unwin.
Miller, G. A. (1951). *Language and Communication.* New York: McGraw-Hill.
Mueller, C. (1965). *Sensory Psychology.* Englewood Cliffs, N.J.: Prentice-Hall.
Open University (1972). *Biological Bases of Behaviour.* (STD 286, Units 5–7), Bletchley, Bucks.: Open University Press.
Over, R. (1968). 'Explanations of Geometrical Illusions', *Psychol. Bull.* 70, pp. 545–62.
Power, R. P. (1967). 'Stimulus Properties which Reduce Apparent

Reversal of Rotary Motion in Depth', *J. Exp. Psychol.* 73, pp. 595–9.
Power, R. P. and Day, R. H. (1973). 'Constancy and Illusion of Apparent Direction of Rotary Motion in Depth: Tests of a Theory', *Percept. and Psychophys.* 13, pp. 217–23.
Power, R. P. and Graham, A. (1976). 'Dominance of Touch by Vision: Generalization of the Hypothesis to a Tactually Experienced Population.' *Perception.* 5 (2), pp. 161–6.
Rock, I. and Harris, C. S. (1967). 'Vision and Touch', *Scient. Am.* 216 (5), pp. 96–104.
Rosenhan, D. L. (1973). 'On Being Sane in Insane Places', *Science.* 179 (4070), pp. 250–8.
Rosenzweig, M. R. (1961). 'Auditory Localization', *Scient. Am.* 205 (4), pp. 132–42.
Segall, M. H., Campbell, D. T. and Herskovits, M. S. (1966). *The Influence of Culture on Visual Perception.* Indianapolis: Bobbs-Merrill.
Snyder, F. W. and Pronko, N. H. (1952). *Vision with Spatial Inversion.* University of Wichita Press.
Stevens, S. S. (1968). 'Ratio scales of opinion', in *Handbook of Measurement and Assessment in Behavioral Sciences* (ed. D. K. Whitla). Reading, Mass.: Addison-Wesley.
Stratton, G. M. (1897). 'Vision Without Inversion of the Retinal Image', *Psychol. Rev.* 4, pp. 341–60, 463–81.
Tinbergen, N. (1951). *The Study of Instinct.* Oxford: Clarendon Press.
Wallach, H. (1963). 'The Perception of Neutral Colors', *Scient. Am.* 208 (1), pp. 107–16.
Warr, P. (1969). 'Inferences about Personal Characteristics', *Advmt Sci.* 26, pp. 206–14.
Weinstein, S., Sersen, E. A., Fisher, L. and Weisinger, M. (1964). 'Is Reafference Necessary for Visual Adaptation?', *Percept. Mot. Skills.* 18, pp. 641–18.
Woodworth, R. S. and Schlosberg, H. (1954). *Experimental Psychology.* London: Methuen.
Worthington, A. G. (1969). 'Paired Comparison Scaling of Brightness Judgments: a Method for the Measurement of Perceptual Defence', *Br. J. Psychol.* 60, pp. 363–8.

Suggestions for further reading

Abercrombie, J. L. *The Anatomy of Judgment.* Harmondsworth: Penguin 1969.
Gregory, R. L. *Eye and Brain.* London: World University Library 1972.
Held, R. and Richards, W. *Perception: Mechanisms and Models.* San Francisco: Freeman 1972.
Vernon, M. D. *Experiments in Visual Perception.* Harmondsworth: Penguin 1966.

Chapter three

Memory

Harry Kay

We think of remembering as one of the most human qualities. It was therefore inevitable that excitement was generated when man made a computer which was said to have a 'memory'. We had long been accustomed to the idea that most biological systems have the means of retaining information and thereby of allowing the past to influence the present. But before the computer the rough distinction had held that man-made machines did not do this: the car does not remember the road home however often it is driven along it, the old horse does. The introduction of the computer changed this thinking in several ways. In the first place, a machine could be designed to retain information and to use it appropriately. In the second, it was evident that once a certain level of complexity was attained in the basic hardware of the system then the functioning of the machine was dependent upon how it was programmed, upon its software. This distinction between the hardware and software components was most illuminating to our thinking about memory. Thirdly, the computer system highlighted the importance of retrieval, and the significant point that information may well be stored within the system but can be obtained only if it is correctly addressed. Human memory studies had tended to emphasize the input stage to the neglect of retrieval problems. We now had further insights into that most human quality, forgetting.

In this chapter we will distinguish some of the main issues by first considering three stages in remembering: (1) the input, (2) the storage or retention, and (3) the retrieval of information. We will then look at the problem as a whole and discuss some of the theoretical concerns which have been raised around short- and long-term memory, before concluding with a brief reference to ageing and clinical states with related neurological evidence.

Input

When we study the different stages of remembering we are trying to understand what happens to information during its transmission from a physical event in the world to that point in time when it again appears in similar form. There is, say, an auditory or visual stimulus which a subject observes and which subsequently he recalls, either verbally or in writing. We talk of stimulus and response, but the problems begin immediately with trying to identify what really is the stimulus and its relationship to a subsequent response. What is perceived and stored? What is the influence of the sensory mode by which a signal is perceived? How far do other sensory modalities influence a message even when they are not directly concerned with its reception? How is a stimulus encoded? How does previous experience influence the process? And a host of similar questions.

The psychologist is not in any position to give precise answers to such questions, in spite of decades of experimental work, but there are certain broad features which have been established. The first concerns the accuracy of reception. It is misleading to assume that for any given stimulus the brain subsequently makes an accurate recording. This will depend on attendant circumstances such as the state of the organism, the content of the stimulus, its familiarity to the subject and, above all, its expectancy. We are very much in the world of individual differences: how humans get information, not only according to general basic rules governing their biological make-up but also according to individual rules related to their personalities.

One of the first experimenters in this field, Ebbinghaus (1885), appreciated that if he were to make any measurable record of memory it would be necessary both to present material under exactly similar experimental conditions and to ensure that such material was of uniform meaning to a subject. Ebbinghaus felt that he could meet this condition – uniformity of meaning – by inventing a new vocabulary and asking his subjects to learn it. The so-called 'nonsense syllable' was the result. Ebbinghaus made up words by placing a vowel between two consonants and accepting as a nonsense syllable every word which was not already in the language. It was a good first try; and because of the stringent conditions under which Ebbinghaus conducted his experiments, acting as his own subject, results were obtained which are still valid.

We should be clear about what exactly Ebbinghaus was attempting to do. He was trying to invent material which would have the same associative value for learning. He argued that if the words were unknown the associative value would be zero and therefore meet his criterion. In fact this basic assumption is invalid. It is not possible to rid items of associations because they are new. Items are perceived in the context of a subject's previous experiences and often a word is associated with a previously known word, by reason of its sound, or appearance, or shape, even though this is peculiar to the individual subject. Bartlett (1932), more than any other psychologist of his time, appreciated this point and in his book, *Remembering*, reported many experiments on perception to illustrate how far subjects would distort material to accord with their expectancies. Bartlett used commonplace material such as pictures of people or line drawings and brilliantly supported his contention that perceiving as well as remembering is an 'effort after meaning'. When confronted with new material a subject 'casts about for analogies with which to subdue the intractability of the perceptual data'. Thus the psychologist cannot make the assumption that what is presented is necessarily perceived or retained; rather, it is highly probable that where material does not accord with the expectancies or predilections of a subject inaccuracies will creep in at the initial perceptual stage.

The general distortion which can take place in perceiving and continue with retention is one of the firmer generalizations which can be made about remembering, and it points to the interaction which must be taking place between the initial input processes and their interpretation. A subject's perception of events is not determined by chance but very much by reason of his own personal experiences. Hence it follows that there is some interaction between perceptual processes and stored experiences. We perceive in terms of the probable (James, 1890); that is, we perceive by reason of our ability to interpret new events in terms of the old. We shall return to the point when we discuss theoretical models of remembering, but let us be clear that though the arguments continue about the actual models the evidence on this interaction is firm enough.

Its importance can be illustrated from different kinds of experiment. Gomulicki (1956) and Kay (1955) had shown how far subjects in trying to assimilate verbal reports made a perceptual analysis of the material, simplifying it in structure and length but retaining the core of the meaning. Gomulicki called this an abstractive process. More recent papers by Mandler (1967, 1968) have stressed that these organizational qualities are a necessary condition for memory. He showed that subjects who had only to categorize a set of words recalled them as efficiently as subjects who were explicitly instructed to remember them. Bower and associates (1969) have shown the effects of organization even more dramatically: after one trial their subjects recalled seventy-three words out of 112 when they were presented in an organized hierarchy, but only twenty-one out of 112 when presented in random sets. We should note Bower is postulating that the organized structure was used by subjects as a retrieval strategy at recall, and we shall return to the point in the section on retrieval.

Retention

From the discussion on input two obvious questions arise about retention: (1) How much in quantitative terms is retained, and (2) how far does distortion continue during retention?

(1) *The Rate of Forgetting*

Ebbinghaus was trying to answer the first question about retention, and in spite of the objections which can be made to his material he gave an answer that has been supported by a century of research. Figure 3.1 is a typical result. In this study Ebbinghaus learned a set of lists of nonsense syllables; then at the end of different intervals of time after

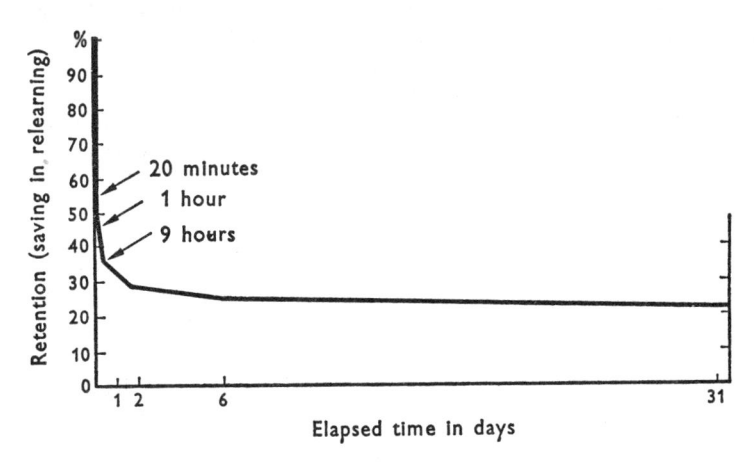

Figure 3.1

learning, varying from twenty minutes to a month, he would relearn the lists. He carefully noted how far the relearning required fewer trials and less time than the original and this was recorded as the percentage savings time. The methodological advantages of the 'savings' method will be mentioned when discussing retrieval, but we should note here that it is a sensitive index for measuring how much has been retained, and the repeatability of Ebbinghaus's results owes much to it. In fact Ebbinghaus's curve of forgetting holds over a surprisingly wide range of conditions, though it must not be generalized too far. It is *not* the curve of forgetting. Nevertheless the finding is widespread that forgetting is at first very rapid and gradually declines, such that the effect may be said to be proportional to the amount of the original material that is being retained at any given moment.

Here then were the first experimental findings that older memories have the greater probability of being retained, that the vulnerable stage is in the early moments after learning. Jost stated this in one of his laws that where associations are of equal strength but of different ages, the older will lose strength more slowly with the further passage of time. Also, further study has greater value for the older memory.

(2) *Distortion During Retention*

Gestalt psychologists were one of the foremost groups who tried to demonstrate that retention was subject to the same influences as visual perception. But their efforts to show that Gestalt laws governed retentive processes in the same way as perceptual processes were not successful. Nevertheless the underlying thesis of the relationship between perception and retention is sound enough.

Bartlett examined retention by a method of repeated reproduction. He read a story of about 300 words to a subject and then asked him to reproduce it as accurately as possible after a given time interval. This might be any time from a few minutes to a day, a week, or even a year. He would continue to ask the same subject to reproduce as much as possible of the same passage after a further time interval. He repeated this many times. If the intervals were short then the reproductions soon took on a stereotyped form: they would shorten the original, often omitting important items and giving names incorrectly, but attaining some internal consistency between one reproduction and the next, in spite of their inaccuracy. When the time intervals were longer the gradual changes in the original story seemed to go on indefinitely.

A number of experiments from Cambridge have illustrated variations on this Bartlettian theme. Davis and Sinha (1950) showed how memories from one source (picture material) would interact over time with memories from another (a story) so that the two originally unconnected events gradually merged and profoundly influenced the retention of each other. In the end subjects who were recalling the picture, which had depicted a happy wedding scene, described how it had the sinister foreboding of an impending tragedy. This, of course, was imported from the story.

Other studies brought out how far memories were indelibly fixed by any responses made by a subject. Let us suppose a picture is presented and a subject is later asked to recall it. What then happens to the subsequent memory of the picture? Belbin (1950) showed that at any further presentation of the original picture, recognition was determined largely by a subject's responses at the time of the first recall. The original material would be confidently but wrongly rejected because it did not conform to the subject's previous recall of it. This process was taken a stage further by Kay (1955), who presented a short story to subjects and asked for its immediate recall. He then re-presented the original story, asked for further recall, and repeated the procedure several times. The frequent presentations did produce some improvement in the reproduction – some further learning did take place – but the outstanding feature was the persistence of those mistakes which the subject had introduced in his original recall. In spite of learning much of the original material it was evident that certain memories had been firmly 'laid down' and were not changed by the discrepancy between them and the presented material.

Decay v. Interference

Experiments such as the above raise one of the oldest problems of remembering: is loss caused by decay of memories or by interference of one with another? The two concepts of decay and interference are generally posed as if they were mutually exclusive, which they are not. Indeed, if memories do not suffer any decay it is hard to see why interference effects should be so prevalent and pronounced. It is much easier to conceive of two events interfering with one another when their original boundaries have become a little blurred. Of course, interference may arise between two items because of certain contextual similarities, as when they are perceived at the same time or place. Confusion may then occur because they both have a common address (the means of locating a particular memory). Most items in store may be located by several different addresses, related to when and where they were perceived, what meaning or associations were attached to them, and so on. For example, if we try to remember the name of an acquaintance we quickly become aware of how many different forms of address may lead us to it, or lead us to that location where there is either a name or some part of it. Often in such cases we may not be sure whether our recall is correct. In these circumstances we may feel that the decay hypothesis suits one set of conditions, the interference the other, and that neither would fully account for all phenomena.

Retrieval

The decay-interference issue has already brought us to the problem of retrieval, particularly in the discussion of the need to address correctly any item in storage if it is to be identified. But a marked feature of human memory is the variety of address systems which may be used. Conditioning experiments have always stressed the biological importance of spatial and temporal contiguity in forming associations, but once we are storing items of meaningful material then the variety of these associations is such that it is conceivable to address them by many different means.

Everyone appreciates that a person cannot always retrieve an item though he has not completely forgotten it. For example, he may be aware that he did know a name but that at this precise moment he cannot identify it. And he may know more than this: he may be able to say, quite correctly, what the name is not. If we suggest names to him they may be rejected with confidence. This negative memory – knowing what it is not, when we cannot say what it is – is exhibiting a threshold phenomenon. Apparently excitation from the retained item is such as to enable a subject to be sure that the proposed name does not match it but is not sufficient to enable the subject to recall the original. In such circumstances we probe for the item by trying multiple modes of address such as the size of the name, its shape, its novelty or nationality, its sound and associated geography. Sometimes these multiple addresses are successful. At others, nothing comes until hours later when the name is, almost unexpectedly, recalled; here it seems as if the address system has suddenly matched and thereby identified the forgotten item.

The psychologist has tried to examine retrieval by several methods. The savings method is a sensitive index of what has been stored, but avoids the retrieval question by re-presenting the items. Another technique is to examine the difference between recall and recognition. Where a subject is asked to recognize an item he is generally shown the original in the context of other items. The difficulty of the task is determined largely by the number of other items which are shown and their similarity to the original. It is easy enough to recognize the picture of a car if there is only one such item and the remainder depict animals. But it may be very difficult if all the pictures are of cars of very similar colour, shape and size. In order to quantify such dimensions of similarity psychologists have tended to use material drawn from a known population size and where the dimensions of similarity might be specified; for example, a matrix of black and white squares.

It might appear that the difference between recognition and recall is that in the former the population size from which an item has to be recognized is known and can be specified, whereas in recall the size is often unknown and may be very large indeed. Thus recall is a measurably more difficult task. It is the case that in certain tasks where the population size can be easily and accurately specified to a subject, as, say in trying to recall or recognize two-digit numbers, there is little difference between the results of recognition and recall, but in other instances the psychological processes involved appear very different. For example, suppose a subject is trying to recall or recognize the picture of a face which he was originally shown. In the recognition case the presented material (the face) is being matched against any stored material, and the retrieval process in such recognition would seem to differ markedly from trying to recall the face without the original stimulus being present.

If we may now refer back to the Bower (1969) example of retrieval through organization, we can appreciate that he is saying retrieval is improved in so far as the retained material is structured and held together in such a way that it is accessible to the particular address system (or probe) which the subject is trying to use in these circumstances. His study seems to verify his point.

Short- and long-term memory

Our consideration of three stages in memory has served to bring out the complexities in the total process and the interaction between the different stages. In their attempts to understand remembering psychologists have conducted thousands of experiments, particularly with verbal material, and it is quite impossible to give the minutiae of their findings. In the following sections an attempt will be made to describe those results which have general theoretical significance. The first refers to the distinction between short- and long-term memory.

Primary Memory: Iconic Memory and Echoic Memory

Philosophers have long puzzled over the problem of the 'specious present' in trying to distinguish that brief time span which may be regarded as happening here and now from that which is a record of past events. James (1890, 1, p. 643) re-called this immediate record 'primary memory', a satisfactory name which has unfortunately been used to mean several other states in recent literature. One question the philosophers had asked themselves was whether an individual could apprehend in a momentary glance more than one object at a time. This had been put to the test first by Hamilton (1859) and then more systematically by Jevons (1871) who demonstrated that the span of apprehension was almost 100 per cent correct when estimating five objects and fell to 50 per cent correct when estimating around eight or nine. His results conclusively showed that in a single glance a subject could apprehend more than one object; and later experiments under more controlled conditions with tachistoscopes (which ensure the presentation could only be momentary) confirmed the findings.

The position rested there until some recent experiments took up a suggestion of Woodworth that 'the true span of apprehension must be larger than the measure which we have obtained' (Woodworth, 1938, p. 695). Sperling (1960) ingeniously demonstrated this by tachistoscopically exposing for fifty milliseconds three rows of letters, four in each row. Only four or five letters were correctly repeated under such stringent conditions. But Sperling then used a partial recall method by giving a signal to instruct his subjects to report any one row of the display. This signal was given immediately after the display was taken off. The results were startling: any row of three letters could be reported with almost 100 per cent accuracy, and a row of four letters with 75 per cent accuracy. The results were much depressed if the signal indicating which row was to be reported was in any way delayed.

This, and further experiments by Averbach and Coriell (1961), have established that there is some brief storage of the visual input which decays very rapidly indeed. A subject can interpret signals for this brief interval before such decay, but it lasts for less than half a second. (Decay takes slightly longer with an auditory signal than a visual.) It is a subject's experience that the letters appear to be visually present when the stimulus has in fact been turned off. This is very similar to a visual image; the experience seems to be perceptual but depends upon retaining the memory of the display.

Here is definite evidence of some form of immediate memory but, as we shall see, this is over a shorter time scale and different from the process which has usually been identified with short-term memory. The names proposed by Neisser (1967) instead of James's primary memory are 'iconic memory' for this visual sensory memory, and 'echoic memory' for the auditory equivalent. In both cases they refer to the preliminary stage of storing sensory information. Such storage, which acts as a sensory buffer, holding signals long enough for them to be processed and transmitted to another store, is essential to a system dealing with time-ordered events. The rates at which signals decay and the speed with which they can be encoded are two important parameters of this immediate memory span.

Short-Term Memory (STM)

There is, however, another form of memory which is also concerned with remembering over short time intervals but is quite different from iconic or echoic memory. We are familiar with this form of STM in the well-known 'span of immediate memory'. If a string of digits is read out at an even rate, say one per second, it is easy enough for most adults to repeat back the string up to about seven items. Individuals vary a little but a span above nine is exceptional.

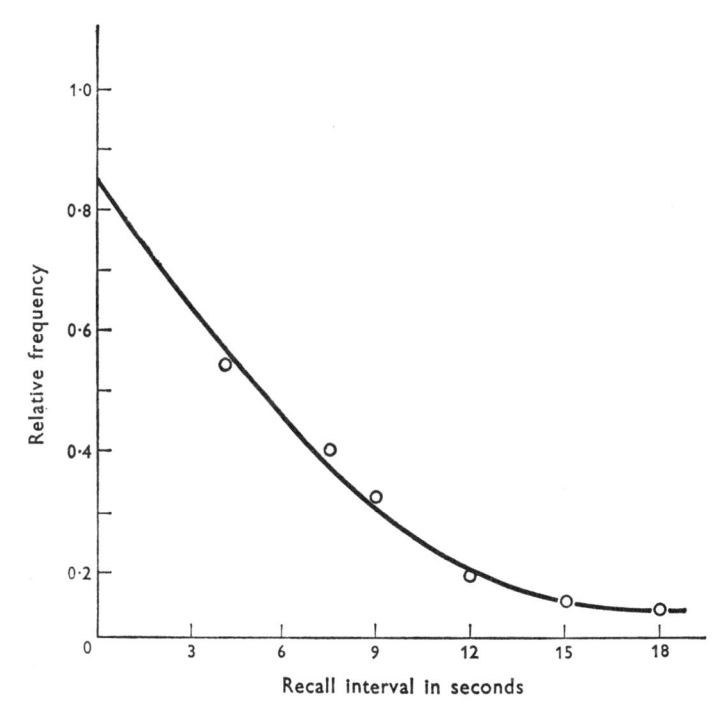

Figure 3.2

The theoretical significance of this limitation both for perception and memory is fundamental. Why can a given individual recall, say, seven digits and not nine? We say this is the capacity of his immediate memory, but it is not clear why it is so limited. Nor is it certain where exactly the limitation occurs.

Many psychologists are trying to resolve this problem by presenting information to subjects under strictly controlled conditions to find out when and how much information is received, how far it is processed, and to what extent it is subject to interference from preceding and succeeding information. Several important methods have been used. For example, Peterson and Peterson (1959) have illustrated the striking effect upon recall of a predictable activity during immediate retention. They presented material to be remembered and then required their subjects to count backwards by threes during the retention interval. Forgetting is very rapid under such conditions and by the time the recall interval reaches eighteen seconds little or nothing is remembered. The negatively accelerating curve is very similar to the Ebbinghaus curve but the loss is more complete (see Figure 3.2).

Another marked effect is achieved by requiring a subject to make a known response before recalling the presented material. Conrad (1960), working on telephone dialling systems, asked his subjects to give the digit zero before recalling a series. Though subjects were well aware of what they had to do, performance was strikingly depressed by this simple response.

The theoretical controversy has focused on where information to the brain is filtered and analysed. In view of the multiplicity of details the reader should consult the work of Broadbent (1958, 1971), Deutsch and Deutsch (1963), Norman (1970) and Treisman (1964, 1969). But certain broad features can be established. Several experiments examine a situation where it would not be possible for a subject to rehearse or even perceive material before recall is required. This is the situation in span of apprehension experiments, or of dichotic listening studies (e.g. Broadbent, 1956). Here series of pairs of digits, each member of a pair differing from the other, are presented to the two ears. A subject cannot hear both messages simultaneously, so he has to store one without having perceived it. He recalls the digits immediately the series ends and his favourite strategy is to give all the digits presented to one ear, and then to switch and give all those presented to the other. It is as if he is perceiving the second list of digits for the first time as he recalls them (we shall mention a different strategy later).

In this situation what we seem to have, though on a longer time scale, is a repetition of the phenomenon of iconic and echoic memory, in so far as information is held in a form of temporary storage before being processed. From there, it is ready to be passed on to a longer-term store; but if no action is taken, or if further items are introduced without processing the older items, then there is rapid loss of the information in the short-term store. The time interval, whilst still only short, is much longer than that of the iconic store. We should note that it is essential that there should be such a form of buffer storage in the system if perception is to take place; for example, in perceiving the temporal order of events it is necessary to retain a number of items over some temporal scale. At the time those items are received they may not be fully identified; indeed, their identification may only be possible after their sequential order and spatial-temporal intervals have been determined. Thus, if the human system is to perceive fully such complex material as is involved in speech, music, or spatial patterns it is essential for there to be a mechanism which can hold signals over a time interval before they have been fully analysed.

But when we turn to experiments on immediate memory span, where there is sufficient time to perceive all items whilst they are being presented successively, the situation is different. Each item is probably rehearsed (aloud in some cases) within the presentation rate before recall is required. Here, though the behaviour may be occurring over a short time interval, we seem to be dealing with examples where a subject is trying to learn the material within the given time constraints. Some series are too long to learn completely, but the failures we observe are due to the long-term system's inability to retain the unconnected material. Hebb's (1961) and Melton's (1963) experiments on immediate memory, where they showed gradual improvement when the same lists were occasionally repeated, illustrate this clearly enough. The distinction between the immediate memory span experiments and the span of apprehension studies is nicely brought out in Miller's (1956) classic paper on 'The Magical Number Seven, Plus or Minus Two'.

For what it is worth the present author does not regard it as helpful to conceive of STM as a separate mechanism. Rather the results over short-term intervals are often a phenomenon of the perceptual analysing system. Signals are passed from the peripheral sensory system to the brain where information is to be processed. We are really discussing the time constants of that analysing system. As we have seen, it is essential that such a system should be able to hold signals which have not yet been fully analysed if their temporal-spatial information is not to be lost. Indeed we can be categorical on this issue that some form of buffer storage is essential to a perceptual system that is capable of analysing signals as complex and varied as the human brain. In the present view the perceptual analysing system has the time constants as revealed by STM experiments and can store information for this limited time. But the act of perceiving involves the translation of signals within the buffer store to the more permanent storage system of the brain. Interaction between the two systems is obviously necessary and, as we have noted, the act of perception is an interaction between what is presented and what has been previously experienced.

We should also appreciate that a subject may adopt different strategies when receiving signals, according to their temporal and semantic characteristics. For example, in the dichotic listening experiment if words are used instead of digits we may find that subjects switch their attention between the different ears so that they construct a meaningful sentence by taking one word from one ear and the next word from the other (Gray and Wedderburn, 1960). This indicates that at comparatively slow rates of presentation it is possible for some perceptual analysis to take place and influence which signals are given priority. The human brain is a flexible system and adapts its strategies to meet contingencies.

One crucial point in the process is the form of retrieval from the long-term store: what determines the actual information which is retrieved, and how does it then influence the act of perception? The speed of the process indicates the flexibility between the two stages, but the extent to which an individual may be completely wrong in his perception if his expectancies (or set) are wrong also indicates the extent to which the stimulus at the stage of perception is under the control of the long-term store.

Long-Term Memory (LTM)

It is fair to say that the underlying concepts of memory have changed remarkably little. The idea of the engram or trace is not fundamentally different from Aristotle's wax tablet impression (see Gomulicki, 1953). Philosophers and then psychologists had written about a trace theory of memory as if the constituent elements were fixed and indelible. But Gestalt psychologists introduced the concept of dynamic trace systems whilst Bartlett (1932) challenged any static view with his schema theory of remembering. We might summarize the present position as follows: most psychologists would think of long-term storage as being represented by a system which allowed one element to interact with another. Any one element might be laid down by one or many different identifying attributes; for example, a word might be stored in terms of when and where it happened, how it sounded, what it meant, what words were related to it, what was its visual appearance, and so on. Some psychologists, such as Norman and Rumelhart (1970) emphasize the contextual significance of attributes. But whilst the identity of the individual element would depend on its perception and how accurately it was initially interpreted, a host of affective factors might well change its subsequent storage, as in the case of an item associated with some highly emotive subject.

The diversity of the phenomena of LTM is well known; the problem is how to account for such variety. For example, are some memories permanently lost? Do they undergo permanent change or is it possible to recover the original 'memory'? These issues are well brought out by contrasting Freud's and Bartlett's positions. Freud (1914) was a pioneer in demonstrating the importance of the nature of mistakes which a person makes during recall. Forgetting was an active process of repression, controlled by the deeper motives and interests of an individual, leading in some cases to an inability to recall any of the original experience and in others to a subtle distortion of it. Bartlett, on the other hand, placed the main emphasis upon the initial coding of the information, and argued that this was primarily determined by the stored experience of the individual. Bartlett's main thesis was that because of a subject's individual experiences acting upon his expectancies and predilections, the perception of an event would be distorted by the individual, and from that point the individual would not be storing an accurate record of the occurrence but his own version of it. This distortion would continue during storage and be subject to the same influences. Thus, for Freud, memory failure would be due to the present repression of a past experience; for Bartlett, present recall was inaccurate because of the result of a past inaccurate perception and the consequent storing of a biased record. The two explanations are not mutually exclusive, but the general ubiquity of the Bartlettian process will be readily appreciated.

What can we say about the details of such storage? For the present very little, beyond guesses. But we have some information about the interaction which takes place within the storage system. For example, clear evidence has emerged about acoustical and visual confusions. Woodworth (1938, p. 37) had pointed to the common experience of acoustic confusions in long-term memory, as in the case of recalling a name which is not correct but which sounds like the original; Cobb for Todd, Walliston for Warburton: 'You get the right kind of name – right in some respect – before you get the right name.' In similar terms, James (1890; 1, p. 251) had described it: 'the gap of one word does not feel like the gap of another'. Conrad (1964) in an important paper clarified this question by demonstrating exactly how this type of error occurred in a memory span experiment. Conrad presented sequences of six letters visually for immediate recall. He was able to show that there were not only systematic errors in recall but that these were the same errors as occurred when subjects listened to the same items in acoustically confusing conditions. Thus, in the first experiment, in spite of the letters for recall being presented visually, subjects were in some way processing them so that in storage their acoustical similarities to other letters were influencing the errors at recall. Here then was an insight into how information was being processed over a short time scale and we already know of similar confusions in long-term memories. Apparently it is not the case that some engram representing visual characteristics is laid down and that this must necessarily be addressed if recall is to take place. Rather the letter and/or its attributes are retained in such a way that the acoustical qualities are as important as the visual.

This type of experiment serves to establish that though mnemonic information may be stored in a way that is related to the sensory mode by which it was received, as in the case of remembering faces or landscapes without verbal mediation, this is not a necessary condition; and that in some cases of recall we have definite examples of interaction between different senses.

Over the years many different kinds of memory confusion have been cited. All tend to illustrate that we are not discussing discrete experiences which are preserved as isolated events; rather they are subject to considerable changes by other mental and emotional activities.

Associations

Older issues such as the role of images or the part played by associations are no longer in the forefront of research, but their importance should not be overlooked. As long ago as Aristotle discussion had raged about how ideas were associated in terms of their similarity or contrast, or their contiguity in space and time. These became known as the laws of association. Later, during the eighteenth and nineteenth centuries, British philosophers, as empiricists, put forward associationism as their main concept to explain mental life in terms of past experience. Much detailed writing was devoted to expounding such laws, but little or no experimental work was done until the time of Galton (1883). As would be expected from Galton, every effort was made to quantify the findings. He measured both the associative reaction time (how quickly a subject can respond to one word with another) and the frequency of repetition of the same associative response. Later experimenters turned from measuring already formed associations between events to studying the formation of such associations in learning experiments. They were particularly concerned with how learning and remembering were influenced by similarity, contiguity, frequency and recency. Such studies, though limited to verbal material, demonstrated that a great variety of associations were being formed; and experimenters took up such problems as serial associations or remote forward and backward associations within a series. One of the oldest findings, not yet explained, occurs when a subject tries to recall a series of items; he recalls most accurately items at the beginning and end of the series and makes most errors or omissions over items in the middle. This serial error curve has been attributed to such factors as a primacy effect (paying most attention to the initial items), and a recency effect (the last items were tested after the shorter lapse in time); but neither fully accounts for the findings.

Memory

Imagery

Another theme, linked with associationism and with Galton's work, was the role of imagery in memories. Again the problem seemed deceptively easy. Many individuals experience things which are not physically present, as in dreams, hallucinations and in different forms of imagery (e.g., eidetic imagery, the very vivid, percept-like images which some individuals and particularly young people may possess; or hypnagogic imagery, which occurs during the state between waking and sleeping). But when Galton (1883) carried out his celebrated investigation by asking people to imagine their breakfast table he found widely differing abilities. Some claimed very clear images whilst other reported no visual pictures at all. Other experiments revealed that some individuals had strong auditory or motor imagery which was an essential component of their remembering, but this type of imagery played only a minor role in the majority of cases. Confusion arises because it is difficult for those individuals who think by using imagery to appreciate that others do not. Visual imagery is the most common form and generally the most vivid, followed by auditory and then by tactile imagery.

Motivation

Psychologists would agree that motivation plays a major role in the remembering of everyday experiences. Yet, in spite of the influences of Freud and Bartlett, who from different standpoints were both stressing the significance of affective influences, comparatively little work has been done. Freud was outstanding in putting forward the clinical evidence from case histories; Bartlett stressed the affective component in perception and storage. We can all cite examples of someone remembering every detail of a subject in which he was interested and having no recollection in another field where he was not. It would seem that a part explanation will be due to the organization of material. Where there is a strong interest component a new experience is often readily understood in terms of already acquired knowledge in that area. There is a clearly defined field of experience; and whether we are thinking in terms of a schema of knowledge (Bartlett) or an interacting engram system the chances are that it will contain a strong internal structure because it has been frequently rehearsed from a particular standpoint. This is indicated when an individual talks on a subject of recurring interest to him; his discourse takes on a set pattern of which his listeners, and often the speaker himself, are aware. He knows he is 'on his hobby-horse'. But such structured organization is only part of the story why motivation can be so influential and we need an explanation that touches other dimensions. In particular, we need to understand why emotions may so charge experience that it becomes wellnigh indelible in time. We can appreciate that at the time of perceiving an event in a vivid emotional context this may have the effect of blocking all other incoming channels, such that the input is totally directed upon the one event. But we do not know how this is achieved, nor how the retentive process continues and is further influenced through the emotions.

Memory defects

Ageing

The subject of memory figures prominently in any account of ageing. Many older subjects complain of loss of memory. Again this is not as straightforward as it might seem. The most obvious deficiency lies in the ability to assimilate and retain events of the immediate past. In learning experiments it is found that old people are much slower than young, and that they persist in repeating their own errors in spite of all the evidence against them (Kay, 1954). It is as if new percepts become harder to assimilate with age, and the events which are retained are those which accord with previous experiences. The well-rehearsed events of early childhood may still be recalled by an older person but the focus of difficulty lies in remembering the inconsequential happenings of the last few hours or minutes (see Welford, 1958; Bromley, 1966). It is the loss of capacity to deal with events over a comparatively narrow time range, such as remembering where an object was placed, who came into the room or what was said, that old people find disturbing.

Clinical evidence

The loss of memory and the slower assimilative abilities of an older person are paralleled by some clinical states, of which the best known is amnesia. In amnesic cases patients with adequate intellectual functions often show marked loss of memory. This is not to be attributed, as in confusional states, to an impairment of consciousness. There are two marked states of amnesia. In anterograde amnesia a patient will show defective learning and retention for on-going events and this may range from total loss to a mild deficiency. The impairment often shows up most strikingly in the inability of the patient to learn to identify hospital staff or his whereabouts within the hospital. In retrograde amnesia there is a loss of memory for events antedating the illness. It is not easy to secure accurate information about such memories, but a patient may be unable to give an account of private or public events which have preceded his illness. This time interval may extend backwards over many years. The syndrome is most striking in accident cases involving head injury and loss of consciousness. When the patient is recovering and is fully aware of his surroundings he may have a retrograde amnesia for all events leading to the accident and, after a severe injury, for some years preceding the accident.

Immediate memory span does not seem to be impaired in amnesic states; so memory failures cannot be attributed to a failure to register events. And such an explanation could not apply to retrograde amnesia where events had been both perceived and recalled previously in a normal fashion. One explanation, but by no means the only one (Warrington, 1971), is that the patient is unable to learn and retain events (anterograde amnesia) because he cannot consolidate the perceived experiences. The transitory immediate state is never transferred to any stable and more permanent condition. Any explanation of retrograde amnesia would have to be along different lines. In so far as memories are often subsequently recalled as the patient recovers from an accident we must look for an explanation in terms of either some temporary disturbance of the previously consolidated memories, or some loss of the ability to retrieve information. The two features may be linked and one possibility is that the injury to the previously organized memory state prevents retrieval. A further point is worth noting: the older the memory the more resistant it is to decay. Amnesic patients may be able to give details of their childhood and preserve the skills which they acquired in early life, but remember nothing about events of a few weeks ago.

Neurological Evidence

Clinical evidence of the above kind is extremely valuable for indicating some of the neurological problems which must be faced in trying to understand human memory. From the point of view of anatomical location it is obvious that memories are not located in any one area. Many different parts of the human brain have been accidentally damaged by trauma, tumour or loss of circulation without causing measurable loss of memory. When we turn to laboratory research on animals, workers from Lashley (1929) onwards have despaired of showing that specific memory losses are associated with specific lesions of the brain. But it should be noted that the ability to learn new events will be disturbed in both human and animal cases long before the recollection of past experience is impaired.

Two types of explanation have been offered to account for the different phenomena found over short- and long-term conditions. It was suggested that STM and LTM represent two different neurological systems. Electrical activity is the starting-point of storage and this might be achieved by some form of reverberating circuit. Accordingly several experimenters disrupted the normal pattern of brain activity at different times after learning, using such methods as hypothermia, electroconvulsive shock, anoxia or drugs. The findings were clear enough: recent inputs were vulnerable to such disturbances. The closer the disturbance to the time of input the greater its effect. Thus it seemed that some time had to elapse after perception for memories to consolidate. On the other hand this disruption was not permanent, for recovery of previously learned habits was observed. This made it unlikely that these memories could have been a function of electrical activity alone. It would seem that some structural change must have taken place to make it possible to regain memories, once the experimental disruption had ceased.

It is generally agreed that structural change would occur at a cellular level and would most likely be biochemical in nature. Attempts have been made to analyse the biochemical correlates of learning, particularly changes in ribonucleic acid (RNA). Early thinking suggested RNA might be the agent responsible for information storage; but later work has suggested that storage is dependent upon the continued synthesis of protein molecules, with RNA acting in the nature of an agent for transforming information into protein (Steele Russell, 1971). Again an alternative explanation is that inhibition of protein synthesis blocks the retrieval of information, rather than its storage. As we have seen, the distinction between retrieval and storage processes is one which is now being made by all workers in the field of memory.

References

Averbach, E. and Coriell, A. S. (1961). 'Short-term Memory in Vision', *Bell System Technological Journal* 40, pp. 309–28.
Bartlett, F. C. (1932). *Remembering*. Cambridge University Press.
Belbin, E. (1950). 'The Influence of Interpolated Recall upon Recognition', *Q.J. Exp. Psychol.* 2, pp. 163–9.
Bower, G., Clark, M. C., Lesgold, A. M. and Winzenz, D. (1969). 'Hierarchial Retrieval Schemes in Recall of Categorized Word Lists', *J. Verbal Learn. and Verbal Behav.* 8, pp. 323–43.
Broadbent, D. E. (1956). 'Successive Responses to Simultaneous Stimuli', *Q.J. Exp. Psychol.* 8, pp. 145–52.
Broadbent, D. E. (1958). *Perception and Communication*. Oxford: Pergamon.
Broadbent, D. E. (1971). *Decision and Stress*. London: Academic Press.
Bromley, D. B. (1966). *The Psychology of Human Ageing*. Harmondsworth: Penguin.

Conrad, R. (1960). 'Very Brief Delay of Immediate Recall', *Q.J. Exp. Psychol.* 12, pp. 45–7.
Conrad, R. (1964). 'Acoustic Confusions in Immediate Memory', *Br. J. Psychol.* 55, pp. 75–84.
Davis, D. R. and Sinha, D. (1950). 'The Effect of One Experience upon the Recall of Another', *Q.J. Exp. Psychol.* 2, pp. 43–52.
Deutsch, J. A. and Deutsch, D. (1963). 'Attention: some Theoretical Considerations', *Psychol. Rev.* 70, pp. 80–90.
Ebbinghaus, H. (1885). *Über das Gedächtnis.* (Translated by H. A. Ruger and C. Bussenins, 1913, as *Memory.*) New York: Columbia Press.
Freud, S. (1914). *Psychopathology of Everyday Life.* New York: Macmillan.
Galton, F. (1883). *Inquiries into Human Faculty.* London: Macmillan.
Gomulicki, B. R. (1953). 'The Development and Present Status of the Trace Theory of Memory', *Br. J. Psychol., Monogr. Suppl.* 29.
Gomulicki, B. R. (1956). 'Recall as an Abstractive Process', *Acta Psychol.* 12, pp. 77–94.
Gray, J. A. and Wedderburn, A. A. (1960). 'Grouping Strategies with simultaneous stimuli', *Q.J. Exp. Psychol.* 12, pp. 180–4.
Hamilton, W. (1859). *Lectures on Metaphysics and Logic.* New York: Alder's Foreign Books.
Hebb, D. O. (1961). 'Distinctive Features of Learning in the Higher Animal', in *Brain Mechanism and Learning* (ed. J. F. Delafresnaye). Oxford University Press.
Hunter, I. M. L. (1964). *Memory.* Harmondsworth: Penguin.
James, W. (1890). *The Principles of Psychology.* New York: Holt.
Jevons, W. S. (1871). 'The Power of Numerical Discrimination', *Nature, Lond.* 3, pp. 281–2.
Kay, H. (1954). 'The Effects of Position in a Display upon Problem Solving', *Q.J. Exp. Psychol.* 6, pp. 155–69.
Kay, H. (1955). 'Learning and Retaining Verbal Material', *Br. J. Psychol.* 46, pp. 81–100.
Lashley, K. S. (1929). *Brain Mechanisms and Intelligence.* University of Chicago Press.
Mandler, G. (1967). 'Organization and Memory', in *Advances in the Psychology of Learning and Motivation: Research and Theory* (eds K. W. Spence and J. T. Spence). New York: Academic Press.
Mandler, G. (1968). 'Association and Organization: Facts, Fancies and Theories', in *Verbal Behaviour and General Behaviour Theory* (eds T. R. Dixon and D. L. Horton). New Jersey: Prentice-Hall.
Melton, A. W. (1963). 'Implications of Short-term Memory for a General Theory of Memory', *J. Verbal Learn. and Verbal Behav.* 2, pp. 1–21.
Miller, G. A. (1956). 'The Magical Number Seven, Plus or Minus Two', *Psychol. Rev.* 63, pp. 81–97.
Neisser, U. (1967). *Cognitive Psychology.* New York: Appleton-Century-Crofts.
Norman, D. and Rumelhart, D. E. (1970). 'A System for Perception and Academic Press.
Norman, D. and Rumelhart, D. E. (1970). 'A system for Perception and Memory', in *Models of Human Memory* (ed. D. A. Norman). New York: Academic Press.
Peterson, L. R. and Peterson, M. J. (1959). 'Short-term Retention of Individual Verbal Items', *J. Exp. Psychol.* 58, pp. 193–8.

Sperling, G. (1960). 'The Information Available in Brief Visual Presentations', *Psychol. Monogr.* 74, no. 11.
Steele Russell, I. (1971). 'Neurological Basis of Complex Learning', *Br. Med. Bull.* 27, no. 3, pp. 278-85.
Treisman, A. M. (1964). 'Verbal Cues, Language and Meaning in Selective Attention', *Am. J. Psychol.* 77, pp. 206-19.
Treisman, A. M. (1969). 'Strategies and Models of Selective Attention', *Psychol. Rev.* 76, pp. 282-99.
Warrington, E. K. (1971). 'Neurological Disorders of Memory', *Br. Med. Bull.* 27, no. 3, pp. 243-7.
Welford, A. T. (1958). *Ageing and Human Skill*. Oxford University Press.
Woodworth, R. S. (1938). *Experimental Psychology*. New York: Holt.

Suggestions for further reading

Lindsay, P. H. and Norman, D. *Human Information Processing*. London: Academic Press 1975.
Neisser, U. *Cognitive Psychology*. New York: Appleton-Century-Crofts 1967.
Norman, D. (ed.) *Models of Human Memory*. New York: Academic Press 1970.

Chapter four

Learning

Dougal Mackay

The aims of this chapter are to define what psychologists mean by learning, to introduce the reader to the basic models and concepts associated with this process, and to indicate some of the ways in which these ideas can be usefully applied in a medical context. No attempt will be made to cover all the intricacies associated with behaviour change methods, or to examine the various issues of theoretical controversy. There are already many excellent summaries of this nature, ranging from the theoretically sophisticated review by Hilgard and Marquis (1961), to Rachlin's (1970) very readable, introductory text. Nor is it the intention to cover the wide range of behaviour modification techniques which have made such an impact on the treatment of various of the psychiatric disorders. Meyer and Chesser (1970) provide a clear and concise introduction to this very promising field of learning theory application. Instead, the emphasis will be very much on showing the relevance of these basic theoretical principles to a wide variety of patient-therapist situations in general medicine.

All members of the caring professions can be seen to be engaged in manipulating the sick individual, by direct or indirect means, in order to make him well again. Although the term 'manipulation', with its anti-humanitarian connotations, may not be a word which usually springs to mind when hospitals, surgeries and clinics are being discussed, a closer examination of the various treatment methods used in medicine will reveal that they all involve 'doing things to people' in order to change them for the better. The point which is to be stressed in this chapter is that the curing process involves subtle psychological manipulations in addition to overt physical interventions (e.g., drugs, physiotherapy, surgery). Everyday clinical activities such as prescribing treatments, general nursing care, and implementing rehabilitation programmes, all involve the staff as agents of behaviour change.

The fact that some people are more capable of organizing wards, handling awkward patients, and obtaining maximum co-operation from professional colleagues than others, is not wholly attributable to personality factors, although they undoubtedly play a part. In many cases it is simply that certain individuals, wittingly or unwittingly, have come to use learning principles more effectively than others. It would seem to follow from this, therefore, that awareness of the processes of learning should help every health care student to be a more skilful manipulator, and ultimately a more efficient clinician.

Some of the medically relevant questions to which learning theory can provide at least part of the answers are as follows:

(1) What are the most effective procedures for preparing a long-stay patient for his return to the outside world?

(2) How can clinical students best be trained to perform their clinical roles?

(3) What measures can be taken to ensure that out-patients follow treatment advice (e.g., taking pills, exercise, eating certain foods)?

(4) What can be done with hypochondriacs who habitually frequent the general practitioner's surgery?

(5) Is it possible to exert close control over the behaviour of ward staff and/or patients while maintaining high morale?

(6) How can patients who are about to go through a traumatic ordeal (e.g., childbirth, renal dialysis) best be prepared for the experience?

There are obviously no simple answers to any of these questions. Nevertheless it is maintained here that a knowledge of learning theory principles, combined with the necessary skills to apply them, have more to offer than the vague notion of 'clinical intuition'. For this reason, the theoretical foundations of learning, as well as their suggested medical applications, are presented in this chapter. Although some mention is made of original experimental work, many of the illustrations are in anecdotal form. By presenting the material in this way, it is hoped that learning theory will not be perceived as a barren intellectual wasteland, with little relevance to any situations outside a rat box, but as an exciting field of study which has obvious implications for all aspects of human existence, not the least of which is illness behaviour.

Basic principles of learning

Definition

Most lay people use the term 'learning' only in those cases where the individual makes a deliberate attempt to improve his performance or increase his knowledge in some way or other (e.g., 'learning' to drive; 'learning' anatomy). Psychologists, while certainly not denouncing the importance of research into psychomotor skills and verbal retention, tend to view these learning situations as artificial and atypical of life in general. Of more interest to them is the general question of how man learns to adapt to his environment. In other words, they are interested in determining what causes him to behave appropriately in different situations, to feel guilty when he transcends social mores, to exert control over his own environment and over his own behaviour, to play his allotted sex role, and so on. In addition, research psychologists interested in abnormal behaviour have been concerned to answer the closely related question of why certain people do not in fact learn to adapt to the demands of their environment, and ultimately 'break down' with psychiatric disturbances or engage in anti-social behaviour. Thus psychologists view learning in a far wider context than the man in the street.

A generally accepted definition is that learning involves a 'relatively permanent change in behaviour that occurs as the result of prior experience' (Hilgard et al., 1975, p. 194). The important points to note here are as follows:

1. *Learning can take place without the subject's awareness.* The author was once effectively manipulated by a group of eighty medical students to whom he had previously lectured on learning. During the first ten minutes of one teaching session, the forty students on his right looked extremely alert, wrote down notes at a furious pace, and behaved impeccably. In contrast, the forty on the left sat looking out of the window, whispered to each other, and appeared totally uninterested in the content of the lecture. The response of the lecturer, so he is reliably informed, was to stand at the end of the platform nearest to the attending group and draw all his diagrams on the blackboard closest to them. Then after ten minutes, on a pre-arranged signal, the groups suddenly changed roles so that those on the left began to take an interest in what was being said while those on the right lapsed into apparent boredom. Predictably, the lecturer gradually moved along the platform until he was addressing the students who now seemed alert. This alteration of group reaction continued for the duration of the lecture with the expected results. The interesting point to note here is that the victimized lecturer had absolutely no idea that he was being manipulated by the group. He believed that he was in complete control over his own behaviour until he was 'de-briefed' at the end of the session by the project organizers. Obviously, even some knowledge of conditioning principles does not render one immune from subtle manipulations of this type.

2. *The change can be in either a positive or negative direction.* Most people think of learning as a process whereby the individual becomes

more knowledgeable or skilful as the result of some educative experience. The above definition, however, does not stipulate that change should necessarily be in a positive direction. Thus, as a result of some traumatic experience or inappropriate training, the individual may learn to behave in a less adaptive or efficient manner than he did previously.

3. *The change has to be lasting.* Only relatively permanent changes are considered to constitute evidence of learning. This condition is a necessary one in order to exclude functional alterations which are directly attributable to other factors such as sensory adaptation, drug intake, or fatigue. The obvious difficulty with this requirement is to determine how long-lasting a change must be before it attains the necessary criterion.

4. *The change has to be due to experience.* Obviously if the individual develops a skill, or functions differently in some way, because of maturational development, then this cannot be attributed to learning. It is not enough just to present evidence of behaviour change in order to maintain that learning has taken place. It is necessary to be able to show that such a change has arisen through certain experiences the individual went through.

One noteworthy point of the above definition is that the concepts can be reduced to physical events which are amenable to observation. In other words, both the independent variable (i.e., practice) and the dependent variable (i.e., behaviour change) are presented in tangible form rather than as conceptual abstractions. Operational definitions of this sort are preferred because experimental procedures can be applied more easily. One difficulty here, however, is that learning is virtually being equated with performance. Despite the obvious advantages of employing a definition which can be easily put to the test, it has to be conceded that there are occasions where a person may learn something without actually showing that he has learned it. For example, if a squash player was to become aware, when playing against a regular opponent, that a recently developed backhand shot could not be returned by his fellow-player, then it is possible that he might, in order to keep their games more interesting, decide not to employ it thereafter. In such a case, behaviour can be seen to have been influenced by motivational factors as well as by learning. An observer, using the above operational definition, would have been unable to conclude that the person had learned how effective the new shot was. Since learning does not always manifest itself at a behavioural level, some writers prefer to talk about 'potential' for responding. In their view, through learning the organism requires the capability to perform certain acts, although sometimes this capability may remain latent and its appearance in

Learning

behaviour change may not be immediate (Hilgard and Marquis, 1961, p. 4). Although this amended version has the advantage of ensuring that covert forms of learning are not excluded, it is obviously a much weaker definition from the strictly empirical viewpoint.

Another difficulty with this operational definition is that the 'prior experience' phrase is not so self-explanatory as it might appear. If by experience is meant the actual participation by the subject in certain preparatory activities, then all the work on learning by imitation would have to be excluded. As will be shown later, it is known that the individual's behaviour can alter through observation of an appropriate 'model' undergoing a particular training procedure. Since it is conjectured that learning in such a case involves certain symbolic processes which are not readily amenable to behavioural scrutiny, the conclusion which must be drawn is either that strict operational criteria are overrestrictive or that experience cannot always be studied objectively. Clearly, therefore, operational definitions must be used with care in psychology.

Classical Conditioning

It is impossible to consider classical conditioning without making some reference to the pioneering work of Pavlov in this field. In his prototypic experiment, he presented a neutral stimulus (a tone) at the same time as a potent stimulus (food) which had previously been shown to elicit a specific autonomic response (salivation). After a number of pairings of this sort, it was found that salivation, which had previously occurred only in the presence of food, could be elicited by the tone itself. Thus, through temporal contiguity (i.e., simultaneous presentation), an association had built up between a stimulus and a response which had previously been shown to be disconnected. In other words, the dogs had been conditioned to respond to a previously neutral stimulus. Before going on to look at the offshoots of this celebrated experiment, it is important to become familiar with the basic terms used in conjunction with this type of learning:

Conditioned stimulus (CS): This is the name given to a stimulus which does not possess response-eliciting powers at the outset, but acquires them as a result of the procedure. In the above example, the tone is the conditioned stimulus.

Unconditioned stimulus (UCS): A stimulus which is consistently followed by a specific outcome before the procedure begins is known as the unconditioned stimulus. This term signifies that no new learning has occurred which directly affects this particular environmental event.

It should be noted that in the Pavlovian example cited above, the sight of food served as the UCS. This is clearly not an unconditioned stimulus in the purest sense of the word, since some learning must have taken place previously during which sight and taste became associated. Nevertheless, since the stimulus-response (S-R) connection had already been established before this particular experiment, it is referred to as the UCS here. Incidentally, when the tone has eventually acquired saliva-inducing properties, it is possible to use it as the UCS and pair it with another neutral stimulus (e.g., flash of light) in a new classical conditioning experiment. As a result of this procedure, the dog will develop a conditioned salivatory response to the light, although that stimulus has never at any stage been associated with food. This phenomenon is known as *higher order conditioning*.

Unconditioned response (UCR): The actual processes of salivation, stomach muscular contraction, pupil dilation and so on which follow the event of food presentation are collectively referred to as the unconditioned response. This term denotes that fact that the S-R connection has not arisen through this particular training procedure.

The fact that so much work has been carried out using salivation as the UCR is due more to the fact that it is an easily measured response rather than because it has any obvious applications to real life. Indeed a semi-successful attempt by the author to condition a friend to prefer claret to Sauternes, in which the red wine was regularly followed by a slice of lemon, is perhaps the only study in which salivatory conditioning has ever been put to any practical use! Of far more obvious relevance to real life are the various studies which have been carried out using anxiety and sexual arousal as UCRs in an endeavour to create various psychological abnormalities experimentally. The reader who is interested in learning theory as applied to psychiatric disorders is referred to Meyer and Chesser (1970).

Conditioned response (CR): This is the name given to the response to the previously neutral stimulus, which has been learned by the subject as the result of this procedure. Although many of the briefer commentaries on classical conditioning may give the impression that precisely the same response is elicited by the CS as by the UCS, this is in fact not the case. In Pavlov's experiments, it was noted that not only was the amount of salivation secreted in response to the CS less than to the UCS, but the various muscular contractions of the stomach, which were such a marked feature of the UCR, did not take place when this new stimulus was presented, even after a large number of association trials. For this reason, it is customary to make a distinction between the CR and the UCR.

One of the most important phenomena associated with classical conditioning is *stimulus generalization*. Pavlov discovered that if a different tone to the original CS was presented, salivation would be elicited, despite the fact that this actual stimulus had never been paired with food. As a rule, the less similar the generalization stimulus is to the CS, the weaker the amplitude of the CR. These are particularly important findings in view of the fact that it is virtually impossible to present the subject with exactly the same stimulus patterns on any two occasions. The laboratory may be slightly more humid, the subject may be more fatigued on some days than on others, the cleanliness of the experimenter's white coat may vary from day to day, and so on. If some degree of stimulus generalization did not occur, then classical conditioning could not take place.

The celebrated case of 'Little Albert' (Watson and Rayner, 1920) provides a clear illustration of stimulus generalization. In this study, a conditioned emotional response to furry animals was induced in a small boy by pairing the presentation of a white rabbit (CS) with a loud noise, produced by banging an iron rod with a hammer (UCS). The suddenness of this noxious stimulus elicited a startle response from the subject. As a result of this procedure, Albert acquired a specific fear, not only of white rabbits, but also of brown rabbits, rats, and other furry creatures. Stimulus generalization of the conditioned emotional response had occurred. It should be noted here that most patients with phobias report a certain degree of anxiety in situations which are similar to the ones that they are unable to cope with.

Obviously there must be a limit to the extent of stimulus generalization, otherwise the individual would end up salivating to, or being frightened of, every stimulus he is confronted with. That this does not happen is due to the fact that the subject learns to discriminate between CS-type stimuli and environmental irrelevancies. Some of Pavlov's most interesting work was that in which difficult discriminations had to be made between CSs and neutral stimuli. In one experiment, carried out by one of his students, a dog was trained to salivate to a circle but not to an ellipse with the ratio of 2:1 between the axes. Once the animal had learned to make this distinction, the shape of the ellipse was gradually altered until it was almost circular (ratio of 9:8). At this point, the subject was not only unable to discriminate between the ellipse and the circle, but was also less capable of differentiating between the CS and the easier ellipses than it had been before. In addition the behaviour of this dog changed dramatically. Whereas before he had been a fairly tranquil animal, he now whined and trembled, refused to eat, and showed signs of general disturbance when in the vicinity of the experimental laboratory. The term *experimental neurosis* has often been employed in such cases, although the analogy with the human psychiatric condition is a weak one (Broadhurst, 1974). Nevertheless there would appear to be little doubt that difficult differentiations can be a source of great distress. Thus, while the phenomenon of discrimination is very necessary in order to offset that of generalization, difficulties can arise where too fine a discrimination is required.

Another important finding associated with classical conditioning is that of *extinction*. If a CS is presented on a number of occasions unaccompanied by the UCS, then the CR will gradually drop in amplitude, and eventually cease altogether. When this occurs, the conditioned response can be said to have been extinguished. That the CR has not disappeared completely, however, is demonstrated by the fact that if the CS is presented again after a certain time interval, the response will re-emerge, but at an amplitude about mid-way between zero and the peak level. The return of an extinguished response after a delay is referred to as *spontaneous recovery*. If the CS is then repeatedly presented by itself over a short period again, the process of extinction will be repeated. Once more, if it is reintroduced after a delay, spontaneous recovery will take place, although the response amplitude will be less than on the previous occasion. After a series of extinction trials of this sort, spontaneous recovery will finally cease to occur and the conditioned response can be considered to have been totally extinguished.

Pavlov also amassed a considerable amount of evidence to demonstrate that the timing of the CS and UCS is crucial in determining the ultimate strength of the CR. In the most effective procedures, the CS is presented just before the UCS and is made to last at least until the onset of the UCS (*delayed conditioning*). A somewhat weaker CR will be obtained if the *trace conditioning* paradigm is employed. Here the CS commences and terminates long before the UCS onset. There is, however, very little evidence for the effectiveness of *backward conditioning*, which involves the presentation of the CS after the UCS has been terminated. Optimally the delayed conditioning paradigm should be employed with the CS preceding the UCS by approximately half a second.

Many specific fears associated with hospitals and medicine in general can be seen to have arisen through the process of classical conditioning. A large proportion of patients who refuse to seek medical help are simply attempting to avoid the anxiety which has developed and spread over the years, following a traumatic event in a clinical setting in their childhood. For instance, if the individual experienced distress when given an injection which was painful or for which he was ill-prepared, then it is possible that, through stimulus generalization, he may not only continue to be anxious about injections, but about white coats, stethoscopes, and hospital disinfectant smells as well. Extinction and spontaneous recovery can be illustrated by reference to those cases where the patient overcomes his anxiety after having been brought into hospital, only to have it return again when hospitalization is suggested some time in the future. The findings on CS/UCS timing are also relevant here. Hospital and dental situations, where the clinical cues both precede and accompany pain, can be seen to constitute examples of the most effective paradigm (delayed conditioning). It is not surprising therefore that specific anxieties concerning medical investigations and treatments are so widespread and persistent.

In conclusion, although classical conditioning constitutes a very simple type of learning, its effects on human behaviour can be quite profound. It is however very limited in its scope. In particular there are two characteristics of this model which limit its range of application: (a) it refers only to situations in which the individual is passive; and (b) only autonomic responses can be modified in this manner. As will be demonstrated below, there are other types of learning which can account for changes in behaviour which is voluntary and governed by the central nervous system.

Operant Conditioning

Skinner's model of operant (or instrumental) conditioning has many more obvious applications to real life than classical conditioning, which is restricted to visceral activity. In contrast, voluntary behaviour is very much the focal point of operant conditioning. This means, in effect, that if the organism does not emit a response of his own accord, then no learning of this sort can take place. Skinner's basic research was carried out with rats and pigeons, because only in this way was he able to exert the necessary control over his subjects to enable him to formulate his basic principles. However, much of the basic research has been repeated with humans, and it is this work which shall be considered here, together with supporting anecdotal evidence from everyday life. Before considering the model in some detail, it is useful to know something about Skinner's basic approach to psychology.

There is no place for question-begging, theoretical abstractions in his model of man. He maintains that the goals of psychology should be, in the first instance, to be able to predict behaviour accurately, and, eventually, to be able to modify it. He is not convinced that it is necessary to invent hypothetical constructs, of either a psychological or physiological nature, in order to achieve these aims. According to him, therefore, psychologists should use their skills to create an applied technology rather than to invent explanatory models of psychological functioning which are not directly testable. This is clearly a controversial position to take and many psychologists, including some eminent behaviourists, have declared themselves to be very much opposed to it. Such a complex issue obviously falls outside the scope of this chapter, and has been mentioned only in order to indicate that Skinner's anti-theoretical approach has by no means been universally accepted by psychologists.

The fundamental principle underlying the Skinnerian model is that an individual's behaviour is governed by its consequences. In other words, a person does not behave in a totally random fashion, but in order to attain certain objectives. Through experience he learns that these are more likely to be achieved if he behaves in one way rather than another. The three outcomes which can affect behaviour have a very central role in the operant conditioning model:

Positive reinforcement (reward) is a consequence of an action which leads to an increase in the frequency of occurrence of that action. It should be noted that, once again, an operational definition has been employed rather than an abstraction such as 'something pleasant', 'an event which produces a particular neural discharge', or 'reduction of a basic drive'. Although it might appear to be somewhat tautological, it is claimed that the circularity of the definition is more apparent than real. Thus if a response-ensuing event has been shown to bring about an increase in the emission rate of that response, it can be predicted that it would produce similar results if applied to another behavioural class.

The work of Ayllon and his co-workers (e.g., Ayllon and Azrin, 1968) provides a clear illustration of the ways in which positive reinforcement can be used to promote behaviour change in an applied setting. They noted that in chronic psychiatric wards there is a tendency for patients to receive positive reinforcement for carrying out socially maladaptive behaviour. The much-sought-after reward of nursing attention is typically provided, in the generally understaffed psychiatric hospital, only when the patient claims to be unable to feed himself, talks in a disturbed fashion, engages in disruptive behaviour, and so on. In contrast, when he is sitting quietly reading, or conversing with other patients, then he is extremely unlikely to receive attention from the staff. Operant conditioning would therefore predict that the probability of disordered behaviour is likely to increase, the longer the patient stays in a ward run along these lines. Ayllon's team have made some attempts to reverse this procedure by instigating ward management programmes whereby positive reinforcement (e.g., cigarettes, food, attention) is made contingent upon socially desirable behaviour (e.g., making bed, going into dining-room unattended, dressing oneself). To make the reinforcers more tangible and immediate, it was decided to allocate special tokens, which could be later exchanged for the reward of the patient's choice, following the successful completion of a specified activity. The results of Ayllon and Azrin's systematic studies of the token economy system strongly indicate that operant conditioning can bring about quite significant improvements in the behaviour of severely disturbed psychiatric patients, in the short term at least.

In those cases where the target behaviour is rarely, if ever, performed, it is customary to employ a 'shaping' procedure. This involves positively reinforcing the organism for behaving in a way which approximates to the desired behaviour. When the frequency of these partial responses has increased to an acceptable level, the criterion of a 'good' response is raised so that vague approximations are no longer rewarded. In this way, the individual's behaviour is gradually 'shaped' until it corresponds to that desired by the experimenter. All tennis coaches, driving instructors, and clinical teachers should employ an ascending scale of response requirements which merit reward.

One of the best-known examples of response shaping with human subjects is the treatment devised by Lovaas (1966), in order to train six mute autistic children to communicate verbally. The positive reinforcements used in this study consisted of both food and social approval (e.g., 'good boy'). Initially the patients were reinforced for emitting any sounds whatsoever at any time. Then, when the frequency of sound production had reached an acceptable level, reinforcement was made more difficult to obtain by making it contingent upon responses produced immediately following an utterance by the therapist. When a subject had learned to do this, rewards were only provided when the sound approximated to that emitted by the therapist. As progress continued to be made, objects corresponding to the words were introduced and the externally provided verbal cues gradually faded out. By the end of the programme, these previously non-communicating children were able not only to name simple objects, but also to string certain words together in a meaningful fashion. It should be noted that although imitation learning (see below) was involved here, the technique of shaping played a very vital role in this treatment.

Punishment can be operationally defined as a consequence of a response which leads to a decrease in the probability of its future occurrence. It is used extremely widely in our society as a method of inducing behaviour change. Criminals are imprisoned for breaking the law, children are scolded when their actions displease their parents, and marital partners shout and/or sulk in their attempts to modify the behaviour of their spouses. One question which is frequently asked of psychologists is why it is that punishment seems to be used as much as reward, when the latter method of behaviour change is obviously far less distressing for everyone involved. In other words, why do we not, for instance, provide positive incentives for criminals to give up antisocial behaviour, allow children to stay up late if they come home on time, and give presents to spouses when they complete unpleasant tasks, instead of applying noxious stimuli when the undesired conduct occurs? The first and obvious reason is that punishment is extremely effective, in the short term at least. If the teacher shouts at the misbehaving pupil, he is likely to cease immediately. This sudden termination of the undesired activity is very reinforcing for the punisher. In the second place, aggression caused by frustration can be incorporated into this method of behaviour change, thus providing the punishment administrator with some extra gratification. Finally, if the potential conduct modifier were to await the occurrence of good behaviour which he would positively reinforce, there would in many cases be a long, if not interminable, delay. Those who wish to exert influence of this sort, particularly when emotionally aroused, generally do not feel inclined to remain inactive in this respect for such long periods. However, despite its widespread use, there are certain problems associated with the use of punishment as a behaviour change strategy, particularly where it is used alone.

So far as actual efficacy is concerned, the sudden cessation of a response does not constitute evidence that a fundamental change in behaviour has taken place. The basic difficulty here is that although aversive consequences are likely to lead to a suppression of the unwanted response, the subject fails to learn the precise nature of a desirable response. If he is not shown an appropriate way to obtain this reinforcer, he may eventually return to his former activities, or alternatively develop an equally inappropriate set of responses. The high incidence of recidivism among criminals is in keeping with this proposition. Similarly, many of the sexual deviants who were treated by aversion therapy many years ago returned to their former undesirable activities after a while, because they had not learned to respond heterosexually. The fact that, nowadays, most treatment programmes of this sort incorporate a sexual reorientation component in addition to punishment-related techniques, would suggest that the negative approach has come to be regarded as insufficient by itself.

It is not being suggested here that punishment has no place in behaviour change. On the contrary, it can play a useful role in stamping out the inappropriate behaviour, thus making it more likely that the individual will emit a more adaptive response which can be shaped accordingly. Although the application of positive reinforcement is necessary in order to train the subject to produce precisely the desired response, punishment of the unwanted behaviour can hasten the learning process.

Leaving aside the question of efficacy, a strong argument against the use of punishment is that it can produce unwanted side effects. If the intensity of the noxious stimulation is relatively low, then this is unlikely to cause problems. Thus every day parents firmly tell their children not to cross the road when the pedestrian light is red, or not to play with matches, without them developing widespread psychological disturbances. Similarly, if the distinction between good and bad is very apparent to the subject, then no behavioural abnormalities are likely to arise (cf. experimental neurosis). For instance, the reasonably intelligent child who is punished for swearing but for no other types of verbal behaviour is unlikely to have his general peace of mind affected by such a régime. If the punishment is very severe, and/or the discrimination between good and bad too subtle for him, then stimulus generalization is likely to take place with highly undesirable consequences. Thus, punishing a child for 'answering back' may not only extinguish this class of response, but also eliminate intelligent discussion behaviour with parents (and perhaps anyone else) as well. Many chronically shy, unassertive individuals report that extremely punitive measures were used against them in childhood, not only when disputing parental commands, but even occasionally when they were only trying to voice their opinions on some issue or other. In extreme cases of this sort, the anxiety elicited by inconsistent punishment for a response which the individual cannot clearly differentiate from others can lead to a general breakdown of behaviour and the disruption of former learning.

A further difficulty with the use of punitive measures is that the administrator of the noxious stimulus, through classical conditioning, may take on the properties of an anxiety-eliciting CS, or alternatively become the target of the offender's hostility. Furthermore, the individual may experience strong emotional reactions when faced with cues which he associates with the punishment situation. Undoubtedly many children have failed to fulfil their scholastic potential because of interfering negative feelings towards teachers and schools which have arisen through earlier traumatic experiences in educational settings. Thus although punishment certainly has a role to play in behaviour change, it should be used sparingly, consistently, and in combination with reward, for both efficacious and humanitarian reasons.

Negative reinforcement is the term used to refer to a response consequence which involves the removal or termination of some unpleasant stimulus. For example, many students work hard not because they are seeking the positive reinforcement of being top of the class, but because they want to avoid the undesirable consequences of failure. Negative reinforcement is also involved in 'escape' learning. Here the noxious stimulus is actually presented, and the individual has to find some way of getting rid of it. The harassed husband who turns to drink, the weak scholar who plays truant, and the elderly couple who retire to the relative peacefulness of the country are all employing escape strategies which are maintained by negative reinforcement. In all these examples, the person does not receive a positive reinforcer, nor a punishment for an undesired response. It is the fact that something unpleasant will be taken away which goads him to action.

Cases where some noxious stimulus is deliberately threatened unless the victim complies with the wishes of the manipulators are examples of a use of negative reinforcement which is referred to as *aversive control*. The parent who threatens to send his child to bed early unless he 'behaves himself' and the wife who will sulk unless her spouse complies with her wishes are illustrations of this much-used method of behaviour change. As a result of this strategy, the frequency of a particular response dramatically alters as the 'victim' attempts to avoid the noxious stimulus. This method can be extremely effective in altering behaviour; but it has the disadvantage that the person who has been manipulated may feel angry about having been coerced, and is therefore likely to retaliate, perhaps in a similar way. This may then lead to an escalation in the intensity of the threatened aversive consequences, and the subsequent creation of a generally noxious environment. When this situation arises, then one or more parties are liable to implement escape procedures, which again are reinforced negatively. The harassed spouse will seek a separation; the unhappy pupil will finish his education as soon as he can; and the rebellious adolescent will leave home and his coercive parents behind. Thus, although behaviour shaping, using positive reinforcement, is a slow and difficult procedure to carry out, it has an advantage over both punishment and negative reinforcement in that the subject is less likely to feel anxious or hostile towards the agent of change and the cues associated with him.

In operant conditioning, stimuli do not serve only as consequences of behaviour. They also set the occasion for responses. People do not carry out responses in a psychological vacuum, but rather in the presence of certain environmental cues. For instance, the student learns that frivolous behaviour in the union bar is likely to be socially reinforced by his friends, whereas the same behaviour is liable to be punished by an angry tutor in the seminar situation. At a more subtle level, the practising clinician may learn that an authoritative stance is likely to be effective with one particular type of patient, whereas a democratic approach is generally more successful with another. It is customary in operant conditioning jargon to turn this round and regard these environmental factors as exerting control over the individual's behaviour (*stimulus control*). The child who is well-behaved in the presence of his father but runs riot when he is absent can be said to be under the control of the stimulus of father's presence. Thus the individual does not just learn that a particular response is likely to be reinforced, but rather that a particular response in the presence of a specific stimulus, called a discriminative stimulus (SD), is likely to lead to reward.

Although much of this work may seem to be merely a more systematic version of the 'carrot and stick' notion which has been utilized by man since time began, one or two findings from the Skinnerian laboratory might not have been predicted by common sense. For instance, it has been convincingly demonstrated that if a response is not reinforced on every occasion it occurs, then it is more likely to persist when the rewards have ceased altogether (extinction) than if continuous reinforcement has been employed throughout. Such a finding is clearly related to the question of why unsuccessful gamblers find it extremely difficult to renounce their self-defeating habit. Presumably the person who begins with a winning streak and then experiences a sudden reversal of fortune, is more likely to give it up than the individual who has had an occasional win amongst a series of losses. Similarly the highly temperamental football star is less likely to get dropped from the team when going through a 'bad patch' than the one who had performed consistently well before a sudden loss of form.

Another important set of findings to emerge from Skinner's work concerns the timing of reinforcements. The sooner the reinforcement follows the response, the stronger will be the S-R connection. One reason why imprisonment is thought to be a fairly ineffective deterrent to the potential criminal is that the positive reinforcement he is likely to receive immediately after carrying out a successful burglary clearly outweighs a less probable noxious stimulus which will follow the response by several weeks. The whole question of response/reinforcement timing has also important implications for child-rearing. Parents must be quick to notice the emission of the desired behaviour (e.g., when toilet training) and immediately follow it with signs of approval and possible 'back-up' reinforcers such as sweets. The importance of timing applies just as much to negative reinforcement as it does to reward and punishment. The child who is attempting to manipulate his parents when bedtime is announced is unlikely to bring about a permanent alteration in his nocturnal retirement arrangements unless he ceases to cry as soon as his parents comply with his wishes. Thus immediacy of reinforcement is essential for quick effective behaviour change, regardless of the type of consequence employed.

There are many obvious points of comparison between classical and operant conditioning. For instance similar kinds of experimental manipulation of the stimuli involved can lead to acquisition or extinction of a response. In fact some authors actually refer to the UCS in classical conditioning as the reinforcement. Stimulus generalization occurs in the operant conditioning paradigm as well as in the classical one. For instance, the child who strokes his cat in order to hear him purr may cause his parents some concern by attempting to stroke the lions in the zoo. Furthermore, an equivalent of Pavlovian higher-order conditioning can also be demonstrated with operant methodology. The child who works hard at school in order to get good grades so that he will be praised by his parents, may continue to work for educational achievements even when parental approval is valued less highly by him. In this example, the previously neutral stimulus, academic success, has, through a process of association, become a reward in its own right (a *secondary reinforcer*). Finally, in both cases, the timing of the various stimulus-response events is an important determinant of the eventual conditioned response.

Until comparatively recently it was felt that despite these common features, classical and operant conditioning procedures were two quite distinct methods of learning. This was largely because it was thought that the Pavlovian type could only operate with autonomic responses, whereas Skinner's instrumental variety was appropriate only for bringing about changes in the voluntary musculature. It had always been recognized, of course, that individuals could deliberately produce an increase in their heart rate or make the blood rush to their heads. However, these autonomic reactions were known to be brought about by changes in responses controlled by the central nervous system (e.g., deep breathing, tensing certain groups of muscles). The work of Miller (e.g., Miller, 1969) and his associates on the instrumental conditioning of visceral responses by direct means has served to blur the distinction, and has opened up a whole new field of experimental investigation.

In the early experiments in this area, rats were given the drug curare, which has the effect of paralysing the skeletal musculature. This was necessary in order to exclude interference from non-visceral sources, thus ensuring that any autonomic effects which took place were due to direct operant conditioning of these responses. One obvious problem when attempting to condition a totally immobile organism, using an operant approach, is to find an effective positive reinforcer. The standard laboratory rewards of food and water are obviously impracticable in such a case. Miller's team therefore decided to adopt the procedure developed by Olds and Milner (1954) of passing a current through electrodes which had been inserted in the brain, in the vicinity of the limbic system. It had been shown in previous experiments that rats will press a bar at an extremely fast rate in order to receive a reward of this kind. Using this method of reinforcement,

Miller and his co-workers were able to demonstrate that rats could be trained to control their heart rate, gastric activity, intestinal contractions, peripheral circulation, and even kidney functions, without using voluntary muscles. For obvious practical and ethical reasons, it has not been possible to replicate this work exactly with humans. Although the whole area of biofeedback (see below) has demonstrated that people can learn to exert a considerable degree of control over so-called autonomic functioning, it is not clear how much of this is due to voluntary muscular activity. Nevertheless, since it is the theoretical issue which is being considered at this stage, the fact that it has been shown to be possible to shape visceral responses directly would seem to make the long-accepted classical/operant distinction less clear than had been hitherto supposed.

In view of the overlap between these two types of learning, some psychologists have gone so far as to suggest that classical conditioning is just a branch of operant conditioning. Once again this is obviously too complex an issue to be considered in depth here. In their excellent review of this area, Hilgard and Marquis (1961) conclude that the distinction is still justified, although it should be noted that the work on instrumental conditioning of autonomic responses had not been published by that time. One of their strongest arguments for maintaining the division rests on the evidence that while partial reinforcement leads to an increase in resistance to extinction in operant conditioning, non-continuous procedures seriously interfere with the learning process in the classical variety. In fact Pavlov himself found that giving food after the CS only on every second or third trial made conditioning impossible. This would seem to lend some support to the argument that they are two quite different types of learning paradigm.

Self-Control

An extension of the operant conditioning work is the development of procedures designed to help subjects exert control over their own behaviour. Where over-indulgence or under-responding with regard to a particular activity is causing concern, then the individual can be said to have failed to exert the necessary degree of control over his behaviour. Insufficient regulation of study habits, alcohol consumption and food intake are common examples of ways in which the frequency of a response deviates markedly from that which the individual considers to be appropriate.

In order to train a person to control his behaviour more effectively, it is important to determine the stimuli which are controlling the behaviour, and the reinforcers which are maintaining it. When this has been achieved, attempts can be made to modify the individual's environment in such a way as to interfere with the old S-R connections. Changing stimulus control is something which can be achieved relatively easily in many cases. Most of us carry out temptation-avoiding manoeuvres in an attempt to regulate our lives. The student who wishes to revise for an important examination may refuse to go anywhere near his friends in order to ensure that they do not exert the sort of stimulus control which would lead automatically to social behaviour, and the inevitable reduction in frequency of studying. The person who cannot get up in the morning when the alarm clock rings either buys a repeater alarm device or places the clock several paces from the bedside so that he has to get out of bed to switch it off. Once this task has been carried out the undesired response of over-sleeping will be less likely to occur. These are everyday examples of ways in which people modify their environment in order to break undesired habits.

It is not always possible, however, to eliminate the SDs so easily as this, since very often they are not under the exclusive control of the individual. In the case of cigarette smoking, for instance, it is difficult for a habituee to cut down his rate of consumption because he tends to be offered cigarettes by other people all through the day. Since this is one of the strongly established signals for the smoking response, he may find himself accepting before he is aware of his actions. Although one possible solution here would be to change his friends, this is clearly a rather drastic measure to take! He could, of course, ask his various acquaintances not to brandish cigarette packets in front of him, and perhaps even refrain from smoking in his presence, but this would be unlikely to prove a reliable method of environmental control. A more satisfactory approach is to teach him to apply cognitive stimulus control over his own behaviour. In other words to train him to think of a dissuasive phrase, which has been well-rehearsed, whenever the external stimulus presents itself. Behaviourists have become increasingly aware of the important role played by self-induced negative thoughts in maintaining maladaptive behaviours. It is claimed (e.g., Meichenbaum, 1973) that this position can be reversed and that people can be trained to modify their internal environments, and thereby learn to produce more appropriate sets of responses.

In addition to modifying the precipitating environmental stimuli, it is important to incorporate new reinforcement schedules into the programme. The individual should be trained to reward himself when he achieves the target that has been set. For example, he could allow himself to buy a new article of clothing or gramophone record, provided that he, say, smokes less than fifteen per day for a week. Alternatively he could remove the pleasurable stimulus which is freely available (e.g., watching television) and use it as an incentive. As in all behavioural procedures, it is essential to specify exactly what the target behaviour is ('try to cut down' is not enough), and the amount of the reinforcer which a particular set of responses warrant.

One point which is particularly relevant here is the timing of reinforcement. As mentioned in the section on operant conditioning, it is essential that the consequence should follow the response as quickly as possible, for reasons of efficacy. This matter is very relevant to the apparent paradox of why it is that a person who wants to pass an examination does not study, and why someone who is desperately seeking to lose weight over-indulges himself when presented with food. The immediate reward which follows entering the union bar or eating a cream cake is far stronger at the time of decision making than the more remote rewards of passing second M.B., or reaching the target weight. Of course, if the individual was faced with the choice of a pint with his friends or an examination pass now, or a piece of cake or instant slimness, there is no doubt as to which of the options he would select. But if there is a long delay between a response and a reinforcer then, despite the strength of the latter, a weaker reward which is immediately available following an alternative response may serve as a more powerful incentive. When attempting to carry out self-control therefore, it is helpful to introduce intermediary reinforcers. Recording daily achievements or crossing completed items off a specially prepared list of objectives are useful ploys. Once again back-up reinforcers, along the lines suggested above, can be incorporated here. One of the most effective reinforcers is social approval from a doctor, tutor, or group of fellow-sufferers (cf. Alcoholics Anonymous) following a behavioural improvement.

Thus, in order to attain a greater degree of control over one's own functioning, it is important to eliminate the discriminative stimuli, set attainable and clearly defined targets, and provide positive reinforcements when they have been achieved. Once again, although the ideas may seem rather commonsensical, it must be emphasized that the difference between success and failure here ultimately depends on how rigidly and systematically the whole programme is carried out.

Imitation

All the learning paradigms described so far have assumed that the individual has actually to respond behaviourally on a number of occasions before learning will take place. However, it is possible for learning to occur as a result of experience of a non-participatory sort. Bandura and Walters (1963) have demonstrated experimentally that subjects will learn a response after having had the opportunity to watch others being rewarded for behaving in this way. In other words, practice is not essential for behaviour change. In fact Bandura and his co-workers maintain that a high percentage of social responses are acquired through vicarious no-trial learning of this sort. For example, the child does not learn to speak simply by emitting random noises which are shaped by the reward of parental approval. Imitation of linguistic sounds, produced by adult models, is clearly involved as well. Similarly at an adult level, modelling is involved when learning to carry out a clinical examination, drive a car, or interact with members of the opposite sex. From the theoretical viewpoint, Bandura does not consider that classical or instrumental conditioning can provide a sufficient explanation for the sudden appearance of a novel response after observation of a model. In his view, learning of this sort takes place through contiguity of stimuli which arise through perception of the model, and the images and thoughts which they give rise to. It is these symbolic processes which act like SDs and set the occasion for responding in imitative learning.

Applications of learning principles to medicine

It has to be conceded at the start that, up to the present time, the contributions made by psychology to medicine (with the exception of psychiatry) have been modest so far. True, some psychologists have become employed as diagnostic-cum-research workers in the fields of paediatrics, geriatrics, and neurology; but firms which utilize psychological services are still the exception rather than the rule. It is surprising that psychologists have not become more involved as advisers on such matters as ward organization, admission procedures, and the preparation of patients for routine tests or operations. Certain large industrial concerns have been quick to recognize the skills of psychologists in modifying environmental conditions in order to raise morale, improve communications, and increase the efficiency of their work team. Since hospitals are, as a rule, highly complex social structures, it would seem that psychologists might well have a lot to offer from the practical and administrative side as well as the clinical. In this section, some of the ways in which basic principles of learning might be usefully applied in general medical settings are considered.

Ward Management Problems

Throughout the course of the illness, the patient is required to modify his behaviour to fit in with the expectations of the medical staff. Each stage of the curing process he goes through (admission, tests, treatment, recovery, discharge) makes a different set of demands on him. For example, when he first enters the hospital, he is expected to play a passive and helpless role as the various diagnostic and therapeutic procedures are carried out. Any attempts at independence or autonomy, on his part, are considered to be obstructive to the whole programme of medical care which is being applied. If he does not conform in this way, then he is labelled a 'difficult patient', and various attempts are then made to coerce him into submission. This is in marked contrast to the latter stages of hospitalization when the physical disturbance has been dealt with and the staff are attempting to speed up recovery (in the widest sense of the word) prior to discharge. In this case, passivity is thought to be a sign of non-co-operation on the part of the patient. Once again, attempts are usually made to modify the patient's behaviour until it corresponds to that considered to be appropriate by members of the clinical team.

An interesting observation that has been made on many occasions is that certain wards tend to get their patients better more quickly than others which are their equivalent in every way. Since the actual physical treatments are identical, and the qualifications and experience of the staff very similar, one can only conclude that these discrepancies are attributable to differences in the less specific aspects of patient care. Undoubtedly the way in which the patient's behaviour is controlled on the ward is a vital factor here. Some clinical staff have a very clear notion as to the way they want their patients to behave, at any one point in time, and proceed to apply reward and punishment in a consistent fashion in order to bring this about. Others, however, fail to define their objectives so clearly and, as a result, there is a lack of uniformity in their method of handling the individual patient.

There are two undesirable outcomes which might emerge as a result of a disunited management policy. In the first place, the patient may feel anxious, confused, and perhaps even hostile towards the ward staff in general, and to certain members in particular. This may severely retard the recovery process. In the second place, inconsistent handling provides the perfect opportunity for the patient who is in no hurry to leave hospital to start exploiting this weakness on the part of the staff. Many patients wish to prolong their stay in hospital because they are protected in this haven from the occupational, marital, and personal stresses which await them in the outside world. Others, particularly elderly patients, enjoy being looked after and cared for in a way which they are not in their everyday settings. They are certainly in no hurry to be discharged and, in fact, may do all in their power to stay in hospital for as long as possible. For example, a patient could adopt the 'sick role' when the consultant carries out his ward round, but appear to be fully recovered so far as the nursing staff are concerned. Any attempts the latter might wish to make to prepare him for discharge would therefore be thwarted by this implicit collusion between the patient and the consultant. In this instance, the patient is actually controlling the behaviour of the staff rather than the reverse. Thus it is essential that the nurses and doctors should communicate with each other, decide on a common policy, and implement it as a team, in order to manage the patient in the optimal fashion.

The principles of operant conditioning are particularly relevant to the process of actually carrying out the policy. If the patient is considered to be fully recovered physically but is still complaining of weakness and pain, and moreover seems unable to co-operate with the physiotherapist, occupational therapist or whoever, the systematic administration of rewards and punishments should be carried out. Under these circumstances the powerful positive reinforcer of nursing attention should not be applied when the patient is talking in a negative fashion about his symptoms. Instead, approval from the staff should immediately follow any positive steps towards recovery the patient may take, thus shaping his behaviour in the desired fashion. In a way this may seem contrary to the traditional unspoken nursing principle of spending more time with the patient when he seems distressed. Nevertheless, in such a case, it is clearly in the patient's best interests ultimately for this procedure to be reversed. Once again it should be emphasized that all members of the team should work together here, otherwise the system is likely to fall down. The same principles should be applied in all circumstances where the patient fails to co-operate with the staff.

Modifying Health Habits

Many clinicians get angry and frustrated with those of their patients who continue to eat certain foods, smoke or drink excessively, or avoid exercise, when such maladaptive behaviour is undoubtedly impairing their health and ultimately shortening their lives. Attempts at aversive control (e.g., 'Well if you don't heed my warning you will die') are generally ineffective. This is largely because the eventual noxious stimulus, which is inevitable in any case, is presumed to be far removed in time from the actual response. If the subject knew that a second glass of sherry would immediately be followed by cirrhosis of the liver, nothing would persuade him to touch it. But, in reality, the immediate reward following a double aperitif seems more powerful to him than the far-removed negative consequence of this action.

The best solution here is to train patients in the self-control methods as described above. Teaching them to avoid or nullify the discriminative stimuli and to make specified reinforcers contingent upon the achievement of certain stipulated sub-goals will help them to break up their old maladaptive habits. This has already proved itself to be a successful method of improving standards of patient self-care. For instance, research with patients at risk of developing cardiovascular disease has indicated that self-control training is more effective here than other psychological methods which have been attempted (Meyer and Henderson, 1974). This is therefore one extremely important area of illness-related behaviour where learning principles have very obvious applications.

The Prevention and Elimination of Medical Phobias

As indicated above, irrational or exaggerated medical fears can arise through a process of traumatic conditioning, particularly in childhood. There are two main types of stimulus occurrence which, through pairing with a neutral stimulus, are particularly likely to produce conditioned anxiety responses. These are pain, and the unexpected. Aversion therapy, where an electric shock is paired with a stimulus associated with a deviation, is an example of the former; while the 'Little Albert' experiment (see above) illustrates the latter. The medical treatment situation can involve both of these noxious stimuli.

Pain, either as the result of injury or through a clinical treatment (e.g., injection), is very often experienced in the presence of clinical cues. Although this can often be reduced by gentle handling, many doctors, with a busy clinic, may carry out these procedures with a minimum of ceremony. Although this may mean that the immediate task is accomplished, the danger here is that rough handling can give rise to a life-long fear of clinics which may manifest itself in hospital avoidance behaviour on the part of the patient, leading in some instances to risk of serious illness through lack of appropriate treatment at the right time. It is important therefore to remember that, although the infliction of a particularly noxious stimulus may have few immediate repercussions, the long-term effects can be quite severe.

However, it is probably the fear of the unexpected which gives rise to most of the anxieties concerning doctors and hospitals. Again many clinicians, perhaps because of lack of time or because the patient seems too young to understand, may suddenly carry out an action, without any forewarning, in order that the job might be completed as quickly as possible. If this involves some pain infliction as well, then it is quite likely that the 'victim' will respond autonomically whenever he is faced with clinical cues in the future. It is advisable therefore, as so many doctors in fact do, to explain carefully to the patient what is going to happen, and then proceed at a pace appropriate to his level of anxiety. Although this may consume precious clinical time in the short term, both the patient and subsequent clinicians will ultimately benefit from it.

As well as ensuring that specific anxiety responses do not arise through traumatic conditioning, it is possible to go further and reduce the risk of an anxiety response developing by systematically preparing the individual for an expected unpleasant event. Just as the administration of a carefully controlled dose of a disease can be used to produce resistance to infection, so it is argued (e.g. Henderson et al., 1972) that 'psychological immunization' can be carried out with high-risk individuals before an anxiety-eliciting ordeal.

The immunization procedure which Henderson and his co-workers favour is that of *systematic desensitization* (Wolpe, 1958), which has proved itself useful in the elimination of specific phobias in the psychiatric field. The patient is first of all asked to draw up a list of situations or objects he fears and to rank them in hierarchical order, with the most feared at the top. He is then trained to relax himself. When he has reached the required standard of relaxation, the stimulus at the bottom of the hierarchy is presented to him, either in imagination or in real life. When he is able to face up to this stimulus without feeling tense, the next item is presented, and so on. If at any stage he should feel anxious, he should communicate this to the therapist, who will immediately substitute for that item a less stressful one. If the deconditioning programme is carried out methodically in this way, then the fear response will eventually be extinguished. Wolpe stresses that it is important to ensure that the items are presented in the fixed order, and that the individual is relaxed throughout.

One area of medicine where psychological immunization would appear to be particularly appropriate is that of childbirth. Many antenatal clinics, of course, carry out some rudimentary programmes to help prepare expectant mothers for the ordeal which lies ahead. Typically this involves relaxation classes, didactic teaching on the stages of childbirth, a film of someone giving birth, and a tour around the maternity unit. Although such programmes are obviously preferable to nothing at all, they can often be criticized on the grounds that they fall far short of the standards proposed by Wolpe for systematic desensitization procedures. It would seem to follow that a closer adherence to his basic principles would mean that the patient would be less anxious and more able to cope during the birth process. Although post-partum depression is generally thought to have a physiological basis, it is by no means clear what effect a traumatic birth has on the patient's mood and her attitude to her child. What is more certain is that a traumatic birth will make it less likely that the woman will choose to have another child.

Another area of medicine where 'psychoprophylaxis' would seem to be relevant concerns the admission of young children to hospital. Much has been written about the long-term psychologically damaging effects of bringing a child into hospital at an early age, and thereby separating him from his parents (e.g., Bowlby, 1961). Although the case is now known to have been overstated, few would deny that a sudden entry into hospital can produce a lot of distress in the young child, and perhaps cause him to fear hospitals in the future. Once again it is conjectured that a preparatory programme, involving increasingly regular visits to the hospital prior to becoming an in-patient, might prevent much of the trauma which accompanies the usual practice of sudden admission of the young child.

So far as the elimination of hospital fears is concerned, it would appear that systematic desensitization is the treatment of choice. Certainly, in view of the fact that the maladaptive response is an autonomic one, there would seem to be little point in trying to reason with the individual in an attempt to persuade him to comply. Systematic desensitization has shown itself to be effective with fears of this kind. Patients with specific fears of blood, injections, losing consciousness, choking, dialysis equipment, have all been treated successfully by this method. Once again it must be emphasized that a haphazard programme is unlikely to produce positive results, and that the Wolpeian principles should be adhered to. Thus learning theory has a part to play both in preventing hospital fears from arising, and in eliminating those which have become established.

Clinical Role Training

One of the highly questionable assumptions apparently made by those responsible for the education of medical students, nurses, physiotherapists, occupational therapists, and even psychologists, is that a degree of knowledge combined with the necessary practical skills is all that is required to enable one to become an effective clinician. While it is recognized that some individuals can exert more influence over their patients than others, these differences are typically attributed to 'personality', 'maturity', 'clinical intuition', or something equally vague. Thus both teachers and students tend to assume that this is a quality which is largely pre-determined.

Psychologists, however, prefer to talk about the *social skills* of the clinical practitioner, rather than about such nebulous concepts as those cited above. The word 'skill' implies an ability which can be developed through practice, rather than a stable characteristic. It is argued here that all health care students should have the opportunity to undergo specific training to help them learn, as quickly and as painlessly as possible, how to behave in the appropriate manner for their profession. This should help them to apply their skills more effectively, to communicate optimally with members of other professions, and, at the same time, to reduce much of the distress which they experience when faced with patients they cannot handle. Many students, and some qualified clinicians, feel obliged to seek psychiatric treatment to help them overcome the anxiety caused by their social incompetence in the clinical setting. It would seem essential, therefore, to prepare people properly for arguably the most important aspect of their work, rather than to leave them to learn by the arduous process of trial and error.

It would be incorrect to argue that no attempts at all have been made to coach students in the non-specific skills of clinical work. All medical students, for instance, have many opportunities for observing consultants relating to patients in the context of the ward round. In addition, the majority of medical schools run a short introductory clinical course which typically includes a lecture on 'the psychology of the interview'. However, observation combined with advice is insufficient in itself to teach the individual how to play his clinical role, and to prepare him to deal with the diverse and complex behavioural patterns provided by the patient population. A more structured approach, geared to the needs of each individual, is clearly required.

The 'behaviour rehearsal' procedure, devised by Lazarus (1971) for those who have problems in interacting in specific social situations, would seem to be ideally suited for this purpose. Essentially this involves providing people with the opportunity to practise interpersonal skills in the relative safety of a small group consisting of similarly deficient individuals. The various components involved here are modelling (imitating a competent person), role playing (acting in simulated scenes), systematic desensitization (working with increasingly stressful situations), and knowledge of results (receiving accurate feedback as to performance). This latter is particularly important since it is quite impossible to improve at any skill unless one has some means of gauging the degree of success achieved by a particular act. Video-tape, which provides a record of non-verbal behaviour (body posture, facial expressions), in addition to verbal behaviour, is particularly useful in this context. 'Action replays' and 'freeze-frame' techniques can be employed to help demonstrate to the individual both good and bad aspects of his performance. In addition, the comments of other group members on the less tangible aspects of the individual's behaviour can prove useful here. It would be extremely easy to adapt this approach to meet the needs of clinical students. Thus, the principles of learning can be applied in the interests of the therapist as well as those of the patient.

Biofeedback

The recent research on the operant conditioning of autonomic responses has opened up completely new areas of application for psychological techniques. Until the work of Miller (1969), it had been assumed that psychosomatic disorders such as migraine, certain types of dermatitis, duodenal ulcers, and essential hypertension could not be dealt with by direct methods. However, the findings that certain visceral responses can be shaped in a similar manner to more overt types of behaviour has led to frequent attempts to use operant conditioning with a whole variety of autonomic responses. 'Biofeedback' is the name given to the procedures which are used here. What happens is that the subject receives instantaneous knowledge of results, in auditory and/or visual form, of a particular psychophysiological response he has produced.

To date, these techniques have been used predominantly in the psychiatric field. One of the best-known pieces of apparatus (the relaxometer) emits a tone, the frequency of which is made contingent upon the level of electrical resistance of the skin. This response is known to be sensitive to changes in the general arousal level of the organism. Although the non-feedback precursor of this technique was colloquially referred to as the 'lie-detector', it is now known that changes in skin resistance can arise through curiosity, sexual arousal and anger, as well as through anxiety and guilt. Despite the risk of intrusion from such artefacts, this type of biofeedback has been found to be particularly useful with patients who find it difficult to control their general level of anxiety. Similarly, the electromyograph (EMG), which gives precise information as to the degree of tension in specific groups of muscles, has been employed to eliminate those 'nervous headaches' which arise through overactivity of the frontalis muscle.

The most promising area of application, so far as non-psychiatric medicine is concerned, would seem to be that of essential hypertension. This is a disorder where raised systolic blood pressure is not directly attributable to renal dysfunction. Patel (1973), for instance, attempted to treat twenty hypertensive patients using a combination of yoga and biofeedback techniques, in this case using the relaxometer. As a result of this therapy, more traditional anti-hypertension treatment was terminated in five cases, and significantly reduced in a further seven. Of the remaining patients, four were better able to control their blood pressure as a result of this treatment, and the remaining four did not respond at all. One problem with this study is that no attempt was made to modify the blood pressure directly itself. The reason which the author gives for this is that continuous monitoring of this response requires the introduction of a transducer directly into an artery, which is obviously both unpleasant for the patient and a relatively hazardous procedure to carry out. There are reports in the literature of blood pressure having been reduced through direct instrumental conditioning, using hypertensive patients as subjects (e.g., Benson et al., 1971), but there is a dearth of follow-up data in most cases.

Other areas of medicine where biofeedback procedures have been applied with some preliminary success are in modifying the brain waves of epileptics (Sterman and Friar, 1972), and in eliminating premature ventricular contractions of the heart (Weiss and Engel, 1971). It is, however, too soon to evaluate this approach properly, or to speculate as to how great a contribution it will ultimately make to medicine as a whole. The advice given in a recent editorial of the *British Medical Journal* (1974) that 'clinicians should keep a keen but critical watch on this research' would seem to be the most appropriate at this point in time.

Conclusion

Throughout this chapter it has been emphasized that there is more to medical practice than healing tissues, eliminating diseases, and intervening physically in other ways. It also involves dealing with the complex patterns of behaviour which characterize each individual who requires health care. Patients do not all automatically seek help when they are ill, agree to undergo treatment when they are advised to, cooperate with ward staff when they are admitted to hospital, follow the doctor's recommendations, and recover when physical criteria dictate that they should. It is therefore important that all medical and allied staff should be fully aware that the subject-matter of their professions is people with illnesses, not just illnesses. It would seem to follow from this that a general understanding of human behaviour, together with some knowledge of how to modify it most effectively, should be one of the primary objectives of clinical education. In this chapter an attempt has been made to indicate how the principles of learning, which have emerged from intensive experimentation, can be utilized to this end.

References

Ayllon, T. and Azrin, N. H. (1968). *The Token Economy: A Motivational System for Therapy and Rehabilitation.* New York: Appleton-Century-Crofts.

Bandura, A., and Walters, R. H. (1963). *Social Learning and Personality Development*. New York: Holt, Rinehart & Winston.
Benson, H., Shapiro, C., Tursky, B. and Schwartz, G. E. (1971). 'Decreased Systolic Blood Pressure through Operant Conditioning Techniques in Patients with Essential Hypertension', *Science*, *173*, pp. 740–2.
Bowlby, J. (1961). *Child Care and the Growth of Love*. Harmondsworth: Penguin.
British Medical Journal Editorial (1974), 17 August, pp. 427–8.
Broadhurst, P. L. (1974). 'Animal Studies Bearing on Abnormal Behaviour', in *Handbook of Abnormal Psychology* (ed. H. J. Eysenck), 2nd ed. London: Pitman.
Henderson, A. S., Montgomery, I. M., and Williams, C. L. (1972). 'Psychological Immunization: a Proposal for Preventative Psychiatry', *Lancet*, 20 May, pp. 1111–2.
Hilgard, E. R., Atkinson, R. C. and Atkinson, R. L. (1975). *Introduction to Psychology*, 6th ed. New York: Harcourt, Brace & World.
Hilgard, E. R. and Marquis, D. G. (1961). *Conditioning and Learning*, 2nd ed. New York: Appleton-Century-Crofts.
Lazarus, A. (1971). *Behaviour Therapy and Beyond*. London: McGraw-Hill.
Lovaas, O. I. (1966). 'A Program for the Establishment of Speech in Children', in *Early Childhood Autism*, ed. J. K. Wing. New York: Pergamon.
Meichenbaum, D. H. (1973). 'Cognitive Factors in Behaviour Modification: Modifying what Clients Say to Themselves', in *Advances in Behavior Therapy* (eds R. D. Rubin, J. P. Brady and J. D. Henderson), Vol. 4. New York: Academic Press, pp. 21–36.
Meyer, A. J. and Henderson, J. B. (1974). 'Multiple Risk Factor Reduction in the Prevention of Cardiovascular Disease', *Prevent. Med. 3*, pp. 225–36.
Meyer, V. and Chesser, E. S. (1970). *Behaviour Therapy in Clinical Psychiatry*. Harmondsworth: Penguin.
Miller, N. E. (1969). 'Learning of Visceral and Glandular Responses', *Science*, 163, pp. 434–5.
Olds, J. and Milner, P. M. (1954). 'Positive Reinforcement Produced by Electrical Stimulation of the Septal Area and Other Regions of the Rat Brain', *J. Comp. and Physiol. Psychol.* 47, pp. 419–27.
Patel, C. H. (1973). 'Yoga and Biofeedback in the Management of Hypertension', *Lancet*, 10 November, pp. 1053–5.
Rachlin, H. (1970). *Introduction to Modern Behaviorism*. San Francisco: W. H. Freeman.
Sterman, M. B. and Friar, L. (1972). 'Modifying Abnormal Electrical Activity in Epileptic Patients', *Electroencephalography and Neurophysiology*, *33*, pp. 89–91.
Watson, J. B. and Rayner, R. (1920). 'Conditioned Emotional Reactions', *J. Exp. Psychol.*, 3, pp. 1–14.
Weiss, T. and Engel, B. T. (1971). 'Operant Conditioning of Heart Rate in Patients with Premature Ventricular Contractions', *Psychosomatic Medicine*, *33*, pp. 301–3.
Wolpe, J. (1958). *Psychotherapy by Reciprocal Inhibition*. Stanford University Press.

Suggestions for further reading

Bolles, R. C. *Learning Theory*. London: Holt, Rinehart & Winston 1975.
Campbell, B. and Church, R. M. (eds). *Punishment and Aversive Behavior*. New York: Appleton-Century-Crofts 1969.
Hilgard, E. and Bower, G. H. *Theories of Learning*. New Jersey: Prentice-Hall 1975.

Chapter five

Emotion

Irene Martin

Plato likened the emotions to a dark unruly horse, violent yet harnessed to the chariot in which we sit and which we try to manage. What to do with this creature has occupied philosophers and religious teachers for thousands of years to the present day; then, as now, we are uncertain whether to advocate discipline and suppression or permissiveness and fulfilment. And having decided on one or another, the debate continues as to how it should be brought about, by what kind of externally imposed authority or what variety of personal adjustment. Contemporary awareness about the function and significance of emotions is leading to attempts to study them objectively, and there is a greater sophistication in matters of definition and measurement. But we are still concerned about methods of modifying those emotions which are distressing and disruptive, and enhancing those more positive feelings which contribute to well-being.

Sources of information

While some emphasize one or other aspect of the total state which we refer to as 'emotional', it is most widely agreed that this state comprises a complex pattern of subjective experience (often described by means of verbal labels: fear, anger, love, rapture, etc.), physiological changes (altered respiration, increased heart rate, flushing, etc.) and overt behaviour (running, talking, hitting, etc.). The assessment of emotionality has been to a very large extent based on one or other of these three categories: verbal, physiological and overt actions. Thus there are questionnaires which purport to measure anxiety, depression or emotional instability; techniques for recording physiological activity from the surface of the body; and a variety of methods for assessing the individual's visible behaviour.

Such an approach recognizes that in making statements of judgments about the emotional reactions of other people we are using some form of measurement. If we judge someone to be happy or gay, low-spirited or moody, there is an implicit attempt to carry out an elementary form of measurement. The large part of our social interaction involves rough and often inadequate assessments of others. It is a logical step to enquire into the reliability and validity of this assessment, as well as its meaningfulness. Quite likely we should find our personal judgments in conflict with those of other judges. But this is a different problem; whether the attempt was successful or not it has in fact been made, and we cannot argue that measurement is impossible unless we condemn our own common practice. The problem becomes acute in that so much of this practice involves counselling, treatment, selection and assessment; in short, a large set of decisions involving the destinies of individuals. If measurement can be shown to be useful, it cannot easily be dismissed.

The first demand of a scientific approach is that we recognize the difference between having an opinion (a hypothesis) and putting it to the test. It is only too easy to make comments and state conclusions on the basis of purely personal observation. It can be exceedingly difficult and demanding to attempt to verify this observation by critical experiment. The imaginative conjecture of the physician's diagnosis is not enough: it must be followed by the collection of evidence to test the hypothesis.

In such a highly complex area as human emotion it is obvious that no instant measure is ever going to solve our problem. There is no single index we can use to measure anxiety or love, as we can measure body temperature. All we can do is to measure certain aspects of emotion. Usually this amounts to recording some of the many responses which occur concomitantly with emotional experience, and by examining the pattern and sequence of events (the external stimuli which precede the emotional response and the overt behaviour which ensues) we can gradually build up a more adequate picture of the whole event which we call an emotion.

The measurement of emotion

Verbal Methods

These methods typically use words in the form of check lists, mood scales, self-reports and questionnaires, and the subject has to make some judgment about his current or his typical feeling state. Inasmuch as they rely on the use of words they raise a number of issues concerning the way we have learned to use words as labels of emotional states. Many of these labels may be poorly defined and ambiguous, learned in a haphazard way during childhood.

It is an old problem, well exemplified in the ways in which people use such terms as pain and anxiety to describe a variety of subjective experiences. Individuals seem to differ in their sensitivity to internal states such as pain, and also in the extent to which they can finely discriminate different emotional experience. Consider depression: how does it relate to and how does it differ from despair, sadness, melancholy, low spirits, unhappiness, and so on. It might be argued that they are synonyms, but certainly some people seem to be able to make precise and meaningful discriminations among such terms. It is the same with anxiety and the variety of words used to describe allied states: worry, apprehension, feelings of foreboding, tension, and so on.

In the mood scales, the subject is asked to endorse from a large list of adjectives (e.g., enthusiastic, relaxed, drowsy, tense) those which apply to his current state. Extensive use of the scales with large numbers of people have shown how the various items cluster together, and the individual's position on certain factors (e.g., activity – passivity, interest – boredom) can be assessed. Or he may be asked to rate himself along a hypothetical continuum. For example, a mood scale of depression might include a scale ranging from 'feeling cheerful', 'on top of the world' at one end, to 'feeling unhappy and miserable all the time' at the other end. A scale of fear might ask the subject to rate a particular fear along a continuum of 0 as no fear at all to 100 as the most frightened he has ever been. The idea behind these scales is that of a standardized format, to help the subject to describe his own feelings; and they have been useful, for example, in demonstrating changes in attitude with forms of psychological therapy, change in emotional responsiveness to frightening films, and in sensitively reflecting the effects of drugs. Test/re-test studies have found them to be surprisingly reliable.

In order that they can be scored with reasonable objectivity, questionnaires usually consist of simple questions which must be answered by Yes, No, or ? Typical questions from an anxiety scale might be: Do you worry about your health? Do you suffer from sleeplessness? Do you consider yourself rather a nervous person?

There have been many criticisms of this method of measuring emotional states. Many of the items included in these lists are selected quite arbitrarily; a person who scores high on an anxiety scale may also score high on a depression scale or a scale of hysteria, simply because the scales include casually grouped items which were just guessed at in the first place. The *a priori* construction of questionnaires and the naïve notion that because a questionnaire is given a particular label it therefore measures that particular trait have had to be abandoned. Very careful statistical analysis is required to solve this kind of problem.

Attempts have been made to structure the whole field of personality in terms of independent dimensions, for example neuroticism, introversion/extroversion, and psychoticism. Items which characterize neuroticism include nervousness, hypersensitivity, depression, inferiority feelings and many more. The neurotic is emotionally unstable, hypochondriacal, worried, excitable, impatient. Eysenck (1965) postulates that differences between people in emotionality or neuroticism are mediated by inherited differences in the lability and excitability of the autonomic nervous system. Some people are constitutionally predisposed to show a strong reaction of the sympathetic nervous system towards stimuli of various kinds, whereas other people are predisposed to react much less strongly. Differentiated emotional states are seen within this dimensional framework: the introverted neurotic, for example, is predisposed to suffer anxiety and depression. The psychotic is conceived to be emotionally impulsive. All these matters are more fully discussed by Claridge in Chapter 7.

Other criticisms of the questionnaire method concern subjects' biases (e.g., the tendency always to answer 'yes' or 'no'), age and sex factors, and the observation that subjects may deliberately fake their answers. Modern questionnaires have gone a long way towards coping with these difficulties. A great deal of statistical and experimental expertise has gone into their construction, their reliability and validity. Nevertheless, questionnaire responses and self-reports must be interpreted with care: they provide useful information, but this is most profitably considered alongside other sources of information, especially physiological and behavioural.

Physiological Changes

The fact of bodily involvement is one of the rarely disputed aspects of emotion. Its manifestations are diffuse.

> Researches ... have shown that not only the heart, but the entire circulatory system, forms a sort of sounding-board, which every change of our consciousness, however slight, may make reverberate. Hardly a sensation comes to us without sending waves of alternate constriction and dilation down the arteries of our arms. The blood vessels of the abdomen act reciprocally with those of the more outward parts. The bladder and bowels, the glands of the mouth, throat and skin, and the liver, are known to be affected gravely in certain severe emotions, and are unquestionably affected transiently when the emotions are of a lighter sort. That the

heart-beats and the rhythm of breathing play a leading part in all emotions whatsoever is a matter too notorious for proof.

This quotation is from James (1890, p. 450) and illustrates a pre-experimental viewpoint which has proved amply justified.

Many experiments have since provided data for the hypothesis that emotionality is related to excitability of the autonomic nervous system. Its role in emotional states was intensively examined in the decades that followed. Pain, the emotions of fear and rage and also intense excitement are manifested in the activities of the sympathetic division of the autonomic nervous system. Impulses are discharged over the neurones of this division to produce all the changes typical of sympathetic excitation (see Figure 5.1).

Salivation is reduced or stopped; movement of the stomach, secretion of gastric juices and peristaltic movements of the intestines are all inhibited. These effects together slow down digestion. They also interfere with normal parasympathetic functions, giving rise to defecation and urination. (These last two indices often serve in tests with animals as measures of emotionality.) Changes in the circulatory system also take place. Sympathetic impulses to the heart make it beat faster. They also cause constriction of the blood vessels of the gut, and control blood flow in such a way as to direct more blood to brain and skeletal muscle mass.

It has been shown how closely related are the effects of the sympathetic nervous system and adrenal secretion. Adrenaline (epinephrin), secreted from the adrenal medulla, is extraordinarily effective in minute amounts, and affects the structures innervated by the sympathetic division of the autonomic nervous system precisely as if they were receiving nervous impulses. Emotional excitement results in sympathetic (neural) discharges both to peripheral structures and to the adrenal medulla. Thus sympathetic effects are automatically augmented and prolonged through direct chemical action on the organs themselves.

Noteworthy effects of adrenaline include liberation of sugar into the blood stream, relaxation of the smooth muscle of the bronchioles, improved contraction of fatigued muscle, and more rapid coagulation of the blood. The utility of these bodily changes was discussed by Cannon (1929) in terms of mobilizing the organism for prompt and efficient action in the struggle for survival.

Many of the bodily effects of sympathetic arousal can be detected from the surface of the body by means of appropriate transducers and high-gain amplifiers. Active brain, muscles, heart, sweat glands and many other structures produce small voltages which can readily be picked up by means of appropriately situated electrodes placed on the skin.

Fundamental Processes of Psychological Functioning

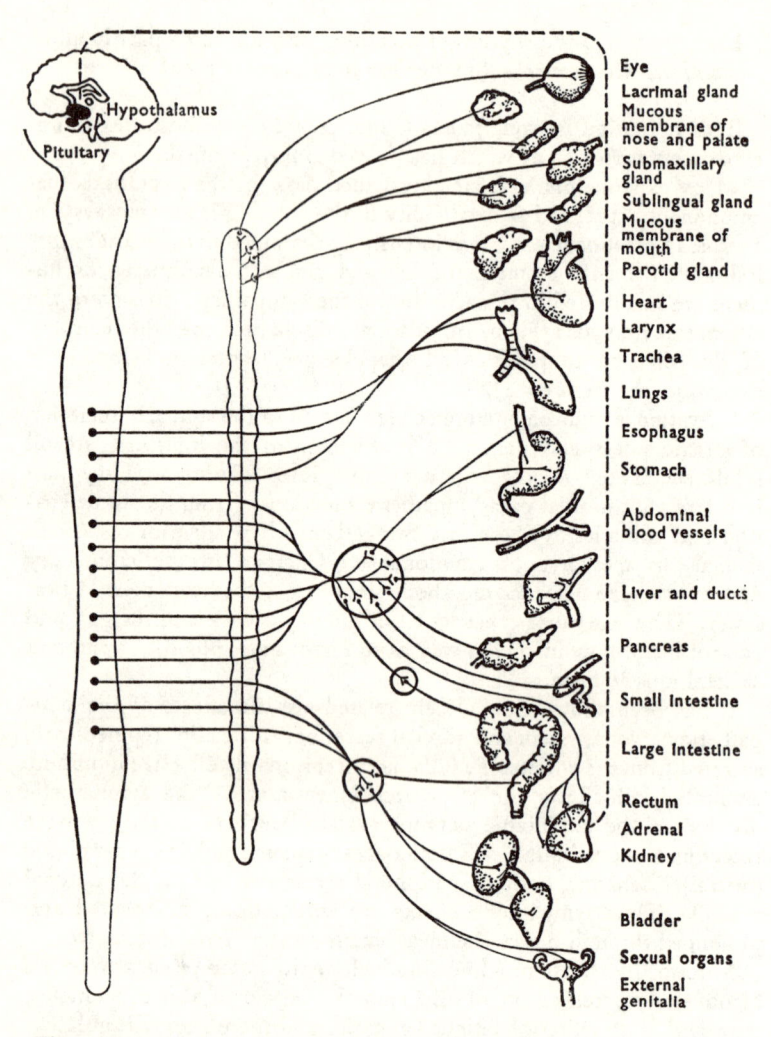

Figure 5.1

In the years following Cannon's work, other classes of compounds have been implicated in various affective states, including normal and pathological anxiety, depression, elation and anger. These include the catecholamines, epinephrin and norepinephrin, and the indole amine, serotonin and other indoles. While norepinephrin functions as a chemical transmitter substance at the terminals of the peripheral sympathetic nervous system, the role of this and other amines in the central nervous system is far from clear. It has been suggested that norepinephrin and serotonin may each function directly as a transmitter substance in the central nervous system, though none of the biogenic amines has yet been definitely established as a chemical neurotransmitter in the brain (see Schildkraut and Kety, 1967, for a review of this area). The adrenal cortex has also been implicated with emotional behaviour in the form of the response to stress, as described previously (see Chapter 1).

Granted that such manifest physiological changes occur within the individual at times of stress and emotional arousal, it is interesting to consider how he perceives and interprets them. Most of the functions described above are well below the level of conscious awareness, but some – cardiovascular and respiratory for example – are accompanied by moderate degrees of awareness. In malfunctioning states the sufferer becomes acutely aware of discomfort and pain, perhaps to the exclusion of all other feelings. But it is doubtful whether, in most normal subjects, increases or decreases in physiological activity are perceived very accurately. Even those changes which might seem fairly obtrusive, like a marked increase in heart rate, or hunger pangs, are not always recognized. The converse is well known: reports may occur of persistent pain and discomfort in the absence of any detectable cause. The ways in which individuals interpret and react to their own internal physiology may well be as dependent upon their evaluation of the external situation as upon actual bodily changes.

This has been recognized in relation to obesity, where one suggestion is that obese people eat not in response to their internal cues (stomach contractions or distension) but in response to the sight and availability of food.

Assessment of Behaviour

We so often pass judgment on other people's behaviour with such complete conviction of our accuracy that we need to be reminded from time to time of the bases on which our judgments are made. If we were asked to judge, from overt behaviour alone, whether a person were suffering from anxiety, anger or depression, what kinds of evidence would we look for? One might suppose that clues could be gained from facial and vocal expressions and direct action. These areas have been at one time or another examined by psychologists, and the results are by no means as clear-cut as one would like.

Darwin was one of the earliest writers to draw attention to the movements of expression (Darwin, 1872). Naturalists have frequently illustrated how rapidly facial expressions of threat are recognized by other members of the group who in turn react – by counter-threats or appeasement – depending upon their position in the group. Parallels can be seen in the display dances of men in different cultures, which frequently follow a pattern of stamping, leaping, and brandishing weapons (see Figure 5.2).

Figure 5.2

Subsequent studies of facial expression carried out with still photographs in the laboratory have been much more cautious and inevitably more limited in their conclusions. Schlosberg (1952), for example, concluded that a series of facial expressions could be described by three major dimensions: pleasantness-unpleasantness, attention-rejection, and level of activation. It was concluded from this work that instead of searching for facial cues associated with specific categories of emotion it may be more profitable to investigate cues associated with dimensions of emotional meaning. Recognition of finer shades of emotion, Schlosberg suggested, will probably depend upon knowledge of the stimulus situation.

Davitz (1964, p. 14), writing some ten years later and summarizing laboratory research on this topic, suggested that while there is some agreement that facial expressions do, indeed, communicate feelings beyond what might be expected by chance alone, large differences in accuracy are reported in the literature:

These differences probably are a function of the stimulus material used, the kinds of discrimination required in the experimental procedure, the categories of emotional meaning considered in a research, and individual differences in ability among those who are asked to identify the expressions.

A variety of techniques have been used to investigate the communication of emotional meaning by vocal expression. These in general attempt to eliminate or control the verbal information conveyed by speech and to express different feelings through vocal rather than verbal cues. Regardless of the techniques used, all studies of adults thus far reported in the literature agree that emotional meanings can be accurately communicated by vocal expression. Analytical studies (e.g., on vocal characteristics of rate, pitch and pauses) have not much extended this fundamental observation. There is some slight evidence concerning the kind of person who is more successful in identifying emotional expression in terms of simple perceptual and cognitive processes (e.g., ability to discriminate pitch, loudness, time and timbre of auditory stimuli) but little in the way of significant personality variables (Davitz, 1964).

Some of the earliest work on ratings of emotionality was carried out by Burt (1937) on schoolchildren. He attempted to rate children on various traits: anger, assertiveness, sociability, curiosity, joy, sex, disgust, tenderness, sorrow, fear and submissiveness. The findings were assessed by means of factor analysis, in an attempt to discover the principal factors in terms of which human behaviour can best be described, an attempt very analogous to work which at that time was being carried out with intelligence. Three factors were extracted, the first of which was called general emotionality, the second appeared to be a bipolar factor opposing the aggressive to the inhibited emotions, and the third another bipolar factor opposing the pleasurable to the unpleasurable emotions.

This type of rating is common to psychiatric descriptions of patients' symptoms such as delusions, mood disturbances, suspicions, depression or anxiety, an exercise which often shows little reliability. Some of the dangers inherent in ratings have been outlined by Eysenck (1965). They are:

(1) Differential understanding of trait names. For example, do the terms 'persistence', 'anxious' mean the same to different judges?

(2) The halo effect. Whether we like (or dislike) someone, admire or

despise him, is likely to colour all the judgments made of his behaviour. We may unwittingly attribute all the virtues to our friends and the vices to our enemies.

(3) Difference in rating ability. Persons who rate others may differ with respect to their ability to carry out this task.

(4) Influence of unconscious bias. Biases for or against certain traits in others may be deeply rooted in the personality organization of the rater.

(5) Influence of acquaintanceship. Contrary to common belief, relatively superficial knowledge seems to give better predictive accuracy than more thorough knowledge.

(6) Raters' preconceptions. Kendell (1968) has shown how psychiatric ratings of clinical features of depression are significantly affected by raters' preconceptions about the classification of depressive illnesses (whether there are two distinct entities or only one), in such a way as to conform with, and so to confirm, these opinions.

With so many factors influencing the rating, it is not surprising that reliability between ratings - either made by the same person at different times or by different raters - tends to be rather low.

The judgment of whether a person is affectionate or co-operative is obviously a highly complicated one, and limited to the samples of behaviour which we are able to observe. It is simpler to measure more specific components of behaviour such as smiling, amount of time spent in proximity to others, vocalization, and so on. These can be fairly precisely defined among a group of observers, criteria decided on, and checks made on the measures obtained. This indeed is the position which contemporary ethologists have moved towards in their detailed observation of animal behaviour in natural surroundings. This work has been described in a number of popular books: e.g., Lorenz (1967) on geese and fish; Tinbergen (1953) on the herring gull; and Jane van Lawick-Goodall (1971) on chimpanzees.

The technique of detailed behavioural sampling is a valid and informative approach to the study of behaviour. It has been successfully applied to human studies, especially of young infants and children. As an example, fear of strangers (which in human infants usually appears in the second half of the first year of life and may extend long into the second year) can be studied by measuring such elements as facial expression (smiling, frowning, etc.), visual fixation, vocalization, and motor activity in response to different types of strangers.

The attachment behaviour of young mammals can be seen as the tendency for both mother and young to seek and to maintain close proximity to each other. In young animals that are born fairly mature, approach is readily elicited by any stimuli of moderate or low intensity that change gradually; for example, a quiet, repetitive sound or an object that moves slowly. Conversely, escape is readily elicited, though a little later, by stimuli of high intensity that change abruptly, for example, sudden loud noises or fast-moving objects. Once a young animal has gained some experience, moreover, another very important factor enters in. Whatever has become familiar tends to be approached, whilst everything else, namely the strange, tends to be avoided, or at least treated with caution (Bowlby, 1969, p. 84).

Some ethologists have extended their naturalistic approach to human behaviour in different societies and cultures. Posture and gesture can

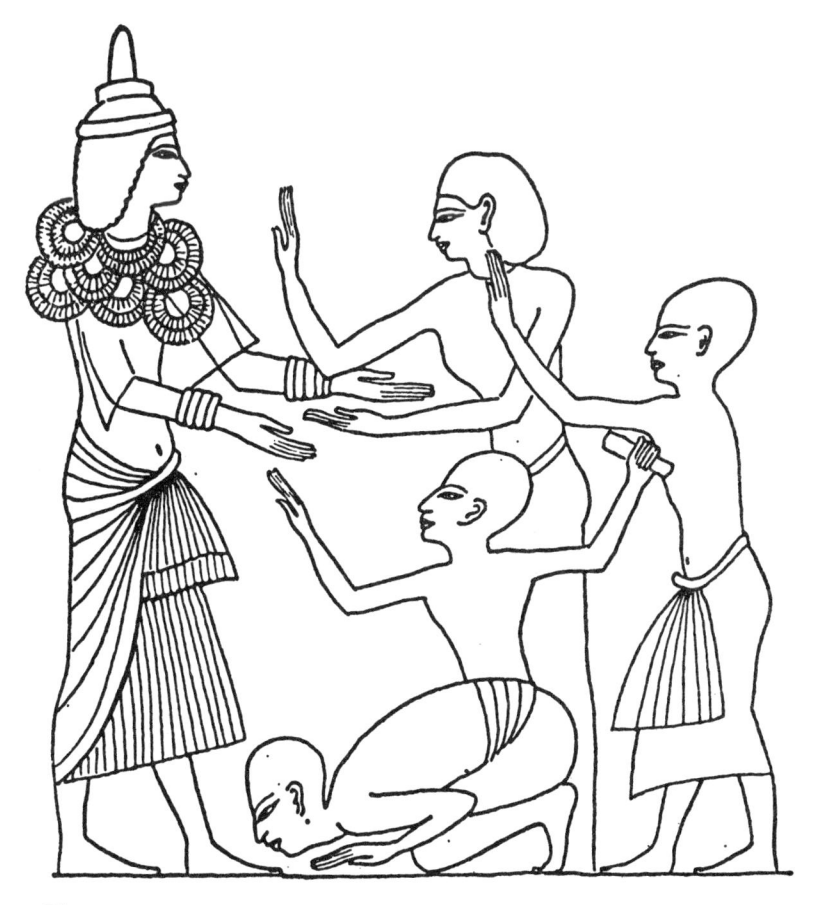

Figure 5.3

be seen as non-verbal ways of conveying information and have important social functions. The role of postures such as bowing, curtsying, falling to one's knees, etc., is that of making oneself small and thereby appeasing (see Figure 5.3); threatening postures on the other hand typically involve making oneself larger.

Argyle (1969) describes in a very readable and comprehensive way the varieties of non-verbal behaviour which occur in social situations. These include bodily contact, proximity, posture, facial and gestural movements, and direction of gaze. At this non-verbal level a great deal of social interaction is carried out and accurately interpreted by both parties. Thus we are well able to judge a sympathetic gaze from a hostile stare, we are conscious when a person comes too close or remains too distant, and adjust our own behaviour accordingly. Seemingly strict social norms prevail about how near to other people we should be, where and how much we should touch them and how we should look at them. These standards, which may differ in different societies, are unwittingly assimilated by the members of each group, such that we feel uncomfortable when members of the group deviate from them.

Differentiation of emotional states

Early Instinct Theories

We confidently use a large number of words to describe our emotional states: anger, fear, love, and many more. How valid are these distinctions? What are the cues, internal and external, which cause us to identify and label different emotions?

One of the first attempts to specify and list different kinds of emotion was based on the instinct theories current at the beginning of this century (McDougall, 1910). It was fashionable at that time to describe human behaviour by analogy with the behaviour observed in other animals, in terms of instincts. These were held to comprise three parts: the cognitive, the affective and the conative. An instinct was defined as an inherited disposition which determines us to perceive and pay attention to objects of a certain class, to experience an emotional excitement of a particular quality, and to act towards the object in a particular manner.

McDougall cites a long list of instincts, each with its own associated emotion: the instinct of combat, associated with an emotion of anger, rage or fury, the instinct of curiosity, of food-seeking, of escape and mating. The point to emphasize is that the emotion was held to be innate, ready-made as it were to serve the instinct by providing the appropriate driving force. McDougall, in common with many writers of the period, was guilty of frank anthropomorphism, and did not hesitate to read the attributes of human emotions into his observation of lower animals.

The modern concept of 'instinctive' behaviour is very different. Indeed, it differs so radically from earlier 'instinct' theory that many modern ethologists do not use the term because of its undesirable connotations, especially with regard to the fixity of inherited behaviour. Much more is learned than was formerly recognized; and the immensely important factor of prolonged experience has to be taken into account.

Physiological Theories

A second view of emotional differentiation is that it relates to differential patterns of physiological activation. Following James's emphasis on the role of physiological changes in emotion, a number of studies were undertaken in search of the physiological differentiators of the emotions. Relatively few of these studies have provided positive results. Among those that have, Wolf and Wolff (1943) found that fear regularly reduced gastric activity and blood flow, while other emotions (annoyance and anger) seemed to produce a different pattern. At one time it seemed that anger and resentment resulted in cholinergic excitation, while fear and anxiety excited adrenergic nerves. Again, subsequent studies were not overwhelmingly clear. One of the difficulties is to reproduce situations in the laboratory which do reliably elicit fear or anger. Using ingenious means to arouse these emotions, Ax (1953) showed that anxiety or fear (the subjects were afraid of a possible shock from defective electrical wiring) produced a cardiovascular pattern like that seen after adrenaline injection, while anger produced a pattern like that appearing after noradrenaline injection.

These and other findings cited by Arnold (1960) offer the best evidence available that fear and anger may be differentiated in terms of the pattern of physiological arousal. Some of the other findings are, for example, that animals which prey upon others, and attack and fight a great deal, show a predominance of noradrenaline from the adrenal medulla, while rodents and other plant eaters that need not attack other animals for food, but flee from predatory enemies, show more adrenaline.

There is much current interest in the relationship of catecholamines to depression. Briefly, the hypothesis relates depression to a relative deficiency of norepinephrin at certain central synapses, and manic states to a relative excess of norepinephrin. Other investigators favour a competing indoleamine hypothesis, implicating serotonin systems in the brain. They argue that lowering brain serotonin tends to produce hyper-responsivity to both internal and external stimuli, manifested in disturbances of sleep, increased susceptibility to convulsions, heightened sexuality, greater irritability and aggressiveness. It may well be that balances or interactions between catecholamine and indoleamine mediated neurons will prove to be important in the regulation of mood and the emotional experiences of anger and depression (Hamburg, Hamburg and Barchas, 1975).

Cognitive Theories

In most of the emotional states experimentally manipulated using human subjects, results have shown a general pattern of excitation of the sympathetic nervous system. Schachter and Singer (1962, pp. 379–381) comment, however:

> Whether or not there are physiological distinctions among the various emotional states must be considered an open question. Recent work might be taken to indicate that such differences are at best rather subtle and that the variety of emotion, mood and feeling states are by no means matched by an equal variety of visceral patterns.

This rather ambiguous state of affairs has led many to suggest that cognitive factors may be major determinants of emotional states. Schachter and Singer continue:

> Granted a general pattern of sympathetic excitation as characteristic of emotional states, granted that there may be some differences in pattern from state to state, it is suggested that one labels, interprets and identifies this stirred-up state in terms of the characteristics of the precipitating situation and the general perceptual state. This suggests that an emotional state may be considered a function of a state of physiological arousal and of a cognition appropriate to this state of arousal. The cognition, in a sense, exerts a steering function. Cognitions arising from the immediate situation as interpreted by past experience provide the framework within which one understands and labels his feelings. It is the cognition which determines whether the state of physiological arousal will be labelled as 'anger', 'joy', 'fear', or whatever.

Schachter and Singer examined the implications of this formulation experimentally. First they asked whether the state of physiological arousal alone is sufficient to induce an emotion. Available evidence, in which patients were injected with adrenaline and then asked to introspect, suggests that it is not. A large percentage of subjects simply reported their physical symptoms (e.g., accelerated heartbeat) with no emotional overtones: a few responded in an apparently emotional fashion. Of these the majority described their feelings in a 'cold' or 'as if' way; that is, they made statements such as 'I feel as if I were afraid'. Only a very few cases reported a genuine emotional experience.

In the early studies, the subjects may have known that they were receiving an injection of adrenaline. Consider now a person in a state of physiological arousal for which no immediate explanatory or appropriate cognitions are available. The authors argue that the subject would be aware of the symptoms associated with a discharge of the sympathetic nervous system, and that the way he labelled these bodily feelings might depend upon situational pressures: 'Should he be at a gay party he might decide that he was extremely happy and euphoric. Should he be arguing with his wife, he might explode in fury and hatred.' It is the basic assumption of the authors that emotional states are a function of the interaction of cognitive factors with a state of physiological arousal, and their results seem to confirm the hypothesis.

Thus the earlier psychological theories that emotions are simply bodily changes – of the heart, sweat glands, muscles, respiration and so on – must be expanded to include mental activities like perception, remembering and evaluating. This more inclusive view would hold that 'love', for example, is probably not an entity in itself, but a range of attitudes and values towards different objects which are uniquely coloured by previous experience and by the contexts in which they occur. In any model of human behaviour, this store of expectancies, of labels and preformed judgments, must loom as large as, if not larger than, the accompanying bodily reactions which constitute only one part of an emotional experience. Indeed, a case could be made for the view that these more mental events *are* the emotional experience, in the sense that they are the elements which make one emotion distinguishable from another.

Emotion and motivation

Motivators as Energizers of Behaviour

Historically, a whole range of viewpoints have converged on the idea that purpose determines evolutionary development and behaviour. This emphasis has kept alive, and made of central importance, the belief that organisms are active rather than passive participants in their interactions with the environment. This active participation is attributed to innate, impulsive forces, important to survival and development.

An opposite viewpoint insists on the sufficiency of physico-chemical forces for the explanation of animal conduct and proposes a relative rigidity of animal behaviour. It is illustrated in tropistic behaviour, whereby a plant will orient 'mechanically' towards light. This view has little or no place for internal sources of behaviour like drives; it stresses the role of external stimuli in guiding behaviour.

Most theories of motivation have held to the former view and postulate a variety of innate drives related to eating, drinking, escaping from pain, attacking, exploring, care of the young and the like. These are conceived as changes in the internal physiological state and as energizing restless activity which is terminated only by various consummatory acts. It was assumed that organisms would not act in any significant way without such drive mechanisms, and motivation has tended to be identified with them. A deprived animal has certain tissue deficits which goad it into activity: it will cross obstructions, travel distances and learn pathways to obtain food, for example. The goal having been achieved, activity decreases and a period of quiescence occurs.

These descriptions carry the implication that motivated behaviour is an attempt to preserve organismic integrity by homeostatic restorations of equilibrium. The term homeostasis was originally coined by a physiologist to describe the steady states attained at any particular moment by the physiological processes at work in living organisms. Since then, the term has been applied to many psychological conditions. The homeostatic position in general is that the organism (and each of its sub-systems) tends to resist changes in its environment that are of a magnitude large enough to upset its equilibrium or threaten its survival as a stable system. The theory does not require that a disturbed system return to its prior state of equilibrium; by assuming that biological systems are open and have continuous energy exchange with the environment it allows for a variety of means and states through which stability can be reached.

The learning theorist Hull (1943) assumed that all behaviour is motivated by homeostatic drives or secondary drives based upon them. He also assumed that all rewards are ultimately based on the reduction of a primary homeostatic drive. A reward of food reduces the homeostatic imbalance produced by hunger; and all animals will rapidly learn quite difficult responses to get a reward. Secondary rewards, such as social approval, are effective because they have been associated with food and other primary rewards in the past. In this sense, drive is conceived as arising from a tissue need and having the general function of arousing or activating behaviour. Direct tension reduction becomes the critical reinforcement factor in the process of learning.

The essence of the drive doctrine can perhaps be summarized in the form of two propositions:

(1) Organisms act only to reduce their drives; thus all activities are interpreted as direct or indirect attempts at drive reduction.

(2) Activities that are accompanied by a reduction in drive are strengthened, and such drive reduction is a necessary condition for learning to occur.

Drive theory, in one form or another, still stands at the centre of modern thinking about motivation and learning, and has been extended to the analysis of emotional states such as fear and anxiety, aggression and dependency. These emotional states are considered within the theory as logically equivalent in status, character and function to such drives as hunger and thirst. Attempts have been made, for example, to treat frustration as a drive which has particular patterns of behaviour associated with it, typically anger and attacking behaviour. Aggression may be directed toward the frustrating agent or turned against some other object or person, including the self. Although the early suggestion was that aggression always results from frustration and that frustration always leads to aggression, the second half of this hypothesis has been modified to acknowledge that a number of other reactions to frustration, in addition to aggression, are possible. Included among these alternatives are regression, repression, and fixation.

Conflict can be regarded as a special case of frustration, often arising from two or more equal but incompatible response tendencies. In a sense, it is equivalent to a condition of double frustration, each of the competing tendencies serving as the barrier to the completion of the other. As in the case of other frustrations, conflict is a state of increased tension, but by its very nature it is characterized by vacillation, hesitancy, fatigue and often complete blocking. In both clinical observations and experimental studies, conflict has been shown to be an emotional response to a situation requiring incompatible responses, e.g., those involving approach to and those involving avoidance of a goal.

Perhaps the most widely discussed emotion in the context of learning and emotion is fear or anxiety. One influential view is that anxiety is a learned response occurring to signals that are premonitory of situations of injury or pain (Mowrer, 1939). According to this view, anxiety is basically anticipatory in nature, and it has great biological utility in that it adaptively motivates living organisms to deal with traumatic events in advance of their actual occurrence, thereby diminishing harmful effects.

It is in this general biological sense that both 'emotion' and 'motivation' can be viewed as a complex integration of behaviour involving selective attention to certain events, a heightened physiological state of excitement, and certain probable patterns of action. These patterns of action are common to most higher species of animals and have a clear biological utility in coping with environment and survival. Both are linked to environmental stimuli which act as incentives or triggers of behaviour, and to internal organismic conditions. Neither the external incentive nor the physiological state is in itself sufficient for producing any species-typical action: an interplay between them is necessary. This interplay can be illustrated in accounts of sexual arousal which emphasize that sexual behaviour depends on two conditions: adequate hormonal levels and adequate external stimulation.

Arousal and Performance

It has long been evident that the degree of energy mobilization of the body was implicated to a considerable extent in the performance of various psychological activities. For example, we learn better, make better perceptual discriminations and have faster reaction times when we are aroused than when we are sleepy and relaxed. Discovery of the arousing function of certain lower brain centres such as the reticular

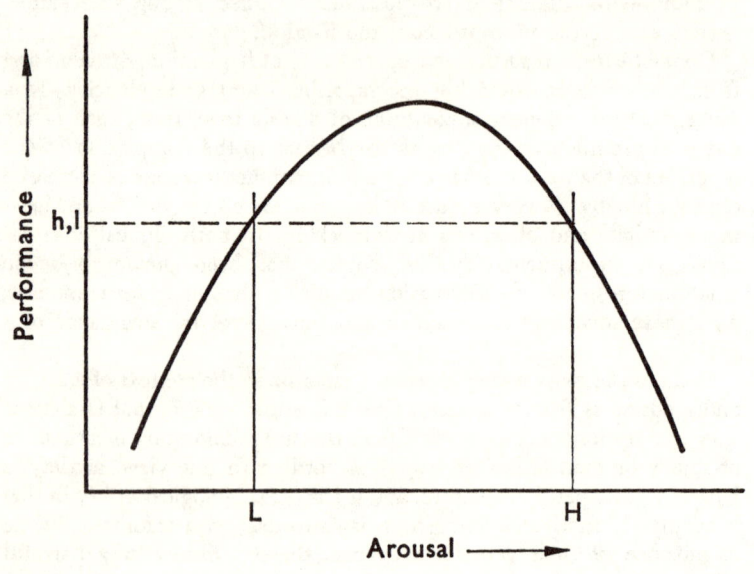

Figure 5.4

formation (Moruzzi and Magoun, 1949) led psychologists to make the connections between these anatomical structures and their own notions of a behavioural arousal continuum, ranging from deep sleep to high excitement.

In general, results have shown that there is an optimal point of activation for best performance, and that on either side of this point performance is relatively impaired. Consider this in the case of anxiety (which is a form of extreme activation) and examination performance. If we are very relaxed and totally non-anxious we shall hardly be bothered or motivated to do well: this would be akin to the 'couldn't care less' attitude. With increasing levels of activation we would feel concerned, keen to do well, all systems ready to go. With still increasing levels of anxiety we should be almost paralysed with fright, possibly shaking, feeling sick, totally unable to verbalize or to organize the knowledge required for examination success. In short, the hypothetical function relating performance to activation is that of an inverted U (see Figure 5.4). These findings apply to many different kinds of performance: degree of activation appears to affect the speed, intensity and co-ordination of motor skills, and also the range of cues which are utilized in making judgments and decisions.

Personality and Arousal

There have been discussions in the literature about whether there is a single dimension of activation, on which emotion can be placed at the upper end, or whether two arousal systems are required to encompass the facts adequately. Recent reviews of the area (Eysenck, 1967; Routtenberg, 1968) settle for two, one the reticular system (as discussed in Chapter 1), and the second, the limbic mid-brain system. This latter includes the hippocampus, amygdala, cingulum, septum and hypothalamus. It is not argued that these two systems are completely independent, but relatively and partially so. As Gellhorn and Loofbourrow (1963, p. 362) have pointed out, it is obvious, since ascending and descending pathways connect the reticular formation with the hypothalamus, that under experimental conditions similar effects may be produced by stimulation of either structure, but this fact should not obscure the fundamental functional difference between the two structures. The complicated nature of the possible mode of functioning and interaction between the two systems is thoroughly discussed in the Routtenberg article.

Eysenck (1967, p. 232) presents a diagrammatic account of the two-arousal schema, relating it to the two personality dimensions of extraversion and neuroticism. He suggests that arousal system 2 (the limbic system) is concerned with emotion, and, in its application to personality differences, with neuroticism/emotionality. According to this outline, cortical arousal can be produced along two quite distinct and separate pathways, i.e., via arousal system 1 or 2:

> It can be produced by sensory stimulation or by problem-solving activity of the brain, without necessarily involving the visceral brain at all; in this case, we have no autonomic arousal, but possibly quite high cortical arousal. A scientist sitting quite immobile and to all appearances asleep, but thinking profoundly about some professional problems, might illustrate this state of affairs; there is considerable cortical arousal but little autonomic activity.

Cortical arousal can also be produced by emotion, in which case the reticular formation is involved through the ascending and descending pathways connecting it with the hypothalamus. In this case, we have both autonomic arousal and cortical arousal.

Such hypotheses concerning individual differences have been put to the test in several experiments which measure sensory thresholds, tolerance for pain, and sensory deprivation. In typical procedures of sensory deprivation, the subject is isolated in a room, eyes blindfolded, ears plugged, covers tied round the hands so that he is unable to feel anything, and left alone. Very few people can tolerate this kind of condition for any length of time, and the absence of stimulation can be as painful as quite considerable degrees of pain. We normally depend upon sensory stimulation to maintain our customary level of arousal. Introvert-type personalities, it is postulated, are better able to tolerate conditions of sensory deprivation because their on-going level of arousal is higher and moreover, whatever small degree of external stimulation is available, as it were, they will get and amplify. But the extravert will receive much less of the very slight stimulation which is still present, because of his lower level of arousal and the inhibitory properties of his nervous system.

This implies the existence of a kind of 'stimulus hunger' on the part of some individuals and 'stimulus avoidance' on the part of others. Recent studies relating 'stimulus hunger' to personality have tended to confirm the predictions both in the tolerance to pain and sensory deprivation experiments; that is, extraverts are more tolerant of pain than introverts, while introverts are more tolerant of sensory deprivation than extraverts.

Motivation and Coping Behaviour

Theories of motivation which have their origins in a biological/evolutionary view of animal behaviour are thinly stretched when it comes to human experience. Various social needs relating to achievement, power, affiliation, etc. have been postulated which do not readily fit into existing drive theories.

The biological view that bodily need is the ultimate basis of motivation has been supplemented by other theorists who stress the fact that many animals (infra-human as well as human) will work to obtain rewards that do not reduce any known biological drives. These theorists have been more likely to study such motivational tendencies as exploration, uncertainty, interest and ambition, and a variety of factors which have no immediately apparent physiological basis. Monkeys, for example, will rapidly learn to press a lever to open a window so that they can look out and around. The tenacity and rapidity with which monkeys work at the task indicate that the activities seen through the window (albeit everyday laboratory routine) are extremely interesting to them. Recent discussion and analysis of the motivation concept illustrate the many uncertainties which exist in relation to this kind of behaviour. Although many theories of motivation refer to inner drive states, others point to the variety of external incentives which motivate behaviour and which are acquired during the individual's lifetime (Cofer and Appley, 1964, review this area comprehensively).

Recently, views of motivational development have been put forward which emphasize the roles of helplessness and mastery in adult life. In the course of infant and childhood experience, some acquire a sense of mastery over their surroundings; others a profound sense of helplessness. Here is an example from Seligman (1975):

> Consider a third-grader who has been beaten in every schoolyard fight he has had. The very first time he fought, he may not have sensed defeat until he was completely subjected. After nine defeats in a row, however, he probably feels beaten early and at only the first hint of defeat. How ready he is to believe himself defeated is shaped by how regularly he has won or lost. So it is with more general beliefs, like helplessness and mastery. If a child has been helpless repeatedly and has experienced little mastery, he will believe himself to be helpless in a new situation, with only minimal clues. A different child with the opposite experience, using the same clues, might believe himself to be in control. How early, how many and how intense the experiences of helplessness and mastery are will determine the strength of this motivational trait.

Most individuals will gradually evolve ways of responding which ensure success, recognition and control over the environment. But some fail to do this. They may learn instead that their responses are ineffective in producing any desired results; they consequently feel powerless to affect this external situation. Attempts to adapt begin to decline; a 'what's-the-use' attitude develops, together with feelings of helplessness and depression (Seligman, 1975).

The basis of such learning is that of operant conditioning. 'Operants' are so called because they 'operate' on the environment; they are voluntary responses, which means that they can be increased in probability by reward and decreased by punishment. The frequency or regularity with which a response is rewarded or punished is called the schedule of reinforcement in learning experiments. People and animals learn readily that their responses are 'sometimes', 'usually' or 'never' followed by rewards and punishments. When an organism can make no operant response that controls an outcome, the outcome can be termed uncontrollable (see Chapter 4).

Experiments with dogs seem to typify what many species do when they are faced with a situation over which they have no control. A dog receiving inescapable shock (i.e., shock from which no escape or avoidance is possible by jumping or moving into a safe compartment) initially shows fear, but after a while stops howling and running and remains silent until shock terminates. It seems to give up and passively accept the shock. Subsequently, when placed in a situation where shock avoidance is possible, the animal makes no attempt to avoid the shock, seeming to have learned a condition of helplessness.

Seligman suggests that humans who experience traumatic events about which they can do nothing to eliminate or mitigate the trauma continue with passive responding to future aversive events. Such helplessness caused by failure can be reversed, however. To do so requires that the individual experience some failure and actively develops a way to cope with it.

The Concept of a Conditioned Fear

A complex human emotion like fear comprises many response elements. These form a complex pattern of autonomic, skeletal-motor and cognitive perceptual factors which are partially independent of one another. One individual may avoid feared objects and display heightened autonomic arousal, but verbally deny that he feels afraid. Another may admit to feeling afraid but be willing to approach and touch a feared object because he does not want to appear cowardly. Thus the individual components of the fear response may have different kinds of interaction with the environment and to some extent are capable of independent change. That is to say, they may have been acquired as a result of different conditioning processes occurring at different times in the history of the individual and they may be modified by separate conditioning treatments. In modifying a complex reaction of fear it may well be necessary to apply a variety of extinction or counter-conditioning techniques to alter the separate autonomic, behavioural and verbal response components.

To state the case simply, one could devise a programme of modification which would seek to lower elevated physiological arousal by means of relaxation or desensitization techniques, or by one of the biofeedback methods in which the person is trained to control aspects of his physiological responding. It could seek to modify overt avoidance behaviour with a retraining programme offering more adaptive types of response strategies, e.g., by learning social skills instead of avoiding social situations. And the individual's attitudes and verbalizations about his fears could similarly be modified by various learning techniques.

It would be expected that training or modifying one component, say the verbal, would have some effect on the physiological and behavioural. Conversely, retraining the physiological, say in terms of learning to relax, should affect the individual's verbalizations about his state ('I feel more relaxed now'), his attitude, and his behaviour. The extent to which alteration in one system affects other systems remains an empirical problem.

Theories of emotion

The emphasis of this chapter has been on a relatively objective, experimental approach to emotion. In considering theories of emotion, however, it is evident that many lie outside the empirical approach adopted, which requires an agreed conceptual system and broad acceptance of experimental operations. Some theories, on the other hand, explicitly reject the experimental method and phrase their hypotheses in ways which are not testable.

Theories of emotion are enormously varied in context and scope and cover widely different aspects of emotion. No single comprehensive theory exists. Some are concerned with the role of instinctual energies; some with the problem of how a single, primitive form of excitement becomes differentiated into specific emotions; others with the delineation of innate emotions which appear ready made, as it were, to serve our purposes. The course of emotional development in the young infant has yet to be analysed. Some theories emphasize the essential subject-object interaction in emotion, i.e., the communicative aspects. Others deal with those central nervous system structures which govern the physiological and behavioural concomitants of emotion.

Obviously, they are dealing with very different facets of the whole problem.

The first important theory was that of James and Lange. This attempted to explain how emotional behaviour and emotional experience were interrelated. It stated that the emotional physiological response comes first, and that emotional experience is the result of that response. The essence of this view is the idea that the experience of emotion is based on the perception of secondary sensations from the viscera. It was therefore capable of experimental verification, in terms of investigating the role of visceral sensation in emotion. What would happen, for instance, if visceral connections were severed. Would we still experience emotion?

Unfortunately most of the subsequent studies purporting to test this, and other theories which emphasized the contribution of peripheral physiological responses, confused emotional experience with emotional behaviour; quite clearly it would only be possible to check on emotional experience by asking the individual what he was feeling; hence only human experimentation would be appropriate. Emotional behaviour, on the other hand, can most readily be studied in infra-human animals and most of the work which tested the theory was carried out on dogs. The results of animal experimentation showed that total separation of the viscera from the central nervous system does not impair emotional behaviour, but no conclusion could be reached concerning emotional experience (see the discussion by Goldstein, 1968).

The next major theory to be put forward related the physiological changes which occur in states of emotion to their biological utility. James had been primarily concerned with emotion as a private experience. Cannon, who worked in the 1920s, was much more experimentally oriented, less concerned with the problem of emotional experience and more with the role of psycho-physiological changes in adapting the organism for life in a world of oft-occurring emergencies.

Many of the functions of the autonomic nervous system in preparation for 'fight or flight' have been outlined above. Cannon argued that the various functions of the parasympathetic division were such as to serve bodily conservation, energy-yielding material being taken into the body and stored. In times of stress, stored energy is made rapidly available so that the animal is ready for immediate and possibly prolonged exertion; secretion of adrenaline calls forth stored carbohydrate from the liver, redistributes blood, and in general mobilizes the body's resources for vigorous muscular activity.

The same adaptive theme runs through Selye's work. He viewed the stress reaction as a defensive response (Selye, 1956). His point was that the adaptive hormones of the pituitary-adrenal system are important in tissue maintenance and repair; they mobilize the defences and energy stores of the body. Together, his and Cannon's scheme provided a powerful framework for viewing the adaptive resources of the body. Through complex interrelationships these mechanisms maintain bodily homeostasis and help the organism in its struggle for survival.

Yet many problems remain obscure. The roles of the pituitary-adrenal axis and the sympathetic nervous system are not clear-cut. Effects of adrenalectomy and sympathectomy on behaviour are not as profound as had been supposed. Sympathectomy in human patients does not eliminate emotional experience. Nor is the overall integration of physiological changes at all well worked out. The main regulator of the bodily components of stress (ACTH release and sympathetic activity) must lie within the central nervous system. Yet it, in turn, is regulated by the level of circulating hormones and feedback from the autonomic nervous system.

A further unsolved problem is the nature of the stimulus which triggers an emotional reaction. We know that only certain environmental stimuli have the property of arousing us, and it is necessary therefore to look for a central screening mechanism which will determine which aspects of the total sensory input will perform this arousal function. We need a mechanism that is able to recognize stimuli which are of significance to the organism (many of which will have been learned rather than innately given), compare events with those which have gone before, and activate somatic and autonomic centres if necessary.

It is increasingly being stressed that an emotional state cannot be inferred from the physiological reaction alone. It is the total pattern of the reaction in relation to the relevant stimulus conditions from which the emotional response is properly inferred.

Thus we find the view being discussed that emotion arises through person-environment interaction, through personal assessment and evaluation. This involves a process of learning, probably along the lines indicated in earlier sections, but it focuses the learning process more sharply in terms of events which are significant for the individual. Basically, though the precise details are unknown, the appraisal of external events seems related to two broad types: of threat or of non-threat (see Figure 5.5 from Lazarus, 1968). The theory suggests that a distinction be made between direct action and reappraisal as ways of coping with disturbing or threatening input. It had for some time been suggested that frustration of on-going behaviour produces aggression and emotionality. To the extent that an act is appraised as feasible, the individual is motivated; 'to the extent that the attempt is appraised infeasible at any moment . . . the individual becomes emotional' (Pribram, 1967, p. 837).

These views reflect the preoccupation of psychologists with the ways in which people process information coming to them from the environment; on how this information is filtered, coded, classified and stored. This, in turn, reflects the general view of behaviour in terms of 'control theory', i.e., the view of living organisms as correcting their behaviour on the basis of information and feedback, as self-regulatory, as operating like a homeostat to maintain a steady state.

Primary appraisal of threat ---> Secondary appraisal

- Direct actions and emotion-arousal
  - e.g., Attack (anger), Avoidance (fear), Inaction (hopelessness-depression)
  - This illustrates rather than exhausts the possibilities
- Benign reappraisal and emotion-reduction
  - Defensive or realistic

Automatized coping without emotion, and no real sense of danger because of the conviction of absolute control

e.g. Attack or avoidance, etc.

Primary appraisal of non-threat ---> Reappraisal of threat ---> Secondary appraisal, etc.

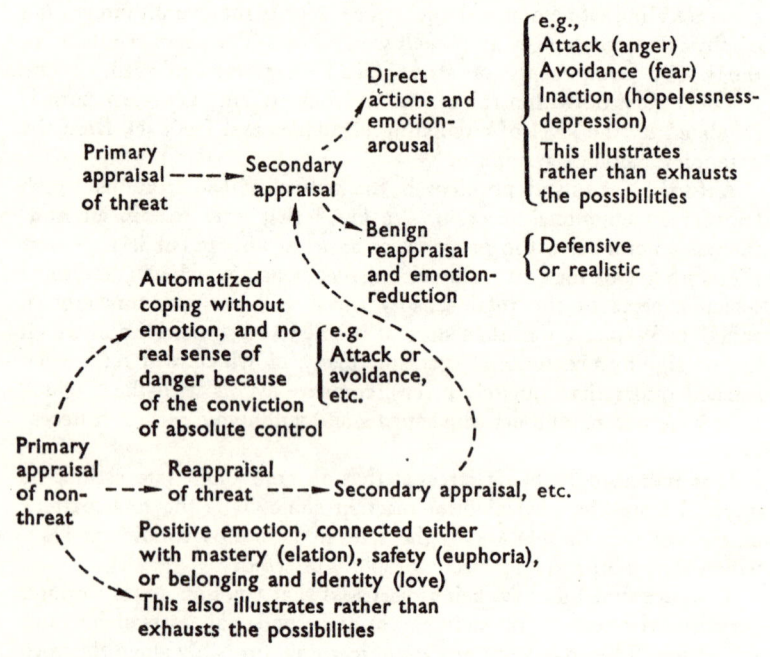

Positive emotion, connected either with mastery (elation), safety (euphoria), or belonging and identity (love)
This also illustrates rather than exhausts the possibilities

Figure 5.5

It is known that experience builds up a set of neuronal models of the events experienced, and a set of expectancies. When incoming stimulation 'matches' our experiences, little in the way of physiological activity occurs; indeed, this is the case when we are well-accustomed or habituated to something. When there is a 'mismatch' there is uncertainty in the system, reflected in physiological arousal. Within this scheme emotions can be seen as responses which cope with the disturbance aroused by uncertainty. Coping may take the form of action or reappraisal, and should eventually result in recovery from disturbance, i.e., a steady state.

Such a view conceives emotion as involving efforts to cope with some particular condition, as trying to promote survival of the individual in a broader sense; that is, in terms of ego-functioning, adjustment and interpersonal effectiveness.

References

Argyle, M. (1969). *The Psychology of Interpersonal Behaviour*. Harmondsworth: Penguin.
Arnold, Magda B. (1960). 'Physiological Effects of Emotion', in *Emotion and Personality* (ed. Magda B. Arnold), 2. New York: Columbia University Press.
Ax, A. F. (1953). 'The Physiological Differentiation between Fear and Anger in Humans', *Psychosom. Med. 15*, pp. 433–42.
Bowlby, J. (1969). 'Psychopathology of Anxiety: the Role of Affectional Bonds', in *Studies of Anxiety* (ed. M. H. Lader). *British Journal of Psychiatry* Special Publication No. 3. Ashford, Kent: Headley, 1969.
Burt, C. (1937). 'The Analysis of Temperament', *Br. J. Med. Psychol. 17*, pp. 158–88.
Cannon, W. B. (1929). *Bodily Changes in Pain, Hunger, Fear and Rage*, 2nd ed. New York: Harper & Row.
Cofer, C. N. and Appley, M. H. (1964). *Motivation: Theory and Research*. New York: Wiley.
Corcoran, D. W. J. (1965). 'Personality and the Inverted-U Relation', *Br. J. Psychol. 56*, pp. 267–74.
Darwin, C. (1872). *The Expression of the Emotions in Man and Animals*. London: Murray.
Davitz, J. R. (1964). *The Communication of Emotional Meaning*. New York: McGraw-Hill.
Eibl-Eibesfeldt, J. (1971). *Love and Hate*. London: Methuen.
Eysenck, H. J. (1965). *The Structure of Human Personality*. London: Methuen.
Eysenck, H. J. (1967). *The Biological Basis of Personality*. Springfield, Illinois: Thomas.
Gellhorn, E. and Loofbourrow, G. N. (1963). *Emotions and Emotional Disorders*. New York: Harper & Row.
Goldstein, M. L. (1968). 'Physiological Theories of Emotion: a Critical Historical Review from the Standpoint of Behaviour Theory', *Psychol. Bull. 69*, pp. 23–40.
Hamburg, D. A., Hamburg, Beatrix A. and Barchas, J. D. (1975). 'Anger and Depression in Perspective of Behavioral Biology', in *Emotions. Their Parameters and Measurement* (ed. L. Levi). New York: Raven Press.
Hull, C. L. (1943). *Principles of Behavior*. New York: Appleton-Century-Crofts.
James, W. (1890). *Principles of Psychology*, 2. London: Macmillan.
Kendell, R. E. (1968). 'An Important Source of Bias affecting Ratings made by Psychiatrists', *J. Psychiat. Res. 6*, pp. 135–41.

Lawick-Goodall, Jane van (1971). *In the Shadow of Man*. London: Collins.
Lazarus, R. S. (1968). *Emotions and Adaptation: Conceptual and Empirical Relations*. Nebraska Symposium on Motivation. Lincoln, Nebraska: University of Nebraska Press.
Levine, S. (1969). 'Psychophysiological Effects of Infantile Stimulation', *Roots of Behavior: Genetics, Instincts and Socialization in Animal Behavior* (ed. E. E. L. Bliss). New York: Hafner (reprint of 1962 ed. New York: Harper & Row, 1969).
Lorenz, K. (1967). *On Aggression*. London: Methuen.
McDougall, W. (1910). *Introduction to Social Psychology*. Boston: Luce.
Magoun, H. W. (1953). 'Physiological Interrelationships between Cortex and Subcortical Structures', *Electroenceph. Clin. Neurophysiol. Suppl. 4*, pp. 163–7.
Moruzzi, G. and Magoun, H. W. (1949). 'Brain Stem Reticular Formation and Activation of the EEG', *Electroenceph. Clin. Neurophysiol. 1*, pp. 455–73.
Mowrer, O. H. (1939). 'A Stimulus-response Analysis of Anxiety and its Role as a Reinforcing Agent', *Psychol. Rev. 46*, pp. 553–65.
Pribram, K. H. (1967). 'The New Neurology and the Biology of Emotion: a Structural Approach', *Am. Psychol. 22*, pp. 830–8.
Routtenberg, A. (1968). 'The Two Arousal Hypothesis: Reticular Formation and Limbic System', *Psychol. Review. 75*, pp. 51–80.
Schachter, S. and Singer, J. E. (1962). 'Cognitive, Social and Physiological Determinants of Emotional State', *Psychol. Rev. 69*, pp. 379–99.
Schildkraut, J. J. and Kety, S. S. (1967). 'Biogenic Amines and Emotion', *Science N.Y. 156*, pp. 21–30.
Schlosberg, H. (1952). 'The Description of Facial Expressions in Terms of Two Dimensions', *J. Exp. Psychol. 44*, pp. 229–37.
Seligman, M. E. P. (1975). *Helplessness. On depression, development and death*. San Francisco: Freeman.
Selye, H. (1956). *The Stress of Life*. New York: McGraw-Hill.
Tinbergen, N. (1953). *The Herring Gull's World*. London: Collins.
Wolf, S. and Wolff, H. G. (1943). *Human Gastric Function*. Oxford University Press.

Suggestions for further reading

Gray, J. *The Psychology of Fear and Stress*. London: World University Library 1971.
Mandler, G. *Mind and Emotion*. London: Wiley 1975.
Strongman, K. T. *The Psychology of Emotion*. London: Wiley 1973.

Part Two

Human Growth and Development

Chapter six

Intelligence

H. J. Butcher and F. S. Stevens

The concept of intelligence

'Intelligence' has been a widely used concept for some seventy years, but the descriptions and interpretations proffered by layman and professional psychologist alike have been various – so various that it hardly constitutes a useful scientific term unless pinned down operationally by some means. For many practical purposes, therefore, we have to equate an individual's intelligence with his score on an established test or battery of tests.

The basic meaning of the word is not in dispute; it refers to the individual's overall capacity in problem-solving and especially in abstract thinking. Some of the debatable issues are:

(1) How can intelligence be most effectively defined and assessed?

(2) Does it operate basically as a unitary trait or by means of several specifiable sub-abilities?

(3) How far is it given at birth and how far are favourable environmental circumstances essential to its development?

(4) To what extent can one legitimately study cognitive abilities in isolation from temperamental and motivational factors?

The organization of this chapter is as follows: the first part deals with the debatable issues exemplified above; the second part is concerned with practical problems, e.g., with the principles of psychological testing and with the interpretation of test scores, and concludes with examples of tests and their application.

As with any scientific concept that corresponds approximately to a popular term of wide connotation, psychologists have been obliged to simplify, to operationalize, and to ensure that the technical usage is narrower than that of common speech. Intelligence testing has often been criticized on the grounds that a test score or quotient does not really provide an adequate description of a person's intelligence, and that various aspects of intelligence as commonly envisaged are not represented. This is fair comment so far as it goes, but it is not a damaging criticism of test scores properly used and interpreted. The doctor, psychologist or social worker requires for many purposes a standardized instrument for diagnosis and prognosis. He should not expect this to provide a complete picture of the client's abilities and aptitudes, but rather an approximate, limited, but none the less highly useful thumb-nail sketch, which will possess the crucial advantage of being interpretable in terms of carefully prepared norms for the population. The layman's attitude tends to expect too much or too little, to alternate between imagining that tests produce perfectly reliable and valid results, and, on the other hand, condemning them as inadequate because they do not embody all the facets of such a vague and wide concept as 'intelligence'.

Nevertheless, the man-in-the-street is right in believing that cognitive tests, as used in the past and as currently available, have tended to omit important aspects or areas of mental functioning. A great deal of research and experimental work has been done in recent years that may be expected to improve this situation. The range of relevant research is wide, but there are two areas that have attracted particular attention: (*a*) the study of divergent thinking and creativity; and (*b*) the analysis of concept formation and development in children, especially in connection with the seminal work of Jean Piaget and his associates in Geneva. But before describing these recent developments, it will be appropriate to sketch very briefly the history of attempts to assess individual differences in intelligence.

During the latter half of the nineteenth century, the writings of Herbert Spencer and of Francis Galton were influential in formulating more clearly the concept of general mental ability. In addition, Galton, who was a polymath experimentalist in biology and in the social sciences, and who may fairly be called the originator both of biometry and of mental testing, was active in developing techniques for the assessment of psychological traits. But the turning-point at which the experimental and statistical study of human abilities commenced in earnest occurred about 1900. Alfred Binet in France and Charles Spearman in England began at that time to conduct experiments and publish papers that have continued largely to determine the theory and practice of intelligence testing. The most widely used individual test of intelligence has been successively adapted and modified from Binet's original scale, and the most widely used group tests have been based on principles clearly formulated by Spearman. Similar work was done in the United States during this early period, notably by J. McK. Cattell and E. L. Thorndike, and in all three countries the assessment of individual differences

Intelligence

in ability has been lastingly influenced by the views of these pioneers. In the three or four subsequent decades, up to about the time of the Second World War, the most important figures continuing this work in Britain and the USA respectively were Sir Cyril Burt and L. L. Thurstone. In particular, they showed that the concept of general intelligence, with which Binet and Spearman were primarily concerned, was in many ways insufficient to account for all the observed data; although important, it required supplementation by the investigation of other abilities, relatively more specific but general enough to enter into quite a wide range of performance.

The main reason why Binet's work was fundamental is that he was the first to attempt a systematic and thorough investigation of what children could do at particular ages and stages of development. Before his enquiries, this was a matter essentially of opinion and speculation. By developing what were the first practicable and satisfactory scales he was able to establish norms of mental performance at each successive year of life, so that it became possible adequately to assess a child's level of intelligence relative to a representative sample of children of the same age. Second, Binet's concept of intelligence was broad and eclectic, so that he aimed to sample skills ranging from fairly abstract reasoning to the handling of practical daily problems. An immediate consequence of the use of the first Binet tests was the reclassification of numerous children who had been labelled as mentally defective, but who were found to be merely backward and susceptible to remedial education. Similar results were obtained by Burt soon after he was appointed as the first psychologist to the London County Council in 1913.

Spearman's researches were of equal importance, but for different reasons. He was less concerned with assessing the individual child than with charting the structure of intelligence and abilities in whole populations, and also to a large degree with developing and improving the appropriate statistical techniques, such as those of correlation and factor analysis. He was especially eager to establish rigorously the existence of a unitary, high-level ability that could properly be described as general intelligence. His method was to demonstrate that most assessable skills and types of intellectual performance were positively correlated. In simple terms, if and only if there is a strong statistical tendency for people who perform well on one cognitive task to perform well on all, will it be possible to isolate a factor of intelligence. This tendency was found, though extensive qualifications were later required; and it is important also to note that such a tendency is only a statistical average. It does not, for instance, preclude numerous individuals from performing well on one kind of intellectual problem and poorly on another.

The extent to which this finding by Spearman was valid is still not finally settled, though there is a fair measure of agreement. Considerable controversy about this issue occurred during the period 1910–40, and it became clear that the finding required some modification, as will be described in the next section.

General intelligence and specific abilities

So far we have skirted around the question of how far intellectual performance can be accounted for by one massive cognitive factor, as strongly urged by Spearman, or how far more specific abilities play an important part. The problem appears akin to problems of taxonomy in medicine and psychiatry. What is the least misleading classification of the neuroses and psychoses? How justifiable is the implicit grouping together of rather diverse conditions under the generic title of schizophrenia? Until the aetiology and causative factors are more fully understood, many of these groupings are debatable, and alternative classifications might be quite defensible.

Since mental tests yield numerical scores, attempts to find an agreed taxonomy and analyses of the structure of cognitive abilities have depended largely upon statistical techniques such as those of correlation and factor analysis already mentioned. To provide even a superficial description of the results obtained, it will be necessary to discuss these methods slightly more technically, but here again one should bear in mind that conclusions drawn from these correlational studies apply on the average to a population and not necessarily to any individual.

The correlation coefficient, which can take any value from $+1 \cdot 0$ through zero to $-1 \cdot 0$, is a measure of the extent to which two variables (e.g., scores on two mental tests) co-vary positively or negatively. If two tests, when administered to a sizeable group of people, yield a substantial degree of positive correlation, this is taken as evidence that they are tapping, probably in varying degrees, a single ability. If however the resulting correlation is zero, this suggests that the tests are measures of two distinct and independent abilities. Spearman generalized this kind of interpretation by devising a more complex type of statistical technique known as factor analysis, whereby the common factor partly measured by each of a number of variables could be isolated. He found that one such common factor emerged from a wide variety of different scores, e.g., on mental tests and school examinations, and described this factor as g. It was interpreted as general intelligence or general capacity for abstract reasoning, but given the alphabetical label to distinguish it from vague popular conceptions. Of the original measures, some were found to have higher 'factor loadings' than others;

that is, to be more satisfactory as measures of *g*. From then on constructors of intelligence tests devoted much of their effort to devising items that would be highly loaded in or 'saturated' with *g*.

Spearman's picture subsequently proved to be too simple. Further research showed that, after the general factor interpretable as intelligence had been 'extracted', further common factors were detectable, these not being common to all the original measures but to several of them. Thus, tasks involving computation tended to yield a factor interpretable as numerical ability, tasks involving manipulation of shapes as spatial ability, and so forth. The accepted picture among British psychologists became one of a hierarchy of abilities of decreasing generality from general intelligence to very specific skills.

Unfortunately, the method of factor analysis cannot unequivocally demonstrate any single taxonomy as correct. Given a set of data such as the correlations between a battery of tests, alternative classifications are possible. If disagreements occur also, as they do, about what selection of variables most adequately represents the entire domain of intellectual skills, the apparent structure of abilities may take many different forms. It must also be remembered that it is quite easy to refer to a particular factor as, say, spatial ability, but quite another matter to demonstrate true isomorphism, i.e., that the factor referred to is identical with the name you decide to give it. The hierarchical model just described legitimately maximizes the importance of general intelligence. Several American authorities, notably L. L. Thurstone and J. P. Guilford, have constructed models that legitimately minimize it.

Thurstone's model comprises some six or seven 'primary mental abilities' (for which tests are available). The pattern differs slightly according to the age-range being considered, but generally includes factors of verbal meaning, spatial ability, inductive reasoning, numerical ability, and verbal fluency. These factors are themselves positively correlated, though to a relatively small extent, and this implies that they can be combined to form an estimate of general intelligence.

Guilford's scheme is harder to reconcile with the retention of a general intelligence factor. In effect, he splits intelligence into no less than 120 independent facets or components; separate tests for most of these rather specific intellectual skills have emerged from his laboratory (Guilford and Hoepfner, 1963). The number 120 derives from his three-way classification of abilities into operations (e.g., cognition, memory, evaluation), products (e.g., units, relations), and contents (e.g., figural, symbolic). One of the 120 abilities will consist, for instance, of cognition applied to figural material to produce a relation. The model is too elaborate to describe in detail here; for an exhaustive account, consult Guilford (1967). For a recent discussion of the advantages and disadvantages of the system and its relation to other models, see also the chapters by Merrifield, by Vernon and by Butcher in Dockrell (1970).

In spite of the existence of these alternative models, and of others not described here, general intelligence is recognized by the majority of psychologists as an important concept. For example, in the very numerous situations in experimental and social psychology where it is necessary to control or allow for variations in ability, the general practice is to use a measure of general intelligence rather than the more specific measures such as those devised by Thurstone or Guilford. Similarly, in the next section, where we shall describe some of the work on hereditary and environmental influences, it will be clear that most of this work has been concerned with general intelligence and that less is known about the relative contributions of these influences to, for example, spatial ability, and very little about their contribution to skills as specific as those defined by Guilford. In clinical and educational work, this applies even more strongly. Measures of general intelligence are extremely serviceable, whereas the employment of measures of spatial or numerical ability has proved on the whole less helpful. Admittedly, many of the general tests used in clinical practice include sub-tests that permit the plotting of individual profiles, but these sub-tests have usually been devised pragmatically and not from models of the kind just described.

It does appear likely, however, that future test development will be influenced by two areas of research briefly mentioned earlier, one of which partly derives from Guilford's model. One of the operations defined by Guilford is 'divergent thinking', by which is meant the kind of activity involved in generating ideas and hypotheses, as contrasted with 'convergent' problem-solving. The latter converges towards an accepted or objectively defined solution, the former is more open-ended and is involved in the sort of situation where there is no single right answer. The recent research into creative abilities has frequently been linked with this concept of divergent thinking. Many new tests have been constructed, notably by Guilford and his associates, to assess divergent thinking abilities; these have sometimes been used in selection procedures, though such use is still experimental. They have so far rarely been used for diagnostic or clinical purposes. The second relatively new influence on the study of intelligence and on the construction of instruments for its assessment is the work of Jean Piaget on concept attainment and the growth of concepts in children (see Chapter 8). Developments in these two areas have, for instance, directly influenced the construction of the new British Intelligence Scale, which will be considered in more detail later.

Intelligence

The relative influences of heredity and environment

The literature on the relative contributions of heredity and environment to human intelligence is extensive, probably amounting to several thousand books and papers. This question has always been controversial and two collections of papers have recently been published by the *Harvard Educational Review* that contain some heated debate between American psychologists of strongly opposed views. (see Jensen *et al.*, 1969, *Environment, Heredity and Intelligence*, and *Science, Heritability and IQ*, reprinted from the *Harvard Educational Review*.)

Extreme views of the issue are not new. John Locke, the English empirical philosopher of the seventeenth century, believed that the mind of the newborn infant was a *tabula rasa* or blank sheet and that individual differences in intellect developed entirely through sense-data. The opposite view was held, for instance, by the French writer Gobineau, who believed that such differences were entirely innate.

No responsible authority would now maintain that the degree of human intelligence was determined only by genetic differences, nor that such differences exercise no effect. Clearly the remaining area of controversy is concerned with the complex interaction of hereditary and environmental influences.

There is good evidence that within the normal range of human intelligence, with which we shall here be mainly concerned, inherited differences exercise a considerable influence. These are due to the combined action of a large but unknown number of genes. The influence of single genes is much less observable in human cognitive psychology, except as causing a few, comparatively rare types of mental defect. Examples are the conditions of phenylketonuria and galactosemia. In the former, a gene mutation results in a metabolic block whereby the amino-acid phenylalanine is not broken down, but accumulates in toxic amounts in the bloodstream. This accumulation causes, in a manner not fully understood, severe mental retardation. If the condition can be diagnosed shortly after birth, the retardation can be prevented or minimized by the prescription of a special diet consisting largely of fruit and vegetables and as low as possible in phenylalanine. Galactosemia is similarly caused by a single defective gene and again may cause severe mental retardation. The patient is unable to metabolize galactose, and treatment is again mainly dietary.

One of the most common forms of severe mental subnormality arises from a chromosomal abnormality. This is Down's syndrome, or mongolism, so called because one of the physical signs is a fold on the eyelid which results in a supposedly Oriental appearance. As recently as 1959 this condition, which had previously been generally ascribed to environmental causes, was found to arise from a trisomy, i.e. from the presence of an extra chromosome (No. 21). The factors that result in the presence of this trisomy have been the subject of considerable recent research. It has been known for a long time that the incidence of mongoloid births rises sharply with maternal age, and evidence is now available that this incidence co-varies with the incidence of some virus infections. It may also be dependent to some degree on maternal exposure to radiation, e.g., from X-rays. Mongolism accounts for about one quarter of all severe mental subnormality in England and Wales, as assessed by a study of the fifteen- to nineteen-year age-group (Kushlick, 1966).

Category		0·00 0·10 0·20 0·30 0·40 0·50 0·60 0·70 0·80 0·90	Groups Included
Unrelated persons	Reared apart		4
	Reared together		5
Fosterparent–child			3
Parent–child			12
Siblings	Reared apart		2
	Reared together		35
Twins Two-egg	Opposite sex		9
	Like sex		11
Twins One-egg	Reared apart		4
	Reared together		14

Figure 6.1 Correlation coefficients for 'intelligence' test scores from 52 studies. Some studies reported data for more than one relationship category; some included more than one sample per category giving a total of 99 groups (from L. Erlenmeyer-Kimling and L. F. Jarvik, 'Genetics and Intelligence: a Review', *Science*, NY, 1963, 142, 1477–9. Copyright 1963 by the American Association for the Advancement of Science)

Within the normal range of intelligence, the effects of heredity can be disentangled only by sophisticated statistical techniques. Even with their aid, conclusions remain tentative, since it is difficult to say how far some of the assumptions are legitimate. The most telling evidence for genetic determination comes from twin studies, and more generally from other comparisons of the similarity in mental level between relatives of varying degrees of consanguinity. This evidence is such that a considerable degree of determination can hardly be denied, as is conveniently summarized in Figure 6.1. Apart from the convincing overall picture, many of the correlations shown correspond fairly closely to the theoretical figures that would be expected if measured intelligence were entirely determined by a polygenic mechanism of inheritance.

From these correlations, and most conveniently from those between monozygotic and dizygotic twins, an index of heritability may be calculated. This index is an estimate of the ratio within a given population of inherited variance in test performance to total variance (excluding error variance). This inherited component can in turn be divided conceptually, and to some extent empirically, into four subcomponents of which the first is the most important. These are genic (additive) variance, variance due to assortative mating, variance due to the dominance of particular genes, and epistasis (interaction among genes at different loci). After the basic additive sub-component, that due to assortative mating is the next most important. The tendency among human beings for like to mate with like in terms of intelligence level is strong, producing an estimated correlation of $+\cdot5$ or $+\cdot6$ between husband and wife, which is higher than for any other known characteristic, including physical ones such as height (Huntley, 1966; Jensen, 1969). Such findings, however, need considerable qualification if they are not to be misinterpreted.

First, any estimate of heritability is specific to a particular population studied and to the environmental circumstances prevalent at the time. An especially important reservation of this kind arises in connection with controversy about differential average intelligence among ethnic groups. Any conclusion that one ethnic group is innately more intelligent than another is at present speculative. Another qualification is that no estimate of heritability is meaningful in the case of an individual; it is quite impossible by any scientific means to estimate how far a single person's intelligence is inherited. Finally, the fact that a quality shows a high index of heritability does not mean that it is not modifiable. The tendency to pulmonary tuberculosis would at one time have shown a high index of heritability, but liability to the disease has during the last two decades become much more influenced by extent of exposure to the bacillus and much less by inherited predisposition.

When questions concerning the relative contributions of heredity and environment to human intelligence are debated theoretically in scientific journals and considered in the most abstract terms, they frequently generate heated discussion. When such issues are narrowed down to the consideration of observed differences between particular ethnic and cultured groups, they become highly inflammable. The reaction to Jensen's long paper (*Harvard Educational Review*, 1969), is ample support for this statement, especially, for instance, the paper by Brazziel published in the next issue of the same journal.

In the preceding sections we have tried to steer a course well away from the extreme and implausible positions that are often adopted on platforms or in the popular press about intelligence and abilities. As we have already conveyed, a position somewhere in the middle is necessary on many of these issues; we emphasize some of the reservations and qualifications one must make in interpreting test results, yet it is necessary also to stress that such results contain valid and important information that it would be foolish to reject entirely. In reviewing work on supposed inter-cultural differences in intelligence and especially work such as Jensen's that claims to demonstrate heritable differences between ethnic groups, it is even more essential to aim at a calm and selective attitude. One of us has analysed the relevant literature up to 1967 in some detail, and has also commented specifically on a paper by Jensen (Butcher, 1968, chapter 10; 1972). Here it will be possible only to select a few salient points to discuss in outline.

We do not believe that the investigation of group differences in measured intelligence should be the subject of moral exhortations or be declared a taboo topic; the same applies to a consideration of whether such differences, if adequately demonstrated, are primarily environmental or genetic in origin. The most discussed example of this issue has been the regularly observed finding that in terms of measured IQ, Negroes in the USA tend to score on average some fifteen points lower than whites. There is ample evidence that a component of this difference is accounted for by environmental factors and cultural deprivation, but Jensen would hold that this component amounts to only about one-third of the observed difference. This is the case that has provoked a considerable furore in recent years, and three or four comments on it may not be out of place.

Jensen is correct in maintaining that those who wish to ascribe the whole difference to environmental factors have not substantiated their case. He also produces telling evidence that Mexicans, for instance, living in a poor and culturally deprived community according to the normal standards of assessment, score markedly higher on intelligence tests than Negroes in the same school system. It is very probable to our mind, however, that more of the difference is due to environmental factors than Jensen would allow, and that the conventional assessments of cultural deprivation are inadequate to make allowance for the long history of Negro oppression, which has been of quite a different order from the other examples of depressed socio-economic status commonly assessed by psychologists and sociologists. Much of the indignation inspired by Jensen's claims has been a generous but misguided reaction. If a proportion of the measured difference between American blacks and whites is due to heritable factors, this does not imply that such differences are immutable (as Jensen himself has pointed out). But it does suggest an even more damning indictment of white American policy towards the Negro (see Eysenck, 1971) than would be implied by a demonstration that the differences were entirely environmental.

Probably the most important recent work on inter-ethnic differences in ability, and on the social and cultural factors that determine such differences, is that of Vernon (1969), as summarized in his book *Intelligence and Cultural Environment*. This extensive series of researches made it fairly clear that for future investigations of this kind the global concept of general intelligence will be too crude, whatever its usefulness as a first approximation. Vernon investigated groups of children in England, in the Outer Hebrides, in parts of Africa, in the West Indies and in Canada (including Canadian Eskimos). His most general conclusion was that each group certainly showed variations in the pattern of abilities. (Compare the similar findings of Lesser, Fifer and Clark, 1965, even within one relatively restricted urban environment). Children in under-developed countries sometimes reached or surpassed western standards on some tests, but fell on others below what would be regarded in western industrial countries on the borderline of mental deficiency. These inter-ethnic differences were paralleled to a considerable degree by social class differences within the countries, although these were complicated by such factors as common schooling and cultural pattern. It was clear also that sheer amount of schooling, even if not of the highest quality, helped to promote both school achievement and the kind of reasoning assessed in non-verbal intelligence tests.

Psychological tests

Before discussing the types of test available an attempt must be made to define the term 'test'. A shortened definition would be that a test is an objective and standard measure of a sample of behaviour. No psychological test can do more than sample behaviour, and it is important for the tester to understand what is meant by behaviour' and how behaviour can be altered, especially under test conditions.

Behaviour can be seen as an interface reaction between the individual and the environment. If people are asked to describe an individual then they will tend to do so in terms of genetics, personality development and past experience. These three broad groups of characteristics fairly adequately describe any individual. Similarly, descriptions of the environment will be made in objective (physical) terms or subjective (psychological) terms. Behaviour will be the resultant of the individual reacting with his environment – this is what a test will sample.

On this basis it is easy to see why the test situation must be properly controlled: both the tester and his equipment will be part of the environment, and if this is allowed to vary, then the behaviour sampled will vary and the result will hardly be standardized or objective.

Tests can be classified in various ways but there are two broad categories: those tests which attempt to make predictions, and those which 'sum up' or provide a kind of inventory of the individual. The predictive type seems a little like the crystal-ball and in effect says things like 'Johnny has a fine brain and should get to the University', whilst the other type says 'Johnny is now aged eight years and yet he can do the arithmetic of an average child of ten years'. This latter type offers you a bald statement about the existing situation; the first type endeavours to be predictive, using the existing situation as a guide.

In actuality the predictive element in testing is always present whatever the test, because of the time element involved and the fact that the test is only sampling behaviour. If one had the time to assess exhaustively all that an individual knew about, say, mathematics, then testing would not be needed. It is for this reason that a number of tests are often used on the one individual in order to provide more information and a greater degree of certainty about the result. It is a matter of balancing the time available against the information required, and tests enable the user to obtain the most information in the least time.

In order to categorize tests more fully it will be necessary to examine not only the type of test, but also the way in which it is administered by the examiner or completed by the person under examination.

Types of Test

General Intelligence Test. The construction of a test to assess the overall level of intellectual functioning has long been the crock of gold at the end of the psychologist's rainbow. A consequence is that this category constitutes one of the largest groups of test. They are available to test from infant to adult level and in practically any form of completion or administration method. Examples: Stanford-Binet Scales; Wechsler Scales, e.g. Wechsler Adult Intelligence Scale (WAIS) and Wechsler Intelligence Scale for Children (WISC); Raven's Progressive Matrices.

Multiple Aptitude Batteries. The advent of factorial analysis has paved the way in contemporary psychology for a differential approach to the measurement of abilities. These tests produce a set of scores in different aptitudes and provide a profile highlighting the intellectual strengths and weaknesses of the person. The obvious application for this type of test is in vocational guidance, where a 'global' intelligence quotient gives less information than a set of scores for individual and non-overlapping aptitudes. Examples: Science Research Associates' Primary Mental Abilities (PMA): this battery was the direct result of the work of Thurstone mentioned in an earlier section of this chapter. General Aptitude Test Battery (GATB), promoted by the United States Education Service and used in vocational guidance.

Special Aptitudes. These tests fill the gap between the general intelligence test and the multiple aptitude battery. They provide additional information to add to an intelligence quotient and are available to test aptitude ranging from manual dexterity to art appreciation. Example: Seashore Measures of Musical Talents.

Achievement or Attainment Tests. These are designed to assess the work done and the knowledge achieved after a certain course of instruction has been taken. Unlike the aptitude test they form an inventory of existing knowledge rather than predict the use an individual might make of a particular ability. Examples: Schonell's Reading, Spelling and Arithmetic Tests; or the Neale Reading Tests.

Personality Tests. In most situations calling for the individual assessment of a person's intelligence it is also valuable to have information about his personality characteristics. Claridge, in Chapter 7, discusses personality and its assessment, and the use of personality tests will not be described separately here.

Manner of Completion or Administration of Tests

Individual Tests. These tests are given on a one-to-one basis: one subject and one tester. They require that the tester should be trained and proficient in their correct administration. It is not possible to concentrate sufficiently on the responses the subject is making if the tester is fumbling with the equipment; he should know the test so well that all his attention is given to the subject. An individual test such as the Stanford-Binet Form L-M is carefully standardized against a large population of children, and the result is meaningful only if the same routine is carried out in every case – the 'Bloggs' Corruption of the Stanford-Binet has no standardization, every test is a unique event, and there will be no point in comparing the result with the age-norms provided for the test. These tests can also perform a useful secondary function and serve as a clinical means enabling the tester to make valuable, though qualitative, additional observations on the ways in which the person tackles the problems, meets frustration, whether he is slow and thorough or quick and careless. Examples: Stanford-Binet Scales; Wechsler Scales; Merrill-Palmer Pre-school Scale.

Group Tests. These tests are given to numbers of subjects simultaneously. Thus, at induction centres large numbers of recruits into the Army may be given the Progressive Matrices Test. The role of the tester is minimal, and this ensures that a degree of uniformity is built into the test situation. An advantage is that the results can be processed rapidly – often by machine – and that large numbers of people can be assessed in a short time. Group tests are often used as a screening device because of this. On the debit side it is not possible to ensure that each individual has full supervision during the test, and information about his manner of working will be lost. Examples: A. Heim's Tests (AH_4, 5 and 6); Raven's Progressive Matrices; National Foundation for Educational Research and Moray House Tests of Intelligence.

Pencil and Paper Tests. Any test where the subject makes a response by writing an answer or making some mark on the question paper or a separate answer paper. Example: Raven's Progressive Matrices.

Performance Test. In contrast to the last, the subject now makes his response by manipulating some apparatus; this might simply be fitting the pieces of a jigsaw together. Usually this test is given on an individual basis, but groups have been assessed in this way, especially in the Armed Forces. Examples: Seguin Form Board; Kohs' Block Design Test; Porteus' Maze Tests.

Language Tests. The medium of communication in most tests is by language; and the instructions, and often the response, require that some language should be used. Sometimes the term 'verbal' test is applied to this category, but this should properly be reserved for the description of the content of a test as opposed to its administration. Examples: Stanford-Binet Scales; Wechsler Scales.

Non-Language Tests. These tests make no use of language and can theoretically be given to the deaf, the illiterate or foreigners. Care must be taken when using this type of test, particularly where cross-cultural testing is involved. Examples: Raven's Progressive Matrices; Porteus' Maze Tests.

The Main Individually Administered Tests

Stanford-Binet. The importance of the contribution made by Alfred Binet (1875–1911) to psychometrics cannot be overestimated. In 1904 the French Minister of Public Instruction set up a commission to consider ways of educating subnormal children in the Paris schools. This necessarily involved the 'discovery' and assessment of these children. To this end, Binet, in collaboration with Simon, produced the first Binet-Simon Scale in 1905. The essence of this scale was that an individual child was assessed against a background of what average children of various ages could do. This has been the fundamental concept underlying the assessment of children ever since. A revised scale was produced in 1908 and for the first time the test items were grouped in 'age years', i.e., the tests passed by the average seven-year-old were grouped as year VII. A child's score was now expressed as a mental age (MA), and would be the age of 'normal' children whose performance was the same as that of the subject. The scale was extended and revised in 1911, the year of Binet's untimely death.

The Binet-Simon Scales achieved wide popularity and were adapted for use in many countries outside France. The first American revision was made in 1916 at Stanford University by Terman and his associates. It was in this test that the concept of the intelligence quotient (IQ) was introduced.

In order to calculate the IQ, the MA, as found from the test, was compared with the chronological age (CA) by means of the formula:

$$IQ = \frac{MA}{CA} \times 100$$

This IQ should not be thought of as a percentage. Although it is tempting to see the IQ in strictly quantitative terms, this can lead to misunderstandings. For example, it is possible to say that a child with an IQ of 100 is more intelligent than a child with an IQ of 50, but *not* that he is twice as intelligent.

The second Stanford-Binet Scale was produced in 1937 and was in two parallel forms, L and M. The idea was that if a child had first been tested using, say, Form L, then he could be re-tested at any time using Form M without invalidating the result. In 1960 the opportunity was taken to amalgamate the best items from both forms and the new Form L-M was produced, often known as the Terman-Merrill Form L-M. It covers an age-range from two years up to adult level but is most commonly used in the mid-range.

The Stanford-Binet has been criticized because it has a large verbal element. This depends on what part of the scale is being used. In the early years the items are mainly performance, as might be expected for children in whom speed and vocabulary are only just developing. It is only towards the adult end of the scale that the verbal emphasis appears. In the mid-range there is a reasonable mixture of verbal and performance items, and it is in this mid-range that the test is most commonly used. A typical verbal item may involve the unravelling of an absurd statement or the explanation of a proverb, whilst performance items include threading beads, drawing, or manipulating pieces of card to form a given shape.

The Wechsler Scales. The original Wechsler-Bellevue Scale was published in 1939 and was designed to provide an intelligence test for adults. Both this scale and the 1955 version (known as the Wechsler Adult Intelligence Scale or WAIS) are part verbal and part performance. The test produces three quotients: one for the verbal scale, one for the performance scale, and one for the two combined or the full scale.

The Wechsler Intelligence Scale for Children (WISC), 1949, was prepared as a downward extension of the Wechsler-Bellevue Scale, and was designed for children from the age of five to fifteen years. Like the WAIS it is part verbal and part performance. In a clinical setting it is not always easy to handle this test with young or dull children, and this has now been remedied by the publication, in 1967, of the Wechsler Pre-School and Primary Scale of Intelligence (WPPSI).

A typical verbal item in the Wechsler Scales might involve giving the meaning of various words or the answering of questions requiring information of a general kind. Performance items include jigsaw type questions or the production of a given pattern from a number of coloured blocks, or the arrangement of pictures in order to make a story.

The British Intelligence Scale (BIS). This scale has been under construction for some ten years and will fill an obvious need. The existing intelligence tests (or batteries) in Britain, designed to be administered individually, are essentially two in number, both developed in the USA. These are the successive derivatives of the scales originally devised by Binet at the beginning of this century, and the Wechsler batteries, both already described here. Although these are widely used, dissatisfaction with them is frequently expressed by practitioners, both because they appear somewhat out of date in terms of present views about the structure of abilities, and because some of the claims about their clinical and diagnostic value now appear to have been overoptimistic.

Ward and Fitzpatrick (1970) describe how the new BIS had its origins in informal discussions, originally convened by Sir Cyril Burt, P. E. Vernon and Gertrude Keir of London University in 1960, which developed into the formation of a more formal committee. By 1964 the views of a considerable number, both of academic and of practising psychologists, had been obtained about what kind of material the proposed scale should contain, and shortly afterwards a large research grant was supplied by the Department of Education and Science to support the project for a period of five years, under the direction of the late Professor F. Warburton at the University of Manchester.

The original plan of the BIS envisaged that it should assess some six factors or components of intelligence, which would correspond to a considerable degree to the 'primary mental factors' first described by L. L. Thurstone in the USA. Its age-range was to run from five to twelve years, and each of the six factors would be represented by two or three sub-tests. It was expected that the entire scale would yield about 120 scorable points and would probably take, on average, about one hour to administer.

As the extensive work of item construction continued, the scheme became enlarged and, it appears, somewhat more complex. The age-range was extended both downwards and upwards, and some of the six factors became considerably differentiated. Thus the factor of 'reasoning' has been interpreted to incorporate 'Piagetian' types of problem-solving, which are described in detail in the paper (quoted above) by Ward and Fitzpatrick.

After considering a number of earlier attempts to quantify problem-solving behaviour and to translate sets of logical operations into psychometric instruments, the test constructors experimented with two new possibilities: 'the TV game' and 'Butch and Slim'. Both these experimental tests attempt to assess the combinatorial analysis of logical propositions described by Inhelder and Piaget as characteristic of the attainment of the stage of formal operations in adolescence.

'Butch and Slim' proved the more successful. These characters are two fictitious criminals who are questioned as to whether they have robbed a bank. They can answer basically in four ways: Butch 'Yes', Slim 'Yes' ($p.q$); Butch 'Yes', Slim 'No' ($p.\bar{q}$); Butch 'No', Slim 'Yes' ($\bar{p}.q$); and Butch 'No', Slim 'No' ($\bar{p}.\bar{q}$). These combinations are again shown on four cards. The subject is then given a true statement made by Butch and has to identify, in the light of this, which of the compound propositions on the four cards would be true. Thus if Butch says 'We robbed the bank together', only the statement where both Butch and Slim say 'Yes' can be true. From this approach thirty-two items have been derived, sixteen of which refer to the condition in which Butch is telling the truth (affirmation), sixteen to the condition in which Butch is telling a lie (negation). 'Butch and Slim' is the game which has been used in the try-out and several associated researches. Preliminary results suggest that it may possess considerable promise for work with intelligent adolescents.

Lack of space unfortunately precludes a fuller description of this test and of the other interesting innovations incorporated in the new scale. A very great deal of work was put into the trying out of such instruments, both by the test constructors and by a panel of experienced educational psychologists who provided several thousand man-hours of their time. The enterprise was greatly slowed down by the tragic death of Professor F. Warburton, but at the time of writing there is every indication that the second part of the project will be recommenced on a similar scale. This latter part will be primarily concerned with the establishment of norms and the production of a manual of instructions for the scale's use.

Factors Affecting Test Performance

Exogenous. These are factors from outside the person being tested, and range from extraneous noises to scoring errors on the part of the tester. One well-remembered test room was ideal, except for the Town Hall clock that struck the quarter hours just over the road. Errors by the tester may be due to unfamiliarity with the test or possibly the doubtful or ambiguous nature of the responses. The only safeguard is to make sure that the tester is properly trained and qualified in the use of the test material.

Endogenous. These are factors arising from within the subject. Severe physical disabilities are fairly easily recognized, but it is possible to overlook partial deafness; even the person himself may not know he suffers from this. *Petit mal* epilepsy is another condition that can be overlooked. An experienced tester is unlikely to miss anything significant. Temporary states due to medication must also be noted, otherwise you may be assessing the effects of the drug and not the performance of the subject!

Personal psychological problems form perhaps the largest group of endogenous factors seen in the clinical setting. The nature of the referral may give a clue to what these are, and the tester is forewarned. If not, the patient must be closely watched in case his poor responses are due to his emotional difficulties and not to the test. The obsessional neurotic is a case in point; he may be particularly handicapped if there is a time limit on the test.

Test Interpretation

Problems of interpretation may arise with intelligence test results. Knowledge of the numerical IQ alone is seldom enough, since a person's potentialities can scarcely be summed up by a number such as 83! Tables of test norms are concerned with the performance of groups of people and with average responses; it would be quite possible for two people to obtain exactly the same score but achieve it in very different ways. It is therefore necessary to analyse the 'global' test result in terms of the relative contributions of different kinds of item in order to make it more meaningful as an assessment of a particular individual. See, in this connection, an excellent paper by Eysenck (1967) in which he discusses the many different variables that contribute to the intellectual performance summarized by the IQ figure; e.g., the way in which the person works, whether quickly, carelessly or accurately and slowly, is easily defeated, or persistent in the face of difficulty, and so on.

A knowledge of test construction and the underlying statistics is also helpful to the proper interpretation of results. If a child scores an IQ of 100, and a year later this drops to 95, then it is hardly evidence of deterioration since both IQs are within the average range and much less than one standard deviation apart.

Care must be used in the interpretation of mental age scores. It may be that a girl of fourteen years has a mental age of ten years, but this is not to say that she should be treated like a ten-year-old child. Admittedly she responds to the test like the average ten-year-old, but in many other respects she will be fourteen.

Psychologists have usually found it helpful, in communicating test results to other people, to describe IQs in verbal equivalents, such as:

145+	Brilliant
130+	Very superior
115+	Superior
105+	High average
95+	Average
85+	Low average
70+	Inferior
55+	Very inferior
55−	Severely subnormal

You will notice that the supposedly normal distribution of intelligence is here being 'sliced' into areas of one standard deviation apiece, except in the average region. About 60 per cent of the population are in the average category, 15 per cent in the superior category, and 5 per cent in the very superior to brilliant. About 15–20 per cent are in the inferior bracket.

References

Ashby, B., Morrison, A. and Butcher, H. J. (1970). 'The Abilities and Attainments of Immigrant Children', *Res. Educ.* 4, pp. 73–80.
Burgess, J. and Jahoda, M. (1970). 'The Interpretation of Certain Data in "How much can we boost IQ and scholastic achievement?"', *Bull. Br. Psychol. Soc.* 23, pp. 224–5.
Burt, C. (1940). *The Factors of the Mind.* University of London Press.
Butcher, H. J. (1968). *Human Intelligence.* London: Methuen.
Butcher, H. J. (1972). Comment on Arthur Jensen's 'Do schools cheat minority children?', *Educ. Res.* 14, pp. 92–5.
Butcher, H. J. and Lomax, D. E. (eds) (1972). *Readings in Human Intelligence.* London: Methuen.
Dockrell, B. (ed.) (1970). *On Intelligence.* London: Methuen.
Eysenck, H. J. (1967). 'Intelligence Assessment: a Theoretical and Experimental Approach', *Br. J. Educ. Psychol.* 37, pp. 81–98.
Eysenck, H. J. (1971). *Race, Intelligence and Education.* London: Temple Smith.

Gesell, A. (1942). *The First Five Years of Life.* London: Methuen.
Gesell, A. (1948). *Studies in Child Development.* New York: Harper.
Gesell, A. (1954). 'The Ontogenesis of Infant Behaviour', in *Manual of Child Psychology* (ed. L. Carmichael). New York: Wiley.
Griffiths, Ruth (1954). *The Abilities of Babies.* University of London Press.
Guilford, J. P. (1967). *The Nature of Human Intelligence.* New York: McGraw-Hill.
Guilford, J. P. and Hoepfner, R. (1963). *Current Summary of Structure-of-interest Factors and Suggested Tests.* From: the Psychological Laboratory, The University of Southern California.
Haeussermann, E. (1958). *Developmental Potential of Pre-school Children.* New York: Grune and Stratton.
Heim, A. (1970). *Intelligence and Personality.* Harmondsworth: Penguin.
Huntley, R. M. C. (1966). 'Heritability of Intelligence', in *Genetic and Environmental Factors in Human Ability* (eds J. E. Meade and A. S. Parkes). Edinburgh: Oliver & Boyd.
Jensen, A. R. (1969). 'How Much can we Boost IQ and Scholastic Achievement?', *Harvard Educ. Rev.* 39, pp. 1–123.
Jensen, A. R. (1970). 'Twin Differences and Race Differences in IQ: a Reply to Burgess and Jahoda', *Bull. Br. Psychol. Soc.* 23, pp. 224–5.
Jensen, A. R. (1971). 'Do Schools Cheat Minority Children?', *Educ. Res.* 14, pp. 3–28.
Kushlick, A. (1966). 'Assessing the Size of the Problem of Subnormality', in *Genetic and Environmental Factors in Human Ability* (eds J. E. Meade and A. S. Parkes). Edinburgh: Oliver & Boyd.
Lesser, G. S., Fifer, G. and Clark, D. H. (1965). 'Mental Abilities of Children from Different Social-class and Cultural Groups', *Monogr. Soc. Res. Child Dev.* 30, 4.
Simon, B. (1971). *Intelligence, Psychology and Education.* London: Lawrence & Wishart.
Stutsman, Rachel (1931). *Mental Measurement of Pre-School Children.* Yonkers: World Book.
Vernon, P. E. (1961). *The Structure of Human Abilities,* 2nd ed. London: Methuen.
Vernon, P. E. (1969). *Intelligence and Cultural Environment.* London: Methuen.
Warburton, F. W., Fitzpatrick, T., Ward, J. and Ritchie, M. (1970). 'Some Problems in the Construction of Individual Intelligence Tests', in *The Psychological Assessment of Mental and Physical Handicaps* (ed. P. Mittler). London: Methuen.
Ward, J. (1970). 'The Factor Structure of the Wechsler Pre-school Scale', *J. Ass. Educ. Psychol.* 2, pp. 31–3.
Ward, J. and Fitzpatrick, T. (1970). 'The New British Intelligence Scale: Construction of Logic Items', *Res. Educ.* 4, pp. 1–23.

Suggestions for further reading

Butcher, H. J. *Human Intelligence.* London: Methuen 1968.
Heim, A. *Intelligence and Personality.* Harmondsworth: Penguin 1970.
Vernon, P. E. *Intelligence and Cultural Environment.* London: Methuen 1969.

Chapter seven

Personality

Gordon Claridge

Some basic concepts

It was once said, 'If all members of any one social group acted alike, thought alike, and felt alike, personality would not exist.' This statement underlines one of the most important facts about people; namely, that each of us (even if we have an identical twin) is psychologically different in one way or another from our fellow men. Most – indeed some psychologists would say all – of this variation constitutes what we recognize in each other as differences in our personalities. Despite the difficulty that individual variation in nature poses for the observer, men throughout the ages have tried to describe, understand, classify and more recently measure, their own personalities. Some of the earliest enquiries arose out of philosophical and theological discussion about the nature of man's identity and a preoccupation with the qualities of the soul. A contrasting, though equally ancient, view of personality is derived from the etymology of the word itself, the *persona*, meaning the mask worn by the early actor to signify his role in the drama. The latter view therefore stressed the more superficial, easily observable features of the behaviour by which an individual's personality is judged; literally the face he presents to the world around him. These two concepts of the personality, or at least the different emphasis they place on the inner as distinct from the outer man, have persisted throughout the history of psychology and can still be seen reflected in contemporary thinking, particularly in the kind of techniques used to study personality.

The more recent history of psychology has given rise to a great variety of approaches to personality, mainly in the form of theories attempting to describe and explain individual differences in the way people think, feel and act. Detailed discussion of most of these theories is beyond the scope of the present chapter. In any case many of them have ceased to influence current psychological thought or have lacked the empirical basis which psychologists, like other natural scientists, now demand of their theories. However, in order to give an idea of the range and kind of data which psychologists working in this field have to explain, it is worth briefly considering some of the different ways in which they have approached the study of personality. In doing so, and indeed throughout this chapter, it should be borne in mind that the differences between various approaches are often largely a matter of emphasis on one facet of personality rather than another.

One aspect of the personality on which opinion has differed has concerned the level of generality at which it is considered useful to describe individual variation. Some writers, largely intent on classification, have searched for clusters or types of personality; that is, groups of individuals who show broadly similar behaviour, feelings and attitudes in a wide range of situations. Others, taking a more analytic standpoint, have tried to break the personality down into its many constituent parts, or traits. A trait is usually defined as a relatively enduring characteristic of the individual which he tends to show in a variety of situations that are likely to elicit the particular behaviour or feeling. Since many thousands of such traits have been described, some psychologists have argued that it is not sufficient to regard the personality as a mere collection of dispositions or habits. Instead they have stressed the integrative nature of personality, which is seen as an organized whole resulting from an interaction between traits.

Turning to the underlying determinants of the personality, here many different opinions have also been expressed. At one extreme, stress has been placed on innate biological factors, either in terms of inherited physiological characteristics or in terms of 'instinctive' drives or impulses. At the other extreme the role of experiences occurring during the psychological development of the individual has been emphasized. Naturally the latter viewpoint has itself been formulated in several different ways. Anthropologists and sociologists have looked towards cultural influences for their explanation of personality differences. Psychologists, on the other hand, have tended to concentrate on the shaping of the personality by the immediate environment, especially the family. Some have done so using psychodynamic, mainly Freudian, conceptions. Others have applied the principles of learning and conditioning as derived from behaviourist psychology.

Although these different approaches to personality have no single distinguishing characteristic, they have tended to vary in one important respect, which is of particular interest to the clinician. It concerns the extent to which they have emphasized, on the one hand, the unique or idiosyncratic nature of each individual's personality; or, on the other, the common elements of behaviour which, in different combinations, account for personality variation. These two approaches to personality have been described as *idiographic* and *nomothetic*, respectively. The idiographic approach stresses the importance of understanding each person as an individual. It therefore focuses on the study of the single case, tends to view personality longitudinally and in depth, and to be less concerned with comparisons across people. In contrast, the nomothetic theorist tends to approach personality cross-sectionally and tries to establish general principles of individual variation by studying large numbers of people, usually at a rather superficial level. Historically, the latter view of personality is derived from the search by scientific psychology as a whole for universally applicable laws and measures of behaviour. The idiographic approach, on the other hand, has been more favoured by those working in a clinical setting because of their greater interest in the observation and description of the individual. Such workers have placed less importance on measurement, though, as we shall see, it is not precluded by the idiographic view of personality.

Before closing this introductory section mention should be made of two other terms often encountered in the early literature on personality: these are *character* and *temperament*. Both have sometimes been used interchangeably with the word 'personality', though it is now agreed that, if either has any useful scientific meaning at all, it refers to only part of the total personality. Furthermore, it is generally assumed that each covers a somewhat different aspect of personality, as can be seen in the popular usage of both terms that has passed into the English language. The word 'character' has taken on two slightly different, though related, meanings. One has ethical or moral connections and describes behaviour as judged against some social norm. Thus, individuals may be referred to as having good or bad characters or as lacking in character. The second meaning considers character from the point of view of its strength or quality, the weak character, for example, being considered as someone with poor impulse control. Neither usage has much scientific validity; and the term is rarely employed by professional psychologists. However, psychiatrists have retained the term in their clinical description, 'character disorder', a somewhat evaluative diagnosis reserved for patients without any obvious mental illness but considered, because of their antisocial and incorrigible behaviour, to have a profound defect of personality.

The term 'temperament' has also provided our language with a number of expressions which we commonly use to describe the personalities of others. A person may be considered 'hot-tempered', 'sweet-tempered', or even just 'temperamental'. These descriptions reflect a traditionally held view that the temperament refers to the emotional aspects of the personality, in particular its physiological and constitutional basis. As will be discussed in a moment, some of the earliest attempts to classify personality were in fact descriptions of temperamental types based on observations about the way people differ in their emotional reactions. Like 'character', the term 'temperament' is now rarely used as a scientific term by psychologists.

Classification of personality

Detailed analysis of any kind of individual variation, whether it be of physical elements, biological species, or personalities, presupposes the existence of some logical and agreed system of classification, or taxonomy. Unfortunately, psychology is not yet in the happy position of having achieved a universally acceptable way of classifying people according to their personalities. This is not to say that suggestions for such a taxonomy have been lacking. Indeed, during psychology's long history many different personality typologies, as they are called, have been devised. Most are now of little more than minor historical interest, but to understand how current views on the problem evolved it is necessary to look briefly at some earlier attempts at classification.

If not the first, certainly the most enduring, taxonomic system was derived from the so-called classic theory of temperaments, which recognized four temperamental types differing in emotional make-up: the melancholic, the phlegmatic, the choleric, and the sanguine. This typology first appeared in the writings of the early Greek thinkers and physicians, notably Hippocrates, though it persisted down the centuries into the modern period. For example, the eighteenth-century philosopher, Kant, referred to it as a fundamental scheme for classifying human temperaments.

More recently developed typologies, of which there were many during the early part of this century, were mostly derived from various attempts to identify a single psychological characteristic which could be considered fundamental enough to form the basis of classification. Some writers chose their distinguishing characteristic as a result of observations made on psychiatric patients, who were considered to represent normal personality variation in an exaggerated form; seen, as it were, under a magnifying glass. The most widely quoted example of this approach to classification is the typology suggested by Kretschmer, who distinguished the *schizothymic* and *cyclothymic* personality types, said to be the normal counterparts of the two major psychotic types, schizophrenia and manic-depressive psychosis, respectively. The schizothyme was described as shy, serious, unsociable, and taciturn; the cyclothyme as friendly, jolly, and sociable, though subject to ups and downs in mood.

Personality

The essential distinction that Kretschmer's typology made was between individuals whose experience and interest are directed inwards and those whose psychological functions are directed outwards. The distinction is an important one because, although labelled differently by different writers, it has formed the basis of most typologies developed this century. Indeed, it can even be seen reflected in the ancient Greek classification of temperaments referred to a moment ago, the inward looking melancholic, for example, contrasting with the outwardly oriented sanguine personality. Among modern typologies distinguishing between people according to the direction of their psychological attitudes, the most influential has certainly been that developed by the famous psychiatrist, Carl Jung. He explicitly referred to the *introvert* and *extravert* types, a terminology now more than familiar, even to the layman. It is also interesting to note that, like Kretschmer, Jung also tried to link his typology of normal personality to variations in the symptoms found among psychiatrically ill patients. However, he chose psychoneurosis, rather than psychosis, as the abnormal counterpart of normal personality differences, suggesting that the introvert, when neurotic, tended to develop psychasthenia, that is obsessional and anxiety reactions. He considered that the extravert, on the other hand, tended to react with hysterical symptoms.

One of the difficulties about the notion of personality type, as described so far, is that, if taken literally, it implies that people can be placed into one of a limited number of discrete categories, or pigeon-holes. In other words, it ignores the great variability in human personality and the fact that most people show a mixture of the characteristics assigned to a particular type. Many typologists were aware of this problem and sought various solutions to it. Jung, for example, considered that introverts and extraverts could be further subdivided into sub-types according to the psychological function through which their introversion or extraversion expressed itself. He described four such functions: thinking, feeling, sensation and intuition; so that one could have thinking introverts, feeling introverts, intuitive extraverts, and so on.

Another approach was to view the typology as representing, not discrete categories, but a continuously variable dimension, or continuum, the opposite ends of which were occupied by the extreme or 'pure' types. This notion is implicit in Kretschmer's classification, schizophrenics and manic-depressive psychotics forming the polar ends of a continuum of schizothymia-cyclothymia. Most normal people would cover the middle range of this continuum; the further they deviated from the centre in either direction the more evidence they would show of schizothymia or cyclothymia, as the case may be. The continuously variable nature of the typological dimension described by Kretschmer is further illustrated by the fact that he reserved a special description for those personalities who were extremely abnormal but not sufficiently so to be regarded as psychiatrically ill. These prepsychotic personalities were described as schizoid and cycloid, respectively, depending on whether they deviated markedly in the direction of schizophrenia or manic-depressive psychosis.

The concept of dimensions is now firmly entrenched in current psychological thinking about personality classification; and the task of psychologists who concern themselves with the problem is seen to be that of providing a dimensional rather than a crudely typological description of personality. However, the efforts of modern psychologists differ from those of their predecessors in two important aspects. First, it is now recognized that more than one dimension must be necessary to account for the rich variety of human personality. Secondly, the discovery of such dimensions is sought through the statistical and experimental analysis of personality, rather than, as hitherto, through simple observation and description. The main statistical procedure used for this purpose is *factor analysis* or some variant of it. Briefly, this technique allows the investigator to take a matrix of inter-correlations between a set of items and reduce it to a limited number of parameters (namely, factors) which can account for much of the variation on the items. For example, part of the score on a particular psychological test will be specific to that test. However, some of the score will be determined by a component which it has in common with many other tests. It is this common component which is isolated by factor analysis. In practice, more than one component, or factor, will be found, though, as we shall see in the next section, these may be many or few depending on the level of generality at which the analysis is carried out. For reasons which will become clear then, studies that have attempted to find statistical equivalents of the old descriptive typologies have tended to look for a small number of personality dimensions of broad generality.

Typical of this approach is the work of Eysenck, who, in a series of studies starting in the late 1940s, has tried to provide a dimensional classification of personality based on the theory that a limited set of independent dimensions, isolated by factor analysis, can account for most of the observed variation in personality (Eysenck, 1947). Eysenck has suggested that it is necessary to propose three main dimensions: *extraversion*, *neuroticism*, and *psychoticism*. According to his view, the task of personality classification is that of describing the individual in terms of his relative position on each of these dimensions. The principle of this is illustrated in Figure 7.1, which shows Eysenck's classificatory model in diagrammatic form. The hypothesized dimensions are drawn at right angles to each other to indicate that they are independent of each other. Together they describe a three-dimensional factor 'space' into which an individual can be placed according to the measured strength of each factor. Thus, individual A would be described as highly neurotic and highly extraverted but very low in psychotic tendency. Individual B, on the other hand, would be highly loaded on psychoticism, but only moderately neurotic and extraverted.

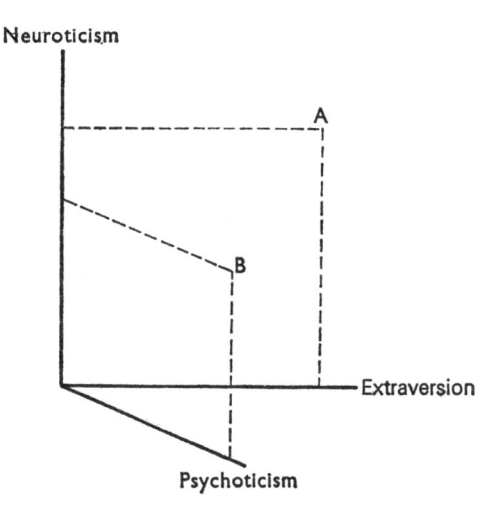

Figure 7.1

(It is worth noting that *intelligence* could be regarded as a further major factor of personality of equal generality and importance as those already described. In that case a four-dimensional space would be generated, which would give the model even greater scope for describing personality variation.)

For some parts of this theory empirical support is considerable; for other parts it is, at best, equivocal. Many clinicians would totally reject the notion of psychoticism as a personality dimension, regarding the psychoses as qualitatively distinct diseases. There is, in fact, much to be said against that view, though most of the relevant evidence is derived from behavioural, genetic and similar data obtained on psychotic patients, and is therefore beyond the scope of this chapter. However, it can be said that factor analytic studies of normal individuals are now beginning to isolate a personality dimension that looks very much like 'psychoticism' and which might ultimately help to define a set of characteristics seen in their extreme form in, say, schizophrenic patients but also observed to a lesser degree in the general population (Eysenck and Eysenck, 1972).

Until recently, though, Eysenck and his followers have tended to concentrate their efforts much more on extraversion and neuroticism, so that what theoretically is a three- (or even four-) dimensional classificatory system has reduced in practice to a two-dimensional one. Statistical analyses of personality data have consistently revealed factors identifiable as extraversion and neuroticism, a finding which is not too surprising in view of the conclusions so often reached by the early typologists on the basis of observation alone. The kind of psychological data subjected to factor analysis in these investigations has varied. Sometimes it has involved objective measurement of aspects of behaviour which, on *a priori* grounds, are thought to reflect personality. Examples are suggestibility, persistence, and reaction to experimentally imposed stress. More convincing in the present context, however, are studies which also include, or are entirely concerned with, items of a questionnaire type in which subjects are actually asked how they would respond in situations which are believed to depend on neurotic or extraverted tendencies in the personality. Figure 7.2 gives a very simple example of the kind of items that may be involved and the results of factor-analysing them. It can be seen that the analysis isolated two factors or dimensions, defined by the way in which groups of items cluster together, having high 'loadings' on (or correlations with) one factor, but low loadings on the other. The factors can be identified as 'extraversion' and 'neuroticism' by inspecting the kind of items that make up each cluster. Thus, items 1–7 appear to be concerned with responses of a neurotic kind, whereas items 8–12 describe behaviour typically associated with extraversion. Of course, in practice many more items than this would be used and, as indicated above, other more objective tests may be included in the analysis. Furthermore, the factors themselves would usually be less easy to distinguish and interpret; that is to say, the clustering of items would be less obvious. Nevertheless, Figure 7.2 does serve to illustrate the basic principles involved in this kind of personality research.

Factor-analytic studies like those described have resulted in the development of personality questionnaires which allow the psychologist to measure an individual's degree of extraversion and neuroticism and so pinpoint his position in the two-dimensional space defined by these two dimensions (cf. Figure 7.1). Indeed the items referred to in Figure 7.2 make up the short version of one such questionnaire, the two clusters forming its extraversion and neuroticism scales.

Personality questionnaires in general will be discussed more fully

Personality

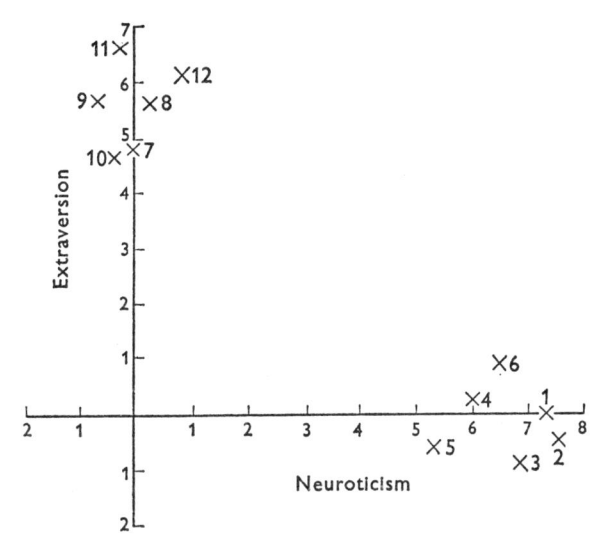

[Scatter plot with axes labeled "Extraversion" (vertical) and "Neuroticism" (horizontal), showing 12 plotted points numbered 1–12]

1. Do you sometimes feel happy, sometimes depressed, without any apparent reason?   N
2. Do you have frequent ups and downs in mood, either with or without apparent cause?   N
3. Are you inclined to be moody?   N
4. Does your mind often wander while you are trying to concentrate?   N
5. Are you frequently 'lost in thought' even when supposed to be taking part in a conversation?   N
6. Are you sometimes bubbling over with energy and sometimes very sluggish?   N
7. Do you prefer action to planning for action?   E
8. Are you happiest when you get involved in some project that calls for rapid action?   E
9. Do you usually take the initiative in making new friends?   E
10. Are you inclined to be quick and sure in your actions?   E
11. Would you rate yourself as a lively individual?   E
12. Would you be very unhappy if you were prevented from making numerous social contacts?   E

Figure 7.2

in a later section. However, there is one aspect of those measuring extraversion and neuroticism that is of relevance here. If the two statistical factors emphasized by Eysenck actually represent important and psychologically meaningful dimensions of personality, then it would be expected that people judged, by some independent criterion, to be extreme on either characteristic would show deviant scores on the appropriate questionnaire scale. In other words, extreme introverts and extraverts should have, respectively, low and high scores on a dimensional measure of extraversion. Similarly, people judged as neurotic should have higher than average neuroticism scores.

There is evidence that Eysenck's system of classification can pass this test of validity. With regard to extraversion it has been found that people nominated by their friends as extraverts or introverts do, in fact, differ in their questionnaire scores of extraversion. In the case of neuroticism the test has been made by examining the questionnaire

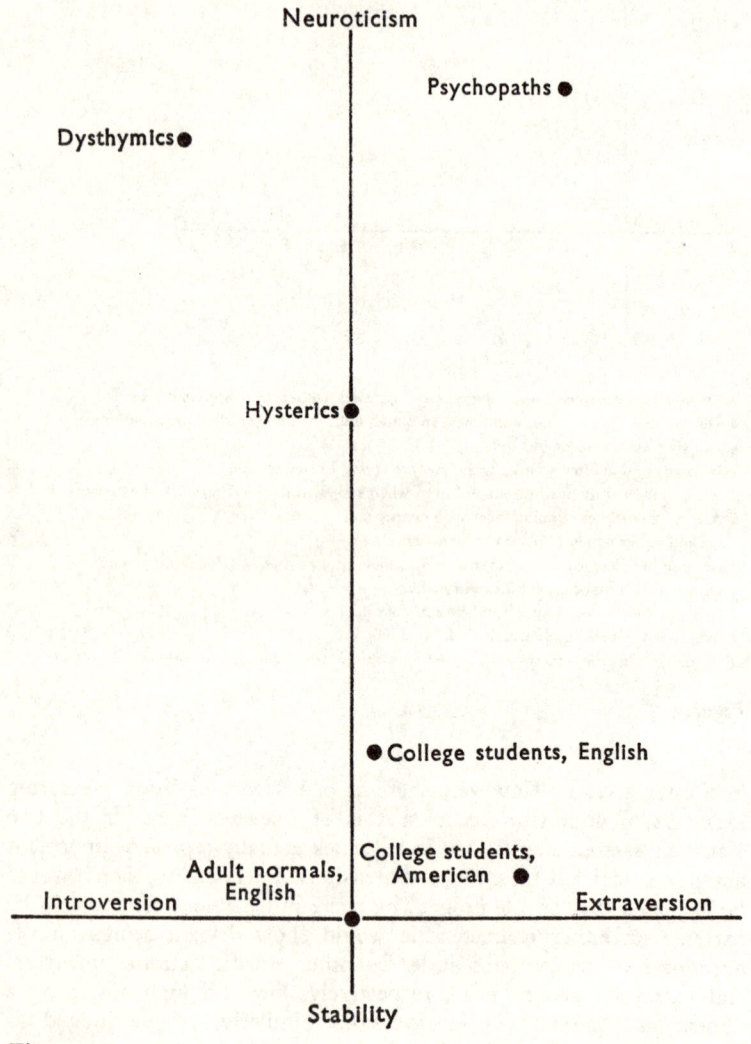

Figure 7.3

scores of patients diagnosed psychiatrically as suffering from neurotic disorders. Typical results are shown in Figure 7.3, where the mean scores of various neurotic groups are plotted for both extraversion and neuroticism. It can be seen that, as predicted, all three neurotic groups chosen (dysthymics, psychopaths, and hysterics) fall towards the high end of the neuroticism dimension, though hysterics are the least 'neurotic' as judged by questionnaire scores. (The description 'dysthymia' was coined by Eysenck to cover those neurotic disorders in which the presenting symptoms are diffuse anxiety, phobic reactions, or obsessionality. It is very roughly equivalent to the older, and now obsolete, term 'psychasthenia'.)

Another point to notice is that the various neurotic groups also differ in extraversion. Thus, dysthymics emerge as extremely introverted and psychopaths as extremely extraverted, with hysterics somewhere in between. In some respects this latter finding supports Jung's clinical observations referred to earlier, though as we saw he would have said that hysterics were more characteristically extraverted than questionnaires show them to be.

Depending on one's viewpoint, Eysenck's system of classification can be regarded as having an elegant simplicity or a simplistic naïvety. In one sense it can be said to point the way towards the principles on which a complete taxonomy of personality might ultimately be based. Furthermore, as we shall see later, even at its present stage of development it has provided a useful framework for investigating some of the fundamental biological correlates of personality. However, some nomothetic psychologists would argue that so far it has advanced little upon earlier, purely typological classifications. For example, they would say that because of its concentration on only two broad personality dimensions the system helps little in describing the individual, perhaps its only advantage being that it adds precision of measurement to descriptions of people as 'neurotic extraverts', 'stable introverts', and so on. Psychologists who take such a standpoint would tend to approach the problem of classification differently. Concerned more with providing a complete description of the person, they would argue that it is necessary to start by looking at smaller units of individual variation, namely the personality traits which form the elements upon which broader types are based. However, a consideration of this view properly belongs with a discussion of the structure of personality, a topic which will be taken up in the next section.

Structure of personality

The approach to personality outlined in the previous section takes as its starting-point the search for dimensions of behaviour having a high level of generality. However, as we saw right at the beginning of this chapter, at a lower level of organization personality is actually made up of a large number of traits or propensities which hopefully are stable enough to be regarded as characteristic of the way in which an individual will behave in a variety of situations that are relevant to the trait in question. For example, a person regarded as persistent will, according to nomothetic theory, tend to be so whenever persistence is demanded of him. The types described by the early personality theorists, and their

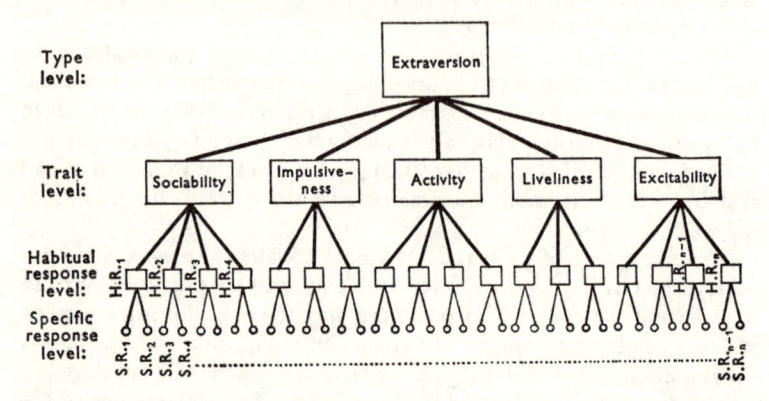

Figure 7.4

modern dimensional equivalents, therefore represent configurations or clusters of traits which together define a particular type or dimension. The scheme suggested by Eysenck and illustrated in Figure 7.4 provides a useful way of visualizing the relationship between traits and the broad dimensions described in the previous section. According to this view personality can be thought of as being organized in a hierarchical fashion, the different levels in the hierarchy representing different degrees of generality. At the lowest level are specific responses which an individual will perform once but which may or may not be characteristic of his behaviour. Such responses will have little value if we wish to try and predict behaviour from one situation to another. The second level refers to habitual responses; that is, responses which are consistent enough to recur under similar circumstances. Thus, given a particular psychological test twice the individual will tend to obtain a similar score on both occasions. (The fact that he may not get exactly the same score will reflect the fact that specific responses will be contributing to his performance). The third, or trait, level of organization represents clusters of habitual responses or, in practical terms, the fact that a particular group of tests will measure a common characteristic such as persistence, another group another characteristic, like shyness, and so on. At the highest level these traits themselves cluster to form types, or broad dimensions which, according to Eysenck, represent the most stable parameters with which to measure personality differences.

Just as the technique of factor analysis has been used to isolate broad dimensions, so it has been applied to personality data in order to identify dimensions at the trait level of organization. In the parlance of the factor analyst, the latter are regarded as lower order, or group, factors. Because these group factors will themselves correlate with each other they can be further analysed to obtain the higher order, or general, factors representing the type level shown in Figure 7.4. Unlike Eysenck, some personality theorists have preferred to work at the trait, rather than the type, level. As it happens they have tended to concentrate less on the typal classification of personality, though, as will be clear from the preceding discussion, their somewhat different approach is not logically incompatible with that of workers like Eysenck. The difference is largely one of emphasis.

In contemporary psychology the foremost exponent of the trait approach is Cattell, who has undertaken an enormous volume of research applying rigorous factor-analytic procedures to personality measurement (Cattell, 1965). In order to identify the main traits that make up personality Cattell has factor analysed three kinds of data. The first consists of *life data*, information about individuals taken from their everyday behaviour. Such information may include, say, a count of the number of societies to which a person belongs, or a rating of his emotional stability by someone who knows him well. The second class of data has come from *personality questionnaires* of the kind already referred to. Third, there are *objective test data* derived from procedures designed to measure the individual's behaviour in a wide range of 'miniature' situations. Just one example is the measurement of suggestibility, using the body sway test in which the experimenter determines the extent to which an individual sways when given the instruction that he is falling forwards.

According to Cattell, many separate analyses of these three kinds of data have revealed the existence of a series of what he calls 'source traits', which, even across cultures, he claims to be surprisingly consistent in both number and character. Including intelligence, sixteen such traits have emerged. These are listed in Table 7.1, together with a brief summary of the psychological qualities associated with high and low scores on each trait factor. A somewhat unusual feature to be noted concerns the rather idiosyncratic names which Cattell has given to some of the traits he has identified. Cattell justifies his practice of deliberately coining words like 'Harria' and 'Threctia' on the grounds that they avoid the vague and often contradictory meanings which more everyday descriptions of traits have acquired through popular usage.

Table 7.1. Sixteen factors of personality described by Cattell

A   *Sizothymia-Affectothymia* (reserved and detached v. outgoing and warm-hearted).
B   *Scholastic mental capacity* (less v. more intelligent).
C   *Ego strength* (affected by feelings and emotionally unstable v. mature and emotionally stable).
E   *Submissiveness-Dominance* (humble and mild v. assertive and competitive).
F   *Desurgency-Surgency* (sober and prudent v. happy-go-lucky and gay).
G   *Superego strength* (expedient and disregards rules v. conscientious and staid).
H   *Threctia-Parmia* (shy and restrained v. venturesome and socially bold).
I   *Harria-Premsia* (tough-minded and self-reliant v. tender-minded and clinging).
L   *Alaxia-Protension* (trusting and adaptable v. suspicious and self-opinionated).
M   *Praxernia-Autia* (practical and conventional v. imaginative and bohemian).
N   *Artlessness-shrewdness* (forthright and artless v. shrewd and worldly).
O   *Untroubled adequacy-guilt proneness* (self-assured and serene v. apprehensive and troubled).
Q_1 *Conservatism-radicalism* (conservative and respecting of established ideas v. experimenting and free-thinking).
Q_2 *Group adherence-self-sufficiency* (group-dependent v. resourceful).
Q_3 *Low integration-high self-concept control* (undisciplined and careless of protocol v. controlled and socially precise).
Q_4 *Ergic tension* (relaxed and unfrustrated v. tense and overwrought).

As the hierarchical organization of personality would lead us to expect, the traits listed in Table 7.1 can be further analysed to produce higher order factors or typal dimensions. One such factor, named *exvia-invia* by Cattell, corresponds closely to the extraversion-introversion factor of other workers. Another is *anxiety*, which is a factor of emotional adjustment very similar to that of neuroticism revealed in Eysenck's research. Although Cattell makes reference to these broader factors, in general he prefers to consider personality from the viewpoint of its trait structure, arguing, unlike Eysenck, that an individual can be most usefully described in terms of the profile of traits that make up his personality. Similarly, the problem of classification is regarded as one of searching for types or 'species' of trait profiles that characterize particular groups of people. In this respect it is interesting, as an example of Cattell's views, to contrast the way he attempts to differentiate neurotic personalities with the approach adopted by Eysenck. It will be recalled that Eysenck is content to specify how neurotics in general and different kinds of neurotic are weighted on two

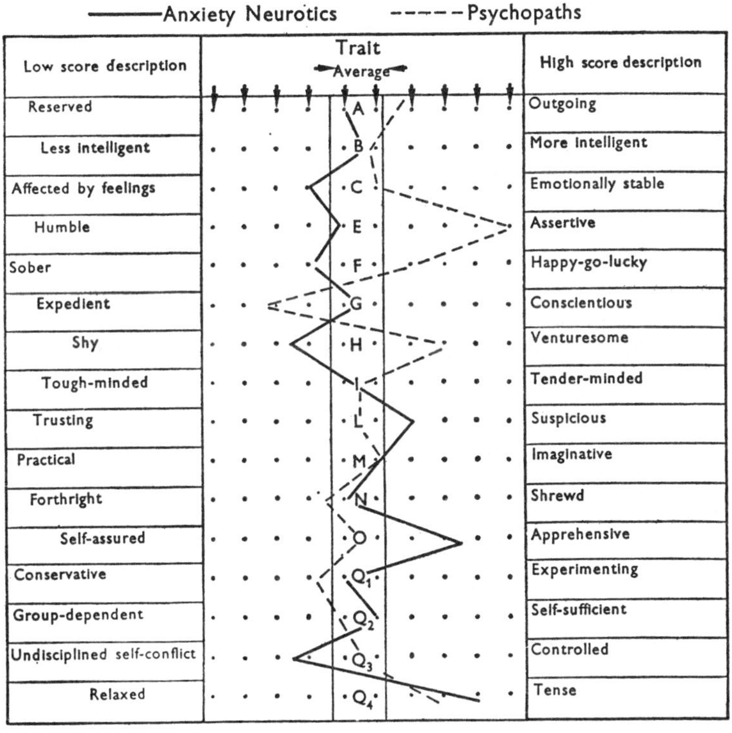

Low score description	Trait ←Average→	High score description
Reserved	A	Outgoing
Less intelligent	B	More intelligent
Affected by feelings	C	Emotionally stable
Humble	E	Assertive
Sober	F	Happy-go-lucky
Expedient	G	Conscientious
Shy	H	Venturesome
Tough-minded	I	Tender-minded
Trusting	L	Suspicious
Practical	M	Imaginative
Forthright	N	Shrewd
Self-assured	O	Apprehensive
Conservative	Q_1	Experimenting
Group-dependent	Q_2	Self-sufficient
Undisciplined self-conflict	Q_3	Controlled
Relaxed	Q_4	Tense

——— Anxiety Neurotics   ----- Psychopaths

Figure 7.5

general factors of extraversion and neuroticism. Cattell, on the other hand, offers trait descriptions of the kind illustrated in Figure 7.5 which shows the average profiles of common forms of behaviour disorder, anxiety neurosis and psychopathy. It can be seen that the profiles for these two kinds of abnormal personality are quite different. Furthermore, the differences can be specified in terms of the relative strengths and weaknesses of particular source traits, in this case mainly those to do with assertiveness, impulsiveness, expedience, and shyness.

It should perhaps be noted that Eysenck does depart slightly from his strict preference for single higher order factors in that he has, for example, recognized the importance of distinguishing between two established components of extraversion, namely impulsivity and sociability. Statistically, however, these are seen as being of greater generality than Cattell's source traits.

As a closing remark to this section it is necessary to make one final and rather important point. The concepts of personality trait and personality type obviously rest on the assumption that people are consistent in the way they behave in different situations; that 'once a rogue, always a rogue'. As one might expect, the picture is not as clear-cut as that (Mischel, 1968). It is known that factors quite specific to the situation will partly determine whether a person behaves 'in character', as it were. Put more technically, there may be only moderate correlations between an individual's actual behaviour in a situation and how strongly he rates himself (or others rate him) on a particular trait; or between what he does in two different situations, both of which are expected to elicit behaviour appropriate to the trait in question. Does this mean that the search for stable personality characteristics is futile? Not at all, because there will be some consistency in behaviour, particularly at the higher order, type, level of generality. On the other hand, some idiographic psychologists have argued that the consistency is not enough to make the notion of trait very useful when one comes to try and predict the behaviour of an individual, as distinct from that of a group of people. Later on we shall see the implications of this viewpoint when we come to look at some applications of personality measurement. In the meantime, it is sufficient to note that whether one chooses to emphasize the specificity of behaviour or the stability of personality depends largely on one's theoretical orientation and on what one is trying to achieve in a particular research or clinical investigation.

Determinants of personality

Biological Basis

A common thread running through many personality classifications has been the notion that people differ in personality partly because of an underlying variation in their biological make-up. This idea was suggested many centuries ago, being an integral part of the classic theory of temperaments referred to above. According to that theory the four temperaments recognized (sanguine, melancholic, choleric and phlegmatic) were due to a predominance of one of four essential bodily fluids or humours; namely, blood, black bile, yellow bile, and phlegm. Of course, humours have no place in modern science, but the general notion of a correlation between personality and biological factors has persisted in various forms. One has been the attempt to relate personality variations to physical body type. Kretschmer, whose personality typology we have already discussed, considered that individuals deviating towards cyclothymia tended to be of pyknic, or thick-set body-build, while those deviating towards schizothymia were of asthenic or leptosomatic body-build. The experimental evidence for this theory was based on rather unreliable data. However, using more sophisticated research techniques, Sheldon subsequently elaborated upon Kretschmer's theory and proposed three dimensions of physique – endomorphy, mesomorphy, and ectomorphy – which corresponded to three personality factors of viscerotonia, somatotonia, and cerebrotonia. The latter terms referred to the fact that individuals were considered to differ in the parts of the body through which the personality is expressed. The viscerotonic personality was thought to be someone whose psychic energy is invested in pleasure-seeking behaviour associated with the digestive tract. Consequently, such people were considered to be of endomorphic, or in Kretschmer's terminology, pyknic body-build. Cerebrotonics, on the other hand, were regarded as being people who are dominated by intellectual function and who have ectomorphic, or asthenic, physique. Despite improved research methodology the relationships between personality and physique predicted by Sheldon have proved to be relatively weak; though in general they have tended to be in the expected direction. Furthermore, when the personality side has been investigated in terms of more familiar and better established dimensions such as extraversion, small but consistent correlations with body type have been found. It is also encouraging that the direction of these correlations is in keeping with the personality descriptions adopted by Kretschmer and Sheldon; that is to say, the introvert tends more often to be of leptosomatic or ectomorphic body-build.

Compared with the somatotype approach to the biological basis of personality, a more important theory, in terms of its influence on contemporary psychology, has been the 'nervous type' view of individual differences derived originally from Pavlovian physiology. Early on in their research on conditioning, Pavlov and his colleagues observed that dogs of different temperamental type varied widely in the ease with which conditioned reflexes could be established and extinguished. Pavlov considered that the reason for this was that differences in temperament were a reflection, at the behavioural level, of underlying variations in central nervous activity, particularly of the cortical processes of excitation and inhibition. Although derived initially from observations on animal behaviour, this theory of temperament was later applied to variations in human personality. Thus, Pavlov himself put forward the view that abnormal deviations in personality were due to disturbances in cortical excitation and inhibition. More recently, intensive experimental work by Teplov and other Russian psychologists has established nervous typological theory as an essential part of the Soviet approach to individual differences in personality (Gray, 1964; Nebylitsyn and Gray, 1972).

In the West a similar approach to the biological determinants of personality has grown up over the years, though until recently and with one notable exception it has developed independently of Pavlovian physiology. The exception was the direct impact of Russian ideas on Eysenck, part of whose personality theory we have already discussed. In the mid 1950s Eysenck (1955) extended his dimensional analysis of the descriptive features of personality by proposing that observed differences in introversion and extraversion were partly due to constitutional variations in the central nervous processes of excitation and inhibition postulated by Pavlov. Furthermore, he suggested that one could examine this relationship between biological and personality variation by comparing the performance of introverts and extraverts on experimental tasks thought to reflect cortical excitation and inhibition. The essential features of this theory are illustrated in Figure 7.6, where it can be seen that what Eysenck proposed was a hierarchical view of personality, the different levels representing links in the causal chain joining the biological substrate of the personality to its various behavioural manifestations. Thus, variations in the balance between cortical excitation and inhibition were said to determine individual differences in the performance of people on a variety of experimental tasks. These performance differences were thought to be related to introversion-extraversion in such a way that introverts and extraverts were considered to show, respectively, high and low levels of central nervous excitation or arousal. Although not of immediate concern here, it should be noted in passing that the theory also proposed a final link in the chain (L4 in the diagram) relating social attitudes to introversion-extraversion.

Eysenck's attempt to combine the Russian notion of nervous typology with the Western dimensional analysis of personality has generated a considerable volume of research, some of which has led to the theory being drastically modified and to other alternative theories being proposed to explain the experimental data obtained. However, the scheme shown in Figure 7.6 remains essentially unchanged, to the extent that it exemplifies the basic principles of the biological approach to personality in which correlations are sought between various descriptive parameters of personality, such as extraversion, and their underlying physiological mechanisms.

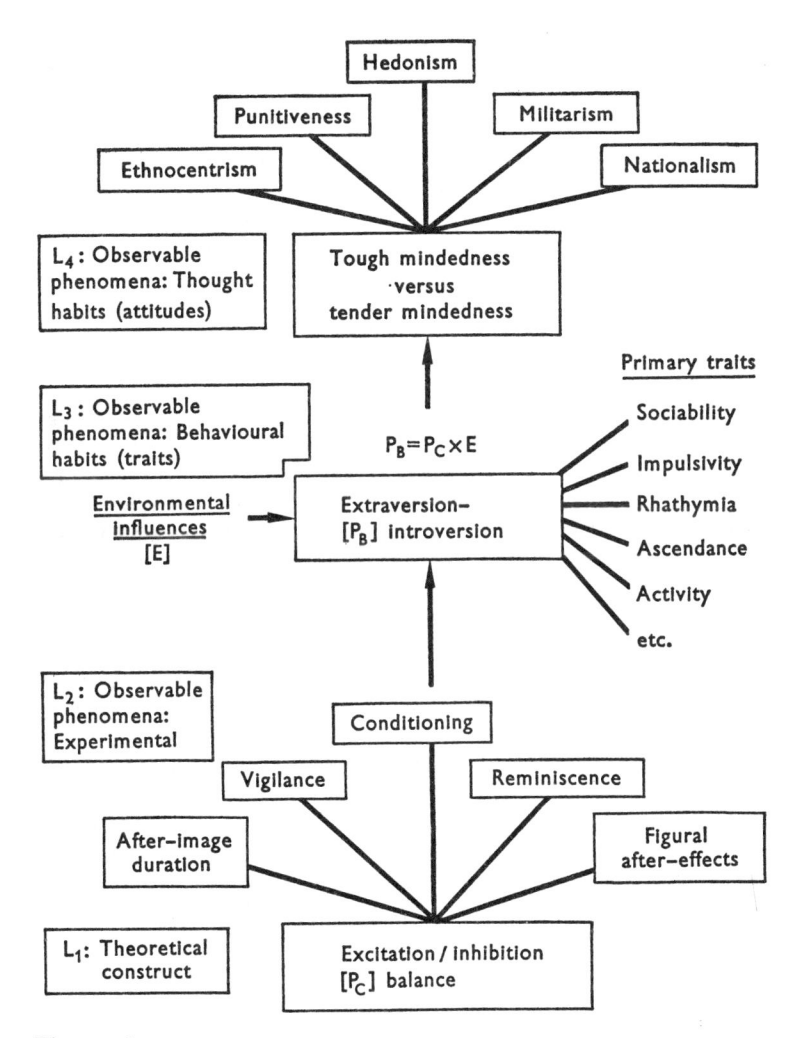

Figure 7.6

To illustrate the kind of deduction that has been made from Eysenck's theory of extraversion, just one example from the experimental literature will be cited. If, as the theory suggests, personalities differ in their levels of cortical excitation or arousal then these differences should appear on tasks which demand a sustained degree of attention or vigilance. Such tasks require of the subject that he attend for a long time to a monotonous display in order to detect 'signals' that appear at infrequent intervals. The problem of vigilance became of interest during the Second World War, when it was discovered that men watching radar screens sometimes missed critical signals after long periods on duty. Work at that time revealed wide individual difference in the ability to maintain vigilance on experimental tasks of the radar-watching type, introverts being superior to extraverts. Although this discovery was made before personality theory had advanced sufficiently to explain it, the finding is consistent with current notions about the biological basis of extraversion and has been confirmed in more recent research.

As mentioned a moment ago, since they were first formulated the original biological theories of personality have been much modified. One reason is the advance that has been made in our understanding of the central nervous mechanisms that mediate such psychological processes as emotion, attention, and consciousness. This work has had great impact on general psychology by allowing it to close the gap between studies of the brain and studies of behaviour. For those psychologists interested in individual differences it was an easy transition to view certain aspects of personality as being related to variations in the activity of identifiable brain circuits. This means that the biological personality theories are now becoming more explicitly physiological, with Eysenck, for example, going as far as to suggest that individual differences in extraversion and neuroticism are directly due to variations in the activity of the ascending reticular formation and limbic system respectively (Eysenck, 1967).

An inevitable consequence of continued research in this area is that the relationships between personality and its biological substrate are proving to be more intricate than was once thought. To take an example from Eysenck's own theory, it is now recognized that variations along his second dimension, neuroticism, may interact with extraversion in a rather complex way (Claridge, 1967). This means that the level of performance on a given nervous typological measure will depend on a particular combination of these two personality dimensions, rather than on either alone. The point is nicely illustrated by some research on drug response in relation to personality.

Because drugs are assumed to act on the same brain mechanisms that are thought responsible for natural variations in personality, their use in nervous typology research has an obvious logic, anticipated by Pavlov himself. In contemporary research a powerful tool for examining the problem in human subjects has been the determination of an individual's tolerance of a drug, usually a sedative like a barbiturate. The way this is done in practice is to administer the drug slowly, usually by injection, until the individual reaches a predetermined level of sedation, as judged by some objective sign, which may be either behavioural or physiological, such as a change in the EEG. The amount of drug administered up to that point is then a measure of his drug tolerance or 'sedation threshold', as it has been called. Extensive work on this technique, both in normal subjects and in psychiatric patients, has revealed consistent relationships between personality and drug tolerance (Claridge, 1972a). However, a particularly interesting finding is that obtained in normal subjects. Originally it was expected that introverts, because of their higher levels of central nervous arousal, would have a greater tolerance of sedatives than extraverts. In fact, it has been found that drug tolerance is related to the way in which neuroticism and extraversion combine in the individual. Thus, in subjects who score highly in neuroticism it is certainly the introverts who have a high tolerance of sedatives, while extraverts are very sensitive to the effects of such drugs. However, in subjects who get low neuroticism scores, the reverse is true. There it is the introverts who have poorer tolerance of sedatives; relationships that have been demonstrated both for nitrous oxide and for the barbiturate, amylobarbitone sodium (Rodnight and Gooch, 1963; Claridge et al., 1973).

Just as results such as these have caused the earlier, rather simple, nervous typological theories to be modified, so future research in other directions is likely to force further revision. A probable important growing-point is the study of the biological basis of psychoticism, the third dimension of personality referred to briefly in a previous section. Work on that topic has only just begun and the results obtained so far are too tentative to justify detailed discussion here. Suffice it to say that there are signs that psychoticism will prove to have distinctive psychophysiological correlates; in which case it will be necessary to modify drastically both present nervous typological models of normal personality and our disease concepts of disorders like schizophrenia (Claridge, 1972b).

Before closing this section it is necessary to comment briefly on an assumption made by nervous type theorists, that genetic factors make a significant contribution to personality variation. It will be clear from the discussion so far that this hypothesis can be tested in two ways: either at the personality dimension or at the nervous type level. There have been numerous studies of the former kind, usually involving the comparison of personality questionnaire scores in monozygotic (identical) and dizygotic (fraternal) twins. The results of different investigations have in fact been highly variable, though there is some evidence that heredity may play a part in determining individual differences in such traits as extraversion and neuroticism (Mittler, 1971).

With regard to extraversion an interesting, though intuitively somewhat surprising, result is that of the two components of that dimension described earlier, sociability seems to be much more heavily dependent on heredity than impulsivity. The questionnaire evidence on that point – based, of course, on samples of adult or adolescent twins – is further supported by the findings of ethological studies of the behaviour of new-born monozygotic twins, who show remarkable similarities in their patterns of social response, including smiling and reaction to strangers (Freedman, 1965).

Of course, personality as we normally measure it with questionnaires is considerably modified by the environment and it is perhaps more logical to expect that, if genetic factors are important, their influence will show up most clearly on measures that reflect the physiological substrate of the personality. Unfortunately, there have been few studies deliberately designed and carried out within a systematic theory of the biology of personality. Most of the relevant evidence comes from isolated experiments in which twins have been compared for their similarity on physiological parameters such as EEG patterns and responsiveness of the autonomic nervous system. The results that have emerged certainly point to heredity being extremely important (Mittler, *op. cit.*), a conclusion supported by a study, recently carried out by the present author, of the sedation threshold in twins (Claridge *et al.*, 1973). There it was found that monozygotic twins were significantly more alike in drug tolerance than dizygotic twins. In so far as biological measures of that type are related to descriptive personality characteristics we can reasonably conclude that certain aspects of the personality are genetically determined to a significant degree.

Learned Factors in Personality

We closed the previous section by calling attention to the role that genetic factors may play in determining the physiological substructure of the personality. However, the actual behaviour through which a person expresses his individuality is the end-result of an interplay between his genetic predispositions and environmental influences, particularly those occurring during the formative years of childhood and adolescence. The role of experiential factors in personality development can and has been looked at from many different viewpoints, though many contemporary psychologists would use a theoretical model derived from learning principles. Even here opinions have differed. Some workers have taken as their starting-point the psychoanalytic theory of personality, translating it into behaviourist terminology, and trying to find learning paradigms of Freudian mental mechanisms. That approach has been popular among American psychologists, though, like psychoanalytic theory itself, it has been less influential in Britain.

A different viewpoint, and the one to be emphasized here, rejects the psychoanalytic model, but has the advantage that it preserves continuity with some of the notions already introduced in this chapter. It would regard the application of learning principles to personality variation as being essentially concerned with an understanding of how, through the interaction of heredity and environment, stable patterns of behaviour arise which allow us to identify, first, traits and, at a higher level of generality, types of personality organization. Viewed in this way the process whereby personality differences emerge can be understood as a logical extension of the nervous type theory outlined in the previous section.

Take, for example, a person who is described as being a characteristically anxious individual. The chances are that he will be genetically predisposed to react to fear-provoking situations with marked physiological arousal, associated with changes in his autonomic nervous system. Such changes may be evoked by even mildly alarming stimuli to which a less reactive person would not respond. It is likely that, according to the usual laws of conditioning, some of these autonomic responses will become attached to quite neutral situations, and so what we see outwardly in his behaviour as the trait of anxiety will gradually be built up.

In practice, of course, whether an individual actually displays a particular trait will depend, not only on his genetic predisposition to react in a certain way, but also on the extent to which the environment has provided him with the opportunity to acquire the behaviour associated with the trait in question. It is possible, for example, that the individual just described might be brought up under conditions in which he is protected from threat and therefore from its physiological consequences. In that case he may be less anxious, as judged by the strength of his acquired habits, than one would predict from his nervous type. Conversely, a more placid person might be reared in a situation where fear reactions are provoked very frequently, with the result that even he acquires a strong trait of anxiety. Actually, in practice, environmental influences will on the whole tend to exaggerate rather than diminish, existing predispositions. This is because most people tend to be brought up by their parents, with whom they share some genetic similarity. Just as intelligent parents more often encourage intellectual activity in their already well-endowed children, so they will tend to act towards them in a way that will reinforce personality traits to which both are predisposed.

The trait of anxiety just described is a particularly important one, since it is believed to be a primary process which mediates the acquisition of many other habit systems that make up the personality. In that case anxiety, or rather its physiological component, can be said to act as a drive which powerfully reinforces learning during the shaping of personality. Thus, responses which lead to a reduction in anxiety will tend to be stamped in and, with further elaboration, eventually become stable behaviour patterns that constitute other personality traits. This process can be seen at work during the socialization of the child, when he is acquiring an ethic of behaviour, learning to judge right from wrong and to act within certain norms laid down by society. The social experience of the very young child, of course, is confined initially to the immediate family circle, in the adult members of which are vested the mores of society as a whole. It is from them that the child learns the rudiments of socially acceptable behaviour. He does so partly through authority figures – usually the parents – punishing socially undesirable habits. Punishment of a forbidden act will induce anxiety the next time it is contemplated, and so the act will be avoided. In our culture, for instance, it is normally required of us that we control extreme physical violence as an expression of anger. Although to begin with it is natural for the child to react in that way when angry, the parents will usually respond with disapproval, either by punishing him or by withdrawing their affection. The consequent anxiety will act to inhibit the display of violent aggression on future occasions and so the child will learn self-control. As he gets older other authority figures in the child's widening social circle will gradually take over the parental role and continue to reinforce the desired behaviour.

An important feature of the developmental process just described is that expression of the conditioned responses that have been acquired – in this case control over aggressive impulses – is not limited solely to the specific situations in which they have been learned. Following the conditioning principle of generalization, a wide variety of other situations, more or less similar to the one in which the original learning took place, will also elicit the appropriate behaviour. Thus, the anxiety and consequent inhibition of aggression evoked on particular occasions in the family setting will tend to spread to other authority figures in other contexts. In the human, of course, the existence of language will extend the possibility for generalization even further, enabling the individual to elaborate his response repertoire at a purely symbolic level, by allowing him to label situations verbally according to their significance to him.

Although the kind of traits acquired by the child will often reflect the norms of the society or sub-culture in which he is brought up, the strength of individual traits will be considerably influenced by early parental conditioning and the models of behaviour presented to him within the family. For example, parents themselves will differ in the extent to which they believe (possibly due to their own upbringing) that the display of anger should be avoided. Parents who believe in extreme self-control will inevitably reinforce this trait in their own children much more than those who take the opposite view. They will do this both explicitly, by reinforcing the desired behaviour when it appears; and implicitly, by behaving in a self-controlled manner themselves, thus providing a model which the child will imitate.

So far we have taken as our example of trait acquisition the instance where learning is mediated by anxiety reduction. Here, if anxiety level is high due to a combination of physiological predisposition and upbringing, the personality that emerges will be one that is generally well conditioned to behave according to the norms of society. Thus it is no coincidence that one of the major personality types we have come across several times previously, the introvert or obsessoid, is characterized behaviourally by a cluster of traits such as social conformity, conscientiousness, self-control, and so on. These traits can be thought of as having arisen on the basis of a high level of physiological arousal, of sensitivity to punishment, and the consequently rapid conditioning of those responses which lead to a reduction of arousal.

What, however, of individuals of a different nervous type, whose physiological predisposition is towards a rather poor degree of responsiveness? Their interaction with the environment during personality development will follow a different course, leading to a different cluster of behaviour patterns, or traits. Part of their behaviour can be said to be due to their relative lack of response to threat, and hence to weak learning of anxiety-mediated habit systems. However, another powerful source of learning in these people will derive from the lack of arousability itself. Just as a very high level of arousal is uncomfortable, so too is a very low level. As a rather extreme example it is possible to quote the mental disturbance that follows severe reduction of stimulation, as occurs during sensory deprivation experiences. This need for the organism to maintain an adequate level of sensory input is called 'stimulus hunger' and is characterized by behaviour which leads to what has been described as 'arousal jag', namely the search for stimulation that increases arousal to a comfortable level. The ability of stimulus hunger to act as a drive which reinforces learning has been shown in a number of experiments. For example, monkeys trained in a sensory-deprived environment will learn to perform tasks that are rewarded by brief periods of visual stimulation. In the human, individual differences have been found in the extent to which the need for arousal jag will motivate learning. In one experiment introverts and extraverts were compared for the rates with which they would press a key in order to receive strong stimulation in the form of bright lights and loud music (Wiessen, 1965). Compared with introverts, extraverted subjects worked much harder for stimulation, increasing their rate of responding as the experiment proceeded. However, the opposite happened when the experimental conditions were reversed and pressing the key was reinforced by the lights and music being switched off. In that case, extraverts responded less frequently than introverts, who gradually increased their effort to reduce stimulation.

We conclude, then, that just as some highly aroused individuals are primed to reduce sensory input, so others are predisposed to behave in a way which will amplify it. This fact is probably extremely important for understanding how certain personality traits arise, particularly those found in extraverts. Thus, extraverts will tend to acquire habits which are reinforced by frequent arousal jags. Such a developmental process is especially likely to occur if, as will probably be the case, the individual is brought up in a family or cultural environment offering constant opportunity for behaviour that satisfies the need for stimulation. Two good examples of the traits in question are the impulsiveness and sociability of the extravert, both of which are aimed at increasing the variety and intensity of experience. At a more pathological extreme the character traits of certain neurotic personalities probably arise in a similar way. Earlier we said that hysterics and psychopaths tend to be of poorly arousable nervous type, and to be more typically extraverted in personality. Significantly, both are characterized by attention-seeking behaviour, while risk-taking is a central feature of psychopathy. Part of the psychopath's lack of socialization can, of course, be put down to his failure to acquire anxiety-mediated habit systems which develop in the more normal individual and to a pathological degree in very highly aroused, anxiety-prone people. However, this is also combined with the psychopath's tendency to acquire behaviour patterns which are reinforced by their pleasurable or arousing consequences.

The above discussion has served only to outline the basic principles of how genetic and learned factors may interact to produce the behaviour by which we identify an individual's personality. It is inevitably sketchy not only because space does not permit it to be otherwise, but also because psychology is only just beginning to establish rational theories which will enable it to analyse in detail how the habit-systems or traits that form the structure of the personality develop. We saw in the previous section how knowledge of the nervous typological basis of personality is far from complete. It is not surprising, therefore, that the immensely more difficult task of disentangling the influence of experiential factors has only just begun. So far its efforts have been confined to relatively crude attempts to understand differences in the behaviour of grossly defined personality types. In this respect it should be mentioned that psychologists have actually paid most attention to the role of learning in the development of abnormal behaviour patterns (symptoms) found among neurotic variants of personality; a practice that contains some logic since it allows the psychologist to see in an exaggerated form developmental processes that are also at work in the more normal individual. Detailed consideration of this aspect of the topic is beyond the terms of reference of the present chapter, though its subject-matter is clearly complementary to that discussed here.

The measurement of personality

Although a great deal of research into personality is concerned with the formulation of viable theories of individual variation, one of its important practical aims is the development of reliable measuring instruments that can be used by the applied psychologist. Actually the latter has at his disposal a wide variety of techniques, a fact which reflects the diversity of approaches that have been taken to the study of personality. Some of these techniques have emerged as natural by-products of basic psychological research; others have been born of practical needs, such as personnel selection or clinical diagnosis. The procedure the psychologist chooses to employ will be decided to a large extent by the purpose of a particular investigation. The clinician may be concerned with gaining a detailed understanding of an individual, the research worker with the precise measurement of a limited characteristic or group of characteristics. Even given this distinction, a number of different personality tests will be available, the choice often being determined by the psychologist's own theoretical orientation.

Despite their variety, all personality assessment procedures have one feature in common. Like most psychological measuring instruments, they aim to sample an adequate cross-section of an individual's real-life behaviour, yet try to do so in a reliable and easily quantifiable form, which has predictive value outside the test situation. Here an element of compromise is inevitably involved. On the one hand, it is necessary to restrict the range of behaviour studied in order to make measurement possible. On the other hand, if too narrow a piece of behaviour is sampled it may, despite being measured with precision, have little to do with personality as observed in everyday life. The most satisfactory solution to this problem might seem to be to observe the behaviour of individuals placed in miniature situations which bear some resemblance to everyday life, yet are sufficiently restricted to make some measurement possible. Such *situational tests*, as they are called, have in fact been commonly used in industry and by military selection boards.

A general technique often used in situational tests and one that has become a personality assessment procedure in its own right is the *rating scale*. Here an external observer records his impression of an individual by rating him on an ordinal scale according to the degree to which he shows a particular characteristic or group of characteristics. Two obvious drawbacks with this kind of procedure are the subjective bias of the rater and the limited sample of the ratee's behaviour to which he usually has access. Another, more technical, problem is the so-called 'halo effect', a response bias found in observers rating more than one trait in the same individual. The halo effect appears as a tendency for persons rated high (or low) on one characteristic to be rated as equally extreme on another, unrelated, characteristic. These and other difficulties can be partly overcome by careful construction and administration of suitable scales; and, when applied to well-defined characteristics, rating techniques have proved to be useful procedures for assessing personality. They have had two main applications in the medical and clinical psychological fields. One is in the assessment of limited affective states, like anxiety or depression, particularly with regard to changes that occur, for example, during drug trials. The other has formed part of an attempt to quantify psychiatric diagnosis. There statistical analysis of symptom ratings has led to the construction of scales purporting to measure objectively definable psychiatric syndromes.

Although useful for special purposes, such as those just mentioned, rating scales have not achieved the status of routinely administered personality tests. By comparison a more widely used technique is the *personality questionnaire*, or *personality inventory*, a type of procedure which we have already encountered. In general format all questionnaires are basically the same, consisting of a series of items describing attitudes, feelings, or reactions to everyday situations. The respondent is asked to indicate whether these are typical or not of himself, the answer required either being in the form 'yes/no' or 'true/false' or also including a middle, 'uncertain', or 'don't know' category.

The actual item content of personality questionnaires, the characteristics measured, and the way these are derived will naturally depend on the psychological theory that gave rise to them. Psychologists concerned with the factor analysis of personality structure have very much favoured questionnaires as measuring instruments; and the two major theorists in this area, Cattell and Eysenck, have both produced inventories that are widely used in the clinical and research fields. Cattell's *Sixteen Personality Factor*, for example, has its most useful application in those situations where it is desirable to obtain a profile of the individual's personality. On the other hand, Eysenck, preferring a more general typological approach, has developed a series of questionnaires measuring a limited number of personality dimensions. The earliest example was the *Maudsley Personality Inventory* (MPI), later replaced by the *Eysenck Personality Inventory* (EPI), both of these being designed to measure the two dimensions of extraversion and neuroticism. Very recently he has introduced another questionnaire, the PQ inventory, which, in addition to extraversion and neuroticism, also purports to measure the dimension of psychoticism.

It will be clear from the previous discussion of the way theorists like Cattell and Eysenck approach the problem of personality description that the characteristics their questionnaires measure are entirely defined by the way in which the items from which they are constructed cluster together in factor analysis. The clusters that emerge are identified and given 'psychological meaning' partly on the basis of the items from which they are constituted and partly in terms of their correlation with some external criterion of the trait or group of traits they purport to measure. An example of the latter is Eysenck's demonstration that his neuroticism scales will differentiate normal subjects from diagnosed neurotics. Other psychologists have adopted a different strategy in constructing questionnaires, approaching the problem from the other end, as it were. They have started with items which it is thought will differentiate defined categories of psychiatric abnormality, eventually arriving at item clusters or scales which, in the normal individual, are said to measure his similarity to the original criterion groups. The outstanding example of this kind of questionnaire is the *Minnesota Multiphasic Personality Inventory*, or MMPI, which contains the following scales:

        Hs: Hypochondriasis
        D: Depression
        Hy: Psychopathic Deviate
        Mf: Masculinity-femininity
        Pa: Paranoia
        Pt: Psychasthenia
        Sc: Schizophrenia
        Ma: Hypomania

It will be realized that, according to an individual's scores on the different scales of this questionnaire, it is possible to arrive at a profile of his personality, in much the same way as with Cattell's 16PF. However, an important difference is that because of the way in which the MMPI scales were derived it cannot be assumed that they measure unitary characteristics. They simply reflect an individual's resemblance to a number of arbitrarily defined psychiatric syndromes which are themselves known to have poor reliability and validity.

Although widely used for measuring personality, questionnaires are not without their drawbacks. In particular, they are subject to various sources of error arising from the test-taking attitudes or 'response sets' with which people approach the completion of any personality inventory. Apart from deliberate faking, subjects may implicitly try to display themselves in a favourable light; or alternatively, as in the case of psychiatric patients, exaggerate their symptoms. An important source of bias has proved to be the social desirability of questionnaire items; it has been shown that items independently judged as describing socially desirable attitudes are much more likely to be endorsed. Another contaminating factor is what has been called acquiescence, the tendency for individuals consistently to endorse or reject items irrespective of content. For example, a statement presented in a particular form may be answered in the affirmative, yet basically the same statement, reworded in its opposite, negative, form may receive the same reply.

The difficulties mentioned can be minimized by adopting certain strategies when constructing questionnaires. These include careful wording of the items and arranging matters so that the answers scored positively on a particular trait are not either always 'yes' or always 'no', but are randomly allocated to both response categories. Additionally questionnaires may be constructed so that they include special scales designed to measure the degree of faking or other distortion of responses to the main items. This technique is used in the Eysenck scales, but more particularly in the MMPI.

All of the assessment procedures considered so far are essentially nomothetic in nature. That is to say, they all place great emphasis on measurement and on the description of personality in terms of universal and relatively superficial characteristics. However, we saw right at the beginning of this chapter that some psychologists have been more concerned with giving an account, in depth, of the personality of an individual. In other words, they have adopted an idiographic approach to personality. In general, because of the theoretical foundation on which their enquiries have been based, such psychologists have been interested less in measurement than in gaining holistic understanding of the person. The traditional assessment techniques to which this viewpoint gave rise were the so-called *projective tests*. These consist of relatively unstructured tasks in which the subject is presented with perceptually vague stimuli which he is asked to interpret, the assumption being that his replies will reflect certain important features of personality dynamics. In other words, he is expected to 'project' on to the test material his wishes, needs, conflicts, and so on. The most famous of the projective techniques is the *Rorschach Test*, comprising a series of inkblots. These are presented in turn, the individual being asked to say what each represents or what he sees in it. A somewhat different approach is to use pictures as the stimulus material, the subject in that case being required to make up a story about each picture. The commonest example of this version of the projective technique is the *Thematic Apperception Test* (TAT).

The main difficulty with all projective tests is that, while they yield a considerable amount of information about the individual, the nature of this information makes exact quantification and reliable interpretation wellnigh impossible. With the Rorschach and TAT detailed criteria are available for scoring and classifying the wide range of responses that can be elicited by the test material, but even so their application is influenced by subjective factors on the part of the examiner. This is not to say they may not be of value in the hands of experienced and clinically intuitive users, who may be able to make sensible statements about an individual's personality on the basis of their accumulated familiarity with the administration of a particular projective test. However, in that case the stimulus material itself is probably only important in so far as it provides the examiner with a standard situation against which to judge behaviour. Because of their poor scientific validity projective tests are gradually falling out of favour in this country, though they are still widely used in the USA.

Although the idiographic approach, and the assessment techniques to which it has given rise, have traditionally been weak in the area of measurement, recent developments suggest that this need not necessarily be so. Some contemporary psychologists believe that it is possible, indeed vital, to maintain an idiographic, person-centred view of the individual, at the same time applying strict quantitative methods to the measurement of personality. This opinion rests on a radically different approach to personality from that so far emphasized here: that of *personal construct theory*, as it is called. Originally developed by the American psychologist, George Kelly, the theory and the approach to measurement derived from it have rapidly achieved popularity in Britain mainly through the work and writings of Bannister and his colleagues (Bannister and Fransella, 1971). The theory itself is complex, and sometimes obscurely stated; but in essence it proposes that personality consists of an organized system of constructs or ways of interpreting, anticipating, or predicting events in the outside world. Constructs are, in effect, concepts like good-bad, friendly-hostile or black-white, though the way an individual uses them and the way they are organized to form his personality are entirely unique. This unique organization of constructs refers to the fact that they will cluster together differently in different people. For example, an individual may construe a coloured stranger as black, bad and hostile. The stranger might construe him, in turn, as white, bad, and hostile.

In addition to being unique to himself a person's system of constructs will have a certain shifting quality about it. This is because, according to the theory, the use of constructs and their relationships to other constructs in the system are constantly being modified in the light of experience, particularly during the development of the personality. Such modification arises out of the predictive nature of personal constructs, the fact that on acting on the basis of the way he currently construes an event an individual may subsequently discover that he needs to construe it differently. In other words, to use our earlier example, on getting to know each other the black and white strangers may begin to construe each other as good and friendly (though still, presumably, as white and black).

It is clear, even from this brief description, that personal construct theory is extremely flexible, a fact which is reflected in its measurement techniques. Instead of trying to measure universal traits or dimensions, which are regarded as trivial or even statistical artefacts, the personal construct theorist uses a procedure called the *repertory grid technique*. This is not a test in the questionnaire or inventory sense; that is, an instrument having norms based on samples of people and against which a particular person can be judged. Instead, it is a range of procedures which can be tailored to the investigation of an individual's personal construct system, aimed at finding out how he uniquely construes the world. Although there are various forms of the technique, the principles of the method are as follows.

The subject takes or is asked to take a series of items or 'elements' to be evaluated. The nature of these elements will depend entirely on the area of experience being investigated. They may consist of people known personally to the individual and nominated by him, or they may be photographs of strangers, institutions, physical objects, and so on. The subject is then asked to sort the elements according to a series of constructs like those illustrated above. The constructs themselves may be supplied to him by the psychologist, although in the most idiographic form of grid testing constructs will be elicited from the subject as a preliminary part of the procedure. One way of eliciting constructs is by the so-called triadic method. Here the person is presented with groups of three elements and asked to say how two of them are alike and therefore differ from the third. For example, asked to rate three members of his family a person may say that two of them (his mother and sister) are similar in being kind and the third (his father) is unkind. This immediately establishes kind-unkind as a construct that that individual uses in evaluating significant people in his environment. Further groups of three elements are then presented until the individual's range of constructs has been elicited.

In the main part of the procedure the subject is asked to use the constructs, whether supplied or elicited, to evaluate the elements being investigated. This may be done by asking him to say about each element whether it belongs to one or other pole of each construct; for example, whether it is judged as intelligent or stupid, friendly or hostile, and so on. Alternatively, and more usually, the subject may be required to rank order the elements on each of the constructs taken in turn. Either way the results of the examination come in the form of a grid or matrix relating elements to constructs. This can then be analysed statistically in order to discover how particular constructs group together or form clusters which may be significant for understanding the individual's personal mode of perceiving people, things, or events. In some cases the statistical methods used may be very sophisticated, involving the very same procedure of factor analysis that we came across in discussing the trait approach to personality. The difference, of course, is that, unlike the nomothetic psychologist, the personal construct theorist is looking for factors within a single individual and hence for dimensions which describe his unique personality structure.

Because of its ability to combine precise measurement with a heavily idiographic view of personality, the approach just described has been much favoured by contemporary psychologists concerned with problems that demand intensive study of the individual, such as those encountered in the clinical setting. There repertory grid testing has found a variety of applications, particularly in conjunction with psychological treatment, where it may serve two purposes. One is that of identifying in the patient areas of attitude or belief upon which therapy can be focused, and the other is of monitoring changes that occur in the construct system with treatment. An example from some work on stuttering by Fransella (1972) will help to illustrate the point.

Fransella's basic assumption was that stutterers construe the world almost entirely from the standpoint of someone whose speech is disfluent. However, she argued that improvement might occur if constructs associated with the infrequent periods of fluency that did occur could be strengthened. Consequently, she had stutterers complete two forms of the repertory grid: one concerned with the meaning of being a stutterer, and one with the meaning of being a fluent speaker. In the 'stutterer' grid constructs were elicited by presenting triads of elements consisting of two photographs of people together with a card on which was printed the words: 'the sort of person people see me as being when I am stuttering.' In the 'non-stuttering' form of the grid the words were changed to: 'the sort of person people see me as being when I am NOT stuttering.' The latter set of constructs was then used as a basis for therapy aimed at strengthening non-stuttering attitudes, the progress of treatment being monitored by repeating the two kinds of grid throughout treatment. The results showed that in a high proportion of patients there was a significant decrease in speech disfluency, accompanied by a gradual shift on the repertory grid towards non-stuttering attitudes.

Before we leave personal construct theory one other, rather special, application of it should be mentioned, and that is its attempts to provide an understanding of the thought disorder that commonly occurs in schizophrenic patients (Bannister and Fransella, 1966). According to Bannister the thought disorder of the schizophrenic reflects a system of personal constructs that is quite chaotic; that is to say, his constructs are so loosely organized in relation to each other that he is unable to use them effectively in evaluating events in the outside world. This is said to be demonstrated in the performance of schizophrenics on a special version of the repertory grid, where subjects are presented with a standard set of photographs of people (the elements) and asked to rank them in order on each of a list of supplied constructs. One measure that is taken from the grid is the overall degree of statistical correlation between the rankings, representing the extent to which the subject assigns extreme ranks to the same photographs on different constructs; or, in other words, how far those people he perceives as most mean are also seen as most selfish, least kind and so on. A second measure derived is the correlation between two successive administrations of the test. Compared with normal subjects schizophrenics get low scores on both measures. This is interpreted to mean that the construct systems of schizophrenics have little predictive value for them, at least in relation to people. Or, to put it more simply, they construe, and hence behave towards others, in an essentially random fashion.

According to Bannister the loosened construct system of schizophrenics originates in the peculiar form of social interaction which they encounter during personality development and which is called 'serial invalidation'. During normal development the construct system becomes established through particular constructs being reliably confirmed; the child discovers that people he construes as good are also usually kind. The serial invalidation hypothesis proposes that the potential schizophrenic is constantly having his constructs disconfirmed, perhaps because of inconsistent behaviour on the part of his family. This eventually results in the whole construct system being pathologically loosened.

This application of personal construct theory is of interest for three reasons. First, it gives some insight into the way the theory views the development of personality; as a process whereby an individual's construct system becomes progressively established through the reactions of others to actions he takes on the basis of his constructs. Second, like the dimensional view of psychotic behaviour mentioned briefly before, but for very different reasons, the serial invalidation hypothesis regards schizophrenia as an, albeit extreme, example of normal psychology. For the normal individual also has his constructs disconfirmed during development; it is simply that the schizophrenic's are loosened to the point where they no longer work. Third, unlike the dimensional view, the theory offers a psychological rather than a biological account of schizophrenia. Thus, the concept of psychoticism assumes, as we have seen, that there is a discoverable physiological basis to the dimension which can account for the peculiarities of thinking and language seen in schizophrenia. The two approaches, however, provide an interesting contrast in the way in which different theories have tried to incorporate data about schizophrenia within the domain of normal personality study.

A procedure not dissimilar to the repertory grid technique is the *semantic differential*, introduced by another American psychologist, Osgood. Derived from a theory of 'meaning' it, too, consists of a series of concepts which the subject uses to rate people, objects, or situations that are significant for him. The concepts are presented as seven-point adjectival scales, like cruel-kind, true-false and so on, the subject being required to rate each item on the selected scales. Unlike the repertory grid, the scales used are always supplied to the subject and are chosen from a list of concepts which, it is claimed, tap important areas of meaning. The list itself was developed from a large-scale study of many such concepts which were subjected to factor analysis. It was found that there were three main dimensions of meaning which could be used as a framework for studying individual differences. These were evaluation, activity, and potency, defined, respectively, by scales such as good-bad, fast-slow, and masculine-feminine. Because of the way it was derived (that is, from the assumption that there is a limited number of universal dimensions underlying behaviour), the semantic differential cannot be considered truly idiographic in origin. However in practice it has often been used in that way, a notable example being a study reported by Osgood in which he examined the case of multiple personality that formed the subject of the commercial film *The Three Faces of Eve*. The examination consisted of administering a form of the semantic differential to the patient on the occasions when she adopted each of her three 'personalities'. Asked to evaluate significant figures and experiences in her life, such as child, doctor, sex and so on, she showed a different attitudinal structure depending on the personality she claimed to be.

To conclude this section it should perhaps be emphasized again that there is no single method of assessing personality. Rather there is a series of quite different techniques from which the psychologist can choose to suit a particular application. For instance, the relatively new idiographic procedures, like the repertory grid technique, may be extremely valuable, indeed the obvious choice, where the purpose of the investigation is the intensive study of the individual, as may be the case when a psychiatric patient is being examined for psychological changes that occur during therapy. On other occasions, for example in psychiatric diagnosis or in research projects aimed at establishing relationships between personality and some other behavioural or physiological variable, it may be preferable to use tests derived from trait theories of individual variation. One final point is that in the space available it has been possible to describe only a few of the methods used to measure personality and to do so only briefly. The interested reader is referred to more complete accounts (e.g., Vernon, 1964).

Personality and medical practice

From time to time throughout this chapter brief reference has been made to one branch of medical practice, namely psychiatry, where knowledge about personality is clearly most relevant. The reader will have gathered that attempts to develop systematic theories of personality have often been inextricably linked with the study of the psychiatric patient. Thus many psychologists, regarding the psychiatric disorders as exaggerated forms of normal personality, have attempted to explain both within the same theoretical framework. Having made this general point, however, the personality field as it relates to psychiatry will not be considered in any further detail here. Instead, this section will be confined to a number of remarks about some other ways in which personality touches upon other aspects of medical practice. In this respect preference will be given to those areas where factual evidence or theoretical expectation suggest that a knowledge about personality may be of value to the doctor.

It is a trite, but often neglected, fact that when an individual comes under medical care he presents, not as a set of symptoms affecting an isolated part of his body, but as a total personality which, according to its nature, will colour the clinical picture in various ways. Perhaps the most obvious way concerns the reaction to the illness itself. Becoming ill can be thought of as a special form of stress, the patient's response to the experience being conditioned by his underlying personality. To take very common everyday examples, the anxiety-prone individual may react by becoming fearful, the hysterical personality by becoming overdependent. A particular facet of this general problem that has been subjected to some research and which is of great importance in medical care concerns a universal accompaniment of physical illness, pain. It has been demonstrated that there are wide individual variations, related to personality, in the extent to which people can tolerate acute pain. It has been found that experimental pain tolerance thresholds are significantly higher in extraverts than in introverts. However, in the clinical situation the relationships between personality and pain reaction are probably more complicated, as demonstrated in a recent study of female patients with advanced cancer of the cervix (Bond and Pearson, 1969). The patients in question were compared in three groups according to their scores on a personality inventory, the extent to which they admitted pain to the doctor, and the frequency with which they were given analgesics by the nursing staff. The first group proved to be pain-free, and in personality to be low in neuroticism and high in extraversion. The second group suffered pain but did not tell the nurses about it. They were high in neuroticism and highly introverted. The third group of patients, who were both highly neurotic and highly extraverted, suffered from pain, communicated this to the nursing staff, and frequently received analgesics. The authors of the study concluded that variations in neuroticism probably reflected differences in physiological arousability (i.e., pain level), whereas extraversion was related to the ability to communicate feelings to others. Thus, although suffering from a similar amount of pain the neurotic introverts were much less likely to complain of it than their equally neurotic but extraverted neighbours.

The results just described are probably not specific to pain but almost certainly apply to other bodily sensations. Thus, an important area of research in general psychophysiology has been concerned with the extent to which bodily activity as measured objectively correlates with subjective report. In fact, it has been found that some people who deny feeling anxious during an experimentally imposed stress may actually show very high levels of autonomic activity, which may be greater than those found in individuals who admit to their anxiety. This work has given rise to the notion of 'repression-sensitization' as a dimension of personality, describing variations in the extent to which people consciously recognize, or alternatively, communicate bodily sensations arising in themselves (Byrne, 1964). Although not clearly established how, it is probable that repression-sensitization is related to one or both of the more familiar dimensions of extraversion and neuroticism. In any event it is obviously a concept that is very relevant to medical practice, which relies a great deal on the patient's willingness, conscious or otherwise, to communicate his symptoms to the doctor.

Another area of medicine where personality will be extremely important concerns the way people react to drugs. There are actually two aspects to this problem. One is concerned with pharmacologically active drugs themselves; the other with the so-called 'placebo response'. With regard to the latter a considerable volume of research has demonstrated that dummy or inert preparations accompanied by appropriate suggestions will produce a wide variety of psychophysiological reactions, including changes in pain tolerance and alleviation of the physical symptoms of disease (Beecher, 1954; Claridge, 1972a). Although there is no evidence for a particular placebo type who will always react in this way, it is known that the presence of certain personality traits increases the likelihood of a placebo response occurring. One such trait is general suggestibility. Another is acquiescence, a feature of personality we came across when discussing the response biases that are found in people completing questionnaires. Thus, it has been found that people who frequently agree with statements that are made to them more often react positively to placebos. Personality will, of course, interact with other factors in the drug-giving situation, as is well illustrated in a study comparing the effects of giving placebos to people when alone and when in groups (Knowles and Lucas, 1960). One of the personality characteristics the investigators were interested in was neuroticism, the subjects being asked to report on the number of side-effects they experienced after taking what they were told was a new psychotropic drug. It was found that in subjects doing this by themselves neuroticism was unrelated to the frequency of reported side-effects. However, when subjects worked in groups the more neurotic of them described many more side-effects. It is interesting to note, incidentally, that one of the primary traits of general neuroticism is suggestibility, which probably accounted for a tendency of the more neurotic people in the group to 'catch' side-effects from others around them. This latter point has important implications in itself, since in practice treatments are often given under group conditions, that is in wards, where patients can communicate their reactions to each other. In this respect it should also be borne in mind that the placebo response is not simply a curious phenomenon found only as a reaction to pharmacologically inert substances but forms a component, often a substantial one, of any situation where drugs, active or not, are administered. The doctor's personality, interacting with that of the patient, is therefore a crucial part of the treatment process.

Quite apart from the placebo response, and the influence of personality factors on it, there are more fundamental ways in which people differ in their reactions to drugs. As discussed previously, these differences are known to be related to personality, work on the topic providing evidence for the concept of nervous type. Naturally, a good deal of the research in this area has been concerned with the psychotropic drugs used in the treatment of psychiatric illness, where it has been found that individuals of different personality types may show totally opposite reactions to the same dose of a drug. Of more general interest, however, is the very wide variation found in the tolerance of sedative/hypnotics, like the barbiturates which may be used for anaesthetic purposes. We saw earlier that experimental psychologists have investigated this particular problem using the technique of sedation threshold which has been developed as a measure of nervous typological variation. Apart from its implications for the understanding of the biological basis of personality, this work is of interest for purely pharmacological reasons. Thus, a recent study by the present writer demonstrated that nervous type, and hence personality, may be by far the most important determinant of the amount of intravenous barbiturate required to induce sedation (Claridge, 1971). Traditionally, of course, pharmacologists have taken account of individual differences in tolerance by correcting drug dosage for some physical characteristic, such as weight or a derivative of it. In fact, the study in question showed, in various samples of people, that the correlations between body weight and drug dosage ranged from negative to only very slightly positive. By comparison, drug amount to induce sedation was consistently correlated with a number of independent measures of nervous type, such as physiological indices of central nervous arousal and performance on tasks like those of vigilance referred to in a previous section.

This work of course complements other research, also discussed earlier, in which drug tolerance has been found to be related to personality as measured more directly, that is through personality questionnaires. Taken together such studies suggest that further research in this area of psychopharmacology might eventually lead to more exact guidelines for prescribing drugs according to the patient's personality.

So far we have examined how an individual's personality may modify his reaction to illness and to some of the procedures to which he may be subjected as part of his treatment. However, it is fitting to end this account with a brief look at probably the most thorny problem of all, namely the role played by personality factors in the aetiology of medical disorder. The field of psychosomatics or psychosomatic medicine is a vast one in itself, and a complete account of it would take us far beyond the confines of this chapter. In any case much of the relevant evidence belongs with a discussion of the topic of emotion, particularly its influences on those physiological mechanisms that might provide vehicles for the so-called psychosomatic diseases. Nevertheless, one aspect of the problem it is appropriate to consider here concerns the extent to which the study of personality factors can throw light on our understanding of physical complaints.

It was a belief long held by workers in psychosomatic medicine that it was possible to identify particular personality types who were especially prone to develop certain kinds of illness, such as coronary heart disease, ulcers or essential hypertension. Unfortunately, this view was based on unreliable evidence derived from clinical observation and has not stood the test of more rigorous experimental investigation. Recent research in the field has therefore tended to narrow down on more carefully defined aspects of personality and to investigate more limited problems in psychosomatics. By way of illustration let us look at two rather contrasting approaches, deliberately chosen to represent the two different (nomothetic and idiographic) views of personality we have come across several times in previous sections.

Nomothetic research in psychosomatics, having abandoned such crude typological notions as the 'coronary personality', has tended to confine itself to the study of established personality characteristics or dimensions, using the personality questionnaire technique to examine people with different illnesses. Several such studies have demonstrated that patients suffering from a variety of diagnosed pyschosomatic disorders tend, with some notable exceptions, to be more neurotic and more introverted than normal (Sainsbury, 1960). Of course, a major difficulty even with this kind of evidence is that it could be argued that the response on personality questionnaires is influenced by the fact that the individuals are currently ill. And certainly increased neuroticism levels have sometimes been found in patients suffering from internal diseases of non-psychosomatic origin. However, the results of some other personality questionnaire studies are more difficult to explain in that way. Some investigators have reported abnormally low levels of anxiety or neuroticism in patients with certain conditions, such as coronary heart disease and lung cancer (Sainsbury, 1960; Kissen, 1966). In line with this is the finding, in one study of blood pressure in normal factory workers, that the hypertensive individuals rated themselves on questionnaire as the least neurotic (Davies, 1970). A possible interpretation of these results is that the lowered neuroticism reflects a denial strategy on the part of certain individuals, an idea which would bring us very near to the popular notion of physical illness being an outlet for repressed or 'bottled' emotion. Alternatively, the differences observed may reflect genuine variations at the nervous typological level which underly such personality dimensions as neuroticism, and which may make certain people prone to physiological responses that are seen in pathological form as physical diseases, such as hypertension. Although nervous typological approaches to personality of the kind discussed earlier have scarcely begun to be applied to the problems of psychosomatics, they are clearly well-placed conceptually for bridging the gap between the personality and the pathophysiological processes responsible for physical disease (Claridge, 1973).

Let us turn now to a very different application of personality theory to psychosomatics. In the previous section we saw how the repertory grid technique is being used to explore individual attitudes, or constructs, in behavioural and psychological disorders. Less commonly, though occasionally, the same technique has been applied to the investigation of physical complaints which can be said to be broadly psychosomatic. A particularly good example is a study of obesity reported by Fransella and Crisp (1970). They investigated changes in the repertory grid structure of two obese women during psychotherapy. Both patients were asked to supply certain elements in the form of people known to them personally and who fitted role titles like 'an admired person', 'a person to be pitied', and so on. Other elements, such as 'like me in character when I'm overweight' and 'like me in character when I am a normal weight', were supplied by the psychologist. As might be expected perhaps, at the beginning of treatment when they were overweight, the patients perceived themselves as being at the 'bad' end of most constructs. Thus, one saw herself as possessive, argumentative, always trying to tell others what to do. During the first phase of treatment, when a gradual reduction in weight was occurring, there was a dramatic shift towards the opposite, 'good', pole of the constructs, the patient just cited now seeing herself when obese as more like herself when of normal weight; that is, confident and understanding of others. Unfortunately both patients later began to put on weight again, though interestingly this was accompanied by a shift back again to the obese attitudes observed at the beginning of treatment. The most striking feature of the results, however, was the temporal relationship between the changes in weight and the alterations in repertory grid constructs that occurred during treatment. Somewhat contrary to expectation the shifts in attitude described above tended to antedate the changes in weight, suggesting a true psychological influence on obesity.

Studies like the one just described are concerned, of course, with the intensive investigation of one or two cases, and the extent to which the results can be generalized is limited; for such is the nature of personal construct theory and of the repertory grid technique. On the other hand, unlike the personality questionnaire studies, they can provide information in depth about the possible psychological mechanisms that may influence the course of physical disorder in the individual. Furthermore, they provide quantitative information. In that important respect they differ from that of earlier idiographic enquiries in the field, which relied heavily on projective techniques and on a now discredited psychoanalytic approach to psychosomatic disease.

Concluding remarks

This chapter started with the comment that there is a great variety of approaches to personality, the particular slant given to the discussion here being only one of many that could have been chosen. It will not have escaped the reader's notice that much, though not exclusive, emphasis has been placed on those facts and theories which try to ground personality variation in its biological basis. No apologies are made for this, since I believe that it is here that knowledge about personality can be most closely integrated with the natural science background of the doctor or potential doctor. The occasional skirmishes into the idiographic field of personal construct theory, with its dislike of biological explanation and universal law, may therefore seem surprising. However, its inclusion, at the risk of losing some coherence and tidiness of presentation, was considered important for two reasons. First, not to have done so would have given a misleading view of the contemporary scene in personality study and of the sharp divisions of opinion that occur over theories such as those of Eysenck. Secondly I believe that idiographic theories, and particularly personal construct theory, do draw attention to data about personality which, as yet, nomothetic workers find difficult to handle. Thus, trait theorists have failed lamentably to find measurement techniques which can say much about the individual; the personal construct theorists have made it their business to do so. Ultimately each will presumably gain something from the other. Just as personal construct theories will have to come to terms with the fact that there are some common rules governing personality and that biological determinants are important, so dimensional theorists will have to recognize the temporal variability and situational specificity of behaviour. Of course, few readers of this chapter will need to bother themselves with such issues. Their main concern will be with what, at the end of the day, the psychologist can say that is relevant to medical practice and research. Hopefully the account given here will have gone some way towards meeting that need.

References

Bannister, D. and Fransella, F. (1966). 'A Grid Test of Schizophrenic Thought Disorder', *Br. J. Soc. Clin. Psychol.* 5, pp. 95–102.
Bannister, D. and Fransella, F. (1971). *Inquiring Man*. Harmondsworth: Penguin.
Beecher, H. K. (1954). *Measurement of Subjective Responses*. Oxford University Press.
Bond, M. R. and Pearson, I. B. (1969). 'Psychological Aspects of Pain in Women with Advanced Cancer of the Cervix', *J. Psychosom. Res.* 13, pp. 13–19.
Byrne, D. (1964). 'Repression-sensitization as a Dimension of personality', in *Progress in Experimental Personality Research* (ed. B. A. Maher). New York: Academic Press.
Cattell, R. B. (1965). *The Scientific Analysis of Personality*. Harmondsworth: Penguin.
Claridge, G. S. (1967). *Personality and Arousal*. Oxford: Pergamon.
Claridge, G. S. (1971). 'The Relative Influence of Weight and of "Nervous Type" on the Tolerance of Amylobarbitone Sodium', *Br. J. Anaesth.* 43, pp. 1121–5.
Claridge, G. S. (1972a). *Drugs and Human Behaviour*. Harmondsworth: Penguin.
Claridge, G. S. (1972b). 'The Schizophrenias as Nervous Types', *Br. J. Psychiat.* 121, pp. 1–17.
Claridge, G. S. (1973), 'Psychosomatic Relations in Physical Disease', in *Handbook of Abnormal Psychology* (ed. H. J. Eysenck, 2nd ed.). London: Pitman.
Claridge, G. S., Canter, S. and Hume, W. I. (1973). *Personality Differences and Biological Variations*. Oxford: Pergamon.
Davies, M. (1970). 'Blood Pressure and Personality', *J. Psychosom. Res.* 14, pp. 89–104.
Eysenck, H. J. (1947). *Dimensions of Personality*. London: Routledge & Kegan Paul.
Eysenck, H. J. (1955) 'A Dynamic Theory of Anxiety and Hysteria', *J. Ment. Sci.* 101, pp. 28–51.
Eysenck, H. J. (1967). *The Biological Basis of Personality*. Springfield: C. C. Thomas.
Eysenck, S. B. G. and Eysenck, H. J. (1972). 'The Questionnaire Measurement of Psychoticism', *Psychol. Med.* 2, pp. 50–5.
Fransella, F. (1972), *Personal Change and Reconstruction: Research on a Treatment of Stuttering*. London: Academic Press.
Fransella, F. and Crisp, A. H. (1970). 'Conceptual Organization and Weight Change', *Psychother. Psychosom.* 18, pp. 176–85.
Freedman, D. (1965), 'An Ethological Approach to the Genetical Study of Human Behavior', in *Methods and Goals in Human Behavior Genetics* (ed. S. G. Vandenberg). New York: Academic Press.
Gray, J. A. (1964). *Pavlov's Typology*. Oxford: Pergamon.
Hall, C. S. and Lindzey, G. (1957). *Theories and Personality*. New York: Wiley.
Kissen, D. M. (1966). 'The Significance of Personality in Lung Cancer in Men', *Ann. N.Y. Acad. Sci.* 125, pp. 820–6.
Knowles, J. B. and Lucas, C. J. (1960). 'Experimental Studies of the Placebo Response', *J. Ment. Sci.* 106, pp. 231–40.

Mischel, W. (1968). *Personality and Assessment*. New York: Wiley.
Mittler, P. (1971). *The Study of Twins*. Harmondsworth: Penguin.
Nebylitsyn, V. D. and Gray, J. A. (1972). *Biological Bases of Individual Behavior*. New York: Academic Press.
Rodnight, E. and Gooch, R. N. (1963). 'A New Method for the Determination of Individual Differences in Susceptibility to a Depressant Drug', in *Experiment with Drugs* (ed. H. J. Eysenck). Oxford: Pergamon.
Sainsbury, P. (1960). 'Psychosomatic Disorders and Neurosis in Outpatients Attending a General Hospital', *J. Psychosom. Res.* 4, pp. 261–73.
Vernon, P. E. (1964). *Personality Assessment*. London: Methuen.
Wiessen, A. (1965). 'Differential Reinforcing Effects of Onset and Offset of Stimulation on the Operant Behaviour of Normals, Neurotics, and Psychopaths', *Dis. Abstr.* 26, p. 1786.

Notes on references

Bannister and Fransella (1966): A description of the development of a repertory grid technique for diagnosing thought-disordered schizophrenia.

Bannister and Fransella (1971): A readable account of personal construct theory and of various applications of the repertory grid technique.

Beecher (1954): An early, but classic, account of research on placebos.

Bond and Pearson (1969): A research paper on the relationships between personality and clinically reported pain.

Byrne (1964): A review of the concept and measurement of repression-sensitization as a personality dimension.

Cattell (1965): A summary, in readable form, of Cattell's theory and approach to the measurement of personality.

Claridge (1967): A research monograph reporting an extensive series of studies of psychophysiological correlates of psychiatric disorder.

Claridge (1971): A research report investigating determinants of individual differences in barbiturate tolerance.

Claridge (1972a): A popular account of some of the experimental evidence about the effects of drugs on human behaviour.

Claridge (1972b): A review article outlining the arguments that schizophrenia is not a disease but a personality 'type'.

Claridge (1973): A review of some basic research on and of strategies for investigating psychosomatic disease.

Claridge, Canter and Hume (1973): A research monograph reporting the results of a study of personality, physiological and cognitive factors in adult twins.

Davies (1970): A research paper on blood pressure and personality in male factory workers.

Eysenck (1947): An early description of Eysenck's factor-analytic approach to personality.

Eysenck (1955): An account of Eysenck's first attempts to examine the biological basis of personality.

Eysenck (1967): An account of Eysenck's revised biological theory of personality, together with a review of the relevant evidence.

Eysenck and Eysenck (1972): A description of the development of a new scale for measuring extraversion, neuroticism and psychoticism.

Fransella (*1972*): A research report and review of work on the personal construct approach to the understanding and treatment of stuttering.
Fransella and Crisp (*1970*): An account of personal construct theory applied to the study of obesity.
Freedman (*1965*): A description of how the direct observation methods of ethology can be used to investigate similarities in the behaviour patterns of new-born twins.
Gray (*1964*): The first authoritative account in English of the Russian work on 'nervous types'.
Hall and Lindzey (*1957*): A review of the major personality theories.
Kissen (*1966*): An account of research examining personality questionnaire responses in patients with lung cancer.
Knowles and Lucas (*1960*): A research report on the interaction between personality and situational factors determining the placebo response.
Mischel (*1968*): A review of current research on personality including a critique of trait theory.
Mittler (*1971*): A popular account of the twin method in psychological research and of the more important results obtained in twin studies.
Nebylitsyn and Gray (*1972*): An edited volume containing representative research studies and theoretical viewpoints about the biological basis of personality.
Rodnight and Gooch (*1963*): A research report of work on the relationship between personality and tolerance of nitrous oxide.
Sainsbury (*1960*): A report of a survey of personality in patients with various psychosomatic and non-psychosomatic medical illnesses.
Vernon (*1964*): A classic text on methods for measuring personality.
Wiessen (*1965*): A research report on personality differences in the extent to which individuals seek out or tolerate physiological arousal.

Suggestions for further reading

Bannister, D. and Fransella, F. *Inquiring Man*. Harmondsworth: Penguin 1971.
Lee, S. G. and Herbert, M. (eds). *Freud and Psychology*. Harmondsworth: Penguin 1970.
Mischel, W. *Personality and Assessment*. New York: Wiley 1968.

Chapter eight

Child Development and Adolescence

B. M. Foss

This chapter attempts to do two things: to give an impressionistic account of the psychology of child development and adolescence, and to bring out in a little detail points which may be of special interest in a volume of this kind. Such points include the stages of development at which different kinds of behaviour might first be expected to appear, and the chapter ends with a table showing some of the more important 'first appearances' in the early years. In describing the psychology of adolescence the writer has put more emphasis than usual on the socal aspects, since these may help to give some insight into present-day society; and there is a longer than might be expected section on moral development, for the same reason.

Early development

Behaviour occurs before birth, in the sense that the foetus moves spontaneously and responds to stimuli. There is also some evidence that the foetus can be conditioned. Immediately after birth fairly complex reflex patterns can be seen: for instance, grasping; the 'rooting reflex', in which a touch on the cheek results in the infant turning its head so that the mouth comes towards the stimulus; and, with appropriate stimulation, it is possible to elicit walking and swimming movements. However, the first impression is that the infant's time is taken up with sleeping (say, 80 per cent), feeding, excreting and crying. Very noticeable at birth are the large differences between individuals in weight and appearance; and also in response; for instance, response to being held. For full-term babies the range of differences in stage of development at birth is large and is sometimes quoted at one month as measured on the Dubowitz scale.

It is important to note that sleeping and waking are not all-or-nothing states, but that several levels of arousal can be discriminated. The way and the extent to which the infant responds to the environment, or to a stimulus, will depend particularly on the level of arousal. For instance, the results of a neurological test will be different if the infant is tested in a state of quiet alertness after being fed or when hyper-excited. (Similarly, with older children, the level of arousal affects the results when a child's stage of development is being assessed.)

What does an infant attend to? At birth it will already attend to clicking sounds; this is shown by its turning its head and eyes in the direction of the click. Later on, for instance at three months, an infant sometimes appears to be attending with only one modality at a time, so that if it is listening it stops looking and if it is looking it stops sucking. When a child first reaches out to grasp an object he does not look at his hands, but attends to the object as though he were concentrating on information from the joint and muscle receptors. There is some controversy as to whether or not very young babies have any sense of object perception. It is possible that one of the most important bits of learning which goes on is that the infant has to co-ordinate information from various modalities, and it is more than likely that there are important consequences if the infant has trouble in such integration. Some people have suggested that as a result of lack of integration in the early months, the infant does not perceive his mother in the usual sense, since he has separate visual, auditory, tactile and olfactory mothers. In many ways perception of the mother is different from perception of objects. For instance, it is late in the second year of life that an object is believed by the child still to exist when it can't be perceived, but judging by infants' behaviour the continued existence of the mother when out of sight seems to be assumed fairly early in the first year of life.

Taking any one modality, something is known of the stimuli which particularly catch a child's attention. In vision, this has been studied by watching the movements of the eyes when the infant is given two objects to look at. It is assumed that the object which is looked at most has attention-getting characteristics. Movement, brightness, complexity of pattern and colour are all important.

There are much-quoted experiments by Fantz (1961), which however are not easy to repeat, showing that infants at even two weeks of age are particularly attracted to representations of the human face. It was thought that an infant could not learn such a configuration so quickly and was assumed that there must be an instinctive basis for the response (by analogy with some of the 'built-in' preferences for stimulus patterns demonstrated by ethologists working with animals other than mammals).

More recent experiments (Carpenter, 1974) have shown that an infant can discriminate its mother's face from that of a stranger in the third week of life. This discrimination must obviously be learned, so that Fantz's assumption turns out to be wrong. It has also been shown recently that an infant at this age can discriminate its mother's voice from that of a stranger. (For additional discussion see Chapter 2.)

We have already mentioned that foetal conditioning may be possible. It is certainly the case that conditioning and other kinds of learning are possible very soon after birth. It has been observed that at the first feed, the way the baby is held, together with other factors such as the shape of the breast and the nipple, may result in the baby being unable to breathe, and aversive conditioning seems to occur very quickly. The interactional nature of human behaviour becomes very noticeable. The baby will struggle and thrash his limbs; the mother will conclude that she is a 'bad mother', and as a result she will become anxious and worse at feeding the baby.

At day 3 experiments have been done demonstrating operant conditioning quite clearly. When a warning sound occurs the infant learns to turn his head to one side rather than the other to obtain food. But, although such simple and rather artificial conditioning is fairly easily demonstrated, what cannot be spelled out are the real-life situations which are important for the infant's learning: that is, the gradual modification of his behaviour as a result of experience. It is quite likely that many responses are under the control of reinforcers, such as food, avoidance of discomfort, possibly warmth and contact; and from an early age, all kinds of outside events (visual and auditory) seem to act like reinforcers so that it is possible to describe the child's learning in terms of operant conditioning. However, it is not so clear that the copying of sounds and other kinds of imitation can be explained in operant terms. Also, although classical or Pavlovian conditioning can be demonstrated in neonates, it is not so clear that this is the way in which, for instance, emotions and motivations become modified through experience. Children pick up emotional responses from parents so quickly that it looks more like contagion than repetitious classical conditioning (see Mackay, Chapter 4).

If the learning situation is looked at more broadly, rather than in terms of the learning processes involved, then there is one rather surprising generalization that can be made. At least for the first few years of life, children develop cognitively more rapidly if they are reared at home with mothers or mother surrogates than if they are in hospitals or other institutions. In one study this was the case for thalidomide babies, even though those which were hospitalized had superior prosthetic devices.

There are of course circumstances in which children do develop better when taken away from home, for instance when malnutrition needs correcting. Presumably also when there is very harsh treatment at home, for instance, baby battering. It seems that many children in institutions suffer from what is sometimes called cultural deprivation. They are often constrained in their cots for long hours and have much less interaction with the environment than do children reared at home. In particular they do not get the many hours of close face-to-face interaction which most mothers provide for their children. Whatever the detailed reasons, it is certainly the case that institutionalized children are delayed in most developmental stages; they are later in smiling, sitting up, walking, talking, and so on.

Crying

As Wolff has shown (1969), there are several different kinds of infantile crying distinguishable by spectrographic analyses, and which mothers may also distinguish. The 'birth cry' is unlike any other. The 'hunger cry' is the commonest and should rather be called a 'basic cry' since it is associated with conditions other than hunger. Most other cries end up as a basic cry, which may pass into drowsiness or sleep. The pain cry, elicited for instance by a hypodermic needle, has an initial yell, followed by several seconds of silence during which the baby maintains expiration which is finally broken by a gasp and loud sobbing. A 'frustration cry' sounds like an excessive version of the basic cry: when it is produced by removing a teat, it resembles a modified pain cry, with a shorter period of expiration. Other causes of crying (usually the basic cry) are coldness, nakedness, internal pain (colic) and 'startle' stimuli. The basic cry can sometimes be stopped by various kinds of repetitive movement, and also by 'white noise' (e.g., the sound of an electric vacuum cleaner). At about four weeks, some mothers notice a new cry which is a sham cry in the sense that it is initiated by no specific need but is simply a call for attention. Presumably it is built up by operant conditioning, and it is probably this kind of crying that several authors suggest can be eliminated by extinction or non-reinforcement.

Separation from the mother is a major cause of distress and crying in a wide variety of animals, and grief is a chronic elaboration of this distress. Whether or not a child is distressed when left by his mother will depend on his age and where he is. Distress at separation is likely to be strongest in the second year, especially if the environment is strange. Anything familiar reduces separation anxiety. It is only when anxiety is low that the child is curious rather than afraid of strangeness. So a child uses his mother or some other familiar safe thing as a base from which to explore. It should be noted that all children pass through a phase when even the briefest exploratory excursion involves temporary separation. Paradoxically it is easier for a child to leave a good mother, because she is a more secure base.

The Robertsons, basing their work on Bowlby's ideas, have demonstrated that a short stay in hospital may have devastating effects on the infant's behaviour towards the mother, to the extent of rejecting her for a considerable time after reunion. It is not certain what the long-term effects may be, but the short-term effects are so pronounced that there has been a widespread acceptance of the fact that separation should be minimal. The Robertsons' later work shows that the effects of separation are much reduced if the child can be gradually introduced to the new situation, so that it is in an environment which has become familiar by the time the separation becomes complete.

Imitation and play

There is anecdotal evidence that a child of five months will imitate putting out the tongue. The claim is hard to credit since it is difficult to see how the infant can 'know' which muscles to move to make its face look like that of the other person. What seems to happen is that the mother imitates the child a great deal from quite early on in the child's life. For instance, the infant will himself put his tongue out and the mother will imitate him and at the same time make noises and smiles which infants seem to find rewarding. The result is that he will learn to put his tongue out when his mother does so on a basis of operant learning.

Imitation of noise is another matter, since the infant can hear himself and match what he hears to the vocalizations of other people. Imitation of noises starts towards the end of the first year, leading to single words, two-word sentences ('Daddy allgone'), then the commoner vocabulary and grammatical structures. During the early stages especially the child 'practises' a great deal on his own. This is true also of much else of his imitation. Play at first tends to be solitary (even when other children are there), but dolls, other playthings and pets are made to stand for parents and children. Play in early childhood is taken to reveal a child's preoccupations, and play therapy is based on the notion that emotional preoccupations can be acted out. Play starts being co-operative at about three to four years, but it is also competitive. The dominance fighting to establish a 'pecking order' which can be seen in all social animals is very marked in children. A great deal of it is symbolic and indirect, especially in girls, where aggression is more likely to be verbal than physical. There have been several demonstrations that boys in particular copy aggressive behaviour which they have seen either in real life or on the screen (Bandura and Walters, 1963; and Bandura, 1969).

Individual differences

It has already been noted that infants differ markedly from each other at birth. There are also consistent differences in speed of conditioning which can be demonstrated in infants only a few days old. Some individual differences, for instance in general reactivity, seem to remain very consistent; but not enough follow-up studies have been done to show what kinds of adult behaviour, if any, may be related to neonatal characteristics. There are tests of 'developmental quotient' (DQ rather than IQ) which depend on assessing the maturational stage which the infant has reached (sitting up, crawling, walking, etc.). Such assessments do correlate significantly with IQ at age eight, for instance, but the correlations are very low and of no use predictively. It is likely that some of the consistent individual differences are related to genetic factors. In one carefully controlled study (Freedman, 1965), the rates of behavioural development during the first year of monozygotic and dizygotic twins were compared, and found to be considerably more alike for the monozygotic.

The table at the end of this chapter makes no allowance for individual differences in developmental rate. Apart from genetic factors, there are many others which are influential. Some of these have been mentioned already.

Home versus institution: Institutionalized children may be delayed in the first appearance of many behaviours, including social responses such as smiling.

Sex: Male-female differences in rate of development are very common, one of the most notable being related to language. On almost any measure of linguistic ability, girls are on the average better than boys, probably up to puberty. On the other hand, boys tend to be better than girls at tests measuring 'spatial' ability.

Social class: This is found to correlate with many things. Before one year of age, middle-class children tend to fixate an object longer than working-class children. In middle and late childhood, middle-class children tend to develop a more complex language (vocabulary and structure); and this divergence is accentuated by the different types of schooling experienced by different social classes.

It has been assumed by most psychologists that the individual differences that develop during the first years of life will be reflected in personality differences in adulthood. On the one hand, Freud and the neo-Freudians have believed that the first five years (say), cover the most important stages of emotional development which produce nearly irreversible changes; and that during this period the foundations are laid for normal and abnormal personality. Rather similarly, experimental psychologists, at least those interested in child development, have assumed that 'early learning' is prepotent, so that habits learned during the first years lay the foundations for later behaviour. The Freudian approach is based mainly on retrospective evidence, from the memories of patients and non-patients, and therefore subject to all the distortions due to the selectivity of memory, especially selection due to having too strong a hypothesis (see Harbison, Chapter 10).

Social development

Compared with other primates, man is born at a very immature stage of development, so that a long period of nurturance is necessary; and for several years after an individual is in principle able to fend for himself, and even for several years after sexual maturity, he cannot adopt adult roles in most societies. There are several mechanisms which ensure that a tie is built up between the infant and the mother or mother-substitute. The mother is attracted to the infant by its appearance, smell, crying, smiling, eye-to-eye contact, and by social pressure to conform to the role of mother as interpreted by her social group. The infant becomes attached to the mother through reinforcement of bodily needs, including possibly warmth and contact. Physical contact is of primary importance for developing this attachment in rhesus monkeys (Harlow, 1961). But work with monkeys has also shown that it is important that the mother-infant tie should weaken at about the time when the next infant is likely to be born, since then the mother will not be able to give the original infant so much attention. Sometimes the mother actually rejects the infant's advances, but also this is usually the time when the infant starts exploring on his own.

It is possible that analogous changes occur in humans. The infant starts to explore at about the time when another infant might be naturally expected, and, probably as a safety measure, it is at about this time that most infants develop fear of strangers. At this stage, there is the paradox that strangeness or novelty may elicit either curiosity and exploration or fear.

There are large individual differences between children in the degree to which they become attached. In one study (Stevens, 1971) carried out at a large nursery in Greece, it was found that some children developed attachments for several nurses whereas others were, so to speak, monogamous and became attached to one nurse only (curiously the nurses also varied very much in the number of children to whom they became attached). Studies in different cultures have not yet shown whether being attached to one person rather than several is advantageous or disadvantageous to the child later. It is often assumed that if no attachment at all is formed the child's cognitive, emotional and social development will be affected. Such an effect would be predicted from Freudian theory, and writers such as Bowlby give support to this. However the evidence is not particularly clear (see Rutter, 1972) partly because a failure to make an attachment is often associated with cultural and other kinds of deprivation.

Sex Typing

This term is used for all those kinds of learning which serve to emphasize the male and female roles within the child's sub-culture. Already at three years of age children tend to choose toys associated with the appropriate sex role, but this kind of learning becomes most noticeable and even exaggerated between the years of six and, say, twelve. A few years ago scientists made confident statements about the kinds of things which girls did as opposed to what boys did, but it is now clear that a great deal is determined by the particular sub-culture, and cultures now change so fast that statements must be made cautiously. During the beginning of this period at least children tend to play with others of the same sex. Some girls do take part in predominantly boyish pursuits, but it is very unusual for boys to engage openly in what are thought of as purely female ones. However, this may not be the case inside the next decade. It is said that girls during this period talk and think more about love of a romantic kind, whereas boys are more curious about sex. A generalization which may have more validity is that boys tend to be more active and girls talk more. It also seems to be the case, as the anthropologist Ruth Benedict pointed out, that in our society there is more sex role continuity for girls than there is for boys. The sorts of games which girls play are much more closely related to what they will do later in life as a home-maker and parent; whereas boys' games tend to train them to be warriors.

Conformity, deviation and adolescence

Not many generations ago, a person was unlikely to survive if he did not belong physically to a group of people. The need to belong to a group is still as great, though little is known about the psychological mechanisms involved. Avoidance of loneliness is one powerful drive.

In modern man, physical membership of a group may not be as important as seeing oneself as being a member. Some psychologists talk of 'identifying' with a group. A century ago, a person's choice of group was limited usually to the family, the immediate neighbourhood, work, church, perhaps hobbies and sport. Now, especially in cities, or where people are mobile, groups are based more on common interests. Especially where the media carry all the news, it is very easy for a person to discover and meet other people who want to behave in the same way or have common goals. Members of a group tend to come to look alike, talk alike, make the same choices in food, music, beliefs, etc., and these tendencies are much more marked in those people who see themselves as belonging essentially to only one group. Those who have multiple group membership will in general appear more non-committal but nevertheless may make some changes in appearance, etc., between different group activities: work, church, pub, etc. The forming of new groups, especially among adolescents and pre-adolescents, is made much easier when there is increased mobility (e.g., motorbikes) or high population density. Anything which lessens the old group allegiances will also make new groupings easier. So that one would expect gangs to be especially prevalent in new 'high-rise' housing estates or with people who have just left school.

Human groups of all kinds tend to be *for* some things and *against* others, and 'things' includes people, causes, art forms, etc. (It is interesting to speculate on the evolutionary origins of this 'us *versus* them' phenomenon.) It is likely that 'groupiness' is the prime motivation, and that the group's activities and interests are often secondary, and owe their existence to the fact that they increase group cohesion. From this psychological point of view, pop festivals have much in common with earlier revivalist meetings.

Besides these pressures to belong to a group, and to conform to it, there are still the largely competitive tendencies, of obvious evolutionary origin, to be unique, to have a role within the group. Very often such a role involves being best at something. Being best may involve owning things, being most daring, or beautiful, or cleverest. With small boys, competitiveness may show itself in the form of 'dominance fighting' as seen in animals.

The group belongingness, and the individual's position in that group, have an interesting reciprocal relation, in that an individual's status comes partly from the group he belongs to, and not just from his own position within the group. One of the main incentives for a boy to join a tough gang is that he will now be seen as tough to outsiders, although he may individually be nothing of the sort.

The psychology of adolescence has often been discussed mainly in biological and individual terms, with an emphasis on pubertal changes. Perhaps one should put more emphasis on social psychological factors, such as those already mentioned. There is the additional factor often known as 'adolescent revolt'. It has been observed for many years, and across many cultures (though not in all) that adolescence is often accompanied by a reaction against parental ways of life. This may well have evolutionary benefits, but it also leads to stress for children and parents. In fact, classic writers on adolescence have talked of the period as one of storm and stress. Many writers have also noted that adolescence is a period of idealism (at least in some middle-class sub-cultures) and of seeking for one's own identity. As we have already said, the latter may be partly interpreted as looking for a group to belong to and finding a role in that group. However, such an interpretation completely ignores the sexual and economic factors also at work. A few decades ago the situation could be stated in fairly black and white terms: the young adolescent was economically dependent; he was sexually capable but not expected to have, or even legally forbidden from having intercourse; and his social roles were essentially non-adult. In the course of a decade he was expected to go through a fairly clear series of transitional stages until he inevitably reached the desired position in an adult society in which his economic, sexual and social roles would all have changed utterly. The apparent inevitability of this causes some writers to describe a series of developmental 'tasks' which had to be undertaken in a more or less definite sequence for the various metamorphoses to occur within the individual. This particular psychology of adolescence now seems dated, for several reasons. Sexual intercourse is often practised soon after the onset of puberty; many children, including working-class children, have considerably more spending money than their parents had at the same age; and there are now so many 'mini-cultures' all the way from pre-adolescence to adulthood, that at any age a child can find himself fully accepted within a culture, as a full member of a society. Together with this change there is a tendency not to look ahead to the next stage in development, and many adolescents cannot begin to imagine what they will be like as grown-ups.

It is now generally accepted that the onset of puberty occurs earlier as time passes. (See, for example, Eisenberg, 1970.) The psychological consequences of this are not clear; nor is it clear what effect the onset of puberty has on the majority of children, since most information which does exist comes from small or specialized samples. What has become clear is that the effects of puberty are probably largely controlled by what the child and his peers expect those effects to be, and so may also depend on the parents. For instance, there are large cross-cultural differences in the extent of menstrual pain, and these differences seem clearly to reflect the expectations. There is some evidence that menarche interferes with a girl's scholastic performance but, from a different part of the country, there is negative evidence. It is again likely that expectations are very important. The effects of ignorance are uncertain; nor are the effects of knowledge known. No one has yet shown that sex education is a good thing (and it would be extremely difficult to show, since the investigator would have the problem of deciding what sex education is good for). The majority of people might be able to agree on a minimum, in order to prevent unwanted pregnancies and disease, and to prevent unhappiness resulting from an ignorance of the normality of abnormality. However, it would be a mistake to think that there are any good psychological reasons which might help one to decide who should give the information, or how or when.

Socialization and moral development

Socialization is used to describe the way in which a child comes to conform, more or less, with the social groups in which he finds himself. Sometimes its use is restricted to the learning of the mores of society as a whole. Sometimes it is taken to include processes going on throughout life. These processes include the acquisition of skills, such as feeding and clothing oneself, and language skills, vocational skills and learning roles.

Here we will mention one aspect of the development of skills, which is that they make use of previously acquired skills, implying that they must be learned in a certain order. The way in which a baby first holds a pencil will depend largely on the innate grasp reflex. Holding it using finger-thumb opposition has to be learned, partly by imitation, but this learning must occur first before any progress can be made in drawing or writing. Also the infant must learn to press sufficiently hard to leave a mark yet not so hard as to tear the paper. These basic skills are in use, vastly overpractised and automatic, every time a person writes, together with many other basic skills concerned with drawing shapes, right-left progression, language structure, and so on. It is quite useful to think of any sophisticated skills as being hierarchical, with the earliest learned lower-order skills being carried on subconsciously. It is likely that such lower-order skills must be overpractised and automatic before the higher levels of a skill can be attended to. It is occasionally the case when there has been a development failure, as in 'word blindness', or acalculia, that a lower-order skill is missing, such as shape discrimination. However, in general it can be said that a failure to develop educational and other skills may be due to very many causes, including genetic factors, neurological dysfunction, and motivational and emotional factors. To illustrate the latter, there is the case of monozygotic twins in the same school, one of whom had an IQ of 15 points higher than the other. The second twin was dominated by the first. Six months after the first twin was sent to a different school, the second was retested. His IQ had gone up by exactly 15 points (as chance would have it). Too high and too low motivation may both be impediments. The pressure from overanxious parents, or the example set by a too-able or successful father, may result in the child opting out of that particular skill. In cases where goals are set too high there seem to be two extreme kinds of reaction: opting out, 'leaving the field', going ill, staying in bed on the one hand; trying too hard, still failing, getting more anxious, on the other. Low motivation is often the result of the views of the parents or the peergroup. What is the point of learning an intellectual skill if it has no currency or status value with one's mates! Psychological studies of the 'need for achievement' have shown that the need varies very much between cultures and sub-cultures. Other psychological work on the ability to 'postpone gratification' has shown wide individual differences. It is not surprising that the majority are not interested in staying an extra year at school if there is more money and fun to be had immediately, even if on the dole in some cases. A child, or adult, will not enjoy staying in any setting where there are no reinforcements (in the technical sense). For a child to be content at school, he must have been a success at something. It hardly matters what. The result of success appears to generalize: there is a spread of confidence to other activities, and socially. Severe failure (in the child's own eyes) may lead to refusal to go to school at all. (There may, of course, be many other reasons, such as bullying, which a child may be afraid to talk about.)

From the point of view of success and failure, there are crucial stages in most children's lives: going to school for the first time, changing school, taking a first job, or going to university or medical school. When changing environment in such drastic ways, it is difficult to take one's previous successes with one. The child may have been at the top of the child hierarchy in junior school, but is at the bottom in secondary school and has to start the struggle over again.

It is characteristic of development educationally, or in sport, or art, or money-making, or status-seeking, that individuals keep setting themselves new goals, which in some sense are higher as well as new. Otherwise the activity ends up boring. (An exception may be when the reaching of the goal is unpredictable, as in gambling.) Education is partly concerned with getting children to set their own goals, rather than rely on externally given ones. Occasionally one finds a particularly able child who is not being intellectually extended, because neither he himself nor anyone else is setting appropriate goals. The main motive for such a child may become to escape from boredom.

What processes are involved in 'moral' socialization? Freudian theory puts emphasis on modelling or imitation of two kinds: anaclitic identification, which involves modelling oneself on a loved person, and which gives rise to a person's 'ego ideal' and desires to do good works; and 'identification with the aggressor', which involves the internalization of punishment and the development of conscience. For this kind of theory, the evidence is rather strong that an affectional bond between parents and child is important for moral development to take place. (The evidence comes mainly from comparison of the families of delinquent and non-delinquent boys.) On the other hand, theories deriving from 'learning' experiments emphasize the effects of rewards and punishments, and the development of anxiety (fear of punishment) as a result of conditioning. These theories fit much of the evidence rather well, but are not altogether very satisfactory in explaining the importance of a strong affectional bond.

Probably all three mechanisms are involved: rewarding, punishing and imitating. Some of the reinforcements for conformity are obvious, varying from edible or spendable rewards given by parents, to prizes and other forms of accolade given by groups and societies to individuals who exemplify what the group or society stands for. However, some rewards are much more subtle, and some have been described in the previous section.

Perhaps the avoidance of punishment, or learning from punishment, is most potent in producing conformity. Lack of conformity leads to lack of belonging and loneliness, which is punishing. No one has done any counting, but it is likely that avoidance of loneliness is a major reason for conforming to some group or other. Other forms of punishment vary from smacking to being laughed at, raised eyebrows, stony silences, hair-shaving, 'tarring and feathering', and, more generally, being made to feel ashamed.

It is possible that the exact way of presenting rewards or punishment may be important. In experiments on puppies, the investigators (Solomon, Turner and Jessac, 1968) attempted to train the animals not to eat certain food by cuffing them with a folded newspaper. They were later tested alone with the food, to see if they had developed 'consciences'. Some puppies had been punished as they were approaching the food, others were punished when they had already eaten some. The first treatment led to a longer avoidance of eating and an apparent development of conscience. The second treatment did not prevent eating, but led to what looked like guilty behaviour after eating. There are related results obtained from experiments with children.

Some behaviour, for instance exaggeration, may be permitted under some circumstances but not under others. One would expect from experiments with animals that it would be important for the child that situations where certain behaviour is permitted should be made easily distinguishable from situations where it is forbidden.

The third process is imitation, or copying. This may or may not be reducible to classical conditioning, or to the effects of reward and punishment. For present purposes it will be regarded as a process in its own right, or rather several processes, since there are many kinds of imitation. A child may come to conform to certain norms, not as a result of any obvious rewards and punishments but through modelling himself on others. We have mentioned that Bandura and his colleagues have carried out many experiments to show that children are particularly prone to copy aggressive actions, especially if those actions have gone unpunished, or been rewarded, much less so if they are associated with punishment. Behaviour shown on television is copied in this way, even if the actors are cartoon characters. Older children may seek to join groups that have the same interests and ways of behaving that they have; but once in the group, they will imitate further and come to conform: in taste, in clothes, hair-style, make-up, food, drink, entertainment, language, beliefs, values, dislikes and morals. Some prediction is possible, since all of a child's (or adult's) tastes and values are not likely to change together. Predicting what group a child will see himself as joining, or more simply, predicting how a child will come to see himself, is difficult more because of the number of variables involved than through ignorance of the processes. However, some predictions can be made regarding the copying of individual bits of behaviour.

No one ends up as completely conformist, since the various group pressures are balanced by individual drives, for instance in 'dominance fighting', status-seeking, the need to be different, and to be best at something. This jockeying for position can go on within a group or between groups. Once a person has identified with a group, the status of that group will become his own status. Just as an individual may get status in his own group by being the most delinquent, so the group as a whole may be the most delinquent. It may be that these two kinds of seeking to be different are inversely related; so that, if one is a member of a 'way out' group, then one is highly conformist within that group.

Although social approval and disapproval continue to influence people to varying extents throughout their lives, nevertheless a child's avoidance of antisocial behaviour is also partly dependent on a conscience, an internal control which would operate even if one knew that there was no chance whatsoever of being found out. There are several theories to explain how conscience develops, and there is also some empirical evidence on the factors involved. The experiments with puppies were elaborated so as to demonstrate that a puppy's resistance to temptation depended on its early upbringing. They were most resistant if their upbringing was affectionate but involved correction, and least resistant if it was either punitive or permissive. It has already been mentioned that comparisons of the families of delinquent and non-delinquent boys (Bandura and Walters, 1959; Glueck and Glueck, 1950) show fairly reliably that the non-delinquent is more likely to have an affectionate tie with his parents; but it is typical also that the parents have imposed some discipline, such as threatened withdrawal of affection, rather than aggressive verbal or physical punishment. Also, the parents use more explanation; presumably the child is more likely to appreciate underlying principles, if they exist.

Failure to act morally, and becoming delinquent, are both the results of failure to become socialized to society as a whole. Such failures may depend on a large number of factors, including the following: the internalized standards of conduct may be strong or weak; those standards may be conventional or deviant; the person's impulses may be strong or weak; the impulses may be normal or deviant; the conflict between impulses and standards may have been resolved in various ways; there may be a physical or functional abnormality; there may be an important genetic component involved in an inability to behave morally; immediate environmental factors, including social and economic factors, may be particularly strong ('everybody's doing it'). That there are many factors involved is shown by the fact that one can catalogue a score of possible causes of failure to learn from the effects of reinforcement.

The moral attitude and judgments of a child do not relate closely to his own behaviour. They depend on his level of cognitive development, the attitudes and judgments he hears being expressed, the 'psychological distance' of the people and events being judged, and the conditions under which the judgment is being elicited, and who the child is talking to.

The dependence on cognitive development is illustrated by Piaget's experiments (substantially repeated many times) in which a child is required to judge the relative wickedness of various kinds of behaviour. (See Flavell, 1963, pp. 290–7.) A general finding is that a child under eight years old (roughly) does not distinguish between an intentional wrong-doing and one that is a mere accident. For instance, he will judge that the intentional breaking of an object worth so much is not as wicked as the accidental breaking of something worth ten times as much. Motives are not considered and punishment should be inevitable. 'Mature' judgments may be expected at, say, age ten, and adequate thinking processes to produce them develop in most children. However, it may be noted that an adult who is otherwise reasonable may show punitive behaviour towards another adult, even though the other's actions are known not to be intentional.

The actual judgments made will depend on the views which a child hears being expressed around him. It has been shown (Bandura and Walters, 1963) that, even though a child has advanced to basing his judgment on whether or not an action was intended, he may nevertheless revert to expressing the less mature judgment if he hears adults expressing that judgment. Conversely, a child may express maturer judgments earlier by being exposed to them earlier. Whom does a child copy in adopting moral judgments? The answer has to be vague since much of the evidence is not rigorously obtained; but early judgments appear to be copied from other members of the family, and misapplied, since the principles have not been understood. Before adolescence there is some evidence that attitudes are adopted increasingly from outside the family, sometimes from fictional and mass media characters, and, of course, from peer-groups; indeed from any group with which the child identifies himself (though he may not be a member of it). The concept of identification may be little more than a restatement that the child is adopting the attitudes of a certain group. However, some theories of identification do make predictions, for instance that the child may identify with the status person who dispenses rewards and punishments. Many psychologists would use this concept of identification to explain the copying of moral judgments as well as attitudes.

If a child is asked to judge a person's behaviour, the direction and strength of his judgment depends on what can be called the 'psychological distance' of the person being judged. The child's judgment will tend to be neutral if the person he is judging is distant geographically or temporally. The child will be the more involved the easier it is for him to identify himself with the person he is judging, or the victims, if any. The same factor may affect adults' judging. If the person doing the judging does identify himself with the person being judged, then the sign and strength of his judgment – whether it is punitive, or approving, or permissive – is said to depend on whether the judge exhibits that behaviour himself, and, if so, whether or not he has insight into his own motives.

Some theories of child development

Piaget

Piaget, who founded what is sometimes called the 'Geneva School' of child study, set out to discover how logical thinking develops. His great contribution has been to demonstrate the irrationality of a child's 'rational' behaviour. He has little to say about emotion, motivation and social pressures. Even when he is talking about the development of moral behaviour, the focus is on the cognitive processes involved. Another characteristic is that individual differences between children are not really relevant to the system, since Piaget is concerned with the normal progression of development; and much of the early empirical work was done on his own children. The smallness and idiosyncrasy of the samples has often been criticized, but when Piaget's work has been repeated by others on large and very different samples of children (including, for instance, subnormal children) results are obtained which are similar to Piaget's.

Piaget's most important technique is to carry out small experiments or demonstrations on individual children, and to question them when they are old enough. For instance: two identical beakers are filled with the same amount of liquid, and the child agrees that they are equal. If one is poured into a taller, thinner beaker, the child may say that this beaker now contains more liquid. Conversely, if it is poured into a wide, short beaker, he will see it as less. In this case, Piaget says that the child has not attained 'conservation of volume'. Or again, Piaget might ask a boy, 'How many brothers have you got?' 'Two: Peter and James.' 'And how many brothers has Peter got?' 'One: James.' With infants, Piaget relied on observation, but using some manipulation of the situation. For instance, a child might be lying in a cot with a string hanging in front of him which, when pulled, produced a noise from rattles placed over the cover of the cot. When the child had learned to pull the string to shake the rattles, Piaget removed the rattles. He then found that the child would pull the string apparently to cause the recurrence of *any* pleasant event, visual or auditory. Piaget has shown great ingenuity in devising methods. For instance, in part of his investigations of moral judgments, he studied children playing marbles, whether or not they obeyed rules, what happened if they did not, and whether they were prepared to change the rules.

Using such methods, Piaget found that the child's cognitive development could best be described in terms of a sequence of stages which occur always in the same order. (Other workers also find the sequence to be rather stable.) The main stages, each of which can be given subdivisions, are:

The sensori-motor stage (roughly eighteen months), in which behaviour does not seem to involve representation of reflective thought.
The stage of symbolic thought (until about four years), in which

play and language are integrated with other symbolic activity.
The stage of intuitive thought (until about seven or eight), in which language and thinking are integrated, but may still be idiosyncratic, and often dominated by perception (e.g. the child is unable to 'conserve').
The stage of concrete operations, which shows mature thinking except that general, propositional thinking is not reached, if at all, until
The stage of formal operations, at puberty or after.

All of this is concerned with describing actual development. Piaget has also constructed a rather complex theory. It has its own terminology, and some of the terms do not translate easily from French. One reason for the complexity is that the theory relies heavily on 'structures' which are not easy to describe, but which Piaget needs to explain many phenomena. As compared with stimulus-response explanations, which imply that the child is at the mercy of its environment, which supplies the stimuli to which it responds, Piaget sees the child as having a complex of cognitive structures which adapt, more or less, to changes in the environment. Two mechanisms are involved in such adaptations: assimilation and accommodation. Assimilation refers to the incorporation of new environmental events into existing structures, and accommodation refers to changing those structures because of such events. For instance, an infant has an innate mechanism allowing him to suck. Besides sucking for milk, he will also use this mechanism to suck his fingers, blanket, and so on (assimilation), but the sucking may become modified as a result (accommodation). A suitable balance between assimilation and accommodation produces intelligence. When a child imitates, it demonstrates the operation of accommodation in an unrestrained form, whereas much fantasy and play show a preponderance of assimilation. Piaget does not say much which might help educationalists to assist a child's development. For early development, the child needs feedback from his own movements, so that interaction between the child and its environment is a necessity. This has led some educationalists, for instance Froebel teachers, to consider that Piaget's theory supports their belief that learning should come through the child's own activity. Various experimenters have attempted to train or coach children to pass from one developmental stage to the next, and have had some success; but no principles have emerged from these experiments which might be applied to the teaching of illiterate children, for instance.

Freud
Many present-day theories of child development are more or less based

on classical psychoanalytic theory. Although Freud himself did not study the development of children directly (his daughter, Anna Freud, and Melanie Klein initiated much of the work on children) nevertheless his explanations of clinical material coming from adult patients are based on infantile and developmental processes. Many people would consider that Freud's main contribution was to focus attention on the first five years of life as being of paramount importance in determining later personality. He suggested that during this period the infant passes through stages which are determined by the way in which the child gets satisfactions of a bodily and erotic kind, and therefore related to the way in which the libido (instinctual energy) operates. The first stage is the oral stage, in which the child's erotic life (in Freud's rather special meaning) centres on the mouth; this is followed by the anal stage, when life centres on excretion; then the phallic stage in which sexual (but of course pre-pubertal) interest centres on the genitalia and body surface as a whole. There then follows a latent period during which there is little development until the genital period is reached at adolescence. Mental illness in later life was seen as originating from traumatic experiences occurring during these periods. The situation was complicated by the Oedipus situation in which the five-year-old, say, sees himself as competing with his father for the love of the mother. Other psychoanalysts elaborated some of these ideas, especially on the lines of devising adult typologies based on infantile experience. For instance, an orally accepting type would be a lover of food and drink, a smoker, and fond of words, quantitatively or qualitatively. The phallic type might be a lover of the body beautiful, an exhibitionist, or an admirer of sculpture. It is extremely difficult to test the validity of such speculations.

Learning Theory

Learning theories were originally based largely on experiments with animals, especially dogs, cats and rats. Nevertheless there have been many more recent attempts to apply these theories to elucidating child development. Because of their animal origins, one might expect the theories to be good at explaining humans to the extent that humans behave like animals, but not so good to the extent that human behaviour is affected by language, that humans imitate more, that they anticipate more, that they reflect more, and have elaborate continuing cultures. Also, humans are 'rule-following' to an extent not imaginable even among chimpanzees or dolphins. The best known applications to behaviour development and personality are associated with names such as those of O. H. Mowrer, N. E. Miller, R. R. Sears and R. A. Lundin.

(Concerned more with adult personality are H. J. Eysenck, and a group of people using behaviour therapy and its derivatives. See Chapter 7 by Claridge, as well as Chapter 4 by Mackay.) Such theories tend to be based on elaborations of classical (Pavlovian) conditioning or operant conditioning, or both. In Mowrer's theory, which is fairly typical, modifications of autonomic nervous system function are thought to occur by classical conditioning, whereas overt behaviour is modified through operant conditioning. From the point of view of child development, it is particularly useful to bear in mind the part played by reinforcement in the encouragement of behaviour. We have already considered cases such as the reinforcement of attention-getting crying. Consider also the case of the school child who can only get attention by behaving antisocially.

Ethology

There is no ethological theory of child development; nevertheless some ethological ideas have had a considerable effect on some theorists and experimenters. In particular, Bowlby (1969) used ethological ideas to explain the development of the child's tie to the mother, and has recently integrated these with psychoanalytic and other ideas in an attempt to explain attachment and grief. Stimulated particularly by Tinbergen's (1958) early book many psychologists were tempted to draw comparisons between the mechanism of imprinting and the development of all kinds of attachment, so that not only human affection would be explained in this way, but also the development of deviations. Lorenz's idea that, if imprinting was to occur, then it had to happen during a certain critical period has also been influential. (The concept probably originates in embryology, and has also been investigated, for instance in dogs, by non-ethological psychologists.) Developmental psychologists and educationalists have used the concept to explain failure to learn. The value of doing this is doubtful, since failure to learn is simply being given a new label or at best explained in terms of a vague maturational process.

Some early developmental stages

Here are given only rough indications. The normal variation is very large indeed.

First Month (Neonatal Period)

Notable reflexes: Moro, Babinski, sucking, grasping, 'stepping', 'swimming', yawning, blinking, vomiting, hiccoughing, sneezing; penis erections in the male. All these are there at birth, or within a few hours. At one month, when awake, the neonate lies on back with head to preferred side, and brings it to mid-position only momentarily. The chin may be lifted (to illustrate the very large range: some infants can raise their heads at birth; others do not do so until more than two months old, even though they are perfectly healthy). Feet are pressed against the observer's hand.

There are perceptual 'preferences' for moving objects, brightness, colour, pattern complexity, possibly for symmetry and possibly also for patterns resembling the human face. The head is moved to track a moving object, sometimes after only a few days.

'Emotional' reactions are limited to startle (Moro) and varying levels of general distress, shown in tearless crying, thrashing about and turning red. Crying simply to get attention occurs towards the end of this period. 'Pleasure' and 'burp' smiles appear, but not 'social' smiling. Classical and operant conditioning can be demonstrated in the first month.

Months 2 and 3

Head is held up when infant is supported in a sitting position. It comes more often to the mid-line. Child takes some weight on legs if supported in standing position. Transition occurs from hands mainly closed to mainly open. Starts to reach out to dangling objects, but this response may be very much delayed in unstimulating surroundings.

Accommodation of lens of eye is more or less complete by end of period (some exists at birth), and eyes converge on approaching object. Blinking at fast-approaching object occurs at about two months, and eye can track object through wide arc. Head is turned to familiar sound.

Crying is now accompanied by tears. Child feeds a great deal; for instance, still twice at night. Colicky babies are often free of colic by three months.

'Social' smiling, at a face, mask, etc., starts in this period. At about two months, if the infant is in an attentive state, he will react strongly when talked to, as though trying to answer.

Shows considerable anticipatory behaviour, for instance at sight of teat, or when footsteps approach while crying.

Months 4 to 6

Transition from sitting supported to beginning to sit alone. Grasps, but inefficiently. When prone and awake, head tends to be kept in midline, but is turned in direction of unfamiliar sound (i.e., later than to a familiar one). Towards end of this period will continue to smile at familiar face, but react coolly to strange ones. Grasped objects tend to be brought to mouth. Finger-thumb opposition is not yet possible. Arm movements still tend to be ambidextrous or symmetrical. Some bi-manual co-ordination.

Starts to sleep through the night, but this is often accompanied by screaming at bedtime. This particular kind of crying seems particularly susceptible to operant conditioning; it is easily increased by reinforcement, and extinguished by ignoring it. Gurgles and babbles to people.

Yet more anticipatory behaviour, for instance before being picked up. Will wait expectantly for a meal.

Months 7 to 12

Transition from crawling to going rapidly on all fours, and standing by pulling himself up, and walking if led. Now grasps efficiently and can throw with a thrusting movement. May hold out arms to be picked up at the beginning of this period, but some children are much later. In first half of period objects are banged repetitively, and often thrown away repetitively for someone to retrieve. Infant highly amused by 'peek-a-boo'. Many understand 'no' by halfway through period, and many speak two or three words by one year.

Emotional expression becomes much more differentiated. Frustration at being deprived of toy comes halfway through period. Fear of strangers is often shown. Shows definite affection and signs of attachment. Enjoys reciprocal 'games', but will play on his own for long periods. Gives up object when asked. Can put one object in another. Appears to realize that there is more to an object than he can see.

During the first year, much of the child's behaviour seems to be concerned with integrating information from the various senses and with body movements. Also he seems to be learning the limits of his own body, i.e., learning his 'body schema'. For instance, it is only in the second half of the first year that the infant seems to learn that his feet are part of himself, so that when he bites them they will hurt.

According to Freud, the child is dominated by orality during this period. According to Piaget, there is a transition from reflexive behaviour to primary and secondary 'circular reactions' in which repetition plays the important part; e.g., repetition of movements with pleasurable ends. These learned reactions are gradually integrated, and lead to trial and error behaviour which in turn leads to desired goals.

Months 12 to 18

Progresses from walking alone to creeping up and down stairs without help. Begins to jump with both feet. Moves from constantly throwing things to rolling them and piling things on each other. Scribbles. Uses cup and spoon.

Can locate sounds well, knows own name, enjoys nursery rhymes and tries to sing. Enjoys picture books and can identify pictures of well-known things. Changes from few words and much babbling and jargon to use of say a dozen intelligible words. Can obey single orders. Imitates mother at household jobs.

According to Piaget, during this period the child starts problem-solving to some extent symbolically; that is, without actually carrying out the actions in a trial and error fashion.

Months 19 to 24

Becomes able to stoop, and later to kick, without falling over. Runs and jumps well. Imitates walking backwards. Builds up six or seven cubes at beginning of this period; and pours from cup to cup. Later washes and dries hands; dresses himself. Makes circular scribbles rather than just strokes.

Produces two-word sentences, and, towards the end of the period, talks volubly, using pronouns. Plays along with other children, but individually.

During this period, sex differences appear in 'aggressiveness', 'fearfulness' and interest evoked by toys.

During the second year, separation from the mother or mother-substitute is very traumatic.

According to Freud, this is the anal period, during which erotic satisfaction is related to excretion, both expulsion and retention. There is no doubt that in our culture toilet training often leads to conflicts with parents during the second year.

Years 2 to 5

The child progresses in body control until he can skip on both feet (but not hop); gross body movements are replaced by more differentiated fine movements, e.g., tying a shoe-lace becomes possible. Can copy square, triangles, etc. and the drawing of a man changes from a basic circle with long descending, radiating lines to a conventional child's-drawing-of-a-man, with discernible head and limbs.

In about the fourth year the child starts discriminating different orientations of an object and may distinguish left from right in some conditions. Things are often seen animistically and, later, as under the control of outside, mysterious agencies.

Play develops from individual forms, with egocentric monologues, to co-operative play, and then organization into groups with leaders and rapid changes of roles. Play with dolls, etc., is highly imaginative, and imaginary companions are common.

Speech at the beginning of this period usually involves lisping and stuttering.

Years 6 to 12

This is the period during which, especially according to Piaget, there is a great change in a child's thinking ability. At the beginning of this period children are unable to conserve volume, which means that they do not realize that a given amount of liquid does not change when it is poured from a vessel of one shape to one of a different shape. They are also unable to see things from a different point of view. At the beginning of this period they are in general unable to see from the start that it is possible to categorize objects and people in several ways, but at the end of the period children have already achieved or will soon achieve logical thinking. During this period most children in our society stop thinking out loud and often practise deliberate deception. They seem to take pleasure in having a world of their own to which grown-ups cannot have access. During this period too they start playing more in gangs and, if there are sufficient children around to make it possible, these gangs will very often be of a single sex. In many subcultures the differences of role between boys and girls tend to become exaggerated during this period. Hero and heroine worship becomes marked and there is a great deal of emulation of favourite pop singers and sportsmen, and children often build up large collections of pictures, discs and so on associated with them.

References

Bandura, A. (1969). *Principles of Behaviour Modification*. New York: Holt, Rinehart & Winston.
Bandura, A. and Walters, R. H. (1959). *Adolescent Aggression*. New York: Ronald.
Bandura, A. and Walters, R. H. (1963). *Social Learning and Personality Development*. New York: Holt, Rinehart & Winston.
Bowlby, J. (1969). *Attachment and Loss: 1, Attachment*. London: Hogarth.
Carpenter, G. C. (1974). 'Mother's Face and the Newborn', *New Scient.* 61, 890, pp. 742-4.

Eisenberg, L. (1970). 'Student Unrest, Sources and Consequences', *Science, N.Y.*, 167, pp. 1688–92.
Fantz, R. L. (1961). 'The Origin of Form Perception', *Scient. Am.* 204, pp. 66–72.
Flavell, J. H. (1963). *The Developmental Psychology of Jean Piaget*. Princeton, N.J.: Van Nostrand.
Freedman, D. G. (1965). 'Hereditary Control of Early Social Behaviour', in *Determinants of Infant Behaviour, III.* (ed. B. M. Foss). London: Methuen.
Glueck, S. and Glueck, E. (1950). *Unraveling Juvenile Delinquency*. New York: Commonwealth Fund.
Harlow, H. F. (1961). 'The Development of Affectional Patterns in Infant Monkeys', in *Determinants of Infant Behaviour, I* (ed. B. M. Foss). London: Methuen.
Miller, N. E. and Dollard, J. (1941). *Social Learning and Imitation*. New Haven: Yale University Press.
Rutter, M. (1972). *Maternal Deprivation Reassessed*. Harmondsworth: Penguin.
Solomon, R. L., Turner, L. H. and Jessac, M. S. (1968). 'Some Effects of Delay of Punishment on Resistance to Temptation in Dogs', *J. Per. Soc. Psychol.* 8, pp. 233–8.
Stevens, A. G. (1971). 'Attachment Behaviour, Separation Anxiety and Stranger Anxiety in Polymatrically Reared Infants', in *The Origins of Human Social Relations* (ed. H. R. Schaffer). London: Academic Press.
Tanner, J. M. (1962). *Growth at Adolescence*, 2nd ed. Oxford: Blackwell.
Tinbergen, N. (1958). *The Study of Instinct*. Oxford: Clarendon Press.
Wolff, P. H. (1969). 'The Natural History of Crying and Other Vocalizations in Early Infancy', in *Determinants of Infant Behaviour IV* (ed. B. M. Foss). London: Methuen.

Suggestions for further reading

Bower, T. G. *Development in Infancy*. San Francisco: Freeman 1974.
Coleman, J. C. *Relationships in Adolescence*. London: Routledge & Kegan Paul 1974.
Conger, J. J. *Adolescence and Youth*. London: Harper & Row 1973.
Foss, B. M. (ed.). *New Perspectives in Child Development*. Harmondsworth: Penguin 1974.
Mussen, P., Conger, J. and Kagan, J. *Child Development and Personality*. (4th edn). London: Harper & Row 1974.
Sants, J. and Butcher, H. J. *Developmental Psychology*. Harmondsworth: Penguin 1975.

Chapter nine

Adulthood and Ageing

D. B. Bromley

Biological factors in ageing

In studying human development throughout the lifespan, it is difficult to escape the conclusion that all or most of the psychological and social consequences of ageing arise directly or indirectly from an accumulation of defects and failures in the biological foundations of behaviour. This is not to say that there are no contributory psychological or social 'causes' of physical ageing, or that the largely adverse effects of physical ageing on performance are irremediable and inevitable; nor is it to say that social attitudes and policies do not affect an older person's physical health or adjustment. Rather, given our present understanding of human biology, the implication is that, soon after reaching the end of the main phase of juvenile development – in our late 'teens or early twenties – each of us begins to accumulate a variety of physical defects and failures leading to increasingly more deteriorated biological states which have profound effects upon our physical and mental performance, our relationships with other people, and our image of ourself as a person. Such considerations do not loom large in the minds of young people, but, particularly since the industrial revolution in Western society and the advent of public health measures (including the elimination of many major causes of death in children and young people), they have been present in the minds of people who are concerned with the organization and continuation of social institutions. The reasons for this are obvious: (1) as people grow older they become more experienced and tend to move into positions of greater social responsibility; (2) at the same time, they become on average less efficient at certain kinds of jobs: namely, those that make heavy demands related to speed of performance, physical stress, cognitive complexity and conceptual innovation; (3) eventually, if they live long enough, people become physically and mentally incapacitated to the extent that their active roles in society have to be taken over by other, more competent, people.

In other words, because human ageing is a large and inescapable fact of life, society has had to take account of it, and has done so – not particularly satisfactorily to date – by means of social norms relating to pay, promotion, transfer and retirement, as well as by evolving an array of social values, attitudes and policies relating to things like respect for authority (experience) and tradition, concern for the elderly infirm, loyalty to elderly kin, the delegation of authority, schemes for training and retraining, insurance and pension schemes, and so on. The process whereby older persons with presumably poorer functional capacities are eased out of their positions in the social system and replaced by the persons next in line for those positions is called 'disengagement'.

Some of the accumulating biological changes are obvious and commonplace: the hair thins and becomes grey; the skin loses its elasticity and becomes wrinkled; the teeth decay; in women, menstruation ceases. Other biological changes are less obvious but soon become apparent on examination: hearing becomes less acute, especially for high-frequency tones; vision becomes more 'long-sighted' and accommodation poorer; all or most of the special senses deteriorate; several organs of the body are reduced by the loss of irreplaceable cells (of particular interest here is the systematic and cumulative loss of thousands of cells in the nervous system); the capacity of lungs is reduced; the circulatory system is adversely affected by such things as cardiac disease, changes in the walls of the arteries, and varicose veins; sexual capacities are diminished. In these and in many other ways too numerous to mention the whole fabric of the body becomes increasingly dilapidated and poorer as a foundation for behaviour and psychological functions.

At the present time, the causes of biological ageing are not fully understood, and it appears that more than one kind of 'cause' may play a part in bringing about the overall effect:

(1) In so far as an organism fails to rectify any damage arising from wear and tear, disease and disruption, it will accumulate defects and become increasingly inefficient, rather like a motor-car which is not serviced and repaired. Undoubtedly, wear and tear play a part in the process we call 'ageing', but such 'extrinsic' processes are by no means a major part; otherwise we might expect organ transplants and other medical treatments to have more effect on life expectancy, whereas the successful elimination of the major diseases in adult life would have a surprisingly small effect on the average expectation of life.

(2) Evidence relating to the survival of organisms and cells maintained in ideal conditions strongly suggests that a major part of the process which leads living things to age and eventually to die is 'in-

trinsic', i.e., part of the molecular biology of the cell and 'built in' to the organism.

An elementary account of the biology of ageing in relation to human behaviour and psychological processes can be found in Bromley (1974).

The adult phase of the human life-cycle

The main phase of juvenile growth terminates in late adolescence (say, the late 'teens to early twenties), by which time the person has also completed his secondary education and may be pursuing further education of one sort or another, at a college or university, or through some type of vocational training. In some societies, including our own, the combination of rapid biological change accompanied by the conflicts of an ambiguous transitional social status conspire to make late adolescence for some people a particularly stressful period of life, unequalled again, perhaps, until pre-retirement (age sixty to sixty-five years in men); and, like that period, it has its associated forms of physical and mental ill-health. It is well known that many forms of antisocial and delinquent behaviour reach a peak in adolescence, reflecting perhaps the conflicts and ambiguities in the teenager's social role, or perhaps some natural tendency to break away from uncongenial restraints imposed by adults and to move from a largely dependent to a largely independent position in the community. Less well recognized is the surge of adventurism and social concern typical of late adolescence.

The adult phase of the human life-cycle can be conveniently described in terms of seven consecutive stages following late adolescence and beginning at the age of about twenty years. The first of these stages occupies the early twenties when the individual is acquiring his first adult social roles. Within a short period of time he has assumed legal and economic responsibilities, voting rights, marital and family ties. He has become fully 'engaged' in the socio-economic and industrial system of the community in which he lives, and is at about the peak of his physical and mental powers (excluding those which depend on prolonged special training or experience). As we shall see, there are no clearly defined biological markers for adult development and ageing. Consequently there is some ambiguity in the terms used to label the adult stages of life and considerable variation between individuals in the extent to which they exhibit the biological and social features which are supposed to be broadly typical for people of a given chronological age.

The second stage occupies a long segment of the life-cycle from the middle twenties to about the age of forty, and can be referred to as adulthood proper. In our kind of society it is characterized by the consolidation of occupational, domestic and other social roles, and by the accumulation of relatively permanent material standards of living and social relationships. In spite of a slight decline in some physiological and mental capacities (usually apparent only in tests of maximum performance), these years are the peak years for many kinds of intellectual and athletic achievements.

The third stage also occupies a long segment of the life-cycle between the ages of forty and sixty. It may be referred to as 'late adulthood' or 'middle age'. The age of forty happens to be mid-way through the working life of most men. By this age some measure of seniority at work will usually have been attained, although many professional and managerial statuses may not be attained until much later in life. There is usually a continuation of the sort of occupational, domestic and other social roles developed in the earlier stage, although, of course, socio-economic changes and changes in social norms and attitudes may help to bring about radical readjustments at this time of life as at any other. The children have grown up and tend to leave home; this modifies the mother's behaviour particularly, and some women will return to full-time employment. The decline of physiological capacities becomes more pronounced, sexual and reproductive functions diminish, and there is a further decline in some aspects of mental capacity which is masked by high levels of competence in some well-practised intellectual activities, e.g., language and occupational skills. After the stage of early adult life, statistics show a steady cumulative deterioration in a wide variety of indices of well-being. Sickness rates and death rates start to rise, accelerating rapidly after the age of forty-five years.

The fourth stage is an anticipatory 'pre-retirement period' which occupies the few years before actual retirement. It is characterized by a more obvious decline of physiological and mental capacities, although this period coincides with the peak years for some kinds of social achievement and authority. For most people, however, there is a partial disengagement or withdrawal from involvement in occupational roles and community affairs. The transition to retirement is usually more abrupt for men than it is for women.

The fifth stage usually begins with retirement at the statutory age of sixty-five years for men. Many people are fairly healthy, active and alert at this age, and do not think of themselves as 'old' in the sense of being infirm or dependent. Nevertheless, retirement brings a more thorough disengagement from the mainstreams of occupational and community activity, although there may well be a compensating shift towards greater involvement with family members and leisure-time relationships. There is a continued deterioration of physiological and psychological capacities and a heightened susceptibility to physical and mental disorders.

At the present time, the average expectation of life in England and Wales is sixty-nine years for men and seventy-five years for women. However, if we ignore infant mortality, sex differences and 'premature' deaths in adult life, we find a relatively 'normal' distribution in age at death with a peak at about seventy-five years and the range from about forty to ninety-five (the upper limit of human longevity is about a hundred and ten years).

The sixth adult stage of the life-cycle (old age) may be thought of as commencing at the age of about seventy years, when the cumulative effects of irreversible physiological and psychological deterioration bring about virtually complete disengagement from wider society and considerable dependency on others for the maintenance of the ordinary activities of daily life: feeding, dressing, moving about.

The seventh and final stage is the terminal stage, leading to death from a natural cause at a late age. This stage marks the final breakdown of the biological functions necessary to sustain life, and is sometimes but not always associated with senile mental and behavioural impairment.

The several stages of ageing briefly described above are dealt with in greater detail in Bromley (1974) together with a number of related topics. In order to understand adult life and old age one must adopt what is sometimes called a 'biosocial' approach to human nature; i.e., one that takes account not only of the fact that there is a biological basis to behaviour and psychological processes but also of the fact that behaviour and psychological processes are shaped and directed by the social and environmental contexts within which the person is placed and out of which his personality has developed.

Ability and attainment

The developmental curve for general intellectual ability, i.e., native intelligence, begins to level off as early as thirteen years of age and is complete by the end of late adolescence. As we shall see later, the gifted individual is now in a position to start making significant contributions to the arts, sciences, literature and medicine. His rate of output increases steadily to reach a peak in the early thirties and thereafter declines somewhat, for various reasons, until it reaches zero in late life. Psychometric surveys indicate that from the early twenties there is a steady cumulative impairment in some important intellectual functions, especially those involving productive thinking, mental speed and complex attentional and memory functions (see Bromley, 1974). It is, presumably, the combination of high innate intellectual ability and the acquisition of advanced knowledge and technical skills that enables the gifted individual to make his contributions to the fund of human knowledge during the middle years. By and large, contributions more dependent upon native ability occur earlier, contributions more dependent upon acquired skills and knowledge occur later. Lehman (1953), for example, suggests that the relatively slow decline with age in research contributions to the classical description of disease happens because, in many instances, such descriptions require prolonged experience with particular diseases.

Although the years from thirty to forty are peak years for intellectual achievement, there are in fact measurable decreases in several sorts of intellectual function from the high levels reached in late adolescence. On the other hand, other sorts of intellectual functions continue unchanged or even improve, especially if the person is actively engaged in the exercise of these functions. Typically, functions requiring the use of words and the reproduction of acquired skills are well maintained, but functions requiring rapid and complex mental operations in unfamiliar situations show some decline. Such age decrements are not normally apparent in the ordinary everyday behaviour of the individual; or, if they are, one could well suspect some pathological process, superadded as it were, to the deleterious effects of normal ageing. It is usually only in tests of maximum performance that these early and slight diminutions in intellectual capacity are revealed, since most daily activities do not require a person to push himself to the limits of his ability. On those rare occasions, however, when the individual is put in a situation which demands maximum response, he may find that his response is inadequate; e.g., in competitive sport, or as a driver in a rapidly developing traffic hazard, or in a novel problem-solving situation.

It is clear that some intellectual functions are more adversely affected than others by the normal processes of ageing, and that some intellectual functions are more adversely affected than others by the focal or diffuse brain damage brought about by disorders in late life. For example, problem-solving behaviour requiring a grasp of complex relationships, abstract thought, rule forming, and mental transformations making demands upon short-term memory, are functions likely to suffer impairment as a consequence of brain damage or normal ageing. Other functions, however, such as routine verbal skills, factual general knowledge and memory for remote events, seem much more resistant to impairment. Research with psychometric methods reveals a variety of differential effects of normal ageing on intellectual functions, including an increase with age in minor cognitive defects such as concrete thinking and logical errors.

Figures 9.1 and 9.2, taken from Bromley (1963), illustrate the

Adulthood and Ageing

differential effects of age on a variety of intellectual functions. Figure 9.1 shows age trends for eleven sub-tests of Wechsler's first form of his test of adult intelligence. Figure 9.2 includes age trends for several measures of 'fluid' ability (see below): the Shaw test and Vigotski test call for the application of abstract relationships and classifications; the Proverbs tests also call for abstraction and generalization; the Letter Families test involves the temporal organization of symbolic patterns

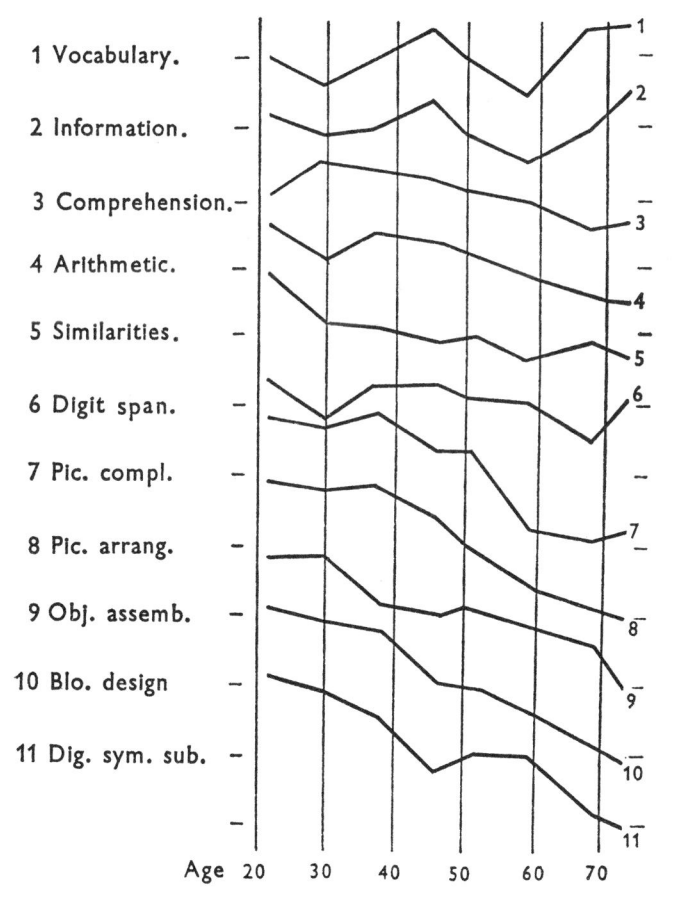

1 Vocabulary.
2 Information.
3 Comprehension.
4 Arithmetic.
5 Similarities.
6 Digit span.
7 Pic. compl.
8 Pic. arrang.
9 Obj. assemb.
10 Blo. design
11 Dig. sym. sub.

Age 20 30 40 50 60 70

Figure 9.1 The relative differential effects of normal ageing on adult intelligence as measured by rank-difference units on the Wechsler–Bellevue test

and relationships and requires close sustained attention and reasoning; W-B cluster 1 represents a sub-set of Wechsler's sub-tests of 'crystallized' ability, whereas W-B cluster 2 represents a sub-set of sub-tests of 'fluid' ability. The measures labelled Shaw D, Vigotski D and Proverbs B (E_2) reflect minor pathologies of cognition, such as concrete forms of thought and abnormal errors. The uneven age trends arise as a consequence of sampling and measurement errors.

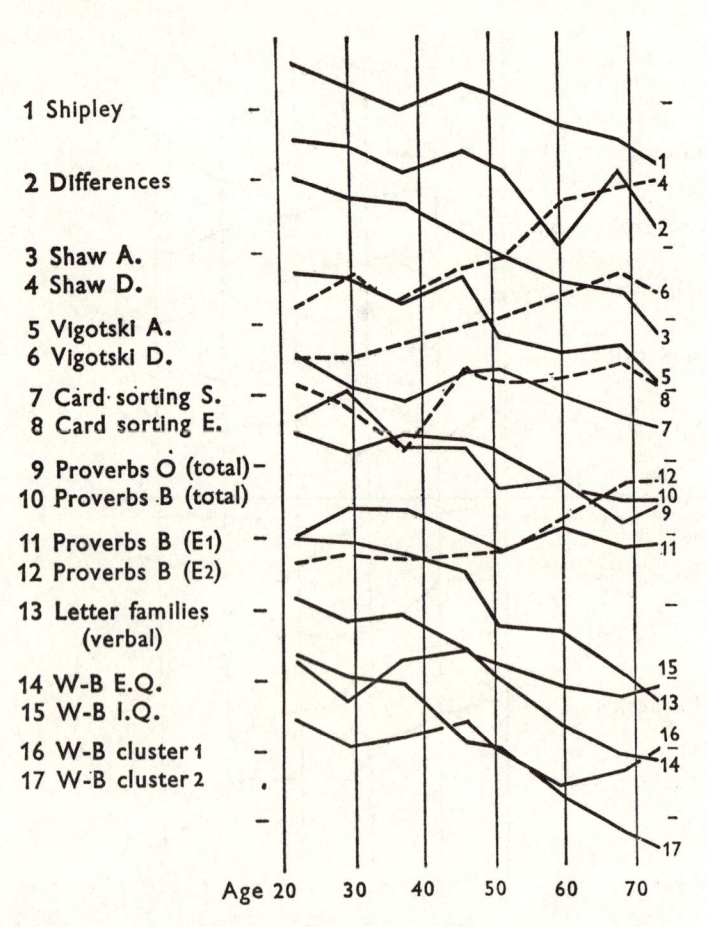

Figure 9.2 The relative differential effects of normal ageing on adult intellectual functions as measured by rank-difference units on various cognitive tests

Diagnostic difficulties in clinical psychology (for example, that of separating out functional from clearly organic factors, and that of assessing the kind and amount of brain damage) make it difficult to say precisely how intellectual changes are associated with clinical conditions (see Williams, 1970). The application of standardized tests of intelligence to large numbers of normal adults, however, as in the work of Wechsler (1955, 1958), and Heron and Chown (1967), provided useful evidence relevant to questions about the normal effects of ageing, and the relationships between normal and abnormal intellectual functions.

Wechsler's tests of adult intelligence sample a number of mental activities in a general way; for example, by assessing the subject's vocabulary, general knowledge, common sense, arithmetic ability and short-term memory, his speed of mental work, and his ability to relate one thing to another logically. On the basis of his surveys of adult intelligence, Wechsler distinguished between intellectual functions which 'hold' with increasing age, and those that 'don't hold'. Although it is possible to demonstrate a differential decline with age in mental abilities, it is difficult to explain exactly why performance on one test declines more than performance on another. In the case of Wechsler's tests, for example, a large part of the decline with age in performance can be attributed to the slowing down of mental operations.

A decline with age in performance can be expected if a task has some of the following attributes: unfamiliarity; time limits; abstract principles; relational complexity; symbolic transformation. In some respects, these same attributes characterize the tasks showing a decline in performance among patients suffering from certain conditions of mental disease and brain damage, but the overlap is not perfect. Vocabulary, for example, seems to be less sensitive to the effects of normal ageing than to the effects of diffuse brain damage (in young adults), whereas functions such as the comprehension of relational complexity and speed of mental operations seem to be more sensitive to normal ageing than to diffuse brain damage. Nevertheless, it remains a convenient, if somewhat approximate, rule to think of the psychological impairment in normal ageing as a function of cumulative diffuse brain damage, which, on average, by about the age of fifty, has produced adverse changes in intellectual capacity; although such changes are usually apparent only when the person is tested to the limits of his mental ability. (See Davies, 1968; and Reed and Reitan, 1963.) In ordinary behaviour in everyday life, however, we rarely face situations which push us to the limits of our mental abilities. More often than not, life situations make routine demands calling for familiar and well-practised reactions to be made at a normal pace. And, since life is geared to the abilities of the average adult, it is not surprising that the adverse effects of normal ageing on intelligence do not begin to become obvious, in the sense of interfering with the ordinary activities of daily living, until quite late in life.

A distinction has been made between 'fluid' and 'crystallized' mental abilities. Fluid abilities are those which more closely reflect inborn potentialities; crystallized abilities reflect the extent to which experience and education have shaped the person's actual abilities. Fluid ability is gauged indirectly by speeded or unspeeded intelligence tests, such as the Progressive Matrices (Raven, 1938), where the 'knowledge' content of each item is reduced to a minimum, but where relational complexity, abstraction and symbolic transformation are progressively increased. Crystallized ability, on the other hand, is gauged more directly by reference to tests of attainments, such as vocabulary, general knowledge and scholastic achievement, where knowledge has to be merely reproduced, and acquired skills put into practice in fairly routine situations.

Naturally, for example in the practice of medicine, most situations make demands upon both fluid and crystallized abilities, since the solution to any problem is likely to require not only a modicum of native intelligence but also some specialized knowledge and training. As we grow old, what appears to happen is that fluid abilities (constitutional intellectual capacities) decrease, whereas crystallized abilities (experience and acquired skills) are relatively unaffected, except in so far as they may improve or worsen by practice or disuse respectively. Thus, as age increases, the fate of any particular behavioural function will be determined in part by the extent to which it depends upon both fluid and crystallized abilities.

What has been said above refers to the general pattern of long-term changes in intelligence in adult life. But, as is well known, there are all sorts of biological and psychological factors, such as fatigue, illness and anxiety, which bring about short-term changes in intellectual efficiency. So that, because of general physical dilapidation, increased susceptibility to stress, and reduced abilities, it is to be expected that older people will show greater day-to-day fluctuations in performance than will younger people, and for this reason greater care is needed in obtaining a reliable index of their capabilities.

Much recent work in the measurement of intelligence has been concerned with isolating relatively independent cognitive functions (analogous to searching for distinguishable physiological functions). It is too soon to say what are the effects of ageing on such primary mental abilities, but the indications so far are that the abilities used in relating and classifying figural stimuli, and in inductive problem-solving, decline with age, whereas verbal and social comprehension do not. These findings are compatible with what has been said above concerning the differential effects of normal ageing on fluid as compared with crystallized components in general intelligence.

We can use the term 'psychomotor performance' to refer to the degree of acquired skill in perception and response, as in driving a car, playing tennis, or performing a surgical operation. Such skills vary all the way from simple dexterities such as one can observe being learned by children to the extremely complex skills just mentioned. When the perceptual process is complex and the motor process simple, it is more convenient to use terms like problem-solving or decision-making, since these more inward complex forms of psychomotor performance can be thought of as mental skills, or intellectual functions.

It is well known that as age advances there is a worsening of sensory functions. Therefore, in so far as a psychomotor skill depends upon fine sensory discrimination, e.g. among tonal or colour qualities, it can be expected to deteriorate in later years, unless the sensory impairment is compensated for by prosthetic aids or by 'sensing' longer or more often. There is a worsening of the motor apparatus in that, later in life, there is a decrease in muscular strength, speed, stamina, co-ordination and fine dexterity. Hence tasks requiring sustained or heavy lifting, or fast detailed manual co-ordination, especially in awkward working conditions, are likely to reveal the older person's disabilities.

Surprising as it may seem, the most serious effects of normal ageing on psychomotor performance relate neither to sensory impairment nor to motor impairment, but to what goes on in between; i.e., to the impairment of organizing processes in the central nervous system (see Welford, 1958). It would take too long to describe the experimental evidence supporting this claim, but it can be shown that whereas changes in, say, the size of the visual stimulus or the loudness of the auditory signal alter the relative difference between the performances of older and younger subjects, this difference is small compared with that brought about by changes in, say, the rate of presentation of the stimuli or in their complexity, or in the kinds of symbolic transformations that the subjects are required to perform. In other words, as far as normal ageing is concerned, the limiting factors in psychomotor performance lie mainly in these central organizing or decision processes. The adverse effects of ageing on these central decision processes may not be obvious from casual observation of older people in everyday life; but in situations which push the individual to the limits of his performance (e.g., by means of a psychological test, or in a complicated surgical operation) the effects of ageing become more obvious. In everyday life, too, older people tend to develop compensatory strategies which minimize their exposure to such demanding situations: they avoid dangerous or congested traffic when driving, they prefer to take a longer time in order to reduce the risk of making errors, or they simply avoid tasks which they feel are getting beyond their abilities. One unfortunate consequence of the older person's poorer psychomotor performance is that he is less likely to detect a danger signal, slower to attach meaning to it, and less able to organize an appropriate response. He is therefore more prone to certain kinds of accident.

The relevance of age changes in psychomotor performance to occupational adjustment should be fairly obvious. In the case of retraining and work study, for example, one would assume that in a properly organized community, a man's work would be adjusted to fit his occupational capacities; and, within limits, through retraining, his occupational capacities would be adjusted to the changing employment needs of the economy. In fact, although a great deal has been achieved in recent years in the direction of job design and occupational retraining, there is still much that could be done to improve the working conditions of older people both in the factory and in the home. As regards retirement, the argument is that on average, by the age of sixty-five, men in most occupations are reaching the stage at which their work is becoming only marginally productive, partly on account of absences through poorer physical health, partly on account of redundant skills, partly on account of the cumulative deterioration in psychomotor performance. The existence of a statutory retirement age of sixty-five years derives from legislation in the earlier part of the present century, but the social and economic aspects of this issue cannot be dealt with here.

Changes in personality and adjustment

Age changes in personality are difficult to deal with separately from age changes in physical health, intelligence and social status. The reason being that personality (the person's unique pattern of adjustment to his individual circumstances) is intimately connected with them.

In the case of physical health, the effects of normal ageing on personality are both direct and indirect. Since the physical structures and functions of the body are gradually impaired by disease and damage, the very physical foundations of behavioural and psychological processes are eroded and disrupted. Thus, for example, we are obliged to change our ways in order to accommodate ourselves to impaired senses, physical disability, an aged appearance, diminished vigour, and so on. Such accommodation calls for appropriate changes in our self-concept if we are to maintain close ties with reality.

Changes in endocrine functions and in the central nervous system bring about more direct effects by subtly altering the organization of a person's behaviour and his states of mind. Unfortunately, individual differences (within the normal range of variation) in the structures and functions of the human body cannot at the present time be correlated in any very meaningful way with individual differences in the more complex behavioural and psychological processes; much less can they be correlated with age changes in these processes. Thus, although it is clear that people react differently to the normal physical processes of ageing, it is difficult to classify these differences and even more difficult to discover their determinants. Attempts to measure 'biological age' independently of chronological age have met with limited success.

The way the person adjusts to changes in his physical condition and social circumstances as age advances is assumed to reflect, among other things, the enduring psychophysical dispositions (traits, abilities, drives) that form the basis of personality; e.g., realism *v.* unrealism, optimism *v.* pessimism, introversion *v.* extraversion. In one sense, growing older is part of the process of 'becoming' a person, since one's life history is this very process. Unfortunately, there are no suitable measures for assessing persisting psychological attributes throughout adult life, and the problem of describing age changes in personality is difficult to deal with. A fuller discussion of concepts, methods and findings in the study of personality and adjustment in adult life and old age can be found in Bromley (1974).

Although the person, by definition almost, remains recognizably the same person throughout his life, he does so not only in virtue of continuities in his physical and psychological characteristics but also in virtue of the social relationships and circumstances he shares with other people. How would one recognize that a person was the 'same person' if his appearance and social identity were different? It would obviously be next to impossible to identify such a person solely on the basis of his behaviour, personal qualities or test performance.

Leaving aside the special difficulties encountered in personality assessment, such evidence as there is suggests that the inability to modify an habitual response – rigidity – seems not to be an invariant accompaniment of ageing; indeed it is not a personal quality that can be easily defined or measured (see Chown, 1961). The rigidity which is supposed to accompany normal ageing is probably a function of a tendency to respond in terms of past experience: 'hardening of the categories', as it has been called. The tendency to think in concrete terms or in clichés, and to use empty verbal formulae, may be associated with diminished intelligence and lack of opportunity for fresh learning.

Evidence based on the use of projective and other psychological methods seems to confirm the common-sense impression that, as age advances, achievement striving diminishes; but see Smith (1970) for contrasting evidence. Active interests decrease, as do assertiveness, emotional involvement, and extraversion. Social relationships become fewer, although possibly deeper and more selective. There seems to be a generalized reduction in responsiveness (separate from sensori-motor impairment), such that a change in stimulation is unlikely to provoke more than a momentary response; it fails, that is, to excite or sustain interest. This, at least, is one way of describing the way in which many older people seem to put up with very unsatisfactory living conditions, and the way in which even a substantial therapeutic endeavour will show only slight and temporary improvement on average in the behaviour of the very old, unless followed up by continued support.

The study of individual differences in personality characteristics as related to changes with increasing age is difficult to pursue because of the unreliability of psychological tests, and the fact that they are rarely standardized over a wide age range. Hence, one cannot know whether a response has the same psychological significance among older respondents as among younger respondents, just as a physical symptom may be given a different interpretation for an older patient from that for a younger patient. Although little is known for sure about systematic adult age changes in personality, such evidence as there is suggests that age changes in measurable characteristics are slight even late in life, between the ages of, say, sixty and eighty years. There appear to be small average shifts towards introversion and neuroticism and towards greater conformity and depressiveness; older women score lower on femininity. So far, therefore, there is little evidence to indicate substantial changes with normal ageing in personal qualities measured by psychometric instruments; certainly nothing to compare with the considerable differential effects of ageing on intellectual abilities (see Bromley, 1963; and Figures 9.1 and 9.2). It may be that a more profitable approach to personality research in adult life and ageing would be to study age changes in strategies of adjustment or to standardize existing tests on a wider age range.

Statistics relating to the incidence of neurosis and psychosomatic conditions among different age groups are difficult to interpret, for a number of reasons. But there appears to be a steady if small increase throughout the adult years, neurosis being about twice as prevalent among women as it is in men. Men, on the other hand, have a higher suicide rate than women. The symptomatology and course of a physical disease may differ somewhat from one age group to another, thus introducing difficulties in medical diagnosis. The effects of drugs, similarly, differ from one age group to another as well as from person to person. It should be readily appreciated then that the diagnosis and treatment of psychological disorders among middle-aged and elderly people present considerable difficulties, particularly when one considers that the 'disease concept' of psychological disorder may sometimes be inappropriate, and that, in any event, the patient's condition is likely to be affected by a multiplicity of psychological and social factors in addition to the biological ones familiar to the physician.

Tune (1969) found a slight decline in the average amount of time spent sleeping in the years between twenty and fifty, followed by an increase in later years, partly arising from naps taken during the day. Extraverts reported sleeping longer than introverts, especially after age fifty. Sleep disturbances increase with age, more so among women. In retirement, release from external social pressures associated with time schedules permits more intermittent sleep episodes. Age changes in energy and arousal naturally affect the nature and distribution of one's behaviour and the adequacy of one's personal adjustment.

In retirement, people develop different strategies in coming to terms with difficult problems of adjustment in late life. The main strategies or reactions are as follows: constructiveness, dependency, defensiveness, hostility and self-hate. There is no one best way of making an adjustment to later life; each person's actions must be considered in relation to his particular qualities and circumstances as they change over time. The study of personality and adjustment, then, deals not only with the description and measurement of personality in general (better referred to as differential psychology), but also with the analysis of individual cases and their associated life histories. The two methods, however, are complementary.

The important thing to remember is that some of the specific behavioural criteria for judging whether a person is well adjusted or poorly adjusted may change with age, although some of the more general criteria of mental health do not. For example, we tend to think of aggressivensss, guilt, morbid anxiety, and unhappiness as being symptomatic of maladjustment at any age, but dependency, passivity, forgetfulness and 'rigidity' may well be excused as being not untypical of older persons, although they might cause concern if exhibited by a younger person. A more difficult problem among middle-aged and older adults is that of distinguishing between justifiable and unjustifiable feelings of depression, anxiety, guilt or other indicators of maladjustment. At the present time, unfortunately, there are available few if any reliable guides to what is psychologically 'normal' in middle age and old age; and until the necessary research has been carried out it will be difficult to assess the extent to which an older person's behaviour deviates from the norm. For the same reason, it is difficult, at the present time, to estimate what improvement should follow from a treatment programme or a change in the living conditions of an older person. It seems therefore that, in the future, personality study (the study of individual cases and individual differences) should play a larger role in the psychological study of ageing. What should be avoided are attitudes of 'therapeutic nihilism' or 'benign neglect', whereby resources are denied to the elderly, or minimized on the grounds that little or nothing can be done to help them – attitudes unfortunately still all too common in hospitals and homes, and attitudes which may even be taken over by the older person himself, thus leading to further withdrawal, apathy and deterioration in standards. Some of the detrimental effects commonly thought of as the products of ageing can be prevented, retarded, and treated.

Middle age

Until recently, middle age was a stage of the life-cycle largely neglected by psychologists, sociologists and biomedical workers alike. Interest, however, is beginning to grow (see Neugarten, 1968; Owen, 1967) and one might expect that preventive medicine in relation to disorders of late onset will be increasingly applied at this stage of life.

One of the obstacles to achieving a rational and constructive view of middle age is the ambiguity of the term itself. The term 'middle age' is construed differently by different people and there is no consensus as to its definition. Most of what we shall have to say will be about the psychological and social aspects of middle age, since the period does not exist as a well-defined biological or chronological segment of the life-cycle. Moreover, there is little evidence of a universal physiological and medical crisis (critical period or 'climacteric') occurring in middle age as is commonly believed, apart from the cumulative effects of damage and disease already referred to. This is certainly true of men: the term 'male climacteric' has little or no medical or psychological meaning, except perhaps in relation to some neurotic conditions. In women, the final cessation of menstruation (the menopause) is the single definite biological marker for middle age; the menopause is associated with irregular menstruation and minor physical symptoms such as hot flushes, and with reduced defence against heart disease. Except in a few instances among women predisposed to psychiatric illness or psychological maladjustment, the menopause seems not to be associated with dramatic psychological or social changes, although it undoubtedly causes some embarrassment and anxiety through its somatic and outward effects.

One reason why the post-developmental period of the human life-cycle is so ill-defined is that evolutionary selection pressures become decreasingly effective (since the main reproductive phase occurs during late adolescence and early adulthood), and the specific characteristics which promote or diminish survival and adjustment in middle and late life – and might act as markers for middle age – are not differentially selected. From the point of view of human social history, we might say that old age is a twentieth-century phenomenon brought about by large-scale improvements in living standards and medical care, particularly the virtual elimination of the fatal diseases of childhood. Looked at in this way, it is not surprising that the maladies of old age are still a problem, since it is only recently that medical studies of them on a large and intensive scale became possible. In recent years, a tremendous amount of scientific research on ageing (biological, psychological and social) has been carried out and considerable changes have occurred in social attitudes and policies. To the average adolescent a person in his middle thirties is likely to be thought of as 'middle-aged', whereas the retired person will think of him as 'young'; the person himself may think of himself as 'young' or as 'middle-aged'. Thus, the term 'middle age' is ambiguous, and to some extent middle age is a state of mind, a set of attitudes and beliefs about oneself which coincides broadly with those held by people in their forties and fifties.

Another source of ambiguity arises because of social class differences. During the working life, occupational status tends to be closely, though not absolutely, tied to chronological age, in the sense that in most occupations there are age limits for entry and normal periods for promotion and transfer. Thus, chronological age tends to be associated with income and standard of living. Income and living standards tend to improve through the working life (except in so far as they may be adversely affected by inflation and other sorts of social change). But the improvements characteristic of working-class men are different from those of middle-class or professional men. Working-class men tend to have an earned income that begins early, climbs steeply but levels off quickly to maintain a relatively shallow and flat course until the age of retirement, when it drops abruptly to the level of a pension. As a consequence, they tend to have few assets, little time and limited resources for leisure-time pursuits and self-advancement. Middle-class men, on the other hand, tend to extend their education and training into the twenties, and to make their way up an extended ladder of promotion; they can often maintain a high earning capacity until retirement or beyond, and their living standards can be maintained at a relatively high level in spite of retirement from their main occupation. As a consequence, they can acquire material assets, and may have considerable time and resources for leisure-time pursuits and self-advancement. It is often possible for them not only to plan and prepare for their retirement but also to carry on rewarding and personally satisfying professional activities well into retirement. This can give a sense of continuity of purpose and personal identity which may contribute a great deal to mental health in middle and late life. Because of these social factors, then, it seems likely that middle age will be experienced differently by working-class men as compared with middle-class men. While 'Too old at forty' might well represent the working man's outlook, 'Life begins at forty' might well represent the professional person's outlook.

Yet another source of ambiguity in the meaning of the term 'middle age' arises as a consequence of sex differences in adult life. The middle age of married women is likely to be closely associated with that of their husband. Women and men in comparable circumstances share the satisfactions (and frustrations) of middle age, and women particularly are affected by the radical changes in family life which ensue when their children leave home for work or marriage. The kind of mid-life and late-life readjustments that a woman has to make are typically as follows: to the menopause, to the independence and departure from home of her children, to her husband's retirement, and to her husband's death. Wide individual differences in personality and circumstances, and lack of research data, make it difficult to generalize about the psychological aspects of these four readjustments.

There are wide differences between individual people: in their physical make-up, in their upbringing, in their psychological characteristics, and in the circumstances to which they are obliged to adapt. We have little or no systematic information on individual differences and norms (or standards) of behaviour in middle age. There are all kinds of ways of being 'middle-aged' and there is no definition or description of 'normal' middle age that is both simple and valid. By middle age, life will have forced its lessons upon all except the most reluctant learners; we will have been made aware of what we are and what we can become; the future has become greatly foreshortened because we can now grasp what it means to have only, at the most, twenty or thirty years of active, healthy life left. Such a realization must have some effect upon our values and tactics of adjustment in middle age.

Lehman (1953) has shown that the peak rates for many kinds of intellectual achievement are in the semi-decade thirty to thirty-five years of age. But the age distribution for intellectual achievements is markedly skewed; so, in most cases over half occur after this age; and, since intellectual achievements beyond sixty form a small part of the total, the middle years contribute over half the total output.

It seems appropriate to consider, in a little more detail, the relationship between chronological age and scientific achievement in medicine, surgery and related fields. The statistical data are again derived from Lehman. Lehman's technique was to consult various historical records and source books, e.g. *An Introduction to the History of Medicine* by

F. H. Garrison (4th ed., 1929), and to extract information enabling him to construct graphs and tables showing the ages at which researchers (now deceased) made significant contributions to their discipline. He could achieve some control over the quality or importance of particular contributions by obtaining ratings from competent judges or by noting the size or frequency of mention of a contribution in history and reference books. Lehman's data for medicine show the average number of contributions per person being made to medicine in each five-year interval. Thus, in the case of bacteriology, 41 persons made 50 contributions; the highest rate of achievement (·050) occurred in the semi-decade 35–39 years, but the years during which achievements were made ranged from 15–19 to 65–69, with a median of 39 years. In another example, 537 persons made 801 miscellaneous contributions to medicine and public hygiene; the highest rate of achievement (·056) occurred in the semi-decade 35–39, but the years during which achievements were made ranged from 15–19 to 90–94, with a median of 41 years. The changes with age in the rate at which significant contributions are being made can be illustrated by converting the rate given for each semi-decade into a percentage relative to the highest rate (e.g. ·055 for pathology) which is set at 100 per cent. The graphs of three age distributions by percentages showing the rates at which researchers (now deceased) were contributing to medical science are shown in Figures 9.3–5. Each ordinate interval is 20 per cent of the output; in each case the peak or maximum is standardized at 100 per cent.

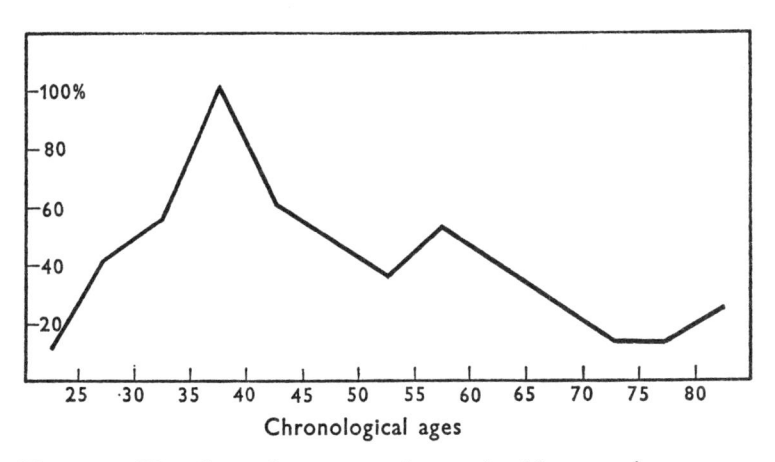

Figure 9.3 The effects of age on rate of research achievement in pathology: data for 170 individuals who made 216 contributions; 52 per cent of the contributions were achieved after the age of 40

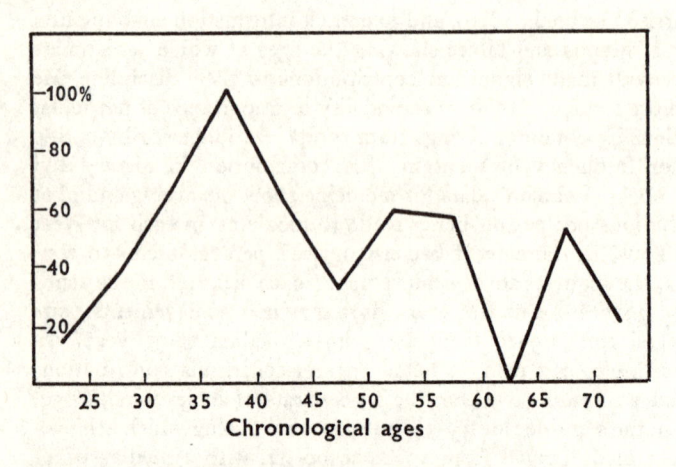

Figure 9.4 The effects of age on rate of research achievement in physiology: data for 55 individuals who made 60 contributions; 52 per cent of the contributions were achieved after the age of 40

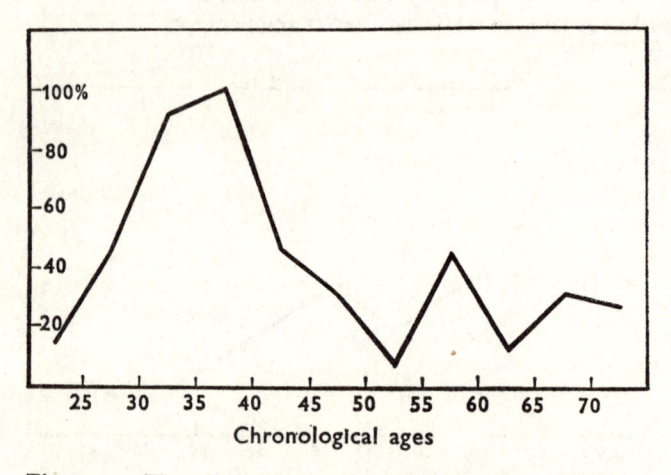

Figure 9.5 The effects of age on rate of achievement in goiter research: data for 40 individuals who made 52 contributions; 37 per cent of the contributions were achieved after the age of 40

For a summary and discussion of Lehman's work, see Bromley (1974). We cannot deal in detail with the above findings; but it is perhaps worth noting that much of the difference between one age distribution and another can probably be accounted for by variations relating to sample size, data sources, historical factors, and so on, apart from any essential connection between chronological age and the kind of abilities needed to make significant contributions to these various medical disciplines. Contrary to Lehman's interpretation, the normal decline with age in speed, power and level of intellectual functions probably plays a considerable part in the reduction after age thirty-five in creative intellectual achievement. It is also worth mentioning that:

(1) In eleven out of twelve medical disciplines the semi-decade marking maximum productivity was 35–39 (the discovery of drugs and remedial agents showed an earlier peak at 30–34).

(2) In all twelve disciplines the median age – the age which divides the total output in half – occurred at or beyond thirty-five years, and, on average, at forty-one.

(3) In medicine probably, as in other disciplines studied by Lehman, for contributions of higher merit (as compared with contributions of lesser merit) the relationship between chronological age and creative achievement is more pronounced; i.e., output starts slightly later, rises more quickly to the same or an earlier peak rate, and then falls more sharply to an earlier termination.

(4) Because of historical changes in the nature of medical research, the larger numbers of people involved, and changes in publishing, it is impossible to say whether or not the relationship between age and creative work in medicine is different now from what it was in previous years. It seems likely, because of changes in education, greater competition, more selective scientific publishing, and so on, that, if anything, the peak years for rates of research output in medical disciplines will have moved downwards, giving rise to an even more pronounced skew in the distribution by age of significant contributions.

Another aspect of achievement in relation to age concerns social leadership and authority. The relevant data, again from Lehman (1953), are as follows:

(1) Adopting the age range 30–59 as the middle years, 68 per cent of the total time spent in office by members of the British cabinets occurred during this period of life; 68 per cent of the total time spent in office by British prime ministers also occurred in this period. Other comparable figures are: military commanders (82 per cent); naval commanders (79 per cent); members of U.S.A. presidential cabinets (75 per cent).

(2) In some types of leadership, of a formal or ritual sort, social

positions are not occupied by people below the age of thirty, although people over the age of sixty are well represented; e.g., presidents of religious organizations and governments, chief justices.

(3) It can be shown that in the Armed Forces, as higher ranks are attained, the age distributions of commissioned officers move systematically along the age scale from the early twenties to the sixties.

(4) In the area of high finance the median age of holders of high office is approximately sixty, with no one below the age of thirty.

If one were to plot the ages at which men attained successively higher ranks in the medical or other professional hierarchy, one would almost certainly obtain a series of slightly overlapping distributions arranged systematically over the career years. It is not surprising that people in their middle years have been referred to as the 'command generation'.

The fact is that authority in social organizations tends to be reserved for the middle-aged and older members, but there are, in many such organizations, practices such as age limits or honorary statuses (or more devious and informal mechanisms) which tend to work against the adverse effects that 'gerontocratic' authority might have. It must be admitted, however, that history provides many examples of social mismanagement apparently associated with undue reliance on elderly leadership, although young leadership has by no means been invariably successful.

From what has been said in connection with intellectual achievement in the arts and the sciences, and in connection with social leadership, authority and material worth, it seems reasonable to conclude that in our sort of society, the middle years are for many people, a rewarding, productive and responsible period of life.

The accumulated experience and stabilized values of the person in middle life should enable him to adopt efficient and economical ways of coming to terms with his environment. He has become established, as it were, in a 'psychological niche'. This allows him to routinize many of his activities and to release his physical and psychological energies for activities which he enjoys and values. He should be able to delimit and schedule his activities far more efficiently than the younger person, although the routine of his 'psychological niche' may deteriorate into the 'rut' so often mentioned as typical of middle age.

The middle-aged person's attitude towards his or her physical condition deserves some consideration. The adage 'By the age of forty a man is either a fool or his own physician' is going too far, no doubt, considering the achievements of modern medicine; but it expresses the point that reasonably intelligent and educated people can generally maintain their physical health without frequent recourse to professional medical advice. For example, they can maintain their proper body weight and muscle tone, and avoid stresses which lead to ill effects. Middle-aged people are usually aware of the value of good physical health; and 'body monitoring' (as the Americans have called it) forms an important part of the middle-aged person's psychological adjustment. That is to say, he is alert to defects and weaknesses in his physical condition, and he is more likely to take common-sense preventive and remedial measures to maintain his health. In some instances, of course, this concern for health slides over into hypochondriasis; but on the whole it seems advisable to encourage people in their early middle years to take a positive pride in their physical condition, through exercise, diet and grooming.

Although the middle years provide a sort of 'pay-off' following the years of 'investment' characteristic of early adulthood, yet they are not without problems even for the relatively fortunate people. There may be health and family problems, and agonizing reappraisals in coming to terms with reality and in making plans for a relatively short further expectation of life. In addition, there is the transition from young adult status to middle-age status, and the transition from middle-age status to old age. In both of these, the anticipation is usually worse than the event. Both transitions, but especially the former, seem to call for a radical adjustment in social values; and this difference in social values is part of what we call the 'generation gap'. It is not only a gap between two different age groups, it is also a gap each middle-aged person must cross.

Data derived from interviews with people in professional and managerial occupations indicate considerable awareness of and adaptation to several aspects of middle age:

(1) Repeated encounters with similar situations enable a person to learn simple but effective strategies for dealing with them; as, for example, a doctor learns to deal with the 'same' disorder in different patients.

(2) The acquisition of techniques for managing others and forming impressions about people means being better able to distinguish promise from performance, and being better able to maintain good relationships with subordinates.

(3) Wider experience tends to give better perspective to the older person's judgments and emotional reactions; he sees the further implications of a decision, and tends not to get upset about small things. Professional competence and personal adjustment vary widely, of course, and it is difficult to establish definite changes in adjustment.

(4) The middle-aged person's wider circle of acquaintances and a better general knowledge puts him into a better position for collecting and disseminating information, and for solving professional problems.

(5) The closing down of opportunities for action modifies the middle-aged person's aspirations, values and attitudes, and helps to bring about changes in his strategies of adjustment. For example, he may abandon his ambitions as a research scientist, and revalue the role of medical administrator.

Successful professional and managerial people in middle life have acquired a range of social skills such as: having realistic standards (or norms) of behaviour; balancing authority, delegation and non-interference; maintaining a social and emotional distance from others, without losing contact and control; being able to manipulate others and enter into favourable 'bargains'; and being able to wait, and to select favourable opportunities for action.

Obviously, not all middle-aged people are well adjusted; but on the whole middle age is a period relatively free of serious biological and developmental stresses, and it provides considerable time and opportunity for most people gradually to come to terms with changes in themselves and their circumstances.

A person's appearance, physical condition and social situation provide him with numerous 'cues' which enable him to make self-assessments in comparison with others or in comparison with some ideal standards. The cues or facts which one person takes into account may well differ from those attended to by another, and we have already seen that there are probably systematic differences between men and women, and between people in different social classes. Unfortunately, we know far too little about this stage of the human life-cycle to be able to do little more than speculate about the problem. One would expect, for example, that doctors become well aware of career structures in medicine. They, like other professional people, come to realize that progress tends to be associated with certain requirements regarding age, experience and performance; they can compare their own progress and rewards with those of others, and take action if necessary to remedy an unsatisfactory state of affairs. Some, naturally, will feel more satisfied, others less – possibly for different reasons, since people differ in what they want from life and differ in their understanding of what has happened. It is to be expected, therefore, that feelings of confidence and self-worth (or their opposites, inadequacy and despondency) will arise as a consequence of these self-other comparisons in mid-life.

Not all self-other comparisons are related to personal appearance, occupational status, material achievements and physical health. Some will be related to sexual activity, social attitudes and leisure-time pursuits. As he lives his life, the middle-aged individual is constantly being reminded of the passage of time: for example, by being called 'Sir', by a photograph taken some years ago, by music which reminds him of former days, by lack of interest on the part of members of the opposite sex, and by the remarks that other people make about him. As far as middle-aged women are concerned, given the present lack of research data and even firm common-sense impressions, one must assume that self-other comparisons also occur, although naturally relating to factors relevant to feminine activities and values. Thus we might expect the average woman to make her self-assessments more in terms of physical appearance, sexual attractiveness, family success, social status and domestic circumstances.

At various times in middle age people will be inclined to think about the position in life they have reached, and to speculate about their limited future. If the individual is at all reflective, he will become aware of the way in which his own actions and the circumstances he has encountered have conspired to lead him into a firm web of circumstances leaving him with little room for manoeuvre; although, no doubt, some individuals will be less inclined to accept their fate than will others. In any event, it becomes increasingly difficult to make radical readjustments; and the realization of this fact can be expected to affect the way a person 'comes to terms' with life and the way he develops strategies of adjustment aimed at realizing his modified life goals. Whether or not this is a painful process depends upon a whole constellation of factors, including the person's predisposition to adjust badly to frustration, and the particular stresses to which he is exposed. For a man, the personal revaluations and readjustments of the mid-life period merge into the reorientations characteristic of pre-retirement, when the prospect of a radical change in circumstances (occupation, income, status, etc.) forces him to make plans (however trivial or tardy) for his retirement. The foregoing emphasis on the benefits and compensations of middle age must not be allowed to obscure the risks and disadvantages of this period of life (see Logan, 1967).

The relationships between chronological age on the one hand and physical and mental health on the other are difficult to determine, partly because of the ambiguities in and variations between medical and social statistics, partly because of a lack of uniformity in diagnosis and treatment, and partly because of age differences, sex differences and social class differences in the behaviour of patients. Among adult patients who visit their doctor with obvious emotional maladjustment or somatic symptoms, about one-third show no apparent organic pathology. If we regard this as indicative of neurosis, then one estimate has suggested that, for women, the rate increases from about 30 per cent at age twenty to twenty-nine to about 50 per cent at age sixty to sixty-nine; for men, the rates are about 15 per cent and 25 per cent respectively. Hence, during middle age, women are twice as likely as men are to seek help regarding neurotic ill-health. On the other hand, men are more likely to kill themselves, although the suicide rate for women has been increasing at all ages, whereas for men it has been relatively steady.

If severe neurotic ill-health is considered, then maximum prevalence occurs in the period twenty-five to forty-five years; but if less severe conditions were taken into account too, then maximum prevalence would probably shift to the period fifty-five to sixty-five years. But because neurotic ill-health, like some sorts of physical ill-health and psychosomatic illness, manifests itself in different ways at different ages, further comparisons are difficult, and firm evidence relevant to this issue seems not to be readily available. Mild neurotic ailments may clear up with treatment in a matter of weeks, but more severe conditions (say, those which make a person unable to work properly) may last for one or several years. In addition, there is a risk of a recurrence of the disorder.

This is obviously not the place for an extended treatment of the problems of social medicine in relation to ageing, but the above remarks indicate something of the complexity of the problem and the relevance of psychological factors.

Pre-retirement and retirement

Retirement has been seen as part of a complex and largely inevitable effect of normal ageing whereby the person gradually 'disengages' from the main streams of social life and is replaced by a younger person (see Cumming and Henry, 1961). Naturally, different societies treat their elderly members in different ways (see Simmons, 1945; and Shanas and associates, 1968).

The pre-retirement period is simply that time of life when the individual is becoming aware of his impending retirement and, if he is sensible, preparing for it. Preparation for retirement and retirement itself obviously depend to a large extent on a person's socio-economic status.

The pre-retirement period is sometimes associated with the achievement of relatively high social authority, prestige and material wealth, coming, as it does, towards the end of the 'pay off' years in late middle age; but, even as some older men are receiving the rewards and recognition due to them because of their contribution to the welfare of the community, they are in many cases delegating, distributing or simply shedding the less essential parts of their social role and disengaging from relationships and activities they find onerous and unrewarding. (See Isaacs, 1972, for an amusing account of 'Homo Dissipiens'.)

Many local authorities and other establishments are setting up courses of instruction aimed at preparing people for retirement. They are often for working-class men (and their wives) and cover topics such as: personal adjustment; financial planning (income, assets, expenditure); physical health and exercise; diet; living arrangements; house maintenance and repairs; gardening; recreation; and the social services (see also Consumer Publication, 1969).

Most men in our sort of society retire from their primary occupational activity at or around the age of sixty-five years. In a proportion of cases, ill-health, redundancy or personal inclination will have brought about an earlier retirement; on the other hand, a number of people will pursue their work for some years beyond this normal retiring age, and a few (particularly men who are self-employed) will work until the end of their days.

The main events in the life-cycle of women are different from those of men. In particular, by the time their husbands have reached the age of retirement, they will already have made two major readjustments: namely, to the menopause and to the departure from their home of the children. To an increasing extent, married women seem to be returning to full-time jobs once their children are at school; and it is to be expected that, given an increase in the scope of further education and retraining programmes, equal pay, and an increase in the number of service occupations, an increasing proportion of older women will return to work. But for many, perhaps most, women at present the occupational role is secondary to the domestic and marital role, so that retirement when it comes does not have the psychological impact that it has for men. That is to say, older women in 'retirement' (i.e., those over the age of sixty and drawing a pension) will usually be exercising their domestic skills and 'working' in much the same way as they have done in their younger days. Moreover, by virtue of their role in the kinship and neighbourhood systems, they are rarely lacking in companionship (or at least opportunities for companionship). Men in retirement, on the other hand, abruptly lose their principal social role, and with it their main sources of interest, prestige and companionship. Because of the usual age difference between men and women, husband and wife will tend to enter the official retirement period (at the ages of sixty-five and sixty years respectively) at about the same time. But it should be noted that, because of sex differences in longevity, many women will live to be widows; women who reach the age of sixty can expect to live about nineteen or twenty years more, men who reach the age of sixty can expect to live about twelve years more. Thus many women have a fourth readjustment to make during the life-cycle: to widowhood.

For men at least, adjusting to retirement is not quite like any other problem of adjustment. But, as might be expected, there are wide differences between individuals in the way problems are tackled, and there is probably a great deal of carry-over from earlier to later forms of adjustment. That is to say, the attitudes and strategies of adjustment that the person has evolved during his adult years will tend to carry over into retirement. In some ways, such transfer of learning may be beneficial; for example, in respect of thriftiness and the avoidance of physical risks; but in other ways, such transfer may be detrimental; for example, in respect of solitariness or laziness.

The broad psychological and social features of retirement can now be sketched in. Like some other problems in life, the anticipation is often worse than the event; and it seems that, probably because of the stigma attached to being old, a good deal of apprehension is aroused in the pre-retirement period by the prospect of what is to come. Before retirement, men tend to focus on its less satisfying features: lower income, poorer health, lack of worthwhile activities. Afterwards they become aware of its more satisfying features: extra rest and relaxation, better attention to physical health, and more time for recreational activities. The release from physical and mental effort and from responsibility can bring about considerable relief, but the increased freedom can be enjoyed to the full only if preparations are made in advance. And, paradoxically, an improvement in morale in the immediate post-retirement period may be accompanied by a slightly higher frequency of attendance at the doctor's surgery, as the person finally gets around to attending to minor physical ailments that he did not care to think about too much in the years before retirement.

The physical environment of people in retirement (including those in residential homes for the elderly and geriatric units) is receiving an increasing amount of attention from behavioural scientists, architects and planners, and medical researchers. But it is important to remember that, excluding medical conditions, the major factor determining the elderly person's adjustment to his circumstances is not the physical surroundings (except in rare and obvious cases) but the psychological surroundings: family life, the attitudes and behaviour of other people, the social management of the residential home, and so on. Among the more obvious environmental factors that have to be taken into account are those relating to the minimization of hazards through the provision of handrails, shallow treads in stairways, nonslip floors, low beds, good illumination especially at floor level, prominent visual notices and indicators, clear and repeated auditory signals, and so on. A distinction can be made between: (1) a 'remedial' environment, which provides the elderly person with temporary supports until he has improved sufficiently to return to his former environment; and (2) a 'prosthetic' environment, which is designed to compensate for the elderly person's chronic biological and psychological deficits, and to maximize his opportunities for self-management in the activities of daily living such as dressing, feeding, moving about. In programmes of rehabilitation, both sorts of environment are arranged, in the sense that the elderly person, having recovered or improved some parts of his functional capacity in a remedial setting (day hospital or clinic), returns to an environment (his own home or a residential home) which has been adapted to some extent to fit his diminished capacities, e.g. by the elimination of stairs, by the provision of special implements for eating and dressing, or by the substitution of showers for bathtubs.

Usually, the elderly person living alone is likely to fare less well than the elderly person living with a spouse or family members. In particular, the person living alone is more likely to suffer as a consequence of an accident or illness, apart from probably failing to maintain an adequate diet or an adequate degree of comfort. Older people differ considerably in their willingness to abandon independent living and go into a residential home which provides adequate warmth and nutrition, and medical care as required. This too may be due in part to the stigma that still seems to be attached to being old, unwell and impoverished, and to the traditional fear of ill-treatment in an institutional setting (unfortunately still with us: see Robb, 1967). Individual differences in attitudes towards dependency arising from deep constitutional factors and early upbringing are also reflected in the adjustment of elderly persons to incapacity. And, as we have seen, old age seems to be typically accompanied by a kind of chronic and generalized habituation, which may be a protective mechanism in that discomforts are felt less intensely but may, at the same time, diminish arousal and flexibility.

Considering the stresses and disadvantages accompanying old age, it is not surprising that a substantial proportion of people become unhappy, maladjusted or mentally sick. In the first place, physical health, vigour and stamina will have become greatly impaired relative to the earlier years, and physical appearance will have deteriorated. Physical health and appearance are highly valued in our society; this partly accounts for the stigma attached to being old. In the second place, these physical changes will have brought about limitations on our mobility and occupational adequacy; this may have serious implications as regards social adjustment, living standards, and feelings of self-worth. Thirdly, there is a risk that our ideas, values and attitudes will have become outmoded. Fourthly, since people in the older generation are dying more frequently, there are fewer and fewer people with whom an older person can share common interests. It seems unlikely, for example, that old people will produce a political movement since they are too diverse a group and, except for a small number of people in high social positions, relatively powerless.

There is considerable variation between individuals in behaviour during late life, although most of the more pressing personal and social problems can be traced directly or indirectly to the common biological facts of ageing. The medical-psychological problem is not simply that of maintaining life, but rather of maintaining functional capacity.

The terminal stage

People are often reluctant to talk about dying and death; they are taboo topics, regarded as morbid and fear-arousing, and so best ignored or avoided. Paradoxically, dying is a mode of life, and has social and psychological, as well as biomedical, aspects.

Most elderly people who are not mentally impaired cannot help becoming aware of the very limited amount of time they have left to live, and they seem to accept the prospect with equanimity. For some, however, the prospect of dying may induce all kinds of anxieties and maladjustments: anger because of things not accomplished, fear of the unknown, guilt over past actions, and confusion, apathy or terror arising from a painful situation for which there is no apparent solution. In some instances, the dread associated with the prospect of dying may well have its origins in long-standing dispositions towards depression and anxiety, and require treatment accordingly. On a more rational level, an old person may very well feel that the benefits of living are now outweighed by the costs.

With regard to what the patient and his relatives should be told (and when and how they should be told) about the likelihood of his dying within a relatively short time, it is obvious that, even without the physician's giving any direct information, the patient is likely to impose his own individual pattern of meaning upon his peculiar circumstances and state of health. He may very well overhear (and misconstrue) doctors and nurses discussing his case; he may pick up scraps of information (and misinformation) from people; he may get obscure and indirect answers to his questions; he may notice that his friends and relatives behave differently towards him; he may be moved, without satisfactory explanation, to different and rather more depressing surroundings. All this may be accompanied by a good deal of anxiety, puzzlement and disturbed interpersonal relationships; so any recommendation which seems likely to ameliorate the patient's unsatisfactory psychological state should be considered. The task of communicating with the dying patient (and being communicated with by him) is not merely a medical responsibility, it is a community or group responsibility (see Ley, Chapter 12). What it amounts to is stating clearly, at appropriate times and in acceptable ways, the dying person's situation and prospects; so that he, and other people – family as well as medical staff and others – can feel that they have done all that is possible, and can come to terms with psychological and social reality as well as with medical facts.

It has been said that for the dying hospital patient, the nurse constitutes the only constant source of emotional support in what may very well be a depressing and dehumanized physical environment. One of the more unsatisfactory aspects of hospital care, by some accounts, is the tendency on the part of the staff to treat the patient as an object rather than as a person, with the result that he begins to feel depersonalized and the victim of events over which he has no control. Nurses, like other medical personnel, are rigorously trained in the technical aspects of life support, but must often find themselves lacking in the psychological and social skills needed for the emotional support of dying patients. Attempts to train medical personnel in such skills have shown that there is a difficult problem here, but one which can be solved. It is of interest that when asked if they themselves would want to know if they were shortly going to die, the majority of medical staff answer in the affirmative; so do most other people.

In our society, social norms for the behaviour of elderly dying people and those associated with them are vague and diverse, particularly nowadays because of the decline in religious sentiments. There are few explicit prescriptions for behaviour under these circumstances and, partly because our society is large, diffuse and complicated, a wide range of reactions is tolerated. Thus we can appreciate, without condoning, the factors which lead in one case to severe and prolonged emotional upset and in another to calm, even humorous, acceptance of the prospect of death. As regards relatives and friends, we can appreciate a range of reactions from relief to rage or grief following a person's death. Historical changes in social custom regarding death are apparent over the past fifty years (see Gorer, 1965); the ritual aspects of dying and mourning have diminished greatly. Since the psychology of dying is a taboo topic, we are rarely given opportunities to observe or talk about it, much less to observe and critically evaluate particular cases. Even literature contains few 'behavioural models' of elderly people dying normally; most are presented because of their dramatic qualities, as illustrating neglect, suicide, forgiveness, implacability and so on. It is not surprising, therefore, that we lack concepts and skills for dealing with the psychological and social problems of death and dying. Most people, having lacked the necessary learning experiences, find themselves at a loss, not knowing how to console or support the dying person, not knowing how to handle their own feelings and reactions, not being able to predict how close kin and friends of the dying person will react. The dying person himself, particularly if the awareness of dying has come abruptly and somewhat prematurely, is similarly at a loss, since he has probably not encountered any 'behavioural models for dying' which he can try to emulate. Instead, he feels himself to be in a painful 'no-solution' situation – a type of frustration which provokes reactions as diverse as rage, apathy, and stereotyped maladaptive responses.

Socially desirable qualities can be exhibited by elderly dying people; and it is these forms of behaviour (like humour, generosity, courage, independence and affection) that constitute the appropriate models. The problem is: how can such virtues be encouraged during the terminal phase, and what sorts of things must the dying person say and do which would make such qualities manifest? This is a difficult issue, because it is unlikely that persons not already predisposed to behave in these ways will do so in their last weeks or months. Nevertheless, counselling similar to that used in psychotherapy could be used to help the elderly dying person to manifest his 'good points', his socially desirable traits, by helping him to see what options were still open to him in coming to terms with his final circumstances. Psychological counselling with the dying, even the elderly dying, is relatively rare; and a great deal of research needs to be done in order to develop suitable psychotherapeutic methods. One interesting approach has been described by Weisman and Kastenbaum (1968) who make use of the 'psychological autopsy'; this refers to an investigation into the psychological and social factors associated with a person's dying. Just as a physical autopsy may reveal important facts about the person's physical condition prior to death, so the psychological autopsy may reveal important facts about the deceased person's prior state of mind, his reactions to treatment and to changes in his condition, the behaviour of other people, and so on. By focusing on the less satisfactory features of a person's demise, one may learn lessons of benefit to another person. The kind of information gained by effective counselling, and the human relationships established with the assistance of a counsellor during the terminal phase, may be of considerable worth to the dying person and those around him, and naturally would greatly affect the findings of a 'psychological autopsy'. Some of the more obvious problems associated with dying, such as pain and discomfort, may be ameliorated by drugs and nursing care. In some instances, the side-effects of infirmity in old age (insomnia, breathlessness and incontinence) and the side-effects of terminal illness and its treatment (vomiting, physical ugliness, and mental confusion) may be more disturbing and depressing than the prospect of dying.

Persons who are mentally confused or under physical stress will not be in a position to benefit from psychological counselling. This is one argument in favour of making preparations well in advance, so that a person will have had time to put his affairs in order, to organize his residual priorities, and to work out some strategy of adjustment to his terminal situation before the physical and mental stress that he may have to encounter make it difficult or impossible for him to think and behave in anything except well-rehearsed ways. A call for discussions about attitudes towards death and non-medical intervention in dying is not likely to have any immediate appeal to medical workers, if only because their training emphasizes the prolongation of life. But it is at least worth considering in what circumstances preparation for death is desirable. In the case of elderly people, it is unlikely that they can use their residual time to best advantage unless they have become adapted to the prospect.

The kinds of non-medical intervention that could benefit the dying person include individual or group psychotherapy, usually of the common-sense counselling variety. Other kinds of non-medical intervention include: (1) social work with the family and friends of the dying person; (2) improvements in the socio-technical aspects of the person's surroundings, including nursing routines, ward placement and cosmetic care; (3) further training of medical, nursing and ancillary staffs in the social and psychological aspects of terminal care, which would include the handling of the repercussions that one patient's death has upon other patients; and (4) the encouragement of appropriate attitudes and activities among medical and nursing staff. One attempt to change the attitudes and behaviour in relation to dying patients of the nursing staff of a geriatric hospital failed when only talks and group discussions were employed; there was even some indication that they had an adverse effect. It was only when practical exercises were introduced (the management of actual deaths, attendance at autopsies, and role playing) that improvements in attitudes and behaviour were noted (see Roche Report, 1968). In the long term we can expect preparation for dying and death to take place through education and socialization in a society with a more humanistic framework of beliefs and values, and through some sort of community support and follow-up care for the bereaved.

One ethical problem is that, while the duty of physician and nurse is to prolong the living functions of the body, this is not to be pursued at all costs, since these costs include: medical and nursing services withheld from other patients; the costs to family and friends in time and money; the emotional distress of the patient and others of living in a painful no-solution situation. Thus while life should be preserved, social and psychological considerations cannot be neglected.

As far as bereavement is concerned, since there are wide individual differences in personal qualities, relationships and circumstances, it follows that there are many sorts of reaction to the prospect of bereavement, just as there are many sorts of reactions to the prospect of dying. This is not to say that there are no broad similarities between people, but rather that consideration of individual differences is a good way of emphasizing the complexity of the issue. For example, the grief one feels following the death of an acquaintance with whom one has almost lost touch is different, in its nostalgic quality, from the grief one feels following the death of a person with whom one has been in close recent contact. Again, bereavement is not necessarily accompanied by sharply defined emotions, but may engender a great deal of ambivalence; it may produce mixed feelings of sorrow, anger, guilt and disappointment. In some instances, bereavement seems to precipitate deviant (pathological) behaviour and suicide. As with the prospect of dying, so with the prospect of bereavement, it seems sensible to argue that discussion, rational anticipation and planning may lessen the emotional impact of the event and enable the bereaved person to make a faster and more effective readjustment. It is not uncommon, for example, for widows to feel some guilt following their husband's death; there is a significant relationship between widowhood and life-expectancy. The psychological and social aspects of dying and bereavement are dealt with in Bromley (1974); see also Brim and associates (1970), Grollman (1970), Hinton (1972), and Parkes (1971, 1972).

Acknowledgments

The author is grateful to the Atherton Press for permission to reproduce the data in Figures 9.1 and 9.2 from *Processes of Aging: Social and Psychological Perspectives. 1.* (1963) by R. H. Williams, C. Tibbitts and Wilma Donahue; and to the Princeton University Press for permission to reproduce the data in Figures 9.3, 9.4 and 9.5 from *Age and Achievement* (1953) by H. C. Lehman.

References

Brim, O. G., Freeman, H. E., Levine, S., and Scotch, N. A. (eds) (1970). *The Dying Patient.* New York: Russell Sage Foundation.

Bromley, D. B. (1963). 'Age Differences in Conceptual Abilities', in *Processes of Aging: Social and Psychological Perspectives, 1* (eds R. H. Williams, C. Tibbitts and Wilma Donahue), pp. 96–112. New York: Atherton Press.

Bromley, D. B. (1974). *The Psychology of Human Ageing*, 2nd ed. Harmondsworth: Penguin.
Chown, Sheila M. (1961). 'Age and the Rigidities', *J. Gerontol.* 16, pp. 353–62.
Consumer Publication (1969). *Arrangements for Old Age.* London: Consumers' Association.
Cumming, Elaine and Henry, W. E. (1961). *Growing Old: The Process of Disengagement.* New York: Basic Books.
Davies, Ann D. M. (1968). 'Measures of Mental Deterioration in Aging and Brain Damage', *Interdiscipl. Topics Gerontol.* 1, pp. 78–90. Basle: Karger.
Gorer, G. (1965). *Death, Grief and Mourning.* London: Cresset Press.
Grollman, E. A. (1970). *Talking About Death: A Dialogue Between Parent and Child.* Boston: Beacon Press.
Heron, A. and Chown, Sheila M. (1967). *Age and Function.* London: Churchill.
Hinton, J. (1972). *Dying*, 2nd ed. Harmondsworth: Penguin.
Isaacs, D. (1972). 'The Fate of Homo Sapiens', *Symposia on Geriatric Medicine*, vol. 1, pp. 121–7. Birmingham: West Midland Institute of Geriatric Medicine and Gerontology.
Lehman, H. C. (1953). *Age and Achievement.* Oxford University Press.
Logan, R. F. L. (1967). 'Health Hazards: 1. The Size and Nature of the Risks', in *Middle Age* (ed. R. Owen). British Broadcasting Corporation.
Neugarten, Bernice L. (ed.) (1968). *Middle Age and Aging.* University of Chicago Press.
Owen, R. (1967). *Middle Age.* British Broadcasting Corporation.
Parkes, C. M. (1971). 'Psycho-social Transitions: a Field for Study', *Social Science and Medicine*, vol. 5, pp. 101–15.
Parkes, C. M. (1972). *Bereavement: Studies of Grief in Adult Life.* London: Tavistock Publications.
Raven, J. C. (1938). *Progressive Matrices (1938), Sets A, B, C, D & E.* London: H. K. Lewis.
Reed, H. B. C. and Reitan, R. M. (1963). 'A Comparison of the Effects of the Normal Aging Process with the Effects of Organic Brain Damage on Adaptive Abilities', *J. Gerontol.* 18, pp. 177–9.
Robb, Barbara (1967). *Sans Everything.* London: Nelson.
Roche Report (1968). *Frontiers of Hospital Psychiatry*, 5 (20), 1, 2 and 11.
Shanas, Ethel, Townsend, P., Wedderburn, Dorothy, Henning, F., Milhøj, P. and Stehouwer, J. (1968). *Old People in Three Industrial Societies.* London: Routledge & Kegan Paul.
Simmons, L. W. (1945). *The Role of the Aged in Primitive Society.* New Haven: Yale University Press.
Smith, J. M. (1970). 'Age Differences in Achievement Motivation', *Br. J. Soc. Clin. Psychol.* 9, pp. 175–6.
Tune, G. S. (1969). 'The Influence of Age and Temperament on the Adult Human Sleep-wakefulness Pattern', *Br. J. Psychol.* 60, pp. 431–41.
Wechsler, D. (1955). *Wechsler Adult Intelligence Scale.* New York: Psychological Corporation.
Wechsler, D. (1958). *The Measurement and Appraisal of Adult Intelligence*, 4th ed. London: Baillière, Tindall & Cox.
Weisman, A. D. and Kastenbaum, R. (1968). *The Psychological Autopsy:*

A Study of the Terminal Phase of Life. New York: Behavioral Publications.

Welford, A. T. (1958). *Ageing and Human Skill.* Oxford University Press.

Williams, Moyra (1970). 'Geriatric Patients', in *The Psychological Assessment of Mental and Physical Handicaps* (ed. P. Mittler). London: Methuen.

Suggestions for further reading

Bromley, D. B. *The Psychology of Human Ageing*, 2nd ed. Harmondsworth: Penguin 1974.

Hinton, J. *Dying*. Harmondsworth: Penguin 1974.

Kimmel, D. C. *Adulthood and Ageing*. London: Wiley 1974.

Parkes, C. P. *Bereavement*. Harmondsworth: Penguin 1972.

Part Three

Social Psychology as Related to Medicine

Chapter ten

Man as his own Observer

J. J. M. Harbison and Joan I. Harbison

Man is no longer regarded as an objective observer and interpreter of his environment. We now know that individuals can respond to the same event in very different ways. There are some situations in which this is immediately obvious: in a fire one person will remain cool and get the fire extinguisher, while another will panic and rush around not able to act in any helpful way. However, there are situations where the differences are not so immediately obvious, and where until very recently such individual differences in responding were not considered important. It was believed that all experimenters were objective in observing, recording and interpreting data, and that in therapeutic situations the relationship between doctor and patient, their expectations of each other, and the environment in which the therapy was administered were irrelevant details having little effect on the successful outcome of treatment. How man responds in a given situation is the result of a complex interaction between his personality and previous learning experience. Since this interaction cannot be the same for any two individuals, then no two people are going to respond to even the same situation in exactly the same way, and this is as true in experimental and therapeutic situations as it is in the case of a fire.

Recent research has indicated that the experimenter and the therapist are important variables in determining the results obtained in an experimental situation and the treatment prescribed in a therapeutic situation. This chapter examines some of the ways these variables influence the results of experiments and treatment. It describes how the experimenter may mis-observe and thus mis-record his data; how the therapist may misinterpret a patient's behaviour or symptoms; and how the expectations of outcome of both the experimenter and the therapist can influence what actually does happen. The influence in the therapeutic setting of other non-specific factors such as placebos (chemically inert drugs) and the therapeutic environment are briefly discussed. Following an examination of the evidence for 'expectancy effects' and 'observer bias' in both experimental and clinical settings, some ways of minimizing these effects are indicated and some suggestions made for improving objectivity in observation. In any scientific investigation and in medicine where valid and successful outcome is dependent on one individual it is important that we maximize any positive effects and minimize the negative influences of that individual.

General observer effects

The first systematic measurement of differences between observers was undertaken, not in psychology, but in the much older science of astronomy. In 1796, Maskelyne, the Astronomer Royal at the Greenwich Observatory, dismissed Kinnebrook, his assistant, because the latter observed the times of stellar transits nearly a second later than he did. The method employed at the time to make such observations was the 'eye and ear' method. This involved not only co-ordination of visual and auditory impressions, but also rather complex spatial judgments. This, the accepted method, was regarded as accurate to one- or two-tenths of a second. In 1816 Bessel, the astronomer at Königsberg, read of this incident and became interested in measuring what came to be known as the 'personal equation' of different observers. Bessel collected and published data on several trained observers and pointed out not only the presence of such a personal equation when comparing any two observers, but also the variability in the equation from time to time. Observer errors have been noted in many sciences (Rosenthal, 1966). For example, Bean (1948) found in nutritional examinations that experienced physicians disagreed in the diagnosis of nutritional deficiency even when objective standards were available. Psychology has been shown to be equally susceptible to observer errors as other sciences (Rosenthal, 1966). One example of an observer error is a computational error; and possibly the most interesting aspect of these observer errors is that it has been reported that three out of every four computational errors are in the direction of the experimenter's hypothesis!

The experimenter observing and recording data has also to interpret it. Identical observations are often interpreted differently by different scientists, and an article by Barber (1961) suggests some of the reasons why this may be so. He points out that such variables as differing theoretical positions or differing status within a profession may lead to some scientists resisting scientific discoveries. In 1914 when Polanyi, a young research worker, published his theory of the absorption of gases or solids it went counter to current theory, and he was publicly castigated by Einstein for his 'total disregard' of what was then known about the structure of matter. Polanyi was later vindicated and his theory accepted; but this example indicates the importance of both the status of the scientist who makes the discovery and whether or not current theory can accept its implications. In a similar way the differing theoretical positions of doctors may influence their observation and interpretation of behaviour. Psychiatry provides a number of examples, including the basic decision as to whether a person is psychiatrically stable or not. During the Second World War, for example, psychiatrists interviewed army recruits for the purpose of rejecting any who might be too severely disturbed to function as soldiers. Extreme differences in the rate of rejection were obtained between different psychiatrists: one induction centre rejected a hundred times as many recruits as another, and there was little to suggest that any actual differences existed between recruits at different centres.

So far the discussion of observer bias has been confined to errors of observation and errors of interpretation. The observer, or experimenter, can also, however, influence the responses given by the subject himself. Rosenthal over the last ten years has carried out research investigating what aspects of the experimenter's behaviour may influence the responses given by subjects in psychological experimentation. He has found that the sex of the investigator can affect the results of his research. He has shown that male and female experimenters conduct the same perception experiment quite differently, so that the different results they obtain may be attributable to unintentional manipulations. He recorded on film and analysed the interactions between experimenters and their subjects. Only 12 per cent of the male experimenters smiled at their male subjects, while 70 per cent of the male experimenters smiled at the female subjects. Rosenthal also showed that smiling by the experimenter affected the subject's responses. Thus the male experimenters were unintentionally carrying out two experiments, one with male subjects and one with female subjects. Other studies in this area have indicated that experimenters who differ along such personal and social dimensions as anxiety, need for approval, status, and warmth, tend to obtain different responses from their research subjects.

Evidence from a wide variety of areas suggests that how the experimenter himself carries out the particular task may affect his subjects' subsequent performance on that task. The situation in which the experimenter's own attributes affect the data obtained from his subjects is known as the modelling effect. Positive and negative modelling effects have been demonstrated over a wide area of behavioural investigations.

In survey research, for example, it has been found that frequently the interviewer's own opinions and attitudes influence the responses he obtains from his sample of subjects. One early example of this was a study in which two interviewers enquired of almost two hundred subjects how much of their time was devoted to various daily activities. One of the interviewers was more athletically inclined than the other, and he found that his subjects reported a greater amount of time spent in athletic activities than did the subjects contacted by the less athletic interviewer.

Other interesting work in this area has been carried out by investigators studying speech behaviour. Goldman-Eisler (1968), for example, has demonstrated that within interviews there are consistent and reliable differences in the amount of speaking time and the amount of hesitation between words shown by different interviewers. There is also considerable evidence that these factors are significantly related to the speaking behaviour of their subjects. The more the experimenter speaks, the more the subject's speaking time increases, irrespective of the content of the interview. Equally, the subject's pattern of hesitation reflects that of the interviewer. These findings have obvious relevance for all interview situations.

Experimenter expectancy effects

When a scientist carries out an experiment, or when a doctor uses a particular method of treatment, the experiment tried or the therapy used are not chosen randomly. Obviously both the experiment and the treatment have been selected because the scientist and the doctor have certain expectations or beliefs about them. The doctor expects that the particular treatment he has chosen will be effective in altering or eliminating the symptoms shown by the patient. The scientist undertakes a particular experiment because he has certain expectations, derived possibly from theory or previous experiments, that the independent and dependent variables he is using are related in a certain way. These expectations of the scientist and the doctor are important in themselves; they may affect the choice of the experimental design, the procedure, or the treatment in such a way as to increase the likelihood that the individual's expectations will be supported. This is obvious. No doctor is going to attempt a treatment which he feels will be worthless for the patient, and no scientist is going to use a procedure which will show that his theory or hypothesis is in error.

Rosenthal (1966) has also shown that in behavioural sciences, where statistical procedures are so generally used to guide the interpretation of results, the expectation of the experimenter may actually affect his choice of statistical tests. He notes that unintentionally the experimenter may use more powerful statistical tests when his hypothesis calls for showing the inadequacy of the null hypothesis, and less powerful statistics may be used when the expectation calls for the tenability of the null hypothesis.

Psychologists have long been aware of the fact that one person's expectation about another person's behaviour may help to determine that behaviour. For example, Merton in 1948 developed the notion of the 'self-fulfilling prophecy', which suggests that when an event is prophesied, the expectation of the event happening then changes the behaviour of the prophet in such a way as to make the predicted happening more likely. Most people can think of everyday examples of this phenomenon. Research into experimenter expectancy effects within the laboratory has increased over the last ten years. Most of this research has originated either directly in Robert Rosenthal's laboratories, or been stimulated by his research. Experiments have been carried out over a wide variety of areas including animal learning, human learning and ability, psychophysical judgments, reaction times, and person perception studies.

Some of the most interesting work has used animal subjects. Rosenthal and Fode (1963) used a class of psychology students who were investigating learning as experimenters. The class was told of studies which had shown that maze-bright and maze-dull rats could be developed by successive breeding of the well and poorly performing subjects. Half the experimenters were told that their rats were highly intelligent in maze situations, while the other half were told that their rats were very dull in maze learning. The animals who were believed to be very intelligent in learning mazes showed from the beginning a daily improvement in their performance, while those believed to be dull actually showed a decline in performance. By the end of the experiment highly significant differences were obtained between the two groups of subjects. Rosenthal and Fode attempted to determine how this difference had occurred. They found that the experimenters who had expected their animals to be intelligent tended to handle their rats more often and also more gently than did the experimenters expecting poor performance from their subjects.

In a review of 94 studies in six or seven different research areas Rosenthal and Rosnow (1969) provide evidence that the experimenter's expectancies do influence both the results he obtains and the responses shown by his subjects. Recently Rosenthal has left the psychological laboratory for a real-life laboratory to try to demonstrate the generality of expectancy effects. He has completed several studies within the classroom in which he has attempted to set up differential expectancies in teachers regarding pupils, and has followed up these teachers and pupils over longish periods of time to determine whether or not these teacher expectancies do alter the pupils' behaviour. Rosenthal and Jacobson (1968) report quite dramatic differential effects on the performance of pupils in the direction of their teachers' expectations. Although this research has created considerable controversy, the importance of teacher expectancy and reliable observation within the classroom is now widely accepted.

The doctor and other non-specific factors in treatment

Most of the studies discussed already are based on work carried out within traditional scientific, and more particularly, psychological laboratory research. In medical practice, however, the doctor or therapist is no less important than the experimenter. In this section it is proposed to look in more detail at such non-specific factors as the doctor himself, the therapeutic situation, placebos and placebo reactors, and to see how these variables may affect both treatment prescribed and responses of the patient to treatments.

Doctors, of course, are just as likely to show observer errors as are other scientists. Bean (1959) describes some of the many kinds of error within medicine. He reports that, for example, interpretation of X-rays by several independent observers is prone to subjectivity. Not only does it vary among different observers looking at the same film, but individual observers show considerable variation over time. He says that 'every aspect of the clinical examination which has had detailed study has similar uncertainty'.

The Therapist

The importance of the therapist in treatment has been examined from two rather differing points of view. (Most of the work has been within the area of psychiatric treatment.) Firstly, the expectations of the therapist regarding either the treatment procedure or the patient himself have been investigated; and secondly, aspects of the therapist's own personality have been looked at to see if they have any bearing on the outcome of his treatment.

The opinions of practising psychiatrists about the place and value of drug treatments vary widely, and in an early study by Feldman (1956) four categories of clinician were found: psychiatrists who were wholeheartedly in favour of drug therapy; those with a moderately conservative attitude towards medication; those showing explicit but partial rejection of drugs; and those completely rejecting drugs as a form of therapy for their psychiatric patients. Feldman showed that the attitudes of therapists towards the use of chemotherapy markedly affected the therapists' evaluations of their patients' progress under drug treatment. Other studies support this. For example, Uhlenhuth (1959) completed a sophisticated study examining different anti-anxiety drugs, including a placebo. Although he obtained no overall difference in the effectiveness of the three drugs, with one doctor's patients active medications were significantly superior to placebos, while with the others they were not. The first doctor expected to find such a difference, the second did not. Sabshin and Ramot (1956) contrasted the use of chlorpromazine at a small private psychiatric service of a general hospital, with the highly favourable reports which were then originating from larger state mental hospitals in America. At the small hospital both the patients and staff regarded such drug treatments as rather inferior. Although chemical therapy was tried in about 80 per cent of patients, this took place in a negative context in which all therapies, other than verbal psychotherapy, were regarded with hostility. As might be expected chlorpromazine failed to show any dramatic results. In explaining these results the authors note the attitudes of the doctors and nursing staff as being of primary importance. These seem to have been communicated to the patients, and the joint negative expectancies appear to have produced a very unsatisfactory result.

The effects of the therapists' expectancies about treatment are not limited only to psychiatric treatments. One researcher found that the attitudes of the therapist had an effect on the blood pressure responses of hypertensive subjects in a placebo control drug study, and this effect emerged regardless of whether subjects were receiving drug or placebo treatment. Another classic study noted extreme differences in gastric acid secretion after placebo treatment, depending on who administered the drug. One of the two physicians in this study consistently obtained increases in acid secretion when he administered a placebo; patients treated by the second physician consistently showed decreased acid secretion after the placebo had been administered. As might be expected, similar or perhaps greater effects of the therapist's expectations have been obtained with verbal and other forms of psychotherapy. A further study may be mentioned in which a group of patients was divided into those who saw their problems as improving over the course of treatment, and those who felt their problems had intensified. The therapists for the two patient groups were then compared in terms of their initial prognostic expectations. This comparison produced a highly significant result, in that the therapists of the patients who had perceived a positive change in themselves over therapy had expected significantly more patient improvement than did the therapists for those patients who perceived negative changes in themselves. There is also some evidence which suggests that the expectancies of the therapist regarding duration of treatment do in fact influence the length of time spent by patients in therapy.

Many studies have looked at the effect the therapist's own personality can have on treatment (Harbison, 1967). Two main areas of investigation will be reported briefly. A number of studies have tried to evaluate the success of therapy with schizophrenics in the light of certain personality characteristics of the therapists. Investigators have isolated two therapist 'types' who have distinct profiles on a fairly simple psychological test. Their feeling is that the more effective therapists established trusting relationships with the patients. They expressed their attitudes towards problems more freely, took initiative for sympathetic enquiry, and made few instructional interpretations of the patients' behaviour. The other sort of therapist was characterized by impersonal, instructional interpretations; they also tended to be either directive or passively permissive. More recent extensions of this work have found, using different diagnostic categories of patients (neurotic patients), significantly more improvement with the second type of therapist. The suggestion has been made, therefore, that the therapist's spontaneity has an adverse effect on patients with self-critical, neurotic personality traits, thus making the rather impersonal style of psychotherapy preferable.

The second series of studies is based on the Rogerian school of psychotherapy, and has been carried out by Truax and his colleagues (Truax and Carkhuff, 1967). Truax has delineated three major areas of therapist personality and interaction which appear crucial for successful outcome of the therapy. These therapeutically potent ingredients were labelled with the self-explanatory terms of accurate empathy, non-possessive warmth and therapist genuineness. Truax and his colleagues have found that high scores on these three measures taken as a group were correlated with improvement in the patients, and that in any one group of patients their improvement depended on high scores on any two of the three variables. A wide range of subjects has been used within therapy, including hospitalized schizophrenics, neurotics receiving out-patient treatment, college students receiving counselling, elementary school children, and female delinquents. Possibly the most sobering of all the findings, however, was that patients treated by therapists low on some of the personality variables showed a loss in psychological functioning – that is, they got worse! Rogers, speaking of the patients who got worse, was moved to say: 'Clinically this is a very sobering finding; scientifically it is of great importance.'

The Environment

Within traditional experimental psychology, the environment or the laboratory within which the experiment takes place is probably a very important variable. Little attention has been paid to this, although Rosenthal (1969) describes some results obtained which suggest that subjects and experimenters behaved rather differently depending on their experimental situation. He varied the professional atmosphere and orderliness of the laboratories and found that experimenters who had been assigned to more professional-appearing laboratories were described by their subjects as being significantly more expressive in terms of their voices and their faces, and more given to the use of gestures. Equally, within treatment the atmosphere of the treatment or the environment seems to be very important. In the experiment of Sabshin and Ramot already described, they noted that the new phenothiazine drugs had much less effect in a small highly-organized psychiatric unit compared with the results obtained in large state or county mental hospitals. Hospital environments obviously vary widely along many dimensions, such as their size, staff ratio, type of patient and finance available. These factors, along with many others, enter into the total therapeutic efficiency of different hospitals, and this evidences itself in the differential patient responses to both active treatments and placebos. The early literature on the use of tranquillizers suggests that the most dramatic results were being obtained in the back wards of large public hospitals where patient neglect was most pronounced. On the other hand, small actively-run hospitals often failed to share this enthusiasm, an example being the Sabshin and Ramot study already quoted.

Other aspects of the therapeutic setting have been found important. One group of investigators attempted to evaluate the effectiveness of carbon dioxide or nitrous oxide therapies on anxiety symptoms. Very pronounced differences in symptom relief were obtained between permissive and non-permissive conditions. In the first case patients were allowed to talk freely with the therapist for fifteen minutes before and after inhaling the gas. Under non-permissive conditions the gas was administered with an absolute minimum of interaction between patient and therapist. Several measures of improvement showed marked differences in treatment effectiveness under the two treatment-setting conditions, with the most pronounced symptom relief being obtained under the permissive conditions.

There is also some evidence to suggest that the effects of drugs may differ when they are administered individually or in groups. Knowles and Lucas (1960) found that placebo effects were more marked in group situations than in individual situations. These workers were studying the relationship between 'side-effects' reported by patients taking a placebo drug and personality factors. They showed that, in group situations, there was a definite positive relationship between neuroticism and the number of placebo side-effects reported. Under individual administration the relationship disappeared. It would appear that if drugs are administered in group conditions such as psychiatric wards, the more neurotic patients are more likely to 'catch' side-effects from other people around them. Some animal experiments have also suggested the importance of the group in altering the effects of drugs. Other work has shown that doses of drugs which were large enough to produce a hypnotic effect in mice, actually exerted a stimulating effect on their spontaneous activity when the mice were grouped together. Similar effects have been observed in humans as the result of alcohol. Finally, there have been some suggestions made that a 'therapeutically' oriented environment is more beneficial for patients (at least for psychiatric outpatients) than is an 'experimental' orientation. In this study, under double-blind conditions with either active or inactive drugs, the therapist role played one of two conditions: that of a treatment-oriented, confident doctor, or that of a research-oriented, objective investigator. The results indicate significantly greater beneficial responses were obtained from the doctors playing the 'therapeutic' role.

Placebos

The final non-specific factor in treatment related to the therapist is, of course, the placebo. The term 'placebo effect' refers to any effect of medical intervention which cannot be attributed to the specific action of the drug or treatment given. It has been said that until the last seventy or eighty years the history of medical treatment was largely a history of placebo effects, and an editorial in the *British Medical Journal* (1961) points out: 'At the present time many of the medicines commonly administered are placebos.' Although it is difficult to determine accurately, it has been estimated that from 20 per cent to 40 per cent of the total prescriptions presently written represent placebos. One well-known physician has said that 'the placebo is probably the most widely used therapeutic device in the armamentarium of the doctor. It should be used with profound respect, for in a very great number of patients it may be all that one has to offer' (Rubinstein, 1961). A vast literature is available on the placebo effect, and the present discussion only examines some of the results of several representative studies and tries to describe the apparent nature and extent of the effect.

A number of studies have attempted to determine the extent of the placebo effect and, since placebo responses are not universal or consistent, the nature of the placebo reactor. One investigator found that, in surgical patients receiving both morphine and placebos for postoperative pain, about 50 per cent received placebo relief when the total number of medication doses was small. These results suggest that both morphine and placebos are less effective in patients where the pain is of long duration, and who thus receive many doses of medication. Beecher (1959) has presented data gathered from several studies in two laboratories, involving patients with acute pain following surgery and chronic pain with cancer. He obtained remarkable consistency in that between 65 and 70 per cent of his patients obtained relief from 10mg of morphine, and 35 to 40 per cent from placebo administration. Beecher (1960) in a later report summarized ten studies of almost 1,000 patients, involving subjects with pain from surgery, cancer, headache and angina pectoris. He again showed that around 35 per cent received satisfactory pain relief with placebo administration.

A further factor accounting for the increasing interest in, and respect for, placebos in recent years is the repeated demonstration of their potency in reducing a wide variety of symptoms. We shall list only a few, but these include reduction of pain, anxiety, headaches, motor-sickness, warts, bleeding, ulcers, arthritic stiffness, gastric hyperacidity, coughing, common cold symptoms, and vomiting. Much work has gone into attempting to identify the sort of person who reacts to placebos, and much controversy still surrounds this area. Such personality variables as suggestibility or extraversion have been suggested as important. While there is little satisfactory evidence to support these suggestions, there appears to be some agreement that it is only patients or subjects who are either highly anxious or are in a highly anxiety-provoking situation who are liable to show a satisfactory reaction to the administration of placebos.

However, it would seem that in some instances there is a place for using the placebo effect. Here the confidence with which the doctor recommends treatment is important. All too frequently doctors are defensive about placebo effects rather than attempting to capitalize on them. Hays (1964) suggests that the ideal pill should be 'as red as possible, as bitter as was compatible with ingesting it successfully, as complicated to take as possible (i.e., take two pills with one-third of a glass of lukewarm water six minutes before each main meal except on Tuesdays), and as unlike the familiar aspirin tablet as the maker could manage'. It has been noted that while most doctors will accept the occurrence of placebo reactions, they are reluctant to admit their existence in their particular specialities, and thus do not make full use of the potential value of such 'ideal pills'.

Conclusion

Just as the infant is no longer regarded as the passive recipient of the stimuli around him but as a positive force interacting with his environment, so man is no longer regarded as an unbiased observer and interpreter or the disinterested initiator of action in his world. This chapter has indicated some of the ways in which events can be influenced by the attributes of the people involved in those events as experimenters or therapists. It would appear that man's beliefs, orientation and expectancies can influence his observation and interpretation of events and his own and others' behaviour as a consequence of those events. There is some debate as to the magnitude of these effects, but there is general agreement that they do exist and that in certain situations they must be considered both relevant and important. In the field of psychological research, where we are as yet very dependent on the human observer in quantifying and explaining behaviour, such phenomena are very important. Even if, at worst, observer bias and expectancy effects account for only 5 per cent of the total variance in any experimental situation, as suggested by Rosenthal (1969), this is an appreciable amount which cannot be disregarded. Equally within the medical field the evidence that not only the therapist influences the outcome of treatment, but also the situation within which he works, and the reactions of his patients both to himself and the situation, warrants serious consideration and further study.

If we accept that man exerts these influences and they are important, we must then try to discover how these influences are mediated. Investigations have looked at the possibility of such effects as artefacts of the situation due to intentional error or faulty recording, and at operant conditioning of responses through selective reinforcement of a particular response. Neither of these suggestions satisfactorily explains the results obtained in experimental investigations. Other workers have indicated the importance of visual and auditory cues. Freud appears to have been aware of this, and stipulated that in therapy the analytic patient should recline on a couch in front of the therapist so that 'my expression will not give the patient indications he may interpret or which may influence him in his communications'. For the moment we must leave the explanation of how these effects occur to the social psychologists who are involved in the whole area of interpersonal communication and who are investigating the verbal and non-verbal aspects of that communication. This does not mean that in areas where the effects of bias or expectancy are important there is nothing we can do. To be aware of such effects is to be able to minimize them in any situation in which we wish to do so.

In traditional scientific experimentation rigorous controls can be introduced to reduce or to assess the effect of any bias or expectancy. It is possible also to include the experimenter as a major variable in experiments by using complex factorial experimental design. In the area of placebo effects their control will be of the greatest importance in drug trials where a new drug is being assessed. A control placebo group will be necessary to ensure that observed effects are the result of the efficacy of the drug and not of any placebo effect. However, in the clinical situation there may be occasions when we may, in fact, want to exploit therapist variables and patient expectations. Truax and Carkhuff (1967) have already indicated how this may be done. Having identified certain crucial variables, such as empathy, in both successful and unsuccessful therapy, they initiated a training programme for therapists in which they demonstrated that it is possible to manipulate the therapist factors in the required direction and thus produce more effective therapists. It has already been suggested that inactive medicaments are the only treatment at present available in some situations, and that in these situations the non-specific factors are highly important and must be utilized.

Thus we can either control expectancy effects or exploit them to maximize the successful conclusion of the experiment or treatment. This still leaves us with the need for controlled and reliable observation of behaviour in both experimental and clinical situations. There are a number of ways by which the reliability and validity of human observation can be improved. These methods of observation take into account the physical and psychological limitations of human observation, and try to minimize their effects. In the past much observation has been of the impressionistic or anecdotal type, and this has meant recording only the most obvious behaviour or running the risk of seeing what is expected. It is also impossible to observe accurately over a long period of time. Both of these effects can be minimized by the use of time-sampling procedures and agreed rating scales or check lists. While observing behaviour over a few seconds for an agreed period on a set number of occasions during the day may not always be appropriate in a clinical setting, it can be very useful in an experimental setting, and can be of value to doctors or therapists when they require a wider sample of the patient's behaviour than they can have in an interview situation. Nurses have been successfully trained in using time-sampling techniques and rating scales or check lists. The use of the latter actually specifies the behaviour which is being observed, e.g., nail biting, and the frequency of that behaviour within the specified time. The behaviour specified must be clearly defined and not open to individual interpretation. There is no point in observing the frequency of aggressive acts when one person may consider an act aggressive and another judge it to be playfully rough. The aggressive acts must be defined so that no value judgments are necessary in recording the frequency of the behaviour.

Recently tape recordings and video-tape or film have been increasingly used to observe and later to analyse and record behaviour. This, of course, has the great advantage that the observation and recording do not have to take place simultaneously. It is also possible, using these electronic aids, to be more accurate about time spent by the patient or subject in a specific act. This time variable has increasingly been used as a means of measuring individual differences in behaviour. The work already mentioned by Goldman-Eisler is a very good example of how useful a tape recorder can be in measuring speech behaviour. Without such equipment it would be impossible to measure the speech hesitations of the individual. Tape-recordings are also useful in any interview situation where it is difficult to record accurately what the patient or subject is saying as he is saying it.

Skilled observation is a necessary technique for both experimenter and therapist if they are to be no longer dependent solely on their own subjective judgments. Means are now available for improving both objectivity and accuracy. Since the evidence is considerable that subjectivity is a significant variable in the observing and recording of behaviour, it is crucial that adequate use is made of such techniques.

References

Barber, B. (1961). 'Resistance by Scientists to Scientific Discovery', *Science N.Y.* 134 pp. 596–602.
Bean, W. B. (1948). 'An Analysis of Subjectivity in the Clinical Examination in Nutrition', *J. Appl. Physiol.* 1, pp. 458–68.
Bean, W. B. (1959). 'The Natural History of Error: Pseudodoxia Endemica', *Trans. Ass. Am. Physns*, 72, pp. 40–55.
Beecher, H. K. (1959). *Measurement of Subjective Responses: Quantitative Effects of Drugs.* New York: Oxford University Press.
Beecher, H. K. (1960). 'Increased Stress and Effectiveness of Placebos and "Active" Drugs', *Science N.Y.* 132, pp. 91–2.
British Medical Journal (1961). 1, pp. 43–4.
Feldman, P. E. (1956). 'The Personal Element in Psychiatric Research', *Am. J. Psychiat.* 113, pp. 52–4.
Goldman-Eisler, Frieda (1968). *Psycholinguistics.* London: Academic Press.
Harbison, J. J. M. (1967). 'The Experimenter Effect: Evidence and Implications', *Pap. Psychol.* 1, pp. 10–16.

Hays, P. (1964). *New Horizons in Psychiatry*. Harmondsworth: Penguin.
Knowles, J. B. and Lucas, C. J. J. (1960). 'Experimental Studies of the Placebo Response'. *J. Ment. Sci.* 106, pp. 231–40.
Rosenthal, R. (1966). *Experimenter Effects in Behavioral Research*. New York: Appleton-Century-Crofts.
Rosenthal, R. (1968). 'Experimenter Expectancy and the Reassuring Nature of the Null Hypothesis Decision Procedure', *Psychol. Bull. Monog. Suppl.* 70, 6, pp. 30–47.
Rosenthal, R. (1969). 'Interpersonal Expectations', in *Artifact in Behavioral Research* (eds R. Rosenthal and R. C. Rosnow). New York: Academic Press.
Rosenthal, R. and Fode, K. L. (1963). 'The Effect of Experimenter Bias on the Performance of the Albino Rat', *Behavl. Sci.* 8, pp. 183–9.
Rosenthal, R. and Jacobson, L. (1968). *Pygmalion in the Classroom: Teacher Expectations and Pupils' Intellectual Development*. New York; Holt, Rinehart & Winston.
Rosenthal, R. and Rosnow, R. C. (eds) (1969). *Artifact in Behavioral Research*. New York: Academic Press.
Rubinstein, M. W. (1961). 'The Placebo'. *J. Nat. Med. Ass.* 53, pp. 61–5.
Sabshin, M. and Ramot, J. (1956). 'Pharmacotherapeutic Evaluation and the Psychiatric Setting', *Arch. Neurol. Psychiat.* 75, pp. 362–70.
Truax, C. B. (1970). 'Effects of Client-centred Psychotherapy with Schizophrenic Patients: Nine Years Pre-therapy and Nine Years Post-therapy Hospitalization'. *J. Consult. Clin. Psychol.* 35, pp. 417–22.
Truax, C. B. and Carkhuff, R. R. (1967). *Toward Effective Counseling and Psychotherapy: Training and Practice*. Chicago: Aldine.
Uhlenhuth, E. H. (1959). 'The Symptomatic Relief of Anxiety with Meprobamate, Phenobarbital and Placebo', *Am. J. Psychiat.* 115, pp. 905–10.

Suggestions for further reading

Armistead, N. (ed.). *Reconstructing Social Psychology*. Harmondsworth: Penguin 1974.
Rosenthal, R. *Experimenter Effects in Behavioral Research*. New York: Appleton-Century-Crofts 1966.
Rosenthal, R. and Rosnow, R. C. *Artifact in Behavioral Research*. London: Academic Press 1969.

Chapter eleven

Attitudes

Alan Richardson

Social medicine and social psychiatry are concerned with the contribution of social factors to the onset of medical and psychiatric conditions, and with the manipulation of social factors for the prevention and treatment of these conditions. Social psychology is concerned 'to understand and explain how the thought, feeling and behaviour of individuals are influenced by the actual, imagined or implied presence of others' (Allport, 1968, p. 3). Along with individual psychology, sociology and anthropology, it may be considered one of the basic social science disciplines of relevance to the social aspects of medicine.

Textbooks on social psychology are readily available (e.g., Secord and Backman, 1974; Brown, 1965) but they cover a wider range of problems than will be discussed in this chapter. The focus of attention in what follows is upon one problem only. It is a central area of research and theory for social psychology and a prime practical issue for much of medicine and psychiatry. The problem to be discussed is that of attitudes: what they are, how they are formed and maintained, how they change, and how they are related to overt behaviour. Some examples will help to make the significance of this problem clear.

In public health programmes a perennial concern is to discover the most acceptable and effective means by which to influence community attitudes and behaviour. How can people be helped to act spontaneously in ways that will benefit their own health and the health of those, like the young and the old, for whom they may be responsible? In particular, how can men and women be persuaded that it is in their best interests to have a periodic cancer check? What is the most satisfactory way of bringing home to people the health risks involved in heavy smoking of cigarettes? Can the prejudices of some sections of a community towards the fluoridation of its public water supply be overcome? How can children be encouraged to develop more positive attitudes towards cleaning their teeth after meals, and adolescents encouraged to develop more negative attitudes towards the taking of 'hard' drugs? In the face-to-face situations of a doctor and patient, how can a child be helped to form positive attitudes to a painful but necessary operation, or an old person helped to maintain a positive attitude towards his own worth as a person when he believes that he is a burden to others? What attitudes do people have towards their own bodies, and how are these attitudes related to post-operative reactions, and to the most appropriate procedures of management to be employed by relatives, nurses and doctors?

Finally, and by no means least among the categories of attitudes with which a doctor is concerned, are those which he holds himself. In the course of becoming a doctor many old attitudes undergo modification and many new attitudes are formed. These changes are part of the process of professionalization; and for the reader of this book, reflecting upon the more detailed discussion of attitudes in later sections of this chapter, it is a useful exercise to examine some of his own attitudes. How did a particular attitude come into being? How complex are the beliefs associated with it? Is it part of a cluster of other attitudes and firmly anchored in an even more complex value system? Under what conditions is his overt behaviour influenced by this attitude? Some attitudes which have been modified since embarking on a medical training may relate to 'people who are ill', 'death', 'transplant surgery', 'a corpse', 'the National Health Service', 'socialized medicine', or 'psychiatry and other specialities'.

The term attitude has been used so far without any attempt at definition. It is now necessary to consider the nature of an attitude in more detail.

The nature of attitudes

An attitude is a predisposition to feel, think and act towards some object, person, group or event in a more or less favourable or unfavourable way. Each of the three components of an attitude varies along the two major dimensions of intensity and complexity. Thus I can feel more or less strongly about an object, and the feeling may be of a simple love or hate variety or it may be a more complex mixture of feelings. My thoughts or beliefs about an object may vary in the degree of certainty with which they are held, and in the number and complexity of the entire set associated with a particular object. Again, my action tendencies in regard to an object will vary in regard to my determination to act for or against the object and in the complexity and range of actions that I am prepared to carry out. For example, my overall attitude to illness might be moderately negative based upon some combination of positive and negative feelings associated with a particular set of beliefs about illness. To varying extents I might believe that illness is a time for relaxing and relinquishing responsibility, for experiencing pain and discomfort, for being a bother to other people, and for not being able to play tennis. My actions might include a wide variety of preventive measures designed to avoid illness.

An attitude, then, is a general state of readiness that under appropriate conditions leads to some form of overt behaviour. However, the connection between the action tendency component of an attitude and actual overt behaviour is a complex one. Overt behaviour, whether physical or verbal, is always the product of a person in a situation and never the result of either set of potential determinants viewed in isolation. For example, a man may be favourably disposed towards his doctor and unfavourably disposed towards his recurrent blackouts at work, yet he may not seek his doctor's assistance. His decision to do nothing may result from his knowledge of the social costs involved. He may believe that his colleagues would regard this particular medical condition as a sign of unreliability and even moral weakness. The objective facts are not relevant to understanding this man's behaviour. One has to view his situation as he views it himself. It is, of course, situations of this kind that ultimately lead to legislation and the requirement of regular medical checks wherever public safety is involved.

The overt behaviour of people in many everyday situations is in part determined by the action tendency component of the attitude and in part upon the extent to which relevant others are seen as opposed to or in favour of this action. By relevant others is meant all those persons and groups that are of importance to the individual because he values his association with them and is sensitive to their good opinion of him and their power to reward or punish. However, it is not only or always a question of the value we place upon our friendships or our group memberships that determines our actions. A further factor is the extent to which an individual regards the expectations of significant others as legitimate. If the expectations are not regarded as legitimate and the attitude is one that is central within the individual's self-concept, the pressures towards acting overtly in a way that is consistent with his attitude will be increased. The behaviour that actually occurs in a particular situation can be conceptualized as the resultant of all the positive and negative forces from within and from without that are operating at that time. Not least among those forces is the attitude itself.

The origin of attitudes

Because the family into which we are born provides us with total environment from which we do not usually escape for any length of time until our school days begin, its importance as the origin of the vast majority of our initial attitudes is very great. Inevitably the family sets limits on the range of objects, people and events to which we are exposed and, by the example and instruction of parents, determines the majority of beliefs that we form and our positive and negative evaluation of them. From the reactions of parents to our own behaviour we develop attitudes towards ourselves which involve a complex set of beliefs concerning our adequacy and inadequacy in every area of endeavour. In this way we come to have an overall evaluation of our personal worth. From attitudes expressed by our parents we come to believe that sitting on public lavatory seats will lead to unmentionable diseases, that old men who have faces like wrinkled cider apples probably drink too much, or that red berries on almost every tree, plant or shrub are almost certainly poisonous.

Whatever the range of attitudes that we learn during these early years at home they are likely to be especially resistant to change. Some of them have a high probability of being learned under conditions of relatively intense motivation. Emotion is more easily aroused in young children, and learning that occurs on such occasions is both more resistant to extinction and more likely to generalize to superficially similar events and objects.

A strong negative attitude to medicines may develop on the basis of having castor oil thrust down one's throat during a highly emotional moment in one's life. One might develop a negative attitude to doctors which generalizes to a variety of associated settings on the basis of an unsympathetically administered injection or of a stomach pump clumsily handled at a time when as a child you were extremely frightened.

Another reason for the persistence of many early attitudes is the almost total absence of any basis from which the child might check on the validity of the beliefs and evaluations provided by his parents. The belief that the best treatment for a bad burn is a buttered bandage dies hard. Even if it occurred to a child that those beliefs are seldom endorsed by the consequences of adhering to them, the absence of an independent frame of reference from which to assess them means that no counter-influences are present to bring about change. Even when counter-evidence does become available at a later period in one's life it may well be discounted or distorted in the service of a general need for consistency.

It is of interest to note that what is sometimes called 'suggestibility' is not so much a general personality trait applying equally to all situations, but rather a more limited response applying to those situations where we lack an appropriate frame of reference from which to judge the probable truth or falsity of a proposition or the rightness or wrongness of a course of action. If a physicist whom we have no reason to distrust tells us that a snark is the very latest particle to be discovered, it is highly probable that we shall believe him. If he goes on to provide an entirely plausible account of its general significance in the field of sub-atomic physics, a definite attitude may be formed which may in turn affect related attitudes. Hoaxes depend for their success not so much upon some general disposition to be suggestible, but on the prestige of the person who provides the information, and on the absence of an appropriate frame of reference in those who are to be hoaxed.

During the second five years of life, when the range of our social contacts is increased as a result of school attendance and neighbourhood play, we increase the number of our attitudes and the complexity of their interrelations. However, it is not until the third quinquennium that we are most likely to come into contact with a vastly increased number of people whose attitudes to many things are very different from our own. This period coincides with a rapid increase in our capacity for abstract thought and the often sudden awareness of our own separateness, our own distinctive identity. To become aware of oneself means to become aware of at least some of the attitudes that have been quietly developing over the years and for which we have had no personal responsibility whatever. Fortunately for our peace of mind these attitudes vary in salience, so that only those which seem most relevant to our immediate concerns are likely to be examined. During these years of adolescence this stock pile of beliefs and evaluations is worked over and often made a little more coherent. What does one really believe about this, that and the other? Even when one is convinced that some belief is false it may still persist as a half-belief. Many superstitions are of this kind. What does one totally reject? People vary in the extent to which they are perturbed by the mass of attitudes that they discover within themselves. When these attitudes are shared by those one likes and admires in the groups to which one belongs, the pressure to evaluate this personal-social inheritance will be less. Often a dramatic shift in *milieu*, as when an individual moves from his birth place to another town or country, or into the army or university, is required before this process of re-evaluation is undertaken.

So far the origin of attitude has been considered in relation to membership in primary groups only. What of membership in secondary groups? Membership in secondary groups, like those of the nation into which we are born, the university in which we learn, the community in which we live or the organization within which we work, is also important. A secondary group is one in which we have at least nominal membership which when known to other people, may influence their behaviour towards us, at least under some conditions. If one is an Englishman abroad then it may be expected that one will act in certain ways and not in others. A university is likely to be a secondary group in which strong normative pressures are applied against anyone who holds strong attitudes which are based on evidence that is demonstrably false or upon arguments that are logically invalid. One's susceptibility to social pressure in any group is partly a function of the extent to which one values one's membership in the group, or the strength of one's motivation to become a member. When identification occurs with a group to which one does not belong that group serves as a reference group as much as any group in which we value our actual membership. For purposes of understanding the origin of a person's attitudes it is as important to know his reference groups as to know his nominal membership groups. Even historical or imaginary groups can serve this reference function. As a result of reading a Utopian novel the reader may be convinced of the desirability of certain forms of social behaviour. Favourable attitudes might be formed towards these behaviours, and the reader might reward and punish himself for deviations from the normative attitudes held by his fictional reference group.

The structure and function of attitudes

Despite the diverse influences to which an individual is exposed in his progress from birth to maturity and beyond, the total set of attitudes that result is not an incoherent jumble. Attitudes to a wide variety of different things show some degree of consistency or structure. Many of them also appear to be the expression of some more general value orientation or ideology.

Structure

In the domain of social attitudes some evidence of structure was obtained by Ferguson (1939). He administered ten attitude scales to 185 university students and found three major clusters which he named Religionism, Humanism and Nationalism. Attitudes towards birth control, evolution and God were associated with the first; capital punishment, treatment of criminals and war were associated with the second; and censorship, communism, law and patriotism with the third. Additional research reviewed by Eysenck (1954) suggested that the structure of the social attitude domain might be described more efficiently in terms of only two orthogonal dimensions. The first of these was called a Radical/Conservative dimension, and the second a Tough-minded/Tender-minded dimension. It was thought that all social attitudes could be described by their unique position in one or other of the quadrants formed by these two orthogonal dimensions. Thus the belief that conscientious objectors are not traitors was located in the Radical/Tender-minded quadrant in association with beliefs in support of pacifism, the desirability of giving up some degree of national sovereignty in the interests of world peace, and opposition to compulsory sterilization of the mentally defective. In the diametrically opposite quadrant defined by high scores on the Conservative and Tough-minded dimensions was another cluster of attitudes involving beliefs in the inferiority of coloured people, the necessity of retaining the death penalty, and the desirability of administering corporal punishment to children and criminals. By using the statistical procedures of correlation and factor analysis it is possible to show that attitudes which are superficially unconnected with each other do in fact form coherent clusters. Individuals who hold one set of attitudes have a high probability of holding another set of attitudes. Though common experience would suggest that this finding is true, the empirical problem is to establish the minimum number of basic value dimensions necessary to account for the largest possible constellation of attitudes present in a particular population. Again, common experience with friends whom we have known since childhood suggests that there are consistencies over time in their value orientation and in the attitudes that express this orientation. The empirical problem in this instance has been to establish an association between present value orientations and the experiences that a child has of himself and his world which derive from the family in which his primary socialization took place. Most well-known among the investigations of this problem are those which have focused upon the origins of authoritarianism (Brown, 1965, provides a useful review of this work), but the example to be discussed here has been taken from Tomkins (1965). He has attempted to show that children become biased in one or other of two main directions as a result of their early experiences in the family. On the one hand the child may learn to do what is expected of him, irrespective of his own wishes, and on the other he may learn to do what he enjoys doing within the limits set by the needs of other people. Basic views of human nature in general may derive from the degree to which a child comes to experience himself in one or other of these ways. To be at the extreme end of the bias mentioned first above, is to develop a view of human nature as basically evil. Humanity is capable of living in what we have come to consider as a civilized fashion only by strict policing and controlling of behaviour. At the opposite extremity a view of human nature develops which sees it as basically good. All that humanity requires for optimum happiness is the opportunity to express itself. Restraints are only justified to ensure that this opportunity is available to everyone. These two value orientations are not dissimilar to some aspects of those already discussed in this section. Their similarity to the basic pictures of man adopted in the classical political doctrines of absolutism and liberalism is also clearly apparent.

Among the studies conducted by Tomkins (1965) and his students is one in which a wide range of attitudes were examined in a mixed sample of about 500 persons. This sample was divided into two sub-samples on the basis of overall view of human nature. One group tended to agree with the proposition that 'human nature is basically evil'; the other tended to agree with the proposition that 'human nature is basically good'. A few of the attitudes associated with each of these value orientations are listed below:

HUMAN NATURE IS BASICALLY EVIL	HUMAN NATURE IS BASICALLY GOOD
Science and education:	
1. The main purpose of education should be to teach the young the wisdom of the remote and recent past.	The main purpose of education should be to enable the young to discover and create novelty.
2. The important thing in science is to be right and make as few errors as possible.	The important thing in science is to strike out into the unknown, right or wrong.
Government:	
3. If an individual breaks the law, he should be punished for the good of society.	If an individual breaks the law, it is not always to his advantage or to the advantage of society that he is punished.
4. A government should allow only such freedom of expression as is consistent with law and order.	A government should allow freedom of expression even though there is some risk in permitting it.
People:	
5. When people are in trouble, they should help themselves and not depend on others.	When people are in trouble, they need help and should be helped.
6. It is disgusting to see an adult cry.	It is distressing to see an adult cry.

HUMAN NATURE IS BASICALLY EVIL	HUMAN NATURE IS BASICALLY GOOD
Children:	
7. Children should be taught to obey what is right even though they may not always feel like it.	Children should be encouraged to express themselves even though parents may not always like it.
8. To act on impulse is to act childishly.	To act on impulse occasionally makes life more interesting.
Feelings:	
9. So called mystical experiences have most often been a source of delusion.	Mystical experiences may be sources of insight into the nature of reality.
10. There is no surer road to insanity than surrender to the feelings, particularly those which are alien to the self.	There is a unique avenue to reality through the feelings, even when they seem alien.

Functions

It might be expected that new attitudes will be formed most readily when they are found to be consistent with pre-existing value orientations. However, the need for consistency is not the only motivational function of importance in understanding the formation of new attitudes. Other emotional and cognitive needs must also be taken into account. For example, if the need for social approval and acceptance is very strong, some attitude clusters might be expected to develop in relation to objects, persons, groups or events for which normative beliefs existed in the most potent social groups to which one belonged. If for some reason, such as migration to another country (Richardson, 1967), one found that the attitude of the new group within which acceptance was sought differed from one's own attitude, conflict would result. The outcome of such a conflict of attitudes would depend upon the relative strengths of the forces involved. Not least among those forces is the extent to which the expectations of the new group carried sanctions for non-conformity.

Another motivational basis for the formation of attitudes is the need for accurate information. Many attitudes are held because the beliefs which they embody provide a more accurate and reliable basis for action. Such attitudes are not easily relinquished unless acceptable contrary evidence provides an even better basis for action. One last motivational basis to be mentioned is what Katz (1960) has called 'ego defence'.

Whenever some cherished value is severely threatened, some non-rational defence mechanism may be brought into play. The new and threatening information may be denied, or the thoughts and impulses stimulated by it may be repressed. Anger and hostility evoked by the message may be unacceptable to the receiver's self-image and may be projected upon the source. Because people fear many things (disease, injury, death to themselves or to those for whom they feel affection and concern), and because intense fear is an unpleasant emotion, the ego defences may prevent some people from becoming aware of information of potential relevance to their circumstances. Negative attitudes may also develop towards the source of messages which are experienced as threatening. Evidence from many studies of ethnic prejudice suggests that one basis for resistance to social influences designed to change attitudes to Jews or Negroes or other ethnic groups is the need to have a group against which hostility can be directed, i.e., a scapegoat. Facts about an ethnic group which might require the relinquishing of some beliefs that currently bolster a negative attitude toward them will be discounted or in some way distorted. Bettelheim and Janowitz (1950) found that among highly prejudiced persons the intensity of their prejudice often increased when attempts were made to present the disliked group in a more favourable light.

As will be seen in the next section on attitude modification, some knowledge of the motivational functions served by attitudes is essential to any understanding of the conditions under which particular attitudes held by particular people either change or remain the same.

The modification of attitudes

Some indication of the factors relevant to the formation, modification and maintenance of attitudes has already emerged in the preceding pages. It remains to complete the description of relevant factors and to place them within a relevant framework. Major variables affecting attitude change have been grouped under four sub-headings: source, message, channel and receiver.

The Source

It obviously matters a great deal who is communicating with us. If we perceive the communicator or the organization, party, institution or other social group to which he belongs as trustworthy and as attractive we are more likely to pay attention to the position that is being advocated on some issue. A public health department that is believed to be accurately informed and whose persuasive communications are seen as motivated, not by self-interest, but by a genuine concern for public welfare, can expect to have its message heard. The first task of the communicator is to have his message received and understood by those whom he wishes to persuade. A million leaflets dropped into a million letter boxes and then placed unopened into a million waste-paper baskets change no attitudes. An educational broadcast on safety in the home is equally ineffective if its only listeners are those who already have the attitudes that are advocated. The message must get through to the intended recipients.

Belief in the trustworthiness of the source is to some extent independent of the degree to which the source is liked or admired. There are occasions on which acknowledged experts of undoubted integrity are unheeded by their listeners because they do not inspire affection. If the source is regarded as having charm, humour and warmth in addition to the possession of accurate information and a disinterested concern for the recipient's welfare, the power of the source to persuade is greatly increased.

It is not surprising to discover that when a doctor makes a treatment recommendation one important determinant of its adoption is the esteem accorded to the medical profession itself. In a study by Brim (1954) the attitudes of fifty-seven mothers towards a new approach to coping with the feeding problems of their infants were investigated. None of these mothers was employed outside the home and all were fully occupied in the care of their child. They were all of Italian, Negro or Jewish background and living with a husband of similar background to themselves. Lastly, they all had an eldest child aged between one-and-a-half and three years of age whom they considered to be a feeding problem, and who at the time of the interview was being forced to eat any food that was refused. The experimenter played the role of a doctor and interviewed the mothers during one of their regular appointments at the local infant health clinic. During the interview it was suggested that they should adopt a permissive approach when their child refused his food. A pamphlet was also provided which outlined the method in more detail. Fifty of the mothers were re-interviewed about three-and-a-half months later. Twenty-six admitted that they had made no attempt to employ the permissive approach, another sixteen had given it up after a few trials, and eight had adopted it. Attitude to doctors as a category was measured by asking each mother how helpful she had found any previous advice received from doctors. Significantly more of those who held doctors in high esteem (i.e., regarded them as helpful) had tried out the recommendation. But of those who tried the recommendation the same proportion of mothers adopted it (about two-thirds) among those who held doctors in high estimation as held doctors in low estimation. All of those who actually adopted the permissive feeding practices were sustained in their decisions by at least two other circumstances. The first of these circumstances was the presence of a supportive husband, and the second was the reported absence of exposure to anti-permissive influences. Experiments on conforming behaviour by Asch (1956) and field studies on the effectiveness of supervisory training schemes designed to encourage democratic as opposed to autocratic patterns of leadership have also shown the importance of receiving some minimal degree of social support if newly formed or newly modified attitudes are to persist and have some chance of influencing overt behaviour. (See Chapter 10 by Harbison.)

This study of Asch's serves to emphasize a recurrent theme in this section, that factors that have been found to play some part in the attitude change process seldom operate alone, but need to be considered in their actual or potential combinations and interactions with other factors.

The Message

Obviously an effective message should be comprehensible by all those for whom it is intended, and it should appear to be relevant to their needs and circumstances. If the sender believes that the position advocated in the message may not be seen as of immediate personal importance to the receiver, he tries to increase its relevance by embedding the message in an appropriate context. The world may be polluting itself and overpopulating itself at a rate that seriously endangers the future of the human race, but how does a government or other concerned source make the relevance of the known facts apparent to all of us? How can the message influence our attitudes to the causes of pollution and overpopulation so that we care sufficiently? Within what context or set of contexts must the message be placed to be most effective in changing our attitudes?

Two aspects of the message will be considered. The first concerns the type of appeal or context within which the message is placed, while the second concerns the amount of attitude change that is being advocated.

A message may be made more effective by implicitly or explicitly arousing appropriate frames of reference within the recipient. One is familiar with the attempts of advertisers to change attitudes towards their products by appealing to particular needs, emotions or interests assumed or known to be present in their audiences. By placing their product within an appealing context such as a beautiful landscape or associating it with beautiful people who are readily identifiable as coming from a salient reference group of the audience, the attempt is made to increase the degree of favour with which their product is regarded.

There is no simple answer to the ancient problem concerning the relative merits of rational and emotional appeals. Where the facts are not in dispute and the recipient has a strong need for accurate information, the rational appeal of a trusted source has a high probability of being effective. If one trusts a consumers' association its reports may be expected to influence attitudes to the range of products in which one is interested. Rational appeals are likely to be successful when they fit in with rational needs to know the world in which we live so that we can function more effectively in it. But of course we are always selective in the kinds of fact that interest us. It may be a fact that the 'best buy' in cars is model X. It is the largest, most comfortable, most powerful, most economical to run and maintain in its price range; but we don't buy it because we don't like its shape or the colours in which it is available. This is not irrational; it merely indicates that aesthetic criteria are being employed rather than utilitarian criteria.

In considering the effectiveness of different appeals it is always necessary to examine the motivations present in the receiver. If he is already concerned with the content area from which the message comes, the information itself will often be sufficient to hold interest and bring about an examination of the position advocated. If the receiver is initially unconcerned, then some means must be found to motivate interest in the content of the message. It is usually the function of an emotional appeal to produce concern where little or none existed before. Some examples of this procedure will now be given.

In a study of emotional role playing by Janis and Mann (1965) a group of women students were encouraged to reduce their cigarette consumption by playing the role of cancer patients. The experimenter took the role of a physician and a series of scenes were acted out in the surgery. Props such as X-ray plates were also employed, and the role-playing patient was obliged to focus attention on the possibility of a painful illness followed by hospitalization and an early death. One control group engaged in cognitive role playing by acting the part of debaters arguing against cigarette smoking. Another control group received exactly the same information as the emotional role-playing subjects by listening to a tape recording of one of the latter's sessions. When re-interviewed two weeks later it was found that the experimental group whose members had engaged in the emotional role playing had become significantly less favourable in their attitude to smoking, and had reduced their daily consumption of cigarettes. As part of a survey conducted for another purpose, eighteen months later, Mann and Janis

(1968) report that the girls in the experimental group still smoked less and had less favourable attitudes to smoking. Some had given up smoking entirely; and spontaneous comments by many of these girls indicated that their attitudes had been strongly influenced by their experiences in the experiment conducted eighteen months earlier.

Given that some degree of emotional concern may need to be aroused if change in an attitude is to occur, what is the optimum amount? Since the original study by Janis and Feshbach (1953) many writers have assumed that the amount of attitude change that had taken place after a persuasive communication is inversely related to the intensity of fear aroused by the message. More recent evidence suggests that where a full range of fear appeals is presented from very weak to very strong a curvilinear relationship may be expected. The amount of attitude change increases with fear intensity up to some maximum and then begins to decrease with each successive increase in fear intensity. Where the theoretical turning point on the curve will be for different categories of source, message content, channel and recipient is not predictable, and must be established empirically. For example, it has been found that relatively high levels of fear arousal are better than moderate or low levels in achieving a reduction in the number of cigarettes smoked, but that relatively low levels of fear arousal are better in getting smokers to have an examination to check on the possibility of lung cancer (Leventhal and Watts, 1966).

An example of a situation where at least a moderate amount of anxiety is naturally present is that of the pre-operative patient. It has been shown in one study that the patient's post-operative attitudes to his own physical condition and his attitudes to the nursing staff are more favourable when he has been informed beforehand of the typical discomforts that can be expected as a result of the operation and encouraged to come to accept them. Egbert *et al.* (1964) conducted an experiment on ninety-seven adult surgical patients at the Massachusetts General Hospital. These patients were allocated 'by random order' to an experimental and a control group. Those in the experimental group were informed in some detail as to the *sequelae* that might occur after their operation, were encouraged to come to terms with them, and instructed how to deal with post-operative pain. No such information or encouragement was provided for those in the control group. To ensure that equivalent nursing care would be given to both groups, the ward nurses and the surgeons were not informed about the experiment until after it was completed. About the same amount of narcotic was administered to the two groups on the day of the operation; but on each of the five days immediately following the operation the requests for pain-relieving drugs were significantly fewer among those patients who had been informed and encouraged. In fact, the narcotic requirements of this experimental group were reduced to about one-half of that needed by the control group. Ratings made on the ward by an independent observer, who was unaware which patients were in which group, revealed significantly better physical and emotional health in the experimental group. These patients also made fewer complaints to the nurses and doctors than those in the control group, and were sent home on average 2·7 days earlier. These results may be explained in part by the reduction of a high level of anxiety to a more tolerable level by the administration of relevant information and the encouragement to come to terms with it. When the anticipated unpleasant experiences do occur after the operation is finished, the patient has an appropriate cognitive and emotional context into which they can be assimilated.

What changes in attitude occur as a result of advocating different amounts of change? It has been demonstrated by Whittaker (1967) that if a message advocates a position on some attitude continuum that is too far from the recipient's own position, there is a tendency to react by rejecting the message and sometimes the source as well. When the source is regarded as trustworthy and moderate change is advocated, the message may be judged as fair and impartial; but as the advocated position becomes more extreme the message is likely to be judged as biased and the source comes to be disliked. For any given person or population there is a definable range of positions which are acceptable. The more extreme the position advocated within this range the greater the change of attitude that can be expected. The new position can be assimilated. The attempt to produce even greater change only serves to emphasize the difference between the recipient's present stand and the one advocated. The new position contrasts with the old and may be rejected. As with findings on fear appeals, it has been found that a curvilinear relationship exists between extremity of position advocated and amount of attitude change that results.

An example will help to make this relationship clear. Let us suppose that attitude to socialized medicine is the topic of investigation. Twenty belief statements are prepared varying in the extent to which they support or oppose government control of medicine. A sample of doctors might then be asked to choose those statements that they found objectionable, those that were unobjectionable and the one statement that best represented their own position. When an individual holds an extreme position, pro or anti, his tolerance for other positions is, of course, very slight. Individuals holding more moderate attitudes, however, have a greater tolerance for other positions. Within this range of tolerance a communicator could expect to produce the maximum amount of change by advocating the most extreme position chosen as unobjectionable by the majority of those in the target population. To advocate change to positions outside the range of tolerance will have the effect of reducing the amount of attitude change produced.

The Channel

There have been many studies designed to find out whether more information is retained or more attitude change occurs after exposure to a printed message (newspapers, magazines, journals), a heard message (radio), a seen and heard message (film and television), or a message conveyed by word of mouth in a face-to-face situation. Distinctions between the mass media will not be discussed in this section. Attention will be focused on the mass media as a whole in contrast with and as an adjunct to face-to-face communication. The general finding has been (Katz and Lazarsfeld, 1955) that attitude change is far more likely to occur as a result of personal influence than as a result of influences originating in the mass media. In a face-to-face situation communication is a two-way process in which the one who is doing the influencing can immediately see the effectiveness of his statements on his listener. He can maintain attention when he sees that interest is flagging, he can anticipate objections and provide immediate counterarguments if these become necessary. All of the mass media are one-way communicating systems in which there is no opportunity of correcting a misunderstanding or an objection made by a recipient. Feedback is achieved slowly and tediously by means of audience surveys or public opinion polls. The critical importance of the mass media in relation to attitude change rests upon the capacity of those who control them to limit the range and quality of the information presented. Beyond this point the influence of the mass media tends to be indirect. Information passes from them to particular persons in the wider community who expose themselves to selected messages because of their specialized interests. These individuals become the potential opinion leaders in those areas of specialized interest within the primary groups of their communities. Some, but not all, are turned to for information and advice on problems where their specialized knowledge and experience is seen as relevant. Whether a potential opinion leader becomes an actual source of influence will depend not only upon specialized knowledge but also upon his position within the relevant social networks. An opinion leader is not only a knowledgeable person, he must also be an accessible person.

A study by Menzel and Katz (1955) will serve to illustrate some of these generalizations. They interviewed almost all the doctors in a particular community to discover the frequency of interpersonal contact, the actual colleagues who were seen and talked to most frequently, and the ones who were turned to for information and advice. Prescription records were then examined for the period during which a new drug had made its appearance and had been gradually adopted by the majority of the doctors in this community. The innovators (opinion leaders) were found to expose themselves more to the relevant mass media than did the other doctors. They read more medical journals, maintained contact with more professional societies, and attended more meetings and conferences connected with medical matters. They also had more contact with other doctors in the community. Apart from the particular opinion leader who was first to adopt the drug, no doctor adopted it unless he had direct contact with another doctor who had used it already.

Though personal influence has more direct impact on recipients' attitudes than do the mass media, it would be foolish to ignore the long-term effects of the mass media on attitudes which are less obviously concerned with decision making. These effects are often difficult to demonstrate but studies like those of Himmelweit et al. (1958) provide evidence that exposure to television does have measurable effects on the beliefs and evaluations of children concerning a variety of social groups and events.

The Receiver

Various characteristics of the receiver have been implicated in the preceding sections. The degree to which the source is trusted, the extent and nature of primary and secondary group affiliations, the complexity and strength of present beliefs, and the overall evaluation of their referents: all these serve to influence the extent to which any change is likely in an old attitude or the probability that a new attitude will be formed. In what follows attention has been focused on the personality characteristics of the receiver. A considerable amount of research effort has been devoted to the discovery of individual differences in persuasibility which are independent of message content. Is it true that some people are more likely than others to agree with any position on any topic that may be advocated by anybody? The evidence reported by Hovland and Janis (1959) suggests that low but positive correlations exist between the tendency to be susceptible to any kind of attitude-change influence and some more enduring personality predispositions. Persuasibility shows a slight but significant association with the tendency to look for cues to appropriate behaviour in social sources outside of oneself rather than to look for them in previously internalized standards. It also shows a slight correlation with low self-esteem. This line of research has not been productive of much in the way of theoretical insights or of findings that could be applied. What is required is a fine-grain analysis which takes into account the needs and interests which sensitize an individual to pay attention to different classes of source and/or message, the cognitive filters or ego-defence mechanisms that may operate to select and possibly distort certain aspects of the message that is received, and finally the particular set of values that may determine whether the implied or advocated change in attitude will be accepted.

In studies concerned with attitudes towards fluoridation, for example, the message that fluoridation will reduce the amount of tooth decay in the children of a community is often received and understood, but rejected for what appear to be non-rational reasons. Those who are most opposed to fluoridation have values which, if not anti-scientific, nevertheless place an emphasis upon the negative aspects of scientific achievement. In concluding their paper on anti-fluoridation attitudes Kirscht and Knutson (1961) suggested by way of explanation that it is general attitudes that set the interpretation framework for the fluoridation issue. Values precede the content of particular issues and form a primary frame of reference within which more specific frameworks are articulated. In a further study by Richardson (1963) it was found that those who were opposed to fluoridation were more likely to have a strong sense of powerlessness in which they felt unable to influence the course of their own lives. It appeared as if their negative attitude to fluoridation was based upon a need to demonstrate their potency by applying a veto. The opportunity to say 'No!' to fluoridation also served to get back at 'Them' by frustrating 'Their' plans, however slightly.

Cognitive consistency theory

Messages which implicitly or explicitly advocate a change in attitude will be more readily accepted and adopted if they are perceived as consistent with a pre-existing value system. Our cognitive structures are developed in the service of making the world and our place in it more intelligible. If from our point of view the adoption of a new attitude or the modification of an old one serves this very general and not too well-defined purpose, change is more likely to occur. If it does not serve this purpose change is more likely to be resisted. Much new information falls midway between these two extremes and sets up tensions (cognitive dissonance), which in turn stimulates the attempt to find some appropriate way of reducing it. Thus, one's response to new and contradictory information is the resultant of the various internal stresses that are created by it. For example, imagine that you have a friend who shares the same set of values as you hold yourself, and imagine that these values are those associated with the more liberal attitudes described by Tomkins (1965) and mentioned earlier in this chapter in the section on the structure and functions of attitudes. One day you discover that your friend is advocating a strong punitive approach to all those who commit offences against people or property. He advocates the flogging of sexual offenders and the reintroduction of capital punishment for murder. These attitudes of your friend appear to be inconsistent with his previous attitudes and with your own. They may even be experienced as inconsistent with your previously felt liking for him.

When such apparent inconsistencies occur, do we merely tolerate them or do we experience a pressure to reduce them? What modes of reducing these inconsistencies are available to us? One mode of achieving harmony might be to maintain a feeling of affection for your friend and to deny that he really meant what he said. However, if the evidence for some genuine change in attitudes became overwhelming, and if his new views were praised by people whom you did not like particularly, cognitive consistency might be restored by a shift in attitudes towards your friend. The need to achieve consistency varies with the amount of dissonance created but even in relatively artificial situations balanced states are preferred to unbalanced states. In a study by Feather (1965), for example, subjects were presented with a series of communications situations involving a source presenting a message about some issue to a receiver. The results showed that the tendency to prefer balanced structures was an overwhelming one.

Inconsistencies may also become apparent as a result of some discrepancy between attitudes towards some object and actions in relation to it; between beliefs about some object and feelings about the object; between an attitude to some object and the direct experience of it. Examples of each kind of discrepancy will be given in relation to its implications for attitude-change procedures.

If we are encouraged to eat a type of food (e.g., frogs' legs or chocolate-covered ants) towards which we have always held a negative attitude, the sensory experience of liking the taste would be inconsistent with the attitude of disliking. If no other cognitions are involved which might support the negative attitude (e.g., a belief that esoteric foodstuffs are bad for one's health, or that significant others disapproved of esoteric foodstuffs), the change to liking these foods reduces the dissonance between expectation and experience in the simplest way possible. If one is encouraged to attend a gymnasium and have a weekly workout, one's previously held negative attitude to exercise may shift if the new experience is found to be rewarding.

Situations in which there is a split between the way in which we think about an object and the way in which we feel about it are very common. A woman may have a set of highly permissive beliefs about Lesbians and their rights, and yet feel personally revolted at what is implied by these beliefs. One way of resolving this kind of dissonance may be compartmentalization, in which the cognitive and affective reactions are held apart and awareness of inconsistency is eliminated. If this resolution is too difficult to maintain, then a more damaging defence mechanism may be brought into play. Negative feelings may be repressed and the positive beliefs asserted, perhaps a little too stridently.

The investigation of the conditions under which dissonance occurs and the conditions under which different modes of resolution are employed is an extremely active area of current research on attitudes (e.g., Insko, 1967; Abelson and associates, 1968).

Concluding comments

In the preceding discussion of social psychology and its implications for medicine, the emphasis has been upon one major problem area only, that of attitudes. Yet it is difficult to avoid discussion of overt behaviour, and the way in which attitudes are related to it. Attitudes predispose to overt forms of behaviour, but because the latter are always a function of a person in a situation and never of a person in a vacuum it is necessary to know something about the way in which the present situation is regarded by the person.

The main purpose of the chapter has been to sensitize the reader to the nature of attitudes, their origins, structure and function, and especially to the conditions associated with their modification. In attempting to fulfil this purpose it is inevitable that some thoughts will have arisen concerning the place of values in a world of fact. Because of the importance of values, especially in areas of the social sciences where applications are being considered, a brief discussion is obligatory.

Assuming that all the findings reported here are eventually substantiated, which is unlikely, and that all the interpretations and explanations are correct, which is equally improbable, are the implications for medicine or any other potential field of application unequivocal? Does the construction of a sound theory to account for the hard facts of a discipline sufficiently define the functions of a scientist? Is it only in the application of knowledge that value judgments must be made and justified? Each of these questions and others like them have been debated a great deal over the years; but as knowledge in all sciences has grown the possibilities of employing it either for life-enhancing or life-destroying purposes has given rise to more intense concern. Many physical and biological scientists, as well as those in the social sciences, have come to feel that the roles of scientist and of citizen can no longer be kept as separate as in the past.

Because an area like that of attitudes is of such general interest, the practical application of any simple generalizations immediately involves the question of values. Underlying many of the examples of attitude modification that have been described is the assumption that it is justifiable to influence others towards a particular way of viewing themselves or their world. Despite alarmist reports of 'brain washing' and popular accounts of the power of 'the persuaders', the conditions that give rise to attitude formation and change are still insufficiently understood. No one yet has the power to make anybody believe anything.

Though we intentionally or unintentionally influence the attitudes of others every time we interact with them, the deliberate attempt to influence large numbers of our fellows to a particular viewpoint requires careful justification and consideration before it is undertaken. A distinction that is not absolute but which serves as a guide to evaluating any communication is the distinction between the polar terms 'education' and 'propaganda'. Educational communications are those which implicitly encourage the receiver to evaluate the evidence from which his conclusions are drawn, or where this is not possible, implicitly to encourage evaluation of the source. Propaganda communications, on the other hand, are intended to bring about a change in the advocated direction by any means available. The difference in the values of those communicators who fall at the two extremes is obvious enough, but the difficulties begin when one considers communicators that fall somewhere in between.

The aim of a doctor or of a public health department is the encouragement of attitudes and actions that will promote the physical and mental welfare of those they serve; but does this justify the use of any means to achieve these ends? We are all aware of the damaging effects of the so-called 'hard' drugs like heroin; but does this justify the attempt to form negative attitudes towards the consumption of hard drugs by implying that soft drugs like cannabis are an equally serious danger to health?

This last sentence like many other sentences in this book implies that the writer holds certain values. The implications need not, of course, be true. Nevertheless, values are always with us in all the decisions we make or fail to make; and, to compound this observation, it might be added that it is right that they should be. The important thing is to be sensitive to the values that are always implied in the ends desired and in the means proposed to reach them. This is equally true whether one is at the sending or receiving end of a persuasive communication. The place of values in the social sciences is an important one (Kelman, 1965), and with the increase in knowledge it will become even more so.

References

Abelson, R. P., Aronson, E., McGuire, W. J., Newcomb, T. M., Rosenberg, M. J. and Tannenbaum, P. H. (eds) (1968). *Theories of Cognitive Consistency: a Sourcebook*. Chicago: Rand-McNally.

Ajzen, I. and Fishbein, M. (1969). 'The Prediction of Behavioural Intentions in a Choice Situation', *J. Exp. Soc. Psychol.* 5, pp. 400–16.

Allport, G. W. (1968). 'The Historical Background of Modern Social Psychology', in *The Handbook of Social Psychology*, 2nd ed. 1 (eds G. Lindzey and E. Aronson). Reading, Mass.: Addison-Wesley.

Asch, S. E. (1956). 'Studies of Independence and Conformity. A Minority of One against a Unanimous Majority', *Psychol. Monogr.* 70, no. 9 (whole no. 416).

Bettelheim, B. and Janowitz, M. (1950). *Dynamics of Prejudice: a Psychological and Sociological Study of Veterans*. New York: Harper & Row.

Brim, O. G. (1954). 'The Acceptance of New Behaviour in Child Rearing', *Hum. Relat.* 7, pp. 473–91.

Brown, R. W. (1965). *Social Psychology*. New York: Free Press.

Egbert, L., Battit, G., Welch, C. and Bartlett, M. (1964). 'Reduction of Post-operative Pain by Encouragement and Instruction of Patients', *New Eng. J. Med.* 270, pp. 825–7.

Eysenck, H. J. (1954). *Psychology of Politics*. London: Routledge & Kegan Paul.

Feather, N. T. (1965). 'A Structural Balance Model of Evaluative Behaviour', *Hum. Relat.* 18, pp. 171–85.

Ferguson, L. W. (1939). 'Primary Social Attitudes', *J. Psychol.* 8, pp. 217–23.

Himmelweit, H. T., Oppenheim, A. N. and Vince, P. (1958). *Television and the Child*. Oxford University Press.

Hovland, C. I. and Janis, I. L. (eds) (1959). *Personality and Persuasibility*. New Haven: Yale University Press.

Insko, C. A. (1967). *Theories of Attitude Changes*. New York: Appleton-Century-Crofts.

Janis, I. L. and Feshbach, S. (1953). 'Effects of Fear-arousing Communications', *J. Abnorm. Soc. Psychol.* 48, pp. 78–92.

Janis, I. L. and Mann, L. (1965). 'Effectiveness of Emotional Role-playing in Modifying Smoking Habits and Attitudes', *J. Exp. Res. Personality*. 1, pp. 84–90.

Katz, D. (1960). 'The Functional Approach to the Study of Attitudes', *Publ. Opin. Q.* 24, pp. 163–204.

Katz, E. and Lazarsfeld, P. F. (1955). *Personal Influence*. Chicago: Free Press.

Kelman, H. C. (1965). 'Manipulation of Human Behaviour: an Ethical Dilemma for the Social Scientist', *J. Soc. Issues*. 21, pp. 31–46.

Kirscht, J. P. and Knutson, A. L. (1961). 'Science and Fluoridation: an Attitude Study', *J. Soc. Issues*. 17, pp. 37–44.

Leventhal, H. and Watts, J. C. (1966). 'Sources of Resistance to Fear-arousing Communication on Smoking and Lung Cancer', *J. Personality*, 34, pp. 155–75.
Mann, L. and Janis, I. L. (1968). 'A Follow-up Study on the Long-term Effects of Emotional Role Playing', *J. Personality Soc. Psychol.* 8, pp. 339–42.
Menzel, H. and Katz, E. (1955). 'Social Relations and Innovation in the Medical Profession: the Epidemiology of a New Drug', *Publ. Opin. Q.* 18, pp. 337–52.
Richardson, A. (1963). 'Attitudes to Fluoridation in Perth, Western Australia', *Aust. Dent. J.* 8, pp. 513–17.
Richardson, A. (1967). 'A Theory and a Method for the Psychological Study of Assimilation', *Int. Migration Rev.* 2, pp. 3–30.
Secord, P. F. and Backman, C. W. (1974). *Social Psychology*, 2nd ed. New York: McGraw-Hill.
Shaw, M. E. and Constanzo, P. R. (1970). *Theories of Social Psychology*. New York: McGraw-Hill.
Tomkins, S. S. (1965). 'Affect and the Psychology of Knowledge', in *Affect, Cognition and Personality: Empirical Studies* (eds S. S. Tomkins and C. E. Izard). New York: Springer.
Whittaker, J. O. (1967). 'Resolution of the Communication Discrepancy Issue in Attitude Change', in *Attitude, Ego Involvement and Change* (eds C. W. Sherif and M. Sherif). New York: Wiley.

Suggestions for further reading

Aronson, E. *The Social Animal*. San Francisco: Freeman 1972.
Jahoda, M. and Warren, N. *Attitudes*. Harmondsworth: Penguin 1966.
Sampson, E. E. *Social Psychology and Contemporary Society*. New York: Wiley 1971.
Wrightman, L. S. *Social Psychology in the Seventies*. Monterey, California: Brooks/Cole 1972.

Chapter twelve

Communicating with the Patient

P. Ley

Many doctors, medical students and others working in health care find it hard to take problems of communication seriously. To some the problem does not seem important, because they feel that they are good communicators themselves and that anyone else of reasonable intelligence can be as well. They believe that if the will to communicate is there all will be well. Others see the human relations side of medicine as being generally of little importance. Accurate diagnosis, correct choice of treatment, and surgical skill seem to them to be the things with which doctors should be concerned. In comparison with these 'hard' aspects of medicine, 'soft' psychological areas such as communication are seen as, at best, optional extras.

Both of these views contain errors. Good communication is rarer than some might think. Without it even the 'hard' aspects of medicine become less efficient. This chapter will try to correct these errors. Specifically, it will be shown that: (1) patients feel dissatisfied with communications; (2) patients frequently fail to follow advice, including advice about medicine taking; (3) satisfied patients are more likely to follow advice; and (4) pre-operative communication with surgical patients can hasten recovery, probably reduce post-operative pain, and lead to earlier discharge from hospital.

So by paying attention to communication variables it is possible to increase patients' satisfaction, increase the possibility that they will follow advice, reduce distress, and reduce length of hospital stay. All of these are laudable aims.

Problems arise in implementing the decision to improve communications. Even when the will to communicate is there, failures still arise from intellectual, situational and psychological factors. Especially important in this last category are failures of comprehension and memory. It is therefore necessary to learn ways of increasing memory and comprehension; and it will be shown that when this is done desirable consequences follow.

Having made these claims it is necessary to look at the evidence on which they are based.

Patients' satisfaction with communications

A number of surveys have been conducted to ascertain the extent to which patients feel that they have been given sufficient information about their condition. One study, for example, found that 65 per cent of patients were dissatisfied with the communications aspect of their hospital stay. However, a more typical figure for such surveys is that about a third of patients are not satisfied (Ley, 1972a). It is worth noting that even in surveys where dissatisfaction with communications is high, patients tend to report high levels of satisfaction with other aspects of hospital stay. The results do not arise from generally disgruntled patients.

The usual explanations advanced to explain the poor communications evidenced above are listed by Ley and Spelman (1967) as: shortage of time; the belief that patients do not want to know; patients' diffidence; uncertainty as to what the patient has been told; reactionary attitudes on the part of hospital staff. All of these explanations assume that the problem can be simply resolved by giving patients information. In the light of the evidence from surveys of patients' satisfaction with communications this plausible assumption appears to be quite false.

Some of these surveys involved patients whose doctors felt that they had made special efforts to inform their patients. When these are compared with surveys of patients whose doctors made no such efforts, it is found that there are no differences between them. A good example of the difficulty of increasing patient satisfaction comes from a comparison of maternity units. In one of these, special steps to improve communication were taken, while another served as a control. Levels of satisfaction with communication were found to be the same in both hospitals (Houghton, 1968). Thus, doctors and other staff having the will to communicate and making special efforts to do so, are no more likely to produce satisfied patients.

Theories to explain this finding include: (1) the personality hypothesis; (2) the psychodynamic hypothesis; (3) the interaction hypothesis; and (4) the cognitive hypothesis.

The personality hypothesis suggests that whatever efforts are made on the patient's behalf there are some patients who, because of peculiarities of personality, will be ungrateful and dissatisfied. This leads directly to the prediction that dissatisfied patients will differ, to their disadvantage, on personality and other characteristics. The evidence fails to support this prediction. No personality differences have been found; and, if anything, dissatisfied patients seem to be younger, more intelligent and of higher social class.

The psychodynamic hypothesis suggests that often the problem that the patient presents to the doctor is a cover for a different conscious or unconscious problem. If the doctor deals only with the patient's presenting problem, and does not spot and cope with the unstated problem, the patient will go away dissatisfied. This view has been ably argued by Balint (1964) in a different context, but there appears to be little hard experimental evidence available to support or reject it.

The interaction hypothesis argues that the whole pattern of interaction in the consultation process determines patients' satisfaction. Thus an attempt to improve communications might be ineffective because the rest of the interaction process is incompatible with satisfaction. The evidence in favour of this hypothesis will be reviewed in some detail below.

The cognitive hypothesis suggests that many of the failures of communication result from the patient's not understanding and not remembering what he is told. This, too, will be considered in more detail later.

Before considering these last two theories further, it is worth digressing slightly to look at the evidence about what patients say they want to know. Also, as both theories apply to patients' failure to comply it is necessary to consider the data on the frequency with which patients follow advice given to them.

The information that patients say they would like

One of the largest surveys on this topic reported that 75 per cent of patients wanted to know as much as possible about their illness (Cartwright, 1964). Other investigations support this finding. Patients want to know the nature and cause of their illness, its seriousness, the reasons for and results of tests carried out, the nature of the treatment, and how they are progressing. This seems to be true even when the illness is cancer, or when the patient is dying (Ley and Spelman, 1967).

Doctors and patients seem to have different views on this last topic. Survey results show that while 77–89 per cent of patients and laymen say that they would wish to be told if they were dying, 69–90 per cent of doctors think that patients should not be told. In terminal illnesses at least, there is some doubt as to the effectiveness of trying to conceal the truth. It has been estimated that 75–80 per cent of patients know anyway (Hinton, 1967). If this is so then all that evasion can do is deprive the patient of the chance of adjusting to and gaining help to face death (Bromley, 1974).

Similarly, in the case of cancer it appears that patients think that it is a good idea for doctors to tell. The vast majority of patients (whether they have cancer and know it, or have cancer and do not know it, or whether they have curable or incurable cancers) think that patients should be told. Amongst the advantages of being told listed by patients with advanced incurable cancers are that it helps them to understand their illness, decreases worry about health, makes for peace of mind, and allows them to make plans for providing for dependants (Ley and Spelman, 1967).

Now that cancer and dying are ceasing to be taboo topics it is likely that there will be adequately controlled investigations of the effects of telling patients, on such variables as distress in dying and adjustment to remaining life. In the absence of these, the best bet is that the patient does want to know, and should be told unless there are strong reasons to the contrary. (For a more traditional but nevertheless enlightened approach to this problem, see Fletcher, 1973.)

The frequency with which patients follow advice

Whatever type of advice is given to patients, be it about medicine taking, dieting, giving up smoking or anything else, it is pretty certain that large numbers of patients will not follow it (Ley, 1974). Evidence from several investigations on this topic is summarized in Table 12.1.

Even in-patients fail to take their medicine where this is under their

Table 12.1 The frequency with which patients fail to follow medical advice

Type of advice	No. of studies	Percentage of patients who did not follow the advice		
		Range	Mean	Median
A. Medicine taking				
(1) PAS and other TB drugs	20	8–76	37·5	35
(2) Antibiotics	8	11–92	48·7	50
(3) Psychiatric drugs	9	11–51	38·6	44
(4) Other medicines, e.g. antacids, iron	12	9–87	47·7	57·5
B. Diet	11	20–84	49·4	45
C. Other advice, e.g. child care, ante-natal exercises	8	30–79	54·6	51
D. All advice	68	8–92	44·0	44·35

control. In one study, in-patients suffering from a variety of gastro-intestinal complaints had antacids prescribed for them. They were told when and how to take it, but it was found that the patients took less than half of the prescribed antacid.

Attempts have been made to identify patients who are likely to fail to follow advice. By and large these have not been very fruitful. Findings of one study fail to be replicated in others. Nor are doctors and other health professionals very good at picking out patients who do not comply. Nor is it known whether patients who fail to comply in one situation fail to comply in others (Davis, 1966). However, patients are less likely to comply adequately with complex medication régimes, and the presence of unpleasant side-effects reduces compliance (Blackwell, 1972).

Interaction in the consultation: patient satisfaction and compliance

The major source of information on this topic is the work of Korsch and her collaborators (Korsch et al., 1971). This research involved a series of 800 consultations at a walk-in clinic for children. Overall 40 per cent of patients (mothers) were rated as highly satisfied with their visit; 36 per cent as moderately satisfied; 11 per cent as moderately dissatisfied; and 13 per cent as very dissatisfied. Satisfaction was associated with the doctor's being seen as friendly rather than business-like; seeming to understand the mother's concern; being a good communicator; and not thwarting the patient's expectations. Patients who expected to be told the diagnosis and cause of the child's illness, or an explanation of the problem, and who were not given this information, were less likely to be satisfied. Similar findings emerged with regard to other unfulfilled expectations about being given injections, tests, medicine; being cured; and being taken into hospital. This seems relatively unsurprising; but, unfortunately for the doctors, 65 per cent of patients' expectations were not communicated to the doctor, and 24 per cent of worries and concerns were not mentioned. Variables which were not associated with satisfaction were the patients' social class; educational level; diagnosis; waiting time; length of consultation.

The extent to which patients followed advice was also assessed: 42 per cent of patients were rated as highly compliant; 38 per cent as moderately compliant; and 11 per cent as low on compliance. The remaining mothers did not receive advice. The relationship between satisfaction and compliance was striking, and is shown in Table 12.2.

Other correlates of non-compliance included the doctor's seeming business-like; unfulfilled expectations about being told the diagnosis and cause of the illness; and having no expectations met.

Table 12.2 The relationship between satisfaction and compliance amongst Korsch's patients

Rating of satisfaction	% of patients showing high compliance
High satisfaction	53·4
Moderate satisfaction	42·6
Moderate dissatisfaction	32·4
High dissatisfaction	16·7

In addition Korsch and her co-workers looked at the content and process of the interaction between mother and doctor. Satisfaction was associated with the doctor's speaking as much or more than the mother, and this was also associated with compliance. Where the mother spoke more than the doctor, both satisfaction and compliance were lower. Not surprisingly, hostility, little expression of positive effect, and high expression of negative effect by the doctor were associated with low satisfaction and compliance. The larger the proportion of the interview devoted to statements not connected with the problem (non-medical statements); and the higher the proportion of time spent in doctor-child conversation, the better were satisfaction and compliance found to be.

However, when the mothers expressed agreement with, and acknowledgment of, the doctor's statements, it was found that while this increased satisfaction it had no effect on compliance. A complex pattern was also found for the mother's asking more rather than fewer questions. This produced less satisfied mothers, but not less compliant ones. On the other hand, when the doctor asked more rather than fewer questions compliance was lower and satisfaction hardly affected.

It is possible on the basis of these findings to draw up a set of rules for doctors to produce satisfied and compliant patients in the pediatric situation:

(1) Be friendly rather than business-like.
(2) Engage in at least some conversation which is not directly connected with the problem.
(3) Spend time talking to the child.
(4) Make sure that you do at least half of the talking.
(5) Discover the mother's expectations, and explain why these are not fulfilled, if they are not.
(6) Discover the mother's concerns and take appropriate action.
(7) Give information as well as ask questions.

There are some difficulties of interpretation in this research, in that the data on which this advice is based are correlational data. For example, perhaps the doctors were business-like when they met a difficult problem that they could not solve, and perhaps it was the fact that the problem was not solved that made the mothers dissatisfied. Before finally accepting that following the rules will make a difference to patient compliance and satisfaction it would be necessary to conduct experiments which compared levels of these amongst patients whose doctors were or were not following the rules. In the absence of such experiments the rules can be treated as plausible guidelines.

The cognitive hypothesis: patients' understanding of what they are told

The cognitive hypothesis states that dissatisfaction and non-compliance stem in part from failures of comprehension and memory. For communication to be effective the message must be understood and remembered. Comprehension and memory are necessary, albeit not sufficient, causes of satisfaction and compliance (Ley and Spelman, 1967). Failures in understanding will have to be examined first.

At least three factors are involved in patients' failures to understand. These are: (1) the material presented to patients is often too difficult; (2) patients often lack knowledge; and (3) patients are very diffident.

The first of these factors has been investigated by examination of written material prepared for patients. Several techniques are available for assessing the difficulty level of written or spoken material. Ley (1974) reports the application of one of these, the Flesch Formula, to some X-ray leaflets issued to patients by a hospital serving a predominantly lower-working-class area. The Flesch Formula enables one to estimate the percentage of the population who would understand a given piece of writing. The results of applying this formula to the X-ray leaflets are shown in Table 12.3.

Table 12.3 Comprehensibility of some X-ray leaflets as measured by the Flesch Formula

Leaflet	% of population who would be expected to understand it
Barium meal	75
Barium swallow	75
Bronchogram	40
Cholecystogram	40
Intravenous pyelogram	75

These investigators also report the application of the formula to a model barium meal X-ray leaflet proposed in the *British Medical Journal*, and showed that only 24 per cent of the population would be expected to understand it. Similar findings have been reported in studies of leaflets issued by a dental hospital (Ley, 1974). The doctors and dentists who made these leaflets were experienced clinicians; and the moral is that it is very easy, even for experienced clinicians, to produce material which is much too difficult for patients.

An impressive study of patients' lack of knowledge is that of Boyle (1970). Boyle used a multiple-choice technique to assess patients' knowledge of the location of some of their major organs. This technique revealed that many patients thought their organs to be in places other than the correct one. The percentage of patients wrongly locating the various organs were as follows:

Organ	Percentage
Heart	58 per cent
Bladder	40 per cent
Kidneys	54 per cent
Stomach	80 per cent
Lungs	49 per cent
Intestines	23 per cent
Liver	51 per cent
Thyroid gland	30 per cent

Unfortunately for the clinician, the patients' areas of ignorance lie behind areas of accurate knowledge. It was found that amongst a sample of the general population asked questions about lung cancer, 91 per cent knew of the connection with cigarette smoking, 56 per cent knew the symptoms, 73 per cent knew the treatment, but that nearly a third of the sample thought that lung cancer was not very serious and easily curable (Ley and Spelman, 1967).

Serious misconceptions on the part of patients have also been discovered by other investigators. In an investigation of patients' beliefs about peptic ulcer it was found that, while many patients believed that acid was involved in ulcer formation and maintenance, only 10 per cent of the group had a reasonably clear idea that acid was secreted by the stomach. Some patients even thought that acid came from the teeth when they chewed, or their brain when they swallowed. Other examples of patients' lack of knowledge can be found in Ley and Spelman (1967).

The importance of these misunderstandings for the communication process is that they are likely to cause confusion which might well militate against satisfaction and following advice. Consider the case of a patient who thinks that (*a*) acid causes ulcers and (*b*) acid is produced by the brain when he swallows. If he is told to eat small, frequent meals, this is in his eyes tantamount to telling him to put into his stomach frequent doses of what is causing his ulcer. He could, of course, ask questions to dispel his confusion, but it has been widely found that patients are very diffident about asking for information from doctors (Cartwright, 1964; Ley and Spelman, 1967; Fletcher, 1973). Because patients are diffident, the clinician receives no feedback when he produces material which is too difficult; so his performance cannot improve, nor does he have the opportunity to learn what misconceptions his patients have. Indeed, a case could be made out for maintaining that the reduction of patients' diffidence would go a long way to solving the communication problem.

Patients' failure to remember what they are told

A number of studies of patients' failures to remember have been conducted. These are summarized in Table 12.4.

Table 12.4 Summary of studies of patients' forgetting of medical information

	Type of patient	Time between consultation and recall	% forgotten
1.	47 out-patients	10–80 minutes	37·2
2.	22 out-patients	10–80 minutes	38·7
3.	22 out-patients	10–80 minutes	40·6
4.	30 out-patients	Immediately after consultation	52·0
5.	24 out-patients	1–4 weeks	54·0
6.	20 general practice patients	Less than 5 minutes	50·0

The number of statements forgotten goes up with the number presented; and Ley (1974) provides the following linear regression equation for predicting patients' forgetting:

$$Y = 0.56X - 0.94$$

Where Y = number of statements likely to be forgotten
X = number of statements made to the patient

Application of this formula to forgetting, found in studies reported by Ley and his co-workers, shows it to predict correctly the number of statements forgotten, plus or minus one, with 77 per cent accuracy. In practice this means that the clinician should expect the patient to forget no statements if only two are presented; one if four are presented; two if six are presented; and if eight or more are presented the patient should forget half of what he is told.

Another finding of the investigations of Ley and Spelman was that advice was more likely to be forgotten than other sorts of statement. Attempts to explain this involved a series of analogue studies in which normal, healthy volunteer subjects were given fictitious medical information to recall. The use of healthy volunteers and fictitious information has great advantages from the point of view of experimental control. It also saves bothering patients with what might turn out to be pointless tasks. The chief danger is that memory for fictitious medical information in volunteers might be quite different from memory for the information amongst patients. This danger has not in fact proved to be a real one. All of the findings of the analogue experiments have been replicable on the real-life situation. Nor are there great differences in the amount of forgetting between patients and volunteers.

The initial analogue studies were designed to test two main hypotheses: (1) that there is a primacy effect in memory for medical information (i.e., that people recall best what they hear first); and (2) that people recall best what they consider most important.

The first of these arose from the observation that the consultant involved in the first investigation of patients' forgetting presented his advice to the patient after he had told the patient the diagnosis and given other information. If there is a primacy effect in recall of medical information, the differential forgetting of instructions would be partly explained.

The second hypothesis was a common-sense one. If patients are presented with more material than they can remember, they will start selecting parts of it to remember and discard other parts. The most likely criterion for this selection is the patient's subjective view of the importance of the different statements made to him. He will tend to forget those he thinks unimportant. To explain the differential forgetting of instructions it was therefore necessary to demonstrate: (*a*) that laymen consider statements giving advice to be less important than other sorts of medical statement; and (*b*) that there is a correlation between a statement's rated importance and the probability of its recall. The analogue experiments revealed a strong primacy effect, and the hypothesized relationship between importance and recall (Ley, 1972b).

The control of patients' forgetting

The attempts to control patients' forgetting arose out of the analogue studies mentioned above. If patients recall best what they are told first, and if they remember best what they consider most important, it should be possible to increase recall of instructions and advice either by presenting them first or by stressing their importance. Accordingly three groups of out-patients were compared. The first received the usual procedure; the second had any advice given before other information; and the third had advice in its usual place, but with the importance of that advice stressed. The mean percentages of instructions recalled in the three conditions are shown in Table 12.5.

Table 12.5 Recall of advice as a function of method of presentation

Method of presentation	% recalled
Normal	44
Advice first	75
Importance of advice stressed	64

However, increased recall of advice was accompanied by decreased recall of other material. It was therefore necessary to find ways of increasing the total amount recalled by patients. Four methods have been tried to date. Three of them stem directly or indirectly from the literature on the experimental psychology of memory, and one was discovered serendipitously.

It is well established that meaningful material is more easily remembered than less meaningful material. It is also possible to use the Flesch Formula to find easier versions of a piece of writing. The formula as given by Flesch (1948) is:

$$\text{Reading ease} = 206 \cdot 84 - 0 \cdot 85 W - 1 \cdot 02 S$$
Where W = average number of syllables per 100 words
S = average length of sentence in words

The higher the Reading Ease the more easily understood and therefore, presumably, the more meaningful a piece of writing is. Material with a score of 90 or more would be expected to be understood by 90 per cent of the population; 70–80 by 80 per cent; 60–70 by 75 per cent; 50–60 by 40 per cent; 30–50 by 24 per cent; and 30 or less by only 5 per cent.

Inspection of the formula shows that to make material easier it is necessary to use shorter words and shorter sentences. A number of experiments have been carried out to assess the effects on total amount remembered of increasing the comprehensibility of material (Bradshaw et al., 1975). The findings of these experiments, which are summarized in Table 12.6, show that in most cases recall can be increased by simplifying material.

Table 12.6 Summary of studies of recall of medical information varying in comprehensibility as measured by the Flesch Formula

Material	Difficulty	% recalled
(a) X-ray leaflet	Easy	73
	Hard	78
(b) X-ray leaflet	Easy	79
	Hard	59
(c) Diet instructions	Easy	31
	Hard	24
(d) Diet instructions	Easy	43
	Hard	25
(e) Diet instructions	Easy	40
	Hard	27

The second method investigated was the use of a technique called 'explicit categorization'. This was based on the finding that clustering of items is associated with greater recall. It was hypothesized that if medical information could be clustered for patients they should recall more of it. The method consists of the clinician providing clusters or categories of information and category names to go with them. Thus he says to the patient:

> 'I am going to tell you
> what is wrong,
> what the treatment will be,
> what tests will be necessary,
> what you must do to help yourself,
> what the outcome will be.
> Now, first, what is wrong with you:
> ....
> Second, what the treatment will be:
> ....etc.'

An analogue study showed that this technique increased recall in volunteers from six to nine out of fifteen fictitious medical statements; and the experiment was then repeated in a general practice situation. Once more it led to significant increases in recall. The results for these patients are shown in Table 12.7 (Ley et al., 1973).

The third technique is repetition. It is clear that the clinician could say everything twice to the patient in the time taken by explicit categorization. Unpublished analogue experiments have shown that repetition leads to increases in recall of the same magnitude as explicit categorization. Which of the two should be used is up to the clinician although arguably the explicit categorization technique flows more smoothly.

Table 12.7 Mean percentage of information recalled by patients in normal and explicit categorization conditions

	Diagnosis	Mean % recalled Advice	Other information
Normal presentation	60·5	28·3	46·1
Explicit categorization	66·7	65·4	70·3

The last technique was discovered by accident. It was noticed during studies of laymen's views of the importance of different types of medical statement that where a specific and a general version of a similar instruction were rated, the specific version was considered the more important. Thus the statement 'you must lose weight' was considered less important than the statement 'You must lose half a stone in weight', and so on. It had already been demonstrated that perceived importance is a determinant of memory; so it seemed reasonable to explore the possibility that specific advice would be better recalled than general advice. Bradshaw et al. (1975) conducted appropriate experiments and found that this was so. Their results are shown in Table 12.8.

Table 12.8 Differences in recall of specifically and generally phrased instructions about dieting

Subjects	Mean % recalled General	Specific
(a) Volunteer subjects given *both* specific and general statements to recall	10·25	45·00
(b) Volunteer subjects given *either* specific *or* general statements	19·00	49·00
(c) Obese women given *either* specific *or* general statements	16·00	51·00

Increasing patients' satisfaction with communications

At this stage it has been demonstrated that failures of comprehension and memory are likely to be, in part, responsible for patients' dissatisfaction with communications and non-compliance.

It is now necessary to review applications of the findings to the improvement of communications. As a first step an attempt was made to increase patients' satisfaction with communications in the hospital situation. Three groups of medical in-patients were studied. The control group received the hospital's normal procedure. In the experimental group patients received an extra visit from the doctor once every ten days or so, in which he tried to ensure that they had understood what they had already been told. No new topics were introduced, and the interview was restricted to simply increasing understanding of information already given. Visits lasted less than five minutes. As the extra medical attention might, in itself, have affected satisfaction, a placebo group was also studied. Patients in this group also received extra visits from the doctor every ten days or so, but the interviews were concerned with how the patient was settling in, privacy, noise, food and other such topics. The results of the experiment showed that increases in understanding led to significantly greater satisfaction with communications. Eighty per cent of the experimental group were satisfied with the communications aspect of their hospital stay as opposed to 41 per cent of the placebo group, and 48 per cent of the controls. Thus, by seeing that patients understood what they were told it was possible virtually to double the percentage of satisfied patients. It has already been pointed out that satisfaction with communications is likely to be justified on practical as well as humanitarian grounds. It will be recalled that satisfied patients were reported to be more compliant by Korsch and her co-workers.

Increasing patients' compliance with advice

Effects of Increasing Comprehension and/or Memory

Two experiments have been carried out by Ley and his colleagues, to see the effects of increasing comprehension and memory on compliance. The first attempted to increase the accuracy with which psychiatric out-patients took their medication. Interviews with patients suggested that patients often did not realize that their medicine might take some time to produce effects, and that they did not know what to do if they forgot to take a tablet. Accordingly a brief leaflet was prepared which gave information on these topics for patients receiving anti-depressants, and for patients receiving tranquillizers. Three versions of each leaflet were prepared, which differed in Reading Ease as measured by the Flesch Formula. One was hard, one moderately hard, and one easy. Eighty consecutive new out-patients, who received either anti-depressant drugs alone or tranquillizers alone, were assigned randomly to receiving one of the three versions of the leaflet, or no leaflet. Patients received a prescription for their medicine and were asked to bring any remaining tablets with them on their return visit, approximately three weeks after their initial visit. The tablets were then counted and an error score worked out. This was the difference between the number of tablets which should have been taken and the number which were taken, as a percentage of the number which should have been taken. Mean error scores for the various groups of patients are shown in Table 12.9.

Table 12.9 The effects of providing information leaflets varying in difficulty to depressed and anxious patients

Type of leaflet	Mean difference between tablets taken and tablets presented as a % of tablets prescribed	
	Depressed patients	Anxious patients
Easy	2·7	5·8
Moderately difficult	8·1	7·8
Difficult	14·5	14·9
No leaflet	16·2	14·6

Provision of comprehensible leaflets can lead to a large reduction in the frequency of patients' medication errors. But, as can be seen, some leaflets are useless. Before writing this off as a mere common-sense finding, remember the evidence reviewed earlier that experienced clinicians tend to produce material which is too difficult for their patients. This study really emphasizes the need to rely on more than common sense when producing leaflets or other material for patients.

The second investigation used obese women as subjects. The obese were chosen as subjects for compliance studies because it was necessary to have a condition of some clinical interest where: (1) there were adequate numbers of subjects; and (2) there was an objective criterion of compliance (i.e., weight loss). In this experiment two versions were prepared of a leaflet designed to motivate and persuade women to start and keep to a low carbohydrate diet. Both versions contained the same content. The control version was moderately easy according to the Flesch Formula. The other version was very easy, and contained explicit categorization and repetition. It should, therefore, have been easier to understand and remember.

Obese subjects who had answered newspaper and television appeals for volunteers were assigned at random to receiving one or other version of the leaflet. In addition, all subjects received an identical low-carbohydrate diet guide. This written material was the only persuasive and technical information given to subjects, except that specific queries about the diet schedule were answered at follow-up visits. Subjects were followed up for sixteen weeks, with the results shown in Table 12.10.

Table 12.10 Weight loss in groups receiving ordinary or experimental (super-memory) leaflet

	Mean weight loss in pounds at			
	2 weeks	4 weeks	8 weeks	16 weeks
Ordinary leaflet	2·7	4·7	7·7	8·2
Experimental leaflet	4·4	8·6	12·3	15·4

The experimental leaflet produced almost twice as much weight loss as the ordinary leaflet. Thus, attempts to increase patients' comprehension of and/or memory for advice can result in substantial gains in compliance in the areas of medicine taking and dieting. By paying attention to these factors patient care can be significantly improved.

Effects of Social Psychological Variables

It was stated earlier that if patients understood and remembered all of the advice given to them it would be unlikely that there would then be complete compliance. Comprehension and memory are necessary, but not sufficient causes of compliance. Other factors need to be investigated in attempts to increase compliance. This might well prove to be difficult, as will be seen. Social psychologists have discovered a number of variables and procedures which appear to facilitate attitude change. Ley and Spelman (1967) suggested that many of these might be applied to the problem of patient compliance with medical advice. The methods they advocated were: (1) use of group decision procedures; (2) use of two-sided communications; and (3) correct use of fear-arousal appeals.

Group decision procedures were invented and studied by Kurt Lewin and his associates in the 1940s and 1950s (Lewin, 1954). In the group decision procedure there is a discussion of the problems involved in following the advice; the discussion is in terms of people like themselves; the members of the group have to make a decision; the members of the group then have to commit themselves to their decision publicly. It is clear that this is a complicated package; but, while there is dispute about which of the variables involved is important, the package seems to produce more reported compliance than the use of straight lecture procedures. This is true even in the two-person situation where the expert 'lectures' to one client or patient.

Thus a study of the effectiveness of advice given to new mothers about including vitamin A, E and C supplement in diets showed that group decision procedures, where the dietician saw a group of six patients for about half an hour, led to greater compliance than a half-hour individual face-to-face interview. The productivity of the dietician could be increased sixfold and better results obtained (Lewin, 1954). It is thus potentially useful in any condition where there are sufficient numbers of patients available to form groups.

When advice is given to patients they are likely to be exposed to counter-propaganda, comments on the advice and conflicting advice, which militate against the original advice being accepted. The effectiveness of such counter-propaganda can be reduced by the use of two-sided communications which not only present the case for following the advice, but also deal with the case against it. Although two-sided communications are less effective initially, the resistance to counter-propaganda that they induce should make them better bets at producing compliance in the long term. Where counter-propaganda is met one would therefore predict an interaction between the sidedness of a communication and the passage of time in producing compliance.

There is considerable dispute about the effectiveness of fear arousal in producing compliant behaviour and attitude change. Some expect curvilinear relationships between degree of fear arousal and compliance, while others expect linear ones. However, there is agreement that different levels of fear arousal can be expected to produce different effects.

To assess the usefulness of these variables in a quasi-medical situation, two sets of experiments have been conducted with obese women by Ley and his co-workers (Ley, 1977). These subjects were chosen because in their case there is an objective measure of compliance. The greater the adherence to their diet, the more weight they will lose. These

Table 12.11 Social psychological variables and compliance

Group	Mean weight loss in pounds at 8 weeks	
	1st series	2nd series
Group decision	9·06	—
Lecture	7·69	—
Low fear arousal	6·75	13·7
Medium fear arousal	8·10	11·0
High fear arousal	7·69	12·0
One-sided communications	6·25	11·9
Two-sided communications	8·63	12·8

experiments have involved comparisons of group decision and lecture procedures, one- and two-sided communications, and three levels of fear arousal. None of these variables has had any greater-than-chance effect on compliance, as assessed by weight loss. The results of these two series of experiments are shown in Table 12.11.

A number of explanations for these negative results can be proposed. Amongst them are the possibilities that the attitude-change variables could not increase our subjects' motivation because it was already at its peak, or that these variables affect attitudes but not behaviour. These possibilities are currently being investigated. It has also been found in our studies that the effects of fear will vary with the position of the fear appeal, and the frequency of the subjects' exposure to it (Skilbeck et al., 1976). Indeed all of these factors will need to be investigated in greater detail and with greater refinement; but as the results stand they suggest that it is not possible at this stage to give clinicians easy, uncomplicated rules for the use of these variables.

Finally, a start has been made on the investigation of situational variables. Ley (1977) reports on experimental attempts to increase compliance with a dietary régime amongst obese women by manipulating group cohesiveness. Two sets of subjects were assigned randomly to membership of nominal or cohesive groups. The cohesive group always attended together, were referred to as a group, were given name badges, and were given a group target. The nominal groups attended together at the first session, but no steps were taken to keep them together as a group. They might or might not meet at follow-up sessions, and none of the special cohesiveness-enhancing measures were taken. Members of the cohesive groups lost significantly more weight than the controls. The results are shown in Table 12.12.

Table 12.12 Mean weight loss in cohesive and control groups

| | Mean weight loss in pounds at | | | |
	2 weeks	4 weeks	8 weeks	16 weeks
Control groups	4·9	6·5	9·0	11·0
Cohesive groups	5·8	8·0	12·6	19·8

Thus, using the simple cognitive model, it has proved possible to account for much of the failure in patient compliance and satisfaction with communication. It has also proved possible to obtain worthwhile improvements in both of these areas. Some suggestions for improving communications can be derived from the work of Ley and his colleagues. These are as follows:

(1) Whenever possible, provide patients with instructions and advice at the start of the information to be presented.
(2) When providing patients with instructions and advice, stress how important they are.
(3) Use short words and short sentences.
(4) Use explicit categorization where possible.
(5) Repeat things where feasible.
(6) When giving advice make it as specific, detailed and concrete as possible.

Patients' forgetting and lack of understanding, complicated by diffidence, resulting in lack of requests for enlightenment, seems to be a major factor in patients' dissatisfaction with communications. It has already been suggested that the reduction of patients' diffidence should produce not only more satisfaction, but also, by providing feedback to the clinician, improve his communicative skills. A series of investigations to find ways of reducing patients' diffidence, and to assess the effects of this on patient satisfaction and clinicians' communicative behaviour, would be well worth pursuing. For the time being Korsch's recommendations about a friendly rather than a business-like approach should be followed. It is a plausible hypothesis that patients will provide friendly doctors with more feedback.

The effects of pre-operative communications on the progress of surgical patients

This is the final area to be examined. But in some ways it is the most impressive one. As will be seen, there is strong evidence that even in the field of surgery attention to the human relations side can make a difference.

Attempts to assess the effectiveness of the use of pre-operative communications to ease distress and promote post-operative recovery were given impetus by the investigations of Janis (summarized by Janis, 1971). Janis reported two main findings. The first was that patients who were not anxious before operation, and those who were highly anxious, had more post-operative problems and distress than those who were moderately anxious pre-operatively. The second was that patients who reported that they had prior information about what to expect showed better pre- and post-operative adjustment than those without prior information. Janis argued that a moderate level of pre-operative fear was necessary to motivate the 'work of worrying' – a mental rehearsal of forthcoming dangers and ways of coping with them. Provision of accurate information aids this process, and ensures that adequate anxiety is aroused to moderate rehearsal.

A great deal of research has centred on these two findings. By and large, the hypothesis that there is a curvilinear relationship between pre-operative anxiety and post-operative complications has not received support; but studies which have attempted to give patients pre-operative information have shown that this can have great effects on post-operative progress and welfare (Ley, 1977).

In these investigations the pre-operative communication has consisted of one or more of the following elements: (1) straight information about what to expect after operation: tubes, drips, days of pain, when the stitches come out, etc.; (2) technical instruction on breathing, coughing, turning over, use of trapeze, what to do when in pain; (3) psychological: letting the patient talk about worries, fears and reactions. Regardless of which of these is used it seems that patients exposed to them get discharged earlier on average than control patients, and usually require fewer analgesics. These studies are summarized in Table 12.13.

Table 12.13 Effects of different types of pre-operative communication on (a) analgesic requirements and (b) days to discharge, in various studies (Adapted from Ley, 1977)

Type of communication	Patients	Require fewer analgesics	Are discharged earlier
1. Instruction	Mixed surgical	Yes	Yes
2. Instruction	Mixed surgical	No	Yes (1·9 days)
3. Information	Mainly hernia	Yes	Yes (2·8 days)
4. Information	Hernia	Yes	Yes (1·6 days)
5. Information	Peptic ulcer	—	Yes
6. Information	Mixed surgical	No	No
7. Psychological	Peptic ulcer	—	Yes
8. Psychological	Hernia	Yes	Yes (2 days)
9. Information + instruction	Abdominal surgery	Yes	Yes (2·7 days)
10. Information, instruction + psychological	Abdominal surgery	—	Yes (1·14 days)
11. Information, instruction + psychological	Mixed surgical	Yes	Yes (2·1 days)

One of the best-known examples of investigations on this topic is that of Egbert *et al.* (1964). Patients who were to have elective abdominal operations were assigned randomly to the experimental or control group.

On the evening before the operation patients in both groups were visited by the anaesthetist, who told them about the operation. The information given included details of the duration of the operation, the type of anaesthetic procedure to be used, and the patients were told that they would wake up in the recovery room. This was all that patients in the control group were told. Experimental group patients received further information. This comprised of a description of the post-operative pain to be expected; assurance that such pain is quite normal; advice on relaxing their abdominal muscles and on how to move; and assurance that they would be given analgesics if the pain was making them too uncomfortable. The surgeons and nurses involved in the patients' surgical care were not informed about the details of the experiment. Post-operative ratings were made by a rater who was also 'blind' as to the experimental conditions. Patients in the experimental group were discharged on average 2·7 days earlier than controls, and required less analgesics after surgery.

As can be seen, Egbert and his colleagues used quite a complicated communication package, complicated, that is, from the point of view of working out which of the elements in it was responsible for the effects they found. Amongst the extra information given to the patients in the experimental group was advice about relaxing muscles and turning over. Technical advice of this sort was found by Lindeman and Van Aernam (1971) to be effective by itself in reducing hospital stay. In their study patients were assigned at random to the normal procedure or to a special instruction programme about breathing, coughing, etc. The control group were discharged on average nearly two days later than the patients who received the special instruction programme.

However, other investigations have shown that patients given extra information, but not extra detailed technical instruction, are also discharged earlier than control patients. Chapman (1969) found that groups of hernia patients given straight information, or a combination of this and discussion about their anxieties, were discharged, on average, 1·7 days earlier than controls. Neither of the experimental groups was given extra technical instruction.

Ley (1977) reviews these and other studies in more detail; and, noting the lack of controls for placebo effects, concludes that although the exact mechanisms involved in producing these effects remain obscure, savings of two days in patient stay are worth achieving. In so far as analgesic requirements can be taken as an index of post-operative distress and adjustment, the value of pre-operative communication in this respect is also clear.

Conclusions

Research on communication in medical settings has a relatively short history, but already it is providing evidence about ways in which patient care can be improved. Apart from what is really the most important argument for communicating with patients (i.e., that patients want this to happen) it has been shown that practical benefits can flow from such communication provided that it is done in the right way. By paying attention to comprehension and memory variables, substantial gains in patient satisfaction and compliance can be obtained. Much more research needs to be done, but it is no longer reasonable to claim that concern with the communications side of health care is merely an optional extra.

References

Balint, M. (1964). *The Doctor, the Patient and his Illness*. London: Pitman Medical.

Blackwell, B. (1972). 'The Drug Defaulter', *Clinical Pharmacology and Therapeutics*, *13*, pp. 841–8.

Boyle, C. M. (1970). 'Differences between Patients' and Doctors' Interpretations of some Common Medical Terms', *Br. Med. J.*, *2*, pp. 286–9.

Bradshaw, P. W., Kincey, J. A., Ley, P. and Bradshaw, J. (1975). 'Recall of Medical Advice, Comprehensibility and Specificity', *Br. J. Soc. Clin. Psychol.*, *14*, pp. 55–62.

Bromley, D. B. (1974). *The Psychology of Human Ageing*. Harmondsworth: Penguin.

Cartwright, A. (1964). *Human Relations and Hospital Care*. London: Routledge & Kegan Paul.

Chapman, J. S. (1969). 'Effects of Different Nursing Approaches upon Psychological and Physiological Responses', *Nursing Research Reports*, *5*, pp. 1–71.

Davis, M. S. (1966). 'Variations in Patients' Compliance with Doctors' Orders: Analysis of Congruence between Survey Responses and Results of Empirical Observations', *J. Med. Educ.*, *41*, pp. 1037–48.

Egbert, L. D., Battit, G. E., Welch, C. E. and Bartlet, M. K. (1964). 'Reduction of Post-operative Pain by Encouragement and Instruction of Patients', *New Eng. J. Med.*, *270*, pp. 825–7.

Flesch, R. (1948). 'A New Readability Yardstick', *J. App. Psychol.*, *32*, pp. 221–33.

Fletcher, C. M. (1973). *Communication in Medicine*. London: Nuffield Provincial Hospitals Trust.

Hinton, J. (1967). *Dying*. Harmondsworth: Penguin.

Houghton, H. (1968). 'Problems in Hospital Communication', in *Problems and Progress in Medical Care* (ed. G. McClachlan). Oxford University Press.

Janis, I. L. (1971). *Stress and Frustration*. New York: Harcourt Brace & Jovanovich.

Korsch, B. M., Freemon, B., and Negrete, V. F. (1971). 'Practical

Implications of Doctor-Patient Interaction: Analysis for Pediatric Practice', *Am. J. Diseases of Children*, *121*, pp. 110–14.
Korsch, B. M. and Negrete, V. F. (1972). 'Doctor-patient Communication', *Scientific American*, August, pp. 66–73.
Lewin, K. (1954). 'Studies in Group Decision', in *Group Dynamics* (eds D. Cartwright and A. Zander). London: Tavistock Publications.
Ley, P. (1972a). 'Complaints made by Hospital Staff and Patients: a Review of the Literature', *Bull. Br. Psychol. Soc.*, *25*, pp. 115–20.
Ley, P. (1972b). 'Primacy, Rated Importance and Recall of Medical Information', *J. Health and Social Behav.*, *13*, pp. 311–17.
Ley, P. (1974). 'Communication in the Clinical Setting', *Br. J. Orthodontics*, *1*, pp. 173–7.
Ley, P. (1977). 'Psychological Research on Doctor-patient Communication', in *Advances in Medical Psychology* (ed. S. J. Rachman). Oxford: Pergamon Press.
Ley, P., Bradshaw, P. W., Eaves, D. E. and Walker, C. M. (1973). 'A Method for Increasing Patients' Recall of Information Presented by Doctors', *Psychol. Med.*, *3*, pp. 217–20.
Ley, P. and Spelman, M. S. (1967). *Communicating with the Patient*. London: Staples Press.
Lindeman, C. A. and van Aernam, B. (1971). 'Nursing Intervention with the Pre-surgical Patient: the Effects of Structured and Instructured Pre-operative Teaching', *Nursing Research*, *20*, pp. 319–32.
Skilbeck, C. E., Tulips, J. G. and Ley, P. (1976). 'Effects of Fear Arousal, Fear Position, Fear Exposure and Sidedness on Compliance with Dietary Instructions', *Europ. J. Soc. Psychol.*

Suggestions for further reading

Korsch, B. M. and Negrette, V. F. 'Doctor-patient Communication', *Scientific American*, August 1972.
Ley, P. and Spelman, M. S. *Communicating with the Patient*. London: Staples Press 1967.
Rachman, S. J. (ed.). *Advances in Medical Psychology*. Oxford: Pergamon Press 1977.

Index

Note: authors mentioned in the bibliographies are not included in the index unless discussed in the text.

abilities, mental, *see* intellect; intelligence
achievement, intellectual, 250, 262–265
action, physiological preparation for, 21, 129, 142, 148
adaptation and adjustment, 4, 26–7, 97, 146, 148–9, 237; to age, 256–260, 262, 267–9, 271–3; to dying, 274–7; General Adaptation Syndrome, 26–7; maladaptation, 29, 112, 116–17; in perception, 51–2, 62–4
adjustment, *see* adaptation
adolescents, 196, 228–30, 238, 247, 302; *see also* children
adrenaline, 21, 25, 129, 131, 137, 139, 148; pituitary-adrenal system, 27, 148–9
advertising, 309–10
advice, medical, compliance with, 324–9, 333–9, 342
affection, 232, 234, 239
age, *see* mental age; middle age; old age
ageing, 90, 245–78 *passim*; biology of, 245–9, 255–6; intelligence and, 249–56; psychology of, 256–60, 272–3; *see also* middle age; old age
aggression, 141, 149, 198, 224–5, 233
Alexander, F., 24
amnesia, 90–1
anaesthesia, 9
anger, 137–8, 198–9, 307
animals: comparison of, with humans, 238; observation of, in natural surroundings, 134
anthropomorphism, 137
anxiety and fear, 4, 21–3, 28, 137, 141, 214, 274, 291, 293, 307; conditioning and, 100–3, 107–8, 117–20, 146–7, 197–200, 232; experimental arousal/control of, 100–1, 311–12, 336–40; measurement of, 7; as personality trait, 197–200
Aristotle, 86, 88

arousal, 19–21, 23, 121, 129, 131, 138–9, 142, 147, 150; in children, 221; performance and, 142–3; personality and, 143–4, 197, 199–200, 211, 213; sexual, 100, 142; *see also under* cortex
association: language and, 16, 75–6; memory and, 88–9
attachment (in children), 226–7, 232, 239
attention, 23, 49–53, 60, 62, 71, 221
attitudes and values, 298–319 *passim*; change in, 307–18, 336–8; definition, 299–300; to human nature, 304–6; moral, 234–5; origin, 300–3; to self, 268–9, 301; structure and function, 303–7; *see also under* behaviour
audition, 34–5, 38–9, 43, 46, 48, 82, 133, 222, 294; auditory imagery, 89
authority, 265–6, 304
autonomic/visceral responses, 13, 23, 103, 110, 119, 121, 144, 146; *see also under* nervous system
aversion therapy, 106, 117

babies, *see* children
Bannister, D., 205, 208
Bartlett, F. C., 76, 78, 86–7, 89
behaviour: attitudes and, 299–300, 317; behaviourism, 4, 176, 196; 'behaviour reversal', 120; brain physiology and, 9–10, 13–14; change/modification, *see* conditioning *and* learning; compensation in, 64; control of, 304–5 (*see also* self-control); environment and, 30, 165, 196–7 (*see also under* culture); expectancy and, 55, 287; explanation of, 139–41; measurement/sampling of, 7, 131–2, 134–6, 201–2, 295–6; non-verbal, 135–6; physiological manipulation of, 8; social norms of, 136, 198–9, 233, 275 (*see also* society); *see also* personality *and under* models

Index

behaviourism, 4, 176, 196
Benedict, Ruth, 227
bereavement, 277-8
bias, *see* subjectivity/bias
Binet, Alfred, 156, 168-9; *see also* Stanford-Binet Scales
biofeedback, 22, 111, 121-2, 147
biology: history of, 4; molecular, 6, 247; nature of, 30; physics and, 30
body, mind and, 3-7
brain: 'brainwashing', 53, 318; as communications system, 6; damage to, 253 (*see also* lesions); evolution of, 11-12; mechanisms of, 8-10, 30, 84-6, 91-2, 194; mind and, 5; parts of, 8-9 (*see also specific parts of brain*); stimulation of, 9-18; techniques for studying, 5, 7-8
'brainwashing', 53, 318
British Intelligence Scale, 160, 170-171
Burt, Sir Cyril, 157, 170

cancer, 323-4, 328
catecholamines, 130-1, 137-8
Cattell, J. McK., 156
Cattell, R. B., 187-90, 202-3
change, perception and, 51
childbirth, 118-19
children: development of, 156-7, 160, 168-9, 196-9, 220-7, 231-243 *passim*, 301, 304, (stages of) 239-43; in hospital, 119, 224; perception in, 58, 60-2; *see also* pediatrics
class, social, 225, 261, 268; intelligence and, 165
cognition: cognitive consistency theory, 315-17; cognitive development, 235-7 (*see also under* children); emotion and, 21-2, 138-9, 146; perception and, 58; *see also* comprehension; judgment
communication, *see* relationships *and under* brain; doctors; hospitals; information; two-sided, 336-8
competition, 224, 228
compliance with medical advice, 324-9, 333-9, 342
comprehension, 323, 327-9, 331-6, 342
computers, 74
conditioning, 14-15, 117, 146-7, 191, 197-9, 220, 232; classical, 99-103, 107, 109-11, 114, 222, 233, 239; operant/instrumental, 22, 103-11, 114, 116, 121-2, 146, 222-4, 239, 294; *see also* stimulation and response
conformity, 228, 232-3, 258, 309
conscience, 232-4
convergence, 160
coronary heart disease, aetiology of, 29
cortex, 9-12, 15, 32-3; cortical arousal, 9, 144, 191-3; decortication, 12
counselling, 276-7
creativity, 156, 160
crying, 223
culture: adolescence and, 229-30; behaviour and, 135-6; cultural deprivation, 223, 227; intelligence and, 163-5; perception and, 58-60; personality and, 176, 187; social development and, 227
cybernetics, 6

Darwin, C., 4, 131
Davitz, J. R., quoted, 133
death and dying, 249, 273-8, 323-4
defence mechanisms, 57, 71, 306-7, 317
delusions, 65, 71
dependence, 273
depression and depressiveness, 23, 137-8, 258; *see also* manic-depressive psychosis
deprivation: cultural, 135-6; sensory, 53, 144, 199-200
Descartes, R., 4
desensitization, systematic, 118-20, 147
development, *see under* children; society, socialization
'developmental quotient' (DQ), 225
deviation, 106, 239
diagnosis, motivation and, 44
diet, assimilation of information about, 324, 332, 335-8
disease, *see* illness *and specific diseases*
divergence, 156, 160
doctors: attitudes of, 299, 312-14; doctor-patient communication, 6, 210-11, 283, 288-94, 299, 308-309, 321-42 *passim*; *see also* medicine

345

Index

dominance fighting, 224, 228, 233
'double-language' hypothesis, 6
drives, 13, 17, 140–1, 145, 176, 199
drugs, 5, 258, 291–2, 318; compliance in taking, 324–5, 334–5; in psychiatry, 288–9; tolerance of, 194–6, 212–13; *see also* placebos
dualism, 4, 6
dying, *see* death

Ebbinghaus, H., 75, 77
economic conditions, age and, 229, 261
education, 165, 230–2, 237, 247, 318; *see also under* medicine
efficiency, *see* performance/efficiency
Egbert, L. D., 340–1
Einstein, A., 285
electrodes, experimental use of, 8, 15–16, 129
emotion, 125–51 *passim*; chemistry of, 130–1, 137–8; cognition and, 21–2, 138–9, 146; illness and, 23–4, 29; learning and, 22, 149, 222; measurement of, 125–6, 133–4; memory and, 89–90; perception and, 55, 57–8; physiology of, 11–13, 21, 26–8, 30, 128–31, 137–9, 148–9; reason and, 310–11; theories of, 147–51; *see also specific emotions*
endocrine system/hormones, 13–14, 26, 142, 149, 256; *see also specific hormones*
energy, 140, 148–9; in perception, 34, 42–3
environment, 13–14, 30, 139–40, 142, 150, 165, 196–7; adaptation to, 97, 237; cognitive assessment of, 21; control of, 112; experimental, 291; intelligence and, 161, 163–5; personality and, 176, 196–7; psychosocial, 29–30; senses and, 32 (*see also* perception); therapeutic, 283–4, 288–95
escape strategy, 107–8
evolution, 139, 144–5, 260–1
expectancy and expectations, 43, 55, 75–6, 86–7, 150, 229–30, 283–284, 286–90, 294–5; of patients, 325–6
experience, human, 7, 89, 97–9, 139, 150, 176; attitudes and, 304; effect of, on perception and retention, 55, 62, 70–1, 75–6, 87, 89–90; measurement of, 7; value of, 267–8
experiment and observation, scientific: factors affecting results of, 43–5, 283–96 *passim*; observer error, 283–8; techniques of, 4–5, 8, 30, 295–6; variables in, 7, 98, 283, 295–6
explanation, scientific, 6
extraversion, *see* introversion
Eysenck, H. J., 165, 180, 183–5, 187–90, 192–3, 202–3, 216; quoted, 144

face, human: expression, 131–3; response of children to, 60, 221–2
factor analysis, technique of, 158–9, 180–2, 187
family: change in, 262, 271; environment, 300–1, 304
fear, *see* anxiety
feedback, 30, 120, 149–50, 237, 313, 329, 339; biofeedback, 22, 111, 121–2, 147
feeding problems, 308–9
Flesch formula, 327–8, 331–2
fluoridation, 315
foetus, responses of, 220
forgetting, 74, 77–9, 83–4, 86–7, 90–1; by patients, of advice, 329–333; *see also* memory
Freud, S., 86–7, 89, 176, 196, 225–226, 232, 237–8, 241–2, 294
frustration, 141, 149, 269, 276

galactosemia, 161
Galton, F., 88–9, 156
General Adaptation Syndrome, 26–27
'generation gap', 267
genetics, *see* heredity
Gobineau, J. A., Comte de, 161
Greeks, 178
groups, 227–9, 233, 235, 302–3; decisions by, 336–8; drugs and, 212, 291–2
Guilford, J. P., 159–60

habituation to stimuli, 20, 23, 51–2, 150, 273
hallucinations, 53, 65, 71
halo effect, 56, 71, 133–4, 202
health, 266–7, 272–3, 298–9; *see also* illness

hearing, *see* audition
helplessness, 146
heredity, 137, 195–7, 225; intelligence and, 161–5, (index of heritability) 162–3
holism, 6
homeostasis, 26, 140, 149–50
hormones, *see* endocrine system *and specific hormones*
hospitals: children in, 119, 224; communications in, 322, 324–5, 333–4; dying patients in, 275; organization of, 114–16; types of, 291
hostility, 107–8, 307
hunger and thirst, 13, 140
hypertension, 121–2, 214–15
hypothalamus, 12–14, 16, 130, 143–144

identification and identity, 232, 235, 302–3
'identity thesis', 6
illness and disease: aetiology of, 6, 23–4, 28–9, 210–16; age and, 248–9, 258–9, 273; attitudes to, 299–300, 323–4; mental, 238, 253; methods of treatment, 95–6, 114–15; *see also* patients *and specific illnesses*
illusions, 64–71
imagery, 89, 114
imitation, 99, 105, 113–14, 120, 199, 222, 224–5, 232–3, 235; *see also* models
imprinting, 239
indole amines, 130–1, 137–8
information: communication of, 307–11, 313–14, 318, 321–42 *passim*; co-ordination of, in babies, 221, 241; retrieval and storage, *see* retrieval/recall; storage/retention; theory, 6; *see also* memory
instincts, 136–7, 176
intellect: achievement, 250, 262–5; age and, 248–55; 'fluid' and 'crystallized' abilities, 254–5
intelligence, 4, 155–73 *passim*, 181, 187, 237; ageing and, 249–56; definition, 155; environment, heredity and, 161–5; measurement/quotient, 155–9, 225, (IQ tests) 165–73, 251–2 (*see also specific tests*); taxonomy, 158–60

interviews, 286, 296, 326
introversion and extraversion, 143–144, 179–85, 188–90, 192–6, 199–200, 203, 211, 214, 258–9
IQ (intelligence quotient), *see under* intelligence
isolation, 53

James, W., quoted, 128–9
Janis, I. L., 339
Jensen, A. R., 163–4
judgment: bases of, 131–2, 301–2; factors affecting, 55–7, 67, 70–1, 133–4; moral, 234–5; *see also* cognition; perception
Jung, C. G., 179, 185

Kant, I., 178
Keir, G., 170
Kelly, George, 205
Korsch, B. M., 325–6, 334, 339
Kretschmer, E., 178–80, 191

language, 198, 225; associations of, 16, 75–6; emotion and, 126–7
learning, 4, 14–16, 77, 90, 95–122 *passim*, 238–9, 287; application of learning theory to practice of medicine, 95–6, 100, 104–5, 114–122; association and, 88; biochemistry of, 92; in children, 222–3, 237, 301; definition, 97–9; drives and, 140–1; emotion and, 22, 149, 222; heredity and, 137; hierarchy of, 230; motor learning, 63–4; perception and, 58–62; personality and, 196–201; *see also* conditioning
Lehman, H. C., 262–3, 265
leisure, 261, 272
lesions of brain, 8–9, 12, 15, 91
Lewin, Kurt, 336–7
Ley, P., 327–30, 332, 334, 336–8, 340–1
libido, 238
life-cycle, human, stages of, 247–9, 271
limbic system, 11–12, 16, 110, 143, 194
'Little Albert' experiment, 101, 117
localization, 34–9
Locke, John, 161
loneliness, 227, 232

maladaptation, 29, 112, 116–17; *see also* adaptation

347

Index

manic-depressive psychosis, 178–80
mass media, 313–14
matter, concept of, 7
meaning, 49, 76, 209, 331
measurement: physiological, 7, 18, 121, 129; psychological, 7; *see also under* behaviour; emotion; intelligence; personality
media, 313–14
medicine: achievement in, 262–5; application of learning theory to, 95–6, 100, 104–5, 114–22; application of personality theory to, 210–16; application of psychology to, 114–22 *passim*; communication in, 321–42 *passim*; education and training for, 119–22, 275, 277; social aspects of, 298, 318; subject matter of, 122; *see also* doctors; patients; therapy *and specific branches of medicine*
memory, 15–16, 20, 74–92 *passim*, 323, 327, 329–36, 342; address system, 79–81, 86–8; chemistry and biochemistry, 16, 92; defects, 90–1; loss, 74, 77–9, 83–4, 86–7, 90 (*see also* forgetting); input, 52, 75–7, 84–7, 89–90, 150; long-term, 86–8, 92; short-term, 81–6, 92; *see also* retrieval; storage
menopause, 260, 271
mental age, concept of, 168–9, 173
middle age, 248, 260–70
mind: body and, 3–7; brain and, 5; concept of, 7
models: behavioural, 99, 114, 120, 199, 232–3, 275–6; modelling effect, 285–6; neuronal, 11, 150; *see also* imitation
mongolism, 161–2
morality, 232–5
motivation, 4, 8, 13, 43–4, 89, 231, 306–7, 310, 338; biological bases of, 13, 140–2, 144–5
motor system, 16, 23, 63–4; motor imagery, 89; psychomotor skills, 255–6
muscles, 110–11; in vision, 35

nervous system, 10; autonomic, 13, 23, 103, 110, 128–9, 144, 146, 149, 197, 239, (parasympathetic) 13, 25, 129, 148, (sympathetic) 13, 21, 23–5, 128–31, 138–9, 149;

central, 8, 15–16, 54, 103, 110, 131, 148–9, 191–2, 194–5, 213, 255–6; chemistry of, 130–1
'neuronal models', 11, 150
neurosis and neuroticism, 179, 258, 269–70; experimental neurosis, 101, 107; groups and, 212, 292; neuroticism as personality dimension, 128, 143–4, 180–5, 188–9, 194–5, 200–1, 203, 211–12, 214
noradrenaline, 137

obesity, 131, 215, 335–6, 338
observation, scientific, *see* experiment
occupation, 245–6, 248, 256, 261–2, 271; *see also* retirement
old age, 249, 261, 272–3
'organ vulnerability', 24, 28

pain, 52, 117, 144, 211–12, 293, 340–1
Papez, J. W., 11
parallax, 35–6, 61
parents: parent-child bond, 232, 234, 239; parent–child separation, 223–4; pressure on children by, 231
patients, 95–6, 114–18, 122, 311–12, 321–42 *passim*; compliance with medical advice, 324–9, 333–9, 342; doctor–patient communication, 6, 210–11, 283, 288–94, 299, 308–9, 321–42 *passim*; satisfaction of, 322–3, 325–8, 333–4, 338–9, 342; surgical, 339–41; *see also* illness
Pavlov, I. P., 99–102, 111, 191–2, 194
pediatrics, 325–6
perception, 10–11, 32–71 *passim*; adaptation in, 51–2, 62–4; constancy in, 40–2, 60–1, 66–7, 70; development of, 58, 60–2; disturbance/distortion of, 53–7, 76 (*see also* illusions); organization of, 45–9, 76–7, 221; subliminal, 57–58; thresholds in, 42–4, 58; *see also* memory, input; senses
performance/efficiency, 20, 53, 98, 285, 287; ageing and, 254; arousal and, 142–3
personal construct theory, 205–9, 215–16

Index

personality, 175–216 *passim*; abnormal, 189, 192, 195, 200 (*see also specific types*); ageing and, 255–260; application of personality theory to medicine, 210–16; approaches to study of, 175–7; arousal and, 143–4, 197, 199–200, 211, 213; attitudes and, 314–15, 322–3; behaviour and, 190, 192; biology of, 176, 190–6, 209, 216; development and traits, 176, 185–190, 196–201, 206, 208–9, 225–6, 238; illness and, 28, 210–11; measurement and testing, 167, 201–10; stimulation and, 19, 75, 197; taxonomy of, 128, 179–87, 192; in therapeutic situation, 290, 293
phenylketonuria, 161
philosophy, 3–6
physics (and biology), 30
physiology: control of, 22–3, 147; individual awareness of, 131; manipulation of, 8; physiological psychology, 8–18; psychology and, 3–30 *passim*; psychophysiology, 18–23, 211; *see also* action
physique, 28, 191
Piaget, Jean, 156, 160, 171, 234–7, 241–3
pictorial techniques, 35–7, 58–60
pilots, 53
pituitary gland, 13, 130; pituitary-adrenal system, 27, 148–9
placebos, 212, 284, 288–9, 291–5, 334, 341
play, 224
Polanyi, M., 284–5
prejudice, racial, 307
projection in personality testing, 204–5
propaganda, 318
protein, 16, 92
psychiatry, 288–9; symptom rating in, 202
psychoanalysis, 24, 196–7, 238–9
psychodynamics, 323
psychology: application to medicine, 114–22; history, 3–4, 175, 178; methods, 4; physiological, 8–18; physiology and, 3–30 *passim*; social, 298; subject field, 4–5
psychomotor skills, 255–6
psychoneurosis, *see* neurosis

psychopathy, 200
psychopharmacology, 213
psychophysics, 42–5
psychophysiology, 18–23, 211
psychosis and psychoticism, 178–182, 195, 203, 209
psychosomatic medicine, 23–30, 121, 213–16, 258
psychotherapy, 276–7, 290
puberty, 229–30
punishment, *see* reward

questionnaires, use of, 126–8, 182–185, 202–4

race: intelligence and, 163–5; racial prejudice, 307
recall, *see* retrieval
recognition, 80–1
recording, electronic, 296
reductionism, 6
reinforcement, 104–13, 116–17, 141, 146, 198–200, 222, 231–2, 239, 294; *see also* conditioning
relationships, interpersonal, 29, 257–8, 313–14
relaxation, 118, 147
religion, 3
repression, 86–7, 214; repression-sensitization, 211–12
reproduction, 14
response, *see* autonomic responses; stimulation and response
retention, *see* storage
reticular formation, 9–10, 15, 142–4, 194
retirement, 248, 256, 261, 269–72
retrieval/recall of information stored in memory, 74, 77, 79–87, 92, 329–33; *see also* memory
reward and punishment, 104–10, 112–13, 115–16, 140, 145–6, 198–199, 232–3
rigidity, mental, 257
Rogers, C. R., 290
role-playing, 120, 310
Rosenthal, R., 285–8, 291

Schachter, S., quoted, 138
schizophrenia, 23, 178–80, 181, 195, 208–9, 290
science: experiment and observation in, *see* experiment; explanation in, 6; potential of, 317–18

Index

self: attitudes to, 268–9, 301; self-control, 111–13, 116–17, 198–9
Seligman, M. E. P., quoted, 145
Selye, H., 26–7
senses and sensory system, 9, 15–16, 18, 32–4; in ageing, 255; in babies, 221, 241; deprivation, 53, 144, 199–200; memory and, 75, 82, 85, 87–8; *see also* perception *and specific modalities*
sensitization, 20–1; *see also* desensitization *and under* repression
separation (of child from mother), 223–4
sex: adolescents and, 229–30; sex differences, 225, 262, 268, 271, (in scientific investigation) 285; sex drive, 13; sex roles, 227; sexual arousal, 100, 142; sexual deviation, 106
Sheldon, W. H., 191
sight, *see* vision
Singer, J. E., quoted, 138
skin, measurements from surface of, 18, 121, 129
sleep and waking, 8–9, 25, 221, 259
smell, 52
smoking, 310–11
society: age and, 245–9, 261, 270; death and, 277; social class, 165, 225, 261, 268; socialization, 224–227, 229–30, 304, (moral) 232–5; social psychology, 298; social roles, 247–9, 265–6, 270–1; social skills, 119–21, 230, 268; socio-economic conditions, 229, 261–2; *see also under* behaviour
space, perception and (localization), 34–9
Spearman, Charles, 156–8
speech, 39–40, 224, 296; in interviews, 286, 326
Spencer, Herbert, 156
Stanford-Binet Scales, 166–70
status, 233, 285, 302
stereotypes, 56, 71
stimulation and response, 4, 18–20, 23, 25–6, 28, 55, 75, 112, 197, 221, 258; of brain, 9–18; proximal and distal stimulus, 34; stimulus control, 111–13; stimulus generalization, 100–2, 107, 110; 'stimulus hunger' and 'stimulus avoidance', 144, 199–200; *see also* conditioning; habituation
storage/retention of information in brain, 52, 74, 76–9, 81–8, 92; distortion, 77–9, 86–8; *see also* memory
stress, 25–30, 57, 118, 120, 131, 148, 210, 269, 273, 275; in adolescence, 229, 247
stuttering, 207–8
subjectivity/bias, 127, 202, 205, 283–96 *passim*, 304
subnormality, mental, 161–2
suicide, 258, 270
surgery, communication in, 339–41
survival, 4, 129, 140, 142, 149; of individual, 151
symptom rating, 202
systems theory, 6

tests, *see* intelligence, measurement; personality, measurement
thalamus, 9–10
therapy, 106, 117, 276–7, 283–4, 288–95
thirst, *see* hunger
Thorndike, E. L., 156
Thurstone, L. L., 157, 159, 167, 170
tolerance, 312–13; drug tolerance, *see under* drugs
touch, 63–5; tactile imagery, 89
trauma, 102, 107, 117–19, 146, 238
twin studies, 163, 195–6, 225, 231

ulcers, peptic, 328–9

values, *see* attitudes
verbalization, 5, 146–7, 198
Vernon, P. E., 165, 170
visceral responses, *see* autonomic responses
vision, 34–8, 40–2, 45–9, 53, 60–1, 78, 82, 221–2, 294; blind spot, 47; distortion, 62–4 (*see also* illusions); visual imagery, 89
vocal expression, 133
vocational guidance, 166–7

waking, *see* sleep
Warburton, F., 170–1
Weber's law, 42–3
Wechsler Scales, 166–70, 251–3
Wheatstone, Sir Charles, 35